Language and
Education

The Collected Works of M. A. K. Halliday

Volume 9 in the Collected Works of M. A. K. Halliday

Language and Education

M. A. K. Halliday

Edited by Jonathan J. Webster

continuum

Continuum

The Tower Building
11 York Road
London SE1 7NX

80 Maiden Lane
Suite 704
New York, NY 10038

First published 2007

British Library Cataloguing-in-Publication Data
A catalogue record for this book is available from the British Library.

ISBN 0–8264–5875–0 (hardback)

Library of Congress Cataloging-in-Publication Data
A catalog record for this book is available from the Library of Congress

Typeset by RefineCatch Limited, Bungay, Suffolk
Printed and bound in Great Britain by MPG Books Ltd, Bodmin, Cornwall

CONTENTS

PREFACE

Translating psyches, achieving metaphors,
Defining room for mutual, fresh realities,
A calculus for fellowship of language
As power, as making, as release.

from *Language and Power*
by Edwin Thumboo

Professor M. A. K. Halliday calls it 'taking language seriously', valuing the role language plays not only in our construal of experience, or as in the words of the poet, "translating psyches, achieving metaphors, defining room for mutual, fresh realities", but also in our enactment of interpersonal relations, i.e. "a calculus for fellowship of language as power, as making, as release".

Not only does Professor Halliday believe in taking language seriously, however, but he also advocates taking seriously "the responsibility of the school towards children's language development". This is something he has been actively practising since as far back as 1964, when he became involved in the "Programme in Linguistics and English Teaching", leading to the development of an innovative curriculum known as 'Breakthrough to Literacy'. This programme and the curriculum that it produced was designed to help young children more fully realize their linguistic potential.

Teachers also need to understand how language as a system functions, and how better to enable children to learn it. What the linguist can offer the teacher is a description of language that takes meaning into account, that relates internal form to function, that is based on "a conception of language as a treasury of resources". No matter whether it is one's first or second language, the learning experience should be an enriching one, as the learner is taught how to explore and exploit the riches of language.

Something else that Professor Halliday takes very seriously is this matter of the social accountability of theory. His commitment to an appliable linguistics is reflected not only in his theory but also in his practice. That much of his work over the years has had an educational focus is clearly evident from the papers appearing in this volume. The papers in the first section, under the heading of *Mother Tongue Education*, chronicle work that got under way in the 1960s, in London, which led to the groundbreaking work on problems of literacy and language development already mentioned above. Subsequent sections include papers that highlight research into second language learning, problems of language education and language planning in multilingual societies, functional variation in language and the place of linguistics in education.

The Introduction to this volume, 'Applied Linguistics as an Evolving Theme' (2002), was originally presented by Professor Halliday on the occasion of his being awarded the AILA Gold Medal Award for exemplary scholarship in the field of applied linguistics. Concluding that lecture, this inaugural recipient of the AILA Gold Medal Award credits his colleagues over the years with having demonstrated "the potential of a linguistics that was functional and systemic: its potential to serve as an abstract tool for those engaging with language in various domains and contexts of application". Those who know the man will recognize his characteristic humility. In fact, it is his pioneering work in systemic-functional linguistics that continues to inspire a new generation of linguists to work towards an "appliable" linguistics such as is described in the papers contained in this volume.

ACKNOWLEDGEMENTS

We are grateful to the original publishers for permission to reprint the articles and chapters in this volume. Original publication details are provided below.

'Linguistics and the Teaching of English' from *Talking and Writing: A Handbook for English Teachers* published by Methuen (London), 1967. Edited by James N. Britton. Reprinted by permission of Taylor and Francis Books (UK).

'A "Linguistic Approach" to the Teaching of the Mother Tongue?' from *The English Quarterly*, published by the Canadian Council of Teachers of English (CCTE), 1971. Reprinted by permission of CCTE.

'Some Thoughts on Language in the Middle School Years' from *English in Australia*, published by the Australian Association for the Teaching of English (AATE), 1977. Reprinted by permission of AATE.

'Differences between Spoken and Written Language: Some Implications for Literacy Teaching' from *Communication through Reading: Proceedings of the Fourth Australian Reading Conference*, published by the Australia Reading Association, 1979. Edited by Glenda Page et al. Reprinted by permission of the Australian Literacy Educators' Association Ltd.

'Language and Socialization: Home and School' from *Language and Socialization, Home and School: Proceedings from the Working Conference on Language in Education, Macquarie University* published by Macquarie University, 1988. Edited by Linda Gerot et al. Reprinted by permission of Professor Theo van Leeuwen.

'Literacy and Linguistics: A Functional Perspective' from *Literacy in*

Society, published by Longman, an imprint of Pearson Education Ltd, 1996. Edited by Ruqaiya Hasan and Geoff Williams. Reprinted by permission of Pearson Education Ltd.

'General Linguistics and Its Application to Language Teaching' from Patterns of Language: Papers in General, Descriptive and Applied Linguistics, published by Longman (Longmans Linguistics Library) an imprint of Pearson Education Ltd, 1966. Reprinted by permission of Pearson Education Ltd.

'Is Learning a Second Language Like Learning a First Language All Over Again?' from *Language Learning in Australian Society: Proceedings of the 1976 Congress of the Applied Linguistics Association of Australia*, published by the Australian International Press and Publications Pty Ltd, 1978. Edited by D. E. Ingram and T. J. Quinn.

Learning Asian Languages, published by University of Sydney Centre for Asian Studies, 1986.

'National Language and Language Planning in a Multilingual Society' from *East African Journal*, 1972.

'Some Reflections on Language Education in Multilingual Societies, as Seen from the Standpoint of Linguistics' from *Report of the 1977 Seminar on Language Education in Multilingual Societies* published by Regional Language Centre (RELC), Singapore, 1979. Edited by Madge Claxton. Reprinted by permission of RELC.

'Where Languages Meet: The Significance of the Hong Kong Experience' from *Teaching Language and Culture: Building Hong Kong on Education* published by Addison Wesley Longman, 1998. Edited by Barry Asker.

'The Notion of "Context" in Language Education' from *Language Education: Interaction and Development, Proceedings of the International Conference, Vietnam, April 1991* published by University of Tasmania (Launceston), 1991. Edited by Thao Lê and Mike McCausland.

'Language Across the Culture' from *Language in Learning: Selected Papers from the RELC Seminar in "Language Across the Curriculum"*, Singapore, 22–26 April 1985, Anthology Series 16 published by SEAMEO Regional Language Centre (RELC) Singapore, 1986. Edited by Makhan L. Tickoo. Reprinted by permission of RELC.

M. A. K Halliday, 'Contexts of English' from *Perspective on English: Studies in Honour of Professor Emma Vorlat*, published by Peeters, Leuven 1994. Edited by K. Carlon, K. Davidse & B. Rudzka-Ostyn. Reprinted by permission of Peeters Publishers.

'A Response to Some Questions on the Language Issue' from *The English Magazine: The Language Issue*, 1981, published by The English

Centre (London). Reprinted by permission of the English and Media Centre.

'Some Basic Concepts of Educational Linguistics' from *Languages in Education in a Bi-lingual or Multi-lingual Setting*, published by the Institute of Language in Education (Hong Kong) 1988. Edited by Verner Bickley. Reprinted by permission of the Hong Kong Institute of Education.

'On the Concept of "Educational Linguistics" ' from *Discipline – Dialogue – Difference: Proceedings of the Language in Education Conference, Murdoch University, December 1989* published by 4D Duration Publications (Murdoch). Edited by Rod Giblett and John O'Carroll.

'A Language Development Approach to Education' from *Language and Learning* published by Institute of Language in Education (Hong Kong) 1994. Edited by Norman Bird. Reprinted by permission of the Hong Kong Institute of Education.

APPLIED LINGUISTICS AS AN EVOLVING THEME (2002)

1 A reflection on "applying" linguistics

I would like to begin by saying, with great feeling, what an honour and a pleasure it is to me to be awarded this first Gold Medal by the International Association of Applied Linguistics. I feel particularly proud that my name should be linked in this way with an enterprise that has always given direction to my own thinking and my own aspirations: the enterprise of describing and explaining the nature and functions of language in ways that are relevant to those who work with language and that can be useful to them in addressing the problems they are faced with. I recall here the two "central perspectives" which Chris Candlin identified, in his paper to the 1987 World Congress, as features of applied linguistics: "one, that [it] is social and two that it is problem-centred" (Candlin 1990: 461). These perspectives are significant, I think, not just in characterizing a general approach, a colouring that is typical of applied linguistic activities, but also in helping us to appreciate the essential coherence of the field – the thematic unity that lies beneath the very diversified forms in which these activities are carried out.

This thematic coherence is not something static and unchanging. What I wanted to suggest by my title was that the field has been continually evolving – as we can see if we look over the history of the last half-century, during which the term "applied linguistics" has been accepted in general usage. I remember that at the 1990 Congress in Halkidiki I referred to the preface that Bernard Pottier and Guy Bourquin had written to the *Proceedings* from the first AILA Colloquium, held at Nancy in 1964: they remarked that they had jeopardized the whole enterprise by adding to the initial theme another one, namely

1

the teaching of modern languages (Pottier and Bourquin 1966: 7–8). Today one would be more likely to jeopardize the whole enterprise if one left modern language teaching out! But what then was the "initial theme" of this first Congress, or Colloquium? It had to do with language automation; they called it "semantic information in linguistics and in machine translation". That does not figure at all among the topics in our present programme, nor is there a Scientific Commission devoted to it. There used to be a Scientific Commission on "Applied Computational Linguistics", listed at the Montreal Congress in 1987, but it seems no longer to be active today.

So while the evolution of "applied linguistics" has been largely a process of expanding into new domains, there has also been a move away from certain areas that initially seemed "central". Of course, this does not imply that such activities are no longer pursued; it is true that machine translation did go out of fashion, in many of the major centres, but some form of natural language processing by computer has been going on ever since. Only, it has taken on a separate identity as a field of research and development, with its own institutional structures and its own discourses: largely, perhaps, because technological advances have transformed both the resources available and the specialist knowledge required in order to exploit these resources. And the original head code, "semantic information", would not be thought of today as an application of linguistics, but rather as a central component in almost all linguistic research. So if we talk of applied linguistics as "evolving", this does not simply mean getting bigger. It means, rather, becoming more complex, both in itself and in its relations with its environment, in ways which reflect – but which also help to bring about – changes in the contexts within which applied linguistic practices are carried out.

But there was another motif in my title: that of applied linguistics as "theme"; and this does perhaps need some further comment – it has seemed to puzzle one or two people who have asked me what I'm going to talk about. Perhaps it was the collocation of "theme" with "evolving" that made it appear problematic. But it seems to me that applied linguistics is a theme, rather in the same sense that mathematics is a theme – mathematics grew out of the activities of counting and measuring things, and likewise gave rise to a concept of "applied mathematics". Here is a definition of applied mathematics, from the *Wordsworth Dictionary of Science and Technology*:

> Originally the application of mathematics to physical problems, differing from physics and engineering in being concerned more with

2

mathematical rigour and less with practical utility. More recently, also includes numerical analysis, statistics and probability, and applications of mathematics to biology, economics, insurance etc.

This is what I mean by an evolving theme. Neither applied mathematics nor applied linguistics is a discipline: a discipline is defined by some object of study and, at any one time, a set of principles and methods for investigating and explaining that object. In that sense linguistics, understood as a set of principles and methods for investigating and explaining language, can be considered a discipline; and if we take this as the point of departure, we can say that applied linguistics has evolved as the use of the findings of linguistics to address other issues – either other objects of study, if we are thinking of research applications, or else other practices, goal-directed activities such as language teaching and machine translation.

But the trouble with that picture, in my opinion, is that it makes too categorical a distinction between (theoretical) linguistics and applied linguistics, with the one creating knowledge and the other making use of that knowledge, as something readymade, in the pursuit of its own agenda. Yet that is not really how things are. Much of our theoretical understanding of language comes from working on and with language in a variety of different contexts, and it is seldom possible to locate a particular body of practice, or of practitioners either, squarely on one side of the line or the other. So in saying that, while linguistics is a discipline, applied linguistics is a theme, I am trying to give a sense of the permeability between the two: language as an object of study, and language – or rather, working with language – as a theme. What is common, as expressed by the common term "linguistics", is that throughout these activities language is being engaged with seriously, studied professionally and above all, perhaps, valued as the critical factor in our construal of experience and in our enactment of interpersonal relationships.

While still in this vein, let me suggest one other way of thinking about the significance of this term "applied". When you do linguistics, you are addressing questions about language that have been posed by linguists. When you do applied linguistics, you are still addressing questions about language, but they are questions that are posed by other people. They are problems that arise in the course of what we might call language-based praxis: all those activities which are undertaken systematically, and often also professionally, in which language is the critical variable. By "systematically" I mean in ways that are based on informed design, with the assumption that given the appropriate technical knowledge – knowledge about language, but also about whatever other domains are involved – it is possible to organize and carry out the activity in a more effective way. "Professionally" means of course that the practitioner is appropriately trained, whether or not they are doing the job for a living. It is particularly the requirement of the professional for well-informed principles to act on that provides the source of energy for the applied linguistic endeavour.

2 Some unifying factors

But we cannot help noting that most of the areas of work that have been recognized as domains of applied linguistics were already, or have now become, independent entities, with their own feet to stand on; and if that is the case, is there any need for applied linguistics? All these specialized activities – language education, translation, speech pathology, and so on – have their own conferences and their own journals; they appear as headings in job descriptions, grant applications and other contexts that confer academic respectability; and they have their own semiotic territory, if I may call it that: domains of meaning whose boundaries are admittedly fuzzy (but that is true of all academic fields) yet whose central concepts and concerns are clearly marked out. One or two sub-disciplines may have been fostered by applied linguistics, or even brought into the world that way, with applied linguistics as midwife; but even if they were, that is no reason why the foster home should remain open once they've grown up and left. So does the world need AILA? Does it need to harbour a virtual entity construed as "applied linguistics"?

I think it does. I think the conception of applied linguistics, and its institutional incarnations such as AILA and the regional affiliates, will have an especially significant function in the decades ahead. In saying this I acknowledge my own personal standpoint, first as a linguist and secondly, also, as a generalist. So let me comment briefly from these two points of view.

First, then, I think it will be critical at this moment for those who work with language, in whatever guise, to continue to engage with language in a principled way, and this means keeping open the dialogue between themselves and those for whom language is an object of study in its own right. Why do I say "at this moment"? The reason is that for the first time in history linguists now have adequate data, in the form of computerized corpuses (or corpora) where large quantities of discourse are assembled and made accessible, and this is likely to provide deeper

4

insight into how language functions in the diverse contexts that applied linguists have to deal with.

Second, as a generalist I believe that the very disparate groups of professionals who come together in the applied linguistics community have benefited considerably from talking to each other, and that this conversation needs to go on. I realize, of course, that in saying I am a generalist I must appear as some kind of a dinosaur, something that ought reasonably to be extinct in this age of specialization. But applied linguistics is a generalizing concept – at least that is how I see it. Not everyone sees it that way, perhaps: after the Eighth Congress, held in Sydney in 1987, we decided, rather than issuing multi-volume proceedings, to publish one volume of selected papers (or two volumes, as it turned out); these were edited by John Gibbons, Howard Nicholas and myself, and we gave them the title *Learning, Keeping and Using Language* (1990). One reviewer, at the end of a review that was factual and entirely fair, concluded by saying that the book should never have been published – the topics covered were too diverse and heterogeneous. The reviewer's opinion was that it was not appropriate to publish a general volume of papers from an AILA Congress.

I disagreed with that view. I enjoyed editing those two volumes particularly because of their diversity: I was able to read about current work in so many interesting domains. But leave aside my personal preference; I do think that such diversity is valuable and constructive in itself. This is true of very many academic contexts, of which applied linguistics must surely be one. Applied linguistics is not simply a collection code, a convenient assemblage of so many disparate modules: the three sub-themes that we identified in our title – learning language, keeping language, using language – seemed to me to suggest very well how the individual papers, through their varied topics and subject matter, did contribute to – did in fact constitute – a coherent theme. And what was true of those volumes is true of the enterprise as a whole, including such instances as the present Congress. This is not a coherence achieved in spite of diversity; it is a coherence that is brought about by diversity. This happens in scholarship just as it does in daily life, where the coherence of language is construed by the great diversity of the functions that languages are called upon to serve.

These two motifs – keeping open the discourse with each other, and keeping open the discourse with their more theory-oriented colleagues – are good enough reasons for people to go on "doing" applied linguistics: locating themselves, and their praxis, in a shared action space having language as the common vector. Or rather: not just language, but

5

a systematic understanding of and engagement with language. But let me suggest two other factors that, while they are present with all forms of intellectual activity, take on special significance in applied linguistic contexts. One is the matter of being accountable; the other is the matter of being available, or accessible; and both are familiar topics in applied linguistic debates. Wherever language is the primary sphere of action, these questions are bound to arise.

Let me recall again Candlin's paper at that 1987 Congress, with its rather mischievously ambiguous title 'What happens when applied linguistics goes critical'. Here Candlin voiced his concern for the social and ethical accountability of applied linguistic research. From one point of view, this is just the general principle that all scholars are responsible to the community. We can argue about whether our work must always have an immediate payoff, or may acquire its value only in the longer term, but as a principle I assume this is not going to be seriously challenged. But much of our research, for example in educational, medical and forensic contexts, makes some rather special demands on other people, when we observe and analyse their linguistic behaviour; how do we bring them in so that they become partners in the endeavour and share in any benefits that flow on from it? There are limits to how far this ideal can be attained, since it is seldom that what we learn from our subjects is going to solve their own immediate problems, but we try to include them as collaborators, not just useful sources of data. Meanwhile, in many places the ethical standards have become bureaucratized: there are ethics committees policing the route, and ethnographic research – so essential to the sciences of meaning – as it has become technologically more feasible has also become almost impossible to carry out. Such issues involve the applied linguistic community as a whole: many of us have to intrude into that most sensitive and personal aspect of people's behaviour, their ways of speaking, and often in quite threatening contexts – where they are struggling to learn new ways, as in adolescent and adult second-language learning; where their old ways have been, or are being, eroded, as in stroke aphasia or Alzheimer's; or where their integrity and even freedom may be at risk, as in confessions and other encounters with the law. It is the shared experience of those engaged in such research activities, with their common focus on language, that gives substance to the rather abstract commitment to being of service to those we learn from.

There remains the question of availability: how widespread are the effects of applied linguistic research? Our 1987 Congress in Sydney (the first, incidentally, to be held outside the orbit of Europe and North

America) had as its proclaimed conference theme "New Approaches to Applied Linguistics as an International Discipline". So: is applied linguistics international? More pointedly, perhaps, what does "international" mean in such a context? I propose to consider this from a somewhat different angle.

3 English at the gate

There is another way of characterizing applied linguists: they are folk who live, or at least who work, in the real world. Not that they don't visit the world of the virtual: they do, and they must, in order to be able not just to operate in the real world but also to think about it. If in addition to acting, say, as a translator, you also think about the relations and processes of translation, you cannot avoid engaging with virtual entities like emphasis and connotation, structure and rhythm, word and clause and sense unit. These are semiotic entities; but then the real world in which applied linguists pursue their trade is, or at least includes, the world of meaning: the semiotic as well as the material realm of human existence. It is none the less real for that: we should not let our scientific and technical colleagues, or our own notoriously gullible common sense, con us into thinking that the material world is the only domain of reality.

The real world of meaning, just like that of matter, has particular properties at any given moment of space-time. We have to understand and work within those constraints. I don't mean we have to accept them without critique; we may use our understanding of the world of meaning to try to bring about change. But it is of no help to us, and still less to our clientele, if we pretend that things are different from the way they are. Now, one feature of the present world of meaning is that, as well as a number of languages that are spread out internationally — English, French, Arabic, Malay, Spanish, German, Russian, Swahili, Mandarin (Chinese) and a few others — we now have one language that has got extended globally, namely English.

There was no linguistic or other necessity that English should assume that role, nor even that there should be any "global" language at all, although it is easy enough to trace the conditions that brought this situation about. Either of these present features may have changed completely 25 years from now. The International Association of World Englishes was founded on the initiative of Braj Kachru, who first used the term "Englishes" to refer to the different varieties of English that are current around the world; it has given prominence particularly to those of Kachru's second group, the "outer circle" of highly evolved Englishes in Commonwealth countries such as India, Nigeria, Kenya, Pakistan and Singapore (Kachru 1990). I recently attended a conference of this Association, held in honour of Braj Kachru on the occasion of his retirement, and I was privileged to listen to, among others, two distinguished Singaporean scholars, Edwin Thumboo and Anne Pakir. Professor Thumboo spoke about E-literatures (English, not electronic!), and the need to study them in their own socio-historical contexts and in terms of their own systems of values. Professor Pakir spoke about "the making of Englishes", the processes by which the NVEs, or "New Varieties of English", have come into being and evolved. Those who visit Singapore soon come to recognize that a new variety of English forms a lectal continuum (in the variationist sense: from basilect to acrolect) just as we find in the Englishes of the "inner circle" (the OVEs, or "Old Varieties of English"), and likewise in other internationalized languages (such as Singapore Mandarin). The new varieties differ from the old in that they seldom serve as mother tongue; they do not get flushed out by a continuing tide of toddlers – immature speakers. But in other respects their functional range is comparable to that of the old varieties; they are self-defining and self-sustaining.

The nature of "global English" is rather different. In Kachru's "expanding circle", English functions in contexts of worldwide commerce and political institutions, and to some extent in education, science and technology; but also, and increasingly, in electronic exchanges: the Internet, the World Wide Web and e-mail. In the former settings, inner-circle Englishes (American, British, Australian) tend to be regarded as norms to be kept within sight (and within earshot); but in e-English, which is a written variety (that is, it uses the written channel), the contexts are evolving along with the language, and innovations of any kind will be accommodated if they are found to work.

So with English having this dual role, both as an international language (one among many) and as the (only) global language, it is not surprising that it figures prominently in applied linguistic activities, with language education at the top of the list. It is prominent even in mother-tongue education, given that English shares with Spanish the second place in number of native speakers (between 300 and 350 million – both way behind Mandarin, which has around 900 million). But in second- or foreign-language teaching it easily predominates: English is way ahead in numbers of people learning it as other than their first language. Figures are impossible to estimate accurately, but on any account the number of people learning English, and even the number being taught English, is a lot.

So for many people "applied linguistics" has meant, simply, TESOL: teaching English to speakers of other languages. In 1987, at the Eighth Congress, out of 550 abstracts submitted, almost half were in some aspect of language education, and the majority of these were concerned with English. I think the proportions have remained fairly constant since that time: I looked through the 900-odd abstracts of paper presentations at the present (2002) Congress, and between 40 and 50 per cent seem to have English as their primary concern. Probably more journals and research papers are devoted to English teaching than to any other region of applied linguistics.

How does this feature, the dominance of English as the language under discussion, square with the aims of AILA, as embodied in the name of the Association? It is not so much the "international" that is problematic: one can always have an international association devoted to the study of one particular language, and there are many such in existence around the world. What I find more problematic is the "linguistics". Linguistics means language, and languages, in general. What has happened in applied linguistics is parallel to what happened in theoretical linguistics following the tenet laid down by Chomsky: that the goal of the linguist was to discover the universal principles of language, and since these were embodied in every language it didn't matter which language you investigated in depth. So those who first followed Chomsky worked on English, which was the language they had native speaker intuitions about; but then other scholars who wanted to take up the argumentation tended to stick with English in order to stay in touch. Now, in applied linguistics too it has been useful to have one language as a testing ground, in this case for practices rather than for arguments, and many ideas on language teaching, for example, have been tried out and evaluated with English. Many of these ideas have had only mixed success, but nevertheless (or perhaps for that very reason) they have provided valuable experience when applied to the teaching of languages other than English.

But there are drawbacks. There are, of course, universal principles of language, but they are much too abstract to be derived from the study of any one language alone. No doubt there are also some universally valid principles of foreign-language teaching, although I'm not at all sure where to look for them, given the almost infinite variety of the situations in which foreign languages are taught. Even here, I suppose, English probably exemplifies most of them: we have moved beyond the stage where we concerned ourselves only with the well-built and well-stocked classroom with its 12 to 20 well-provided students, so as to take account of the very different conditions in which English teachers have to operate in many parts of the world – requiring practices such as the "project-based learning" developed by Zakia Sarwar. So I don't think concentration on English has blocked our view of these wider horizons. But English is only one language among many, and there are other horizons besides those of a language teacher.

Let me make it clear that I am not talking about the status of English as global language. Of course there are many things that can be said about that, as well as the many things that already have been said, but I have nothing new to add to that debate. When I refer to the place of English in applied linguistic studies, I am considering it not as language **of** discussion but as language **under** discussion. And here I would like to make one further comment.

If I was speaking with the voice of a theoretical and descriptive linguist, I would say that, as a locus for the investigation of language, while English is a perfectly valid specimen it is neither better nor worse than any other language in this regard, and no single language should (as we say, in an oddly mixed metaphor) hog the limelight. There should be typological diversity in the languages under discussion.

But, as Edwin Thumboo reminded us yesterday, for applied linguists the issue is not as straightforward as that. There are many Englishes – many e-literatures (and e-languages); and, more significantly, many different cultural and historical contexts within which those languages and those literatures make their meanings. So given the diversity of applied linguistic activities – of the meta-contexts in which we make our own meanings – there is bound to be some imbalance in the languages under discussion, with English likely to predominate because of the extent of its dispersal.

AILA cannot prescribe the topics to be discussed at its congresses. But the question of linguistic diversity is one that could be kept in sight. I think that on this occasion more languages have been under discussion, from a wider range of cultural contexts, than has previously been the case: if so, this is a welcome trend.

4 Evolving themes

I suspect that applied linguistics has always been rather self-consciously in search of its own identity. We can see its scope expanding as new topics have appeared: in section headings for parallel sessions, in the symposia held by scientific commissions, in the titles of keynote and plenary addresses. In the 15 years from Cambridge 1969 to

Brussels 1984 there were new topics within the general field of language education, such as LSP (language for specialized, then special, then specific purposes, itself quite a significant micro-evolution), educational technology, second language acquisition and immersion; and other new areas, such as language and sex (rather coyly renamed language and gender), language and (the) media, pidgins and creoles; language planning, which then expanded to encompass the language problems of developing nations; then language in medical and in legal contexts; and also child language, discourse analysis, lexicology and stylistics.

Some topics have come and gone – some perhaps more than once. Some have changed their names, perhaps reflecting changes in the way they were defined and approached. But many came to stay, as recognized (often professionalized) components of the applied linguistics scene. And I think we can see certain trends, directions of adaptation to changing circumstances. Three such trends seem to me to emerge. One is the movement outwards from the European centre, towards a concern with language problems that are critical in other parts of the world: developing new national languages for education, government and the law, often in highly complex multilingual contexts; and including language rights for linguistic minorities – a recent concern in Europe and North America also, so perhaps one should see this trend as a move outwards from the European **standard language** centre. Second is the movement outwards to other professional commitments: the medical becoming clinical, as linguists began to work with colleagues in language disorders; the legal becoming forensic, as linguists became expert witnesses often where migrants and other disadvantaged citizens were facing charges before the law. (There is still some way to go before these are accepted as applied linguistic concerns. I read an informative article in the latest *European Review*, about the problem of false confessions in criminal courts; it was not suggested that this was in any way concerned with language.) And third, there has been movement outwards from a monolithic conception of language, with recognition that a language is an inherently variable system and that our understanding has to come from observing how folks act and interact via language throughout all the changing scenes in which they are players. (This is where we see the significance of the shift whereby LSP evolved from specialized purposes, through special purposes, to specific purposes, as it was realized that functional variation (variation in register) is not some specialized use or uses of language but a normal concomitant of the linguistic division of labour.)

11

But if we think about these three outward movements, to other societies and cultures, to other professional domains, to other forms of discourse, we can see a deeper and I think more long-term pattern emerging, whereby people's perception of language itself has been changing. We have become more aware of the importance of meaning – of the semiotic aspect of human existence. Perhaps we have become re-aware of it: the awareness may have got lost when the old magical, epic and religious ways of thinking gave way before the forces of technology – I'm not sure; but if so, I believe our awareness may now be at a higher level. Like all living beings, at least all those endowed with consciousness, we inhabit two planes: a plane of matter and a plane of meaning – the material and the semiotic; and we are now more attuned to the power that resides in the semiotic realm, which in a sense is what the applied linguistic enterprise is all about. This is in part what people meant by the "information society", where most of the population-energy is spent moving and exchanging information rather than moving and exchanging goods and services; in part what Chris Brumfit described as taking up the postmodern project (1997: 22ff.), so that we are better able to reflect on the meanings we import, and export, through our own subject positions and their accompanying ideologies; in part our awareness of the awesome power of the media, now not so much reporting on people's doings as actively instigating and manipulating them. As Edwin Thumboo said in his paper, whatever is happening, language is there, and we are now at least coming to acknowledge it. So while as applied linguists our aim may be to intervene, we know that, to intervene effectively, we have to be also linguists; our programme now includes writing grammars and dictionaries, analysing discourse, studying diatypic variation, and so forth. It is this increasing and deepening engagement with language, the recognition of it as critical to our individual and social being, that I see as the central theme around which applied linguistics has been evolving.

But, as we learn more about the power of language, and its penetration into everything we do and think, so we also come to realize that intervening in the processes of language is an extraordinarily complex affair, both in its methods and in its aims. I may assume a certain goal, taking for granted, say, that in teaching a foreign language my aim is to enable the learners to use that language effectively; my problem then is: am I going about it the right way? will what I do help them to achieve that state? and we all know how hard it is to answer that. But we often cannot take for granted what the aim of our intervention ought to be.

5 Problematizing our goals

I once went to an academic lecture on the semiotics of marketing. I was naïve: I assumed that the speaker would tell me about the verbal and other semiotic strategies for selling things that I, as a consumer, had to recognize and learn to resist. But no: what I learnt (or would have learnt, if I'd followed the course) was how to use semiotic strategies to become a more effective salesman. I probably could have turned the lesson round, and made what I learnt serve my own purpose, that of more effective resistance; but that was not the purpose for which the lesson was being taught.

Those encountering forensic linguistics for the first time often assume that the linguist as expert witness is always a witness for the defence. And so they very often are. But the linguist may also be a witness for the prosecution, for example in revealing a forgery, or a fake suicide note that has been put in place by a murderer. We can still assume a common aim, but it has to be stated in more abstract terms: we assume linguistics is being applied in the service of justice.

Recently I started reading a book by the distinguished French linguist Claude Hagège, called *Halte à la mort des langues* "Put a stop to the death of languages" (or "language death", as it has now come to be technicalized) (2000). Like all Hagège's books, it is amazingly broad-ranging, taking in for example cases of language survival ranging from that of English under the "Norman yoke" (the conquest and occupation of England by the Norman French) to that of a variety of Aleut spoken by the 350 inhabitants of a small island to the east of Kamchatka, which is in fact a mixture of Aleut and Russian. Since English was also a mixed language, it seems that in both these cases mixing proved to be a useful survival strategy.

Hagège's provocative title suggests that the message is intervention: something should be done. But this is an area where intervention is an extraordinarily complex issue, raising difficult questions of whether the applied linguistic community should try to act, and if so, how. For example: it is tempting to argue from the biological to the linguistic sphere, and to say that, just as diversity of species is necessary to environmental, ecological well-being, so diversity of languages is necessary to cultural, eco-social well-being. But does the analogy hold? And, before we even ask that question, what is current thinking on biodiversity: does it refer to species, or to groups of species? what is needed for the health of the planet: large numbers of individually differentiated species, or representatives of a smaller number of ecologically defined species types? But then, whatever the preferred interpretation, how do we reason from diversity of species – biodiversity – to diversity of languages – glossodiversity, let us say? And then, is it glossodiversity we should be concerned with, or semodiversity: diversity of forms as well as meanings, or just diversity of meanings? And exactly what is the value that attaches to such diversity, for the human race as a whole?

Then, supposing we find answers to all these questions, we come up against another one, perhaps the most difficult of all, and one to which biology offers no analogies: what is the relation between 'good for the human race in general' and 'good for the specific community whose language is under threat of extinction'? All these are considerations that arise within one component of ecolinguistics: what we might call institutional ecolinguistics, the relation between a language and those who speak it (and also, in this case, those who may be speaking it no longer). There are further questions in what we might call systemic ecolinguistics, some of which I raised at the Ninth Congress of AILA: how do our ways of meaning affect the impact we have on the environment? Which then raises the further question: how are the institutional and the systemic factors interrelated? And so on.

With the problem of language death we are at the other end of the globalization scale from English: here we are concerned with very small languages, many of which are rapidly becoming annihilated. Perhaps this is only a very small concern, in relation to applied linguistics as a whole. But – if we hold on, as I think we should, to the concept of an applied linguistics community – our different spheres of activity are not insulated one from another. At some time in the future the applied linguistics project will be judged by its success, or at least by its efforts, in engaging with all aspects of the human semiotic condition.

6 A personal conclusion

I began my career as a language teacher: I taught my first foreign-language class on 13 May 1945, and this remained my profession (with some interruptions) for the next 13 years. I had already started asking difficult questions about language in my earlier role as a language learner, but now they became more urgent. My students were adults, mainly rather tough-minded adults, and they wanted explanations – which I was generally unable to provide. During those 13 years I was also engaging with language in other ways, and these raised further questions: questions relating to translation, to stylistics, to sociopolitical discourse; but all my questioning was essentially problem-driven – I needed to find out more about language to cope with language-based tasks, some of them more research-oriented, some more immediately practical. That has always been my angle of vision; the difference is that, the older you get the more you realize that the payoff may be quite far away in time, and is often oblique rather than pointing straight towards the target.

Since this is a very personal occasion, perhaps I might be allowed to recall some of those early questions, and the contexts in which they arose. Here are five that occur to me as I think back.

1. I had to translate a play, one or two songs, and some scientific articles into English from the original Chinese. How, and why, does a language vary in different functional contexts? and is this variation preserved in some way across languages?

2. I had to explain to the learners the order of elements in a Chinese clause. How does a speaker decide what comes first and what comes last? What are the different meanings carried by variation in word order? And what on earth does "fixed word order" mean?

3. I had to work out how intonation relates to meaning. Where does intonation figure in the description of a language, given that (a) the meaning of a tone contour varies with the grammatical environment, and (b) meanings expressed by intonation in one tongue (one language, or one dialect) may be expressed by other, grammatical or lexical, resources in another.

4. I had to analyse some poetic texts, in Chinese and in English. How is a text held together? what takes over where grammatical structure leaves off? What is the relation of poetic patterns (e.g. metre) to those of the everyday language?

5. I had to represent a sentence in English, Chinese and Italian for a project in machine translation. Where, and how, could these three languages be brought together: in structure, or in system? and also, although I didn't yet know how to ask this question, in lexicogrammar, or in semantics?

Gradually I built up resources for facing up to questions like these. At some point along the way, I discovered this thing called linguistics; and I was truly lucky in having two of the great linguists of the time as my teachers: Professor Wang Li, of Lingnan University in China, and Professor J. R. Firth at the School of Oriental and African Studies (SOAS) in London. They provided me with a rich store of basic knowledge about language, and, equally important, they taught me how to engage with language in order to find out more. And then, when

I got my first job in linguistics, at the University of Edinburgh, I was again fortunate in having Angus McIntosh and David Abercrombie as the senior scholars in the field; and as younger colleagues two of the founders of applied linguistics in Britain, Ian Catford and Peter Strevens. Catford and Strevens were already collaborating with colleagues in France, such as Paul Rivenc and the other authors of "Français élémentaire" (later "Français fondamental"); they shared the same aim of bringing linguistic theory to bear on the teaching of English and French as second languages, particularly in former colonies (and countries that were about to become former colonies). Ian Catford became Director of the School of Applied Linguistics when it opened in Edinburgh in 1956. Peter Strevens was a founder member of AILA and remained active in the field until 1989, when he died. An important component in the origins of the Association derives from that early collaboration between the French and the British specialists in second-language teaching.

But in accepting this very generous award today, I would like to acknowledge that I do so on behalf of the many colleagues who have worked with me over the succeeding years. They were the ones who demonstrated the potential of a linguistics that was functional and systemic: its potential to serve as an abstract tool for those engaging with language in various domains and contexts of application. I am not a very single-minded person – I tend towards the dilettante rather than the obsessive; but if there is one aim that I have kept fairly constantly in view, it is that of working towards – I won't say an "applied", but rather an "appliable" linguistics; and that would not have been possible without being able to work with people who built on my ideas and then came back to tell me what was wrong with them.

Back in the 1960s, in London, we had a research and curriculum development project entitled the Programme in Linguistics and English Teaching, in which primary, secondary and tertiary-level teachers all worked together in the application of linguistic theory to mother-tongue education. The materials that came out of that project – Breakthrough to Literacy, Language and Communication, and Language in Use – exploited, and explored, specific areas within language such as functional variation (register), writing systems, pattern frequencies, and also the relations between language and other semiotic systems. They were working in the framework of an overall model of language, which in turn continued to evolve in the light of their endeavours: David Mackay, Ian Forsyth, Peter Doughty and the other members of the teams showed clearly in their work the applied linguistic nature of the enterprise. In the 1980s and 1990s in Australia a new initiative in mother-tongue education was led by my colleague Jim Martin. This started with a project on primary children's writing, in which he collaborated with Joan Rothery; Jim Martin subsequently directed a much more broadly based programme, the Disadvantaged Schools Project in the Sydney Metropolitan Region, in which teachers in all subjects – science, maths, history, and so on – participated in a genre-based approach involving close attention to, and analysis of, the critical discourses of learning in school. Geoff Williams has shown how effectively a functional grammar can be taught to primary-school children to develop their literacy skills at any point from Year 2 onwards. Frances Christie has developed powerful language-based teacher educational programmes in various centres in Australia, and has now produced a series of language coursebooks for use in the first years of secondary schooling. Such enterprises are based on the premise that all learning under instruction, whatever the field, is essentially an applied linguistic task, on the part of both teacher and learner: both are applying their knowledge of language, and both can do so more effectively – can add a further dimension to the experience – if they also apply a knowledge of the relevant bits of linguistics.

Accompanying, and also underpinning, the work in language education has been the analysis of text and discourse in systemic functional terms, again starting in the 1960s with the corpus-based work of Rodney Huddleston, Richard Hudson and Eugene Winter at University College London, investigating the discourses of science. At the same time Ruqaiya Hasan began her studies in the analysis first of literary texts and then of children's narratives; and in the 1980s she directed, and carried out together with Carmel Cloran, a large-scale corpus-based study of the verbal interaction between mothers and pre-school children in their homes, showing how semantic variation is the critical factor in differentiating among populations (defined in this instance by sex and social class). The interdependence of theory and description is particularly highlighted in the analysis of natural spontaneous speech, as Hasan's work brings out: it demands a comprehensive approach to lexicogrammar, semantics and context – compare in this regard the important study by Suzanne Eggins and Diana Slade in the linguistic analysis of casual conversation (1997). J.R. Martin's book *English Text: System and Structure* (1992) gave the clearest presentation of the grounding of discourse analysis in linguistic theory; and numerous text studies, both in specific varieties of English and in languages other than English, illustrate how discourse analysis provides an essential interface between theoretical and applied linguistics.

But, as I said at the beginning, I find this line very difficult to draw, and in many of the fields recognized by AILA it seems to me that systemic functional studies typically transcend this distinction: I have in mind, for example, Erich Steiner's work in translation, or Gordon Tucker's in lexicology, or the work of the Clinical Linguistics Research Program instituted by Elizabeth Armstrong and her colleagues. Let me mention just one further domain, that of computational linguistics and natural language processing. Here there has been a great deal of systemic work since the early projects of Terry Winograd and Anthony Davey, and two large-scale projects stand out: that of Robin Fawcett at Cardiff University in Wales, and that directed by William Mann at the University of Southern California, in which Christian Matthiessen was the resident linguist. Both Matthiessen and Fawcett construed the demands made by computational work of this nature into major sources of theoretical insight; and with each new advance in technology the potential of the computer for applying knowledge about language, and thereby for expanding such knowledge, has itself been continually expanding. Examples are the multilingual text-generation work by Christian Matthiessen, John Bateman, Wu Canzhong and others; software for teaching and research in systemic grammar, by Mick O'Donnell in Edinburgh and by Kay O'Halloran and Kevin Judd here in Singapore; grammar databases for language teachers such as that developed by Amy Tsui in Hong Kong, and Michio Sugeno's "intelligent computing" research at the Brain Science Institute in Tokyo. The major work being carried on by Kristin Davidse and her team at Leuven, extending the functional grammar further in delicacy, might be thought of as more oriented towards theory; but it too makes use of a computerized corpus (and it is certainly not divorced from application).

Let me emphasize that this is not a general survey of systemic work; this would not be the occasion for it, and in any case the time is long past when I could attempt to keep abreast of all that is going on. I have wanted just to locate my own work in something of its wider context. As will appear, much of this effort, as in linguistics in general, has been expended on aspects of English; but it has never been anglo- (or even euro-) centric, and my own starting point as a grammarian was in fact the grammar of Chinese. Although I had to switch to English for much of my later career, the experience with Chinese played a significant part in shaping my ideas on language: especially pointing towards a unified lexicogrammar as the resource for the creation of meaning, and towards the importance of system (rather than structure) as the level where languages meet. Many languages have now been and are being interpreted in our systemic terms; but Chinese has remained at the forefront, and our Chinese colleagues, such as Hu Zhuanglin, Fang Yan, Zhu Yongsheng, Zhang Delu and Huang Guowen – and of course my co-presenter at this Congress Hu Wenzhong – are showing how important it is for an appliable linguistics to be grounded in a multilanguage foundation.

These are just some of the people thanks to whom I am able to stand here in front of you today. As long as applied linguistics goes on bringing together, in a spirit of inclusion, diverse questions about language, diverse fields of application, and also a diversity of languages under focus of attention, it will no doubt continue to evolve. My own great privilege has been to have been present and, in a small way, to have participated in half a century of its evolution – especially at a time when we have been forced to become aware of the enormous power that language deploys in maintaining and moulding our lives.

PART ONE

MOTHER TONGUE EDUCATION

EDITOR'S INTRODUCTION

In the first chapter, 'Linguistics and the Teaching of English' (1967), Professor M.A.K. Halliday discusses the relevance of linguistics in the teaching of English as a native language. In particular, he argues that it would be useful for the language teacher – whether teaching the native or a foreign language – to have some knowledge of both 'descriptive' and 'institutional' linguistics. By 'descriptive linguistics' he means "the branch of the subject which is concerned with the organization and meaning of language"; and by 'institutional linguistics', he has in mind the sociological aspects of language, i.e. "the relation between a language and its speakers".

Chapter Two, 'A "Linguistic Approach" to the Teaching of the Mother Tongue?' (1971), focuses on the research and curriculum development work undertaken between 1964 and 1970 as part of the "Programme in Linguistics and English Teaching". Professor Halliday describes their approach as 'linguistic', or, in other words, one that takes language seriously, and gives attention to three significant perspectives on language: language as system, language and the individual, and language and society.

In 'Some Thoughts on Language in the Middle School Years' (1977), Professor Halliday approaches language from a functional perspective, as a 'resource', looking at how language functions "in the many and varied contexts in which it is used", and how language meets the demands that we as its users make on it. "If we take seriously the responsibility of the school towards children's language development," he writes, "we need clearly thought out, professional approaches to language in the classroom, based on teachers' understanding of how language functions, of how its internal form relates to the way it functions, and of how children come to learn it."

Moving on from the discussion in the previous chapter on the middle school years, Professor Halliday, in Chapter Four, 'Differences between Spoken and Written Language: Some Implications for Literacy Teaching' (1979), takes up literacy teaching in secondary education, emphasizing the need to develop sensitivity to and control over register variation, including the differences observed between speech and writing.

In 'Language and Socialization: Home and School' (1988), Professor Halliday credits the fact that Bernstein gives a place in his socialization model to language for enabling his model not only to explain how culture is transmitted, but also to accommodate both persistence and change. Because language plays such a significant role in turning our experience into knowledge, he concludes that "acting on language can change the nature of knowledge – and therefore, the nature of learning and of education as well".

In the final chapter of this section, 'Literacy and Linguistics: A Functional Perspective' (1996), Professor Halliday explores the concept of literacy from a linguistic point of view, or as he puts it, attempting "to trace a course through what Graff called the labyrinth of literacy, while interpreting literacy in linguistic terms".

Chapter One

LINGUISTICS AND THE TEACHING OF ENGLISH (1967)

Any discussion of the role of linguistics in the teaching of English as a native language in our schools presupposes some concept of the aims that English teaching is intended to achieve. There is probably no subject in the curriculum whose aims are so often formulated as are those of English language, yet they remain by and large ill-defined, controversial and obscure. In face of this there might be some advantage in beginning at the opposite end, using linguistic concepts to define the possible goals of English language teaching and the standards that might reasonably hope to be achieved. This in turn may help to circumscribe the role of linguistics in, or rather behind, the teaching operation.

In one rather extreme view, the English class is the only one that contributes nothing to the child's mastery of his native language: he 'learns' English only outside school or in the course of studying other school subjects, such as geography and mathematics. "English" is then reserved for the study of literature, and if explicit attention is paid to language this generally takes the form of linguistic criticism, in which the pupil learns to comment in evaluative terms on what has been written or spoken by others, or even on the language as such. This practice is open to various objections, primarily that it is likely to be either trivial or private: to 'state what is wrong with . . .' is essentially a trivial and negative exercise, while questions such as 'do you think that the English language has gained or lost by the disappearance of its inflexional endings?' can be discussed only in private and subjective terms.

Many teachers who would probably not go so far as to deny that language work has a place in the English class nevertheless appear implicitly to accept this view. If, for example, it is left to the science teacher to teach the pupils how to write "scientific English", the implication is that it is not part of the English teacher's task to help him to do so. There will always be a language component in the science teacher's work: technical terms in chemistry, for example, are clearly not the province of the English teacher, although the general concept of a technical term undoubtedly is his province. But for the English teacher to ignore the language of science, rather as if the mathematics teacher were to leave to the teacher of geography all those aspects of mathematics which were relevant to his subject, can only make things more difficult for all concerned; the science teacher cannot relate what he has to say about the language of scientific experiment to the English language as a whole, or to the child's experience of it. He cannot, in fact, except to the extent that he has deliberately made himself a linguist, teach "scientific English", even in isolation from the rest of the language, in any systematic or structured way. He knows what is acceptable to him and what is not, but that is no more a qualification for teaching the pupils about the English language than the fact that I know what dishes are acceptable to me and what are not qualifies me to teach cookery.

It needs no linguistics to point out that teaching the English language is a highly specialized task, perhaps the most important one in the school, and that only the professionally trained English language teacher can perform it. If it is left in the hands of amateurs – and the English literature specialist who has no linguistic training is almost as much an amateur in this context as is the scientist or mathematician – we can expect the result to be a nation of inarticulates, just as a nation of innumerates would result if mathematics teachers were not trained in mathematics. This is not to question either the importance of the study of English literature or the essential part played by it in the pupil's total experience of the language, nor is it to suggest that the teacher of "English literature" and "English language" cannot and should not be one and the same person. The teaching of literature equally demands a professional approach. But this has always been realized, and the training of the English teacher has equipped him with the necessary knowledge and awareness. It has not usually equipped him to teach the language, which has remained a field for the more or less enthusiastic amateur. The 'English as a foreign language' profession has recognized that it is not enough to be a native speaker of a language (indeed, it may almost be a handicap) in order to teach it to foreigners; the 'English as a native language' profession has perhaps still to appreciate that it is not enough to be able to read and enjoy a poem in order to teach the English language to English children.

26

The English teacher, in fact, if he is regarded as having any responsibility for his pupils' effective mastery of the language, needs to know his underlying discipline in the same way as does any other teacher, to at least the same extent, and the relevant underlying discipline here is linguistics. We are accustomed to reiterating, in the context of our anti-intellectual tradition, the truth – by now a commonplace – that to know a subject does not qualify one to teach it, and this may sometimes lead us to ignore the equally important truth that not to know a subject disqualifies one from teaching it at all adequately. The mathematics graduate who has not done his teacher training may be a menace as a teacher of arithmetic, but nothing would be gained from replacing him by a 'Dip.Ed.' who knows no mathematics. In other words, the teacher of mathematics is a mathematician as well as a teacher, and the teacher of languages, native or foreign, is likewise himself a linguist.

It is worth insisting on this point because the teacher of the native language cannot really define the aims of his work except in the light of what he knows from linguistics about the nature of language and the uses to which it is put. This is not, of course, to say that he is going to teach what he knows about the nature of language to his pupils. Nowhere is the distinction between what the teacher knows – or should know – and what he teaches more vital than in the teaching of the native language. This distinction, obvious as it is, is sometimes forgotten or blurred in the course of educational discussions. The tradition in some colleges of education is to concentrate nearly all the attention on what the teacher is to put over in the classroom; this, like the equally one-sided attention paid to background subjects in some others, has in the past no doubt often been due to pressure of time. But neither extreme is desirable, since both imply that whatever the teacher knows is for him to impart to his pupils. This attitude, whether it takes the form of scholarship without methodology or of methodology without scholarship, is surely one of the shortest roads to educational suicide. The language teacher especially, perhaps, is like an iceberg, with never more that a small fraction of what he knows showing above the surface.

Linguistics is relevant as something for the teacher to know, whether he is teaching the native language or a foreign language, living or dead. How much of it appears above the surface in his teaching is another matter, which can best be examined in the light of what are regarded as the aims of native language teaching. By and large, there are two possible types of aim, which we may call the "productive" and the "descriptive". The productive is the 'skill' side of the subject: the increasing of the pupil's competence in his native language, both the spoken and the written skills, including as an essential component the ability to use the language appropriately and effectively for a wide range of different purposes. The descriptive is the 'content' side of the subject: the understanding of how the language works, of what makes it effective as a means of social interaction, and of the properties of language in general as distinct from those of English in particular. There is no real division here into 'vocational' and 'educational' aims, since both components embrace both: control of the resources of one's native language is as much part of the equipment of the citizen as of the wage-earner, while an understanding of these resources has practical value, for example in drafting and interpreting technical instructions or in the learning of foreign languages, as well as more "cultural" applications – the most important of which is in the appreciation of literature, which perhaps more than anything else points to the inclusion at some level of a descriptive component in the teaching of the native language.

In parenthesis, one should here recognize a third component, the "prescriptive", which consists in teaching linguistic table-manners. It is useful to distinguish prescriptive from productive teaching: unlike the latter, the former adds nothing to the pupil's linguistic abilities; it makes his performance more socially acceptable. To say, as most teachers would agree, that prescriptive teaching has been greatly overstressed in the past is not to deny that it has a place in the teaching of the native language; we all have to be taught to conform, and in fact after a certain age the pupil will accept this as an explicit motive for learning, since it is the only one that makes sense in the context. But this is, or should be, only a very minor part of the total activity of the English class; and it should perhaps not figure at all in public examinations. Indeed, if there is one aspect of English teaching that can safely be taken out of the hands of the English teacher, it is this one, since it needs no specialist knowledge at all.

The language teacher, then, is faced with the need to define the aims of his teaching, to formulate in general terms the range of competence that he expects the pupils to reach by a given stage, and to decide how far "descriptive" teaching has a place either in its own right or as an aid to "productive" attainments. Most important of all, he has to carry out the tasks as he recognizes them to be. This is the context in which to pose the question how much linguistics the English teacher would find it useful to know, and what branches of the subject are relevant to him.

Primarily, he would find it useful to be acquainted with those areas of linguistics that would enable him to interpret and evaluate descriptions of and observations about languages, principally, of course, the language being taught. This means understanding the strengths and weaknesses of our grammatical tradition, the contributions of modern structuralism to our knowledge of the mechanisms of languages, and the importance of the concept of an explicit description. It also means an awareness of the different kinds of patterning in language – grammatical, lexical, and so on – and of the relation among these various "levels". Moreover, he should be able to listen objectively, and to operate accurately with at least a limited range of phonetic concepts. In other words, it is helpful for English teachers to have some knowledge of "descriptive linguistics", the branch of the subject that is concerned with the organization and meaning of language. This is not merely something that might occasionally come in useful, but something that helps to shape and clarify one's understanding of and attitude to language (not least the language of literature); moreover many questions of the sort that the English teacher may have to answer every day demand very considerable linguistic sophistication. Why, for instance, is a particular sentence written by a pupil ambiguous, and is its ambiguity inherent in its own structure or a result of inadequate contextualization? At a higher level, he may need to explain the principles and structure of a dictionary, or to give an accurate account of the rhythm of a line of poetry.

Scarcely less important than the study of language structure, to the teacher of the native language, is the sociological aspect of language: what has been defined as 'the relation between a language and its speakers'. This has been called "institutional linguistics"; under the name "sociolinguistics" it has become a separate, border discipline, linking linguistics and sociology. There is no hard and fast line between descriptive and institutional linguistics, but the latter would include two areas of particular relevance: the study of varieties within a language, both dialects and "registers", and the study of the status of a language in the community, including the attitudes adopted towards it by those who speak and write it.

The distinction between dialect and register is a useful one for the English teacher: the dialect being defined 'according to the user' (the dialect you use is determined, by and large, by who you are), the register being 'according to the use' (determined by what you are using the language for). Note that "standard English" is a dialect like any other socioregional variety. The individual may speak in many dialects, in a linguistically complex community such as ours, but if so this reflects his personal history; he must certainly, however, speak (and write) in many registers, to be a citizen of the community at all. Of course, there is such a thing as 'the English language', and one should not exaggerate the differences among its varieties; nevertheless there are differences between spoken and written, formal and informal, technical and non-technical discourse, and the pupil has to understand and master them.

Some register differences are clearly motivated; they correlate with the purpose for which the language is being used, or with the medium, or with the relations among the participants. When the teacher talks of 'effective English' he can explain why certain patterns are used in certain types of situation, and show that effectiveness is to be assessed in relation to given aims and environments. It is not enough to postulate an idealized English that is 'effective', or 'logical' or 'clear' or simply 'good'. The replacing of the monolithic concept of 'good English', a mythical register assumed to be superior for all purposes and in all contexts, by the notion of an English rendered effective precisely by its ability to assume various styles in response to different needs, has been one of the major sources of advance in English teaching theory and practice. Among the most far-reaching of its consequences has been the readiness to take spoken language seriously, to recognize "oracy", in Wilkinson's terms, as an aim parallel in importance to the aim of literacy.

At the same time other differences between register seem entirely unmotivated: they belong to the region of linguistic table-manners, being conventional markers of acceptable behaviour and nothing more. Here the teacher must be able to stand back (whether or not he takes the children with him) and recognize these linguistic conventions for what they are. Since it is one of the school's tasks to socialize its pupils, no doubt it is as reasonable for the teacher to teach the proprieties of language as those of any other form of social behaviour; he should, however, be aware of the distinction (even if it is fuzzy at the edges, as with any other form of social activity) between the dietetics of language and its table-manners. This is the linguistic basis of the distinction between productive and prescriptive teaching as used above.

The teacher, in fact, needs to be objective in all his social attitudes, and it is because the social attitudes of English people towards their language and its varieties are so marked and vehement that the particular sub-branch of linguistics that deals with the study of such attitudes is relatively of such great importance. The training of teachers in this country seems not yet to make adequate provision for developing objective attitudes towards society; much more progress has been made in inculcating objective attitudes towards the individual. It is assumed that the teacher needs to know some psychology, but not yet that he should be trained in sociology or social anthropology. In fact these three subjects – sociology, psychology and linguistics – are the disciplines that are most crucial to the understanding of one's fellow men; every teacher has to be able to step outside the mythology of his own culture, and the teacher of English as a native language is operating in what is perhaps the most myth-prone area of all.

All this is to demand for language no more than the same standard of objective and accurate thinking as is demanded and assumed for mathematics or the physical and biological sciences. One of the myths, in a sense, is that because we know our language we know how to talk about it, or even that because we 'know' (i.e. read) literature we know how to talk about language. (Most teachers would probably agree that an understanding of literature itself, not to mention an understanding of language, demands more than just the reading of good books.) There is really no more justification for inaccurate statements or fallacious reasoning in the realms of grammar, vocabulary, semantics or phonetics than in the description of a leaf or the conduct of a chemistry experiment. Nor does the mere replacement of old terminology by new add anything of value: "grammar" is no better defined or understood when it is called "syntax" or "structure". Indeed, the teacher who is confident enough of his own knowledge of linguistics to avoid excessive reliance on technical terminology in his teaching is likely to be the most successful of all. There are times when linguistic technical terms are useful and necessary, as a means of structuring the pupils' experience and enlarging it; used in this way they constitute no barrier to children. The danger is that they may become an alternative to clear thinking instead of an aid to it. This peril exists for examiner and teacher alike, and new words are no better or safer in this respect than old ones. Much of the development both of the pupils' understanding and use of the English language and of their conscious awareness of its resources, even their ability to talk about the language if the teacher includes this among his aims, can be achieved without the requirement of a special vocabulary.

The ability to talk about the language belongs primarily to the area of what the teacher should know. But how much of what he knows does he impart? In one sense, one could say he imparts it all the time: whenever he makes a correction in a child's composition or comments on a word in a poem he thereby presupposes his own entire attitude to, and knowledge of, the language.

In another sense, however, none of it is imparted, or need be. There is no implication of 'teaching grammar' in the old sense, of merely replacing an old subsonic grammar by a new supersonic one. Productive teaching does not necessarily involve any overt reference to or discussion of linguistic categories at all; it can proceed without parsing, naming or analysing; and if it is held that the principal aim of teaching the native

31

language is the productive one of developing the child's control over the resources of his language and his ability to use those resources to the greatest effect, then there is not necessarily any place for statements about the language anywhere in the curriculum.

This, of course, is not the whole story, and it would be unwise to dismiss 'teaching about the language' from consideration merely because it does not make the major contribution to the major task. In the first place, there are other tasks; or rather, I should prefer to say, other aspects of the same task. Control over the resources of one's language does not mean (although it includes) the ability to fill in a form, prepare an agenda or follow a recipe. It means also the ability to produce and to respond to language that is creative, in which the pupil is involved as an active participant. Linguistic creativity is a reasonable goal for all children, irrespective of age and 'stream'. Such creativity cannot be attained simply by an awareness of what the language can do, just as an understanding of perspective will not by itself produce creative art; but it may be guided, encouraged and released by it, nor is this necessarily less true for younger than for older children. And at the higher levels of "English", descriptive teaching has a direct and fundamental bearing on the reading and appreciation of literature, where the pupil needs to be able himself to talk in accurate and revealing terms about the language of prose and verse texts.

In the second place it may be that some descriptive teaching can help to further even the more pragmatic aims. A child who has been taught to be aware of his language and has learnt some basic concepts with which to describe it may find this of value even in his more goal-directed use of language. There would be precedents for this in other subjects, given that teaching is based on accurate and objective studies of the facts and is geared to the child's developmental requirements. It should not be doubted that children can get excited about their language. Anyone who has attended classes in a school such as the Junior High School at Westport, Connecticut, and seen 12-year-olds arguing heatedly – and cogently – about the respective merits of different analyses of a given sentence, knows how deeply interested children are in their own language provided they are allowed to approach it with the sophistication of which they are capable.

But this should not be taken as justifying an unthinking acceptance of direct teaching about the language as an essential component of the English syllabus. Many teachers who are aware of recent developments in linguistics are understandably eager to bring the fruits of these into the classroom as quickly as possible. There are two causes for alarm here.

One is that some superficial or partial description may be introduced under the banner of a "new grammar", some representation of the mechanisms of English that, however accurate and explicit, may fail to reveal the underlying patterns of the language. Structure without semantics is as barren as semantics without structure. The other is that new linguistic techniques may be grafted on to an existing pedagogical framework without the re-examination of the fundamental aims of native language teaching that (quite apart from other considerations) linguistics itself demands, with all the old exercises of parsing, correcting and the like simply carried out on new material. Such developments can lead only to disenchantment, disenchantment that will then be transferred to linguistics as yet another 'god that failed'.

Children can learn about their language, and be fascinated by the process. They can become fully involved in the study of its grammar, even in primary school, especially if linguistics can provide a 'concrete semantics' for operations with language leading to the development of basic general concepts, on the analogy of the physical operations used to develop concepts of weight, volume and the like. Is there any place for this approach? I do not know. This is one of the things that current research into the teaching of English as a native language, such as that being carried out by the Nuffield Programme in Linguistics and English Teaching at University College London, is designed to find out. Linguistics alone certainly cannot provide the answer; but the answer will not be forthcoming without account being taken of some of the essential facts about language that only linguistics can provide.

If there is any place for teaching about the native language, for example in relation to the study of literature, it is essential that this should be, and should be seen to be, a public and not a private discipline. For a 'numerate' society, we turn to the most explicit discipline of all, mathematics; so for a literate (and 'orate') society, we need an explicit linguistics, in which the meaning of a grammatical statement, as of an algebraic one, resides in and not between the lines. Behind the third of the three R's lies mathematics; behind the first two lies linguistics, and this is perhaps the place to note that advances in the teaching of reading cannot come about if the problem is treated in isolation from its linguistic foundations. In mathematics, the trend is to bring the underlying principles into the classroom: to oversimplify somewhat, one could say that computations which are surface, abstract and specific (i.e. sums), which can lead only to repetitious 'exercises' of the same specific nature, are being replaced by operations that are deep, concrete and general. The nearest linguistic analogue of doing sums is perhaps parsing; this is likely to be less effective than various operations with language could be expected to be. The object of the English class, in one very real sense, is to make the language work for you, as the object of the arithmetic class is to make numbers work for you. A teacher who can show the language at work, or at play, in a living environment is increasing his pupils' effective control over it, and thereby also their appreciation of the control exercised over it by others, including our greatest poets.

Linguistics, as has been stressed, is not the only discipline underlying the teaching of English as a native language. Closely associated with it here are sociology and psychology. These two subjects are relevant of course to a great deal more than the teaching of English; they underlie the whole educational process. So also does linguistics, since education largely takes place through language, and educational performance, as Bernstein's work makes clear, is closely related to linguistic development. In the teaching of English to English-speaking children, however, linguistics has a more specific and central role to play: it can both build on and contribute to the renewed enthusiasm and informed interest now being shown in the "English" class on all sides of the teaching profession.

Chapter Two

A "LINGUISTIC APPROACH" TO THE TEACHING OF THE MOTHER TONGUE? (1971)

For more than ten years now I have enjoyed a close working association with teachers of English as a mother tongue, first in Scotland and then in England. I am particularly happy, therefore, to have this opportunity of talking with English teachers in Canada.[*]

As a matter of fact, my association with the English-teaching profession began at birth, because my father was a teacher of English at a secondary school in a town in northern England; and one of my early memories, which those among you who are familiar with the British educational system will instantly recognize, is of being almost unable to move in the house in which we lived without falling over piles of examination scripts.

More recently, however, I became concerned with the teaching of English by a different, and somewhat circuitous, route; one that led me through Oriental languages, with a detour into the teaching of English as a foreign language, and into the field of linguistics. As a linguist, I came to be teaching in a university English department, at the University of Edinburgh; from this department many of the graduates went on to teach English in secondary schools, and through them we came to hold regular discussions and study sessions with groups of teachers from different parts of Scotland. This explains the personal nature of these introductory remarks, for which I make due apology. My point is that it was mainly my experience in working with English teachers during that time in Scotland that convinced me of the need to examine more closely the linguistic basis of the teaching of English as a mother tongue.

[*] Keynote address, Ontario Council of Teachers of English Convention, 22 March 1971. The editors have made some changes (mainly, necessary shortening) but have retained the oral tone of the original presentation.

To bring the tale up to date, in 1963 I moved to London, to University College; and for the past six years, up to the end of 1970, I have been directing a research and development project in the teaching of English in English schools. This project, known as the Programme in Linguistics and English Teaching, was financed first by the Nuffield Foundation and subsequently by the Schools Council of the Department of Education and Science. Its work is just now coming to an end.

In one sense this paper could be considered as a report on the work of the programme. But this does not mean that I propose to give a chronicle history of the project, still less a catalogue of the achievements we should like to be able to claim for it. Most of what I have to say is not directly about the project at all. I hope to give some impression of the directions we explored in the course of the work, and of the conclusions we reached concerning the teaching of the mother tongue, as a result of a number of years of reading, thinking and talking; of holding study groups, teachers' conferences, and in-service courses of varying lengths; of writing materials, trying them out, and rewriting them in the light of what the teachers who had used them had to say about them; and finally – the stage that is not yet quite completed – of preparing these materials for publication and launching them on their way.

I use the word "we", but my part was that of non-participating director, creating the conditions in which others could do the work and joining in in what spare time I could set aside. This now has the advantage that it allows me to express satisfaction with the results without being lacking in modesty. If I speak in enthusiastic terms of the materials that have been produced, the praise is entirely due to my colleagues, the people who actually produced them.

The team was a combined force of university, secondary and primary teachers; and having once learnt to understand each other – no easy task in an educational system where the boundaries are clearly marked and usually difficult to cross – we tried to keep in the front of our minds a clear picture of the route by which we had arrived at this mutual com-prehension. I am sure that it was the experience gained from working in such a team which more than anything else helped us to collaborate effectively with the teachers who were trying out our materials, so that they understood what we were attempting to do and we in turn could appreciate and take advantage of their responses.

Our brief was perhaps an unusual one in curriculum research and development. We were the first group of this kind in Britain to work on the teaching of the mother tongue; and for this reason we undertook to survey the whole process, from the infant school right through to the

36

sixth form – ages 5 to 18. Naturally, with this perspective we could not investigate the requirements of any one age group in full detail. But we could hope to obtain an overall view of English in school; and this is valuable because it allows one to think in terms of an integrated or 'strategic' approach to the teaching of the mother tongue, and to develop certain general notions which will underlie the more specific, and very diverse, activities being pursued by students at different maturational levels.

In this context we identified three points at which to concentrate our own curriculum development work; these were, roughly, the beginning, the middle and the end of the school career. The development work thus took the form of three projects: the "initial literacy project", better known by the name under which its materials were finally produced, "Breakthrough to Literacy"; the "middle-school project"; and the project for the upper school, which also came to be known by the name of its materials, "Language in Use". Of these, the middle-school project was late in starting and was unfortunately not complete at the time when the funds ran out; those involved are still hoping to finish it in their own time. *Breakthrough to Literacy* came out early in 1970 and is being used by about a hundred thousand children this year. *Language in Use* is in the press and will be published in September 1971.

The title by which the whole venture was known, "Programme in Linguistics and English Teaching", was intended to suggest that we were going to explore the teaching of English (as a mother tongue) from the standpoint of modern linguistics. We had no wish to neglect developments in other relevant subjects, such as sociology, psychology and literary criticism, or in educational theory in general. But while the approach to English through literature had been thoroughly explored all along, and the place of psychology in education has been well established for most of a century, the theoretical achievements of sociology and linguistics had so far made very little impact. In particular, I felt that there had been hardly any serious consideration, in an educational context, of the real nature of language, so that neither the task faced by the child in mastering his mother tongue nor the role of the school in helping him to achieve this mastery had been adequately understood and assessed.

There have of course been "linguistic approaches" to some of the learning tasks, particularly to initial literacy, although in general they were not very well known in Britain. But this is itself a source of difficulty. What do we mean by a "linguistic approach"? The term has been applied to various techniques, such as that of vocabulary limitation, whereby the total number of new words that is introduced in each of a series of reading primers is carefully controlled; or the techniques of selecting words, on the basis of their relative frequency, or on the principle of phonic-graphic regularity, so that instead of starting on page one with *See Spot run. Run, Spot, run!* we start with *Pick the thick stick off the brick, Chick!* – a principle that was already embodied without the aid of linguistics in the classic sentence "The cat sat on the mat". And later on there is a special type of linguistic approach sometimes known as the "structural approach", in which the more mature student is taken on a voyage through the structures of English; this is liable to leave him feeling rather as if he had been led blindfolded through a maze and then invited to find his own way out. Or else he is taught to analyse sentences into their structures – in other words, to parse them.

Whatever the value of such techniques, they do not, either severally or together, constitute what I would call a "linguistic approach" to the teaching of the mother tongue. That is to say, they do not derive from any general consideration of what language is, of what it means to learn a language, or of what part language plays in our lives. They do not presuppose that any questions have been asked – still less any answers given – about the place of language in education, the respective roles of teacher and student in the student's linguistic development, or the relation between the learning of the mother tongue and the study of the various 'subjects' with which the student is concerned in his working life: history, science, the new maths, foreign languages, and so on. They do not start from what we do with language, as individuals and as social beings.

The analytic or structural approach to English, whatever may be claimed or hoped for from it, seems to have no solid justification in theory or in practice. We may have a new supersonic grammar to replace the old subsonic one, but it is still being used in much the same old way, with hardly any extension to the runways, let alone serious rethinking of the pattern of air travel or the principles of flight control. I do not think that techniques like these will ever make the difference between success and failure in the learning of the mother tongue. And we now realize that we must turn failure into success; we are aware of a massive level of linguistic failure in our schools, and of the disastrous social consequences that this failure brings in its train.

We are convinced that, in the teaching of the mother tongue, whether English to English-speakers, French to French-speakers, or any other, language should be the central theme.

Whether our approach is to be regarded as a "linguistic" approach or not depends on how broadly one is prepared to define the term. If it is defined narrowly, for example as the study of the phonological and grammatical structure of language, or as the study of an aspect of the human mind – as "a branch of theoretical psychology", in Chomsky's characterization – then our approach is definitely **not** through linguistics. It has relatively little to do with theoretical psychology, although this does play some part in it, and it is certainly not confined to considerations of linguistic structure.

I myself would define linguistics very broadly, to include all facets of the study of language. But in order to avoid misunderstanding we have tended to use the term "language study" rather than linguistics in relation to our work, thus emphasizing our opinion that the successful teaching of the mother tongue is founded on an exploration of language in all its aspects, and not bound by the limitations of any one interpretation of what linguistics is or ought to be.

Breakthrough to Literacy and *Language in Use* represent an approach to the teaching of the mother tongue that is 'linguistic' in this broad sense. It is an approach through language, and through "language study". In other words, it is an approach that takes language seriously. I should like to highlight this concept today as my central theme. 'Taking language seriously' is not as easy as it sounds. It demands that most elusive quality: a sense of proportion, a feeling for what is important and what is less important in the context of what one is doing. I sometimes feel that what is most lacking in our attitude to English is a linguistic sense of proportion.

Perhaps I can illustrate this best by referring to grammar, since grammar always tends to occupy a prominent place in our deliberations – whether or not it is central to the English curriculum, it is usually central to discussions among English teachers. Presumably, if we take language seriously, we should pay due attention to the rules of language, and particularly to those of grammar.

Or should we? I would suggest, without wanting to take this to extremes, that paying attention to the rules of grammar is often a way of **not** taking language seriously. It may be precisely a way of avoiding having to take language seriously. If the rules of grammar come to dominate the scene, we have lost our linguistic sense of proportion. The reason is quite straightforward. The rules of grammar are the mechanics of language; if we concentrate on the rules of grammar, therefore, we are concentrating on the mechanism, or even in some instances on the wrapping and the packaging, instead of on language for what it really is – a field, perhaps the most important field, of human potential.

39

It is true that there can be no language without grammar. If my reference to the rules of grammar as the "mechanics" of language leaves an impression of something that is flat and unimportant, I will gladly adapt the metaphor and say, as I did once in talking to members of your fraternal association in London, that grammar is the harmony and the melody of language. (I suggested on that occasion, I remember, that if I was a writer of science fiction, my invaders from outer space would have just one secret weapon: a degrammatization ray, which had the effect of depriving all who came in contact with it of their grammatical faculties. To be grammarless is to be totally powerless.) But then, harmony and melody are the mechanics of music. To know the rules of harmony is not the same thing as to take music seriously; and to study nothing but the rules of harmony would not by itself bring about a deep sensitivity to music. It might even bring about an aversion to music; and this is equally likely to happen whether the rules are studied in the old way, as immutable norms, or in the new psychologistic way through investigations of the reaction of experimental subjects to different musical intervals. Nether is an alternative to listening. In just the same way, excessive concentration on the rules of grammar has caused generations of students to be resentful at the mere thought or mention of language.

We should try to put this in perspective. I am a grammarian myself, and I think grammar is an illuminating and exciting object of study. I am writing a grammar at the moment; or rather, I am writing a description of a language, and this naturally includes a description of its grammar. The language is that of my small son, who is now aged 16 months; and the description I am writing just at present is the fifth in the series. The first four descriptions, incidentally, were to the best of my knowledge complete; if so, they are the only complete accounts of a language I have ever written or almost certainly ever shall write. It is a chastening thought that by the time he is 18 months old his language will in all probability have become too rich for a linguist (or at least this particular linguist) to give a total account of.

However, these descriptions are not sets of grammatical rules. In fact in the narrow sense of grammar, where "grammar" equals "structure", my little boy still has no grammar at all: he has grammatical systems, but no structures. What I am describing is what I would call his "meaning potential": that is, the range of meanings he is able to express. And these meanings, in turn, are related to the purposes he uses language for. He has mastered certain elementary but very fundamental linguistic functions, certain systematic uses of language; and within each of these functions he is building up what I referred to just now as a "meaning potential". In other words, he has control of various sets of options, and these represent what he is able to do with language in each particular context of use.

The list of functions is very short – there are only four or five – but these are very general functions, of great significance for the child as he becomes a social being. We can recognize, at this stage, an "instrumental" function, a "regulatory" function, an "interactional" function, a "personal" function and an "imaginative" function. The first of these, the instrumental function, is the use of language to satisfy his material needs: to obtain some object or some service he requires. So he makes general demands, like [na], on a mid-falling tone, which means simply 'I want that thing you've got there', and specific demands like [ə'ɹoᵂ], also on a mid-falling tone, which means 'I want a rusk'. We might describe this informally as the 'I want' function.

The regulatory function, the second on my list, is the use of language to control other people's behaviour, a function that is not difficult for him to appreciate because language is used that way by others speaking to him. Again there are general commands, such as [ɛ] (high-falling) 'do that again', and specific ones such as [????] (very slow glottal friction) 'let's go for a walk'. While in the instrumental function the focus is on the object or service needed, and it does not matter who acts to satisfy the need; in the regulatory function the focus is on the person addressed and it is the behaviour of that particular person that the child is seeking to control. We could call this the 'do as I tell you' function of language.

In the interactional function, he is using language to interact with those around him, through greetings, valedictions and the like, e.g. [anna], high level tone, 'Iona!' (personal name), [ɛ:'dɛ] (high rise and fall) which means really 'nice to see you, and shall we look at this picture together?'. The personal function, on the other hand, is language in the expression of his own individuality: his feelings of pleasure, interest, impatience and so on. Here we have for example [a'ʸiː], on a high tone, which is said only in front of a mirror and means 'look, that's me there!'; various exclamations at particular objects of interest, such as [œ] (low-falling tone) 'listen, an aeroplane!'; and [bᵂgabᵂgabᵂga], also on a low-falling tone, which means 'what's all that gibberish?' when the radio comes out with talk instead of music. The interactional function is that of 'me and my mum', perhaps, while the personal is the "here I come!" function; the two overlap somewhat, as do almost any pair of functions, but the general distinction is clear enough.

Finally there is language in the imaginative function, that of 'let's pretend'. Here language is being used to create a world of fancy; this may be in pure sound, like [gɔg!gɔg!gɔg!ga] (mid-narrow fall), or in pretend-play, for example [gʷəigʷəigʷəi], also mid-narrow fall, meaning 'I'm pretending to go to sleep' accompanied by the appropriate posture on the floor.

Notice how the intonation patterns vary, not only with the individual utterances but corresponding in part to the different functions. The range of meanings within each use of language is very limited, but this little child has effectively grasped the fact that there is a great deal he can do with language. Language has many kinds of meaning. The functions we have identified, the 'I want', the 'do as I tell you', the 'me and my mum', the 'here I come' and the 'let's pretend', are the different kinds of meaning that language has for him.

I do not think we can seriously doubt that this little boy has language. He can, and does, produce utterances that are both systematic and functional. They are systematic, in that there is a constant relation between the content and the expression: sounds retain their meanings from one day to the next, the meanings go on being expressed by the same sounds. The utterances are functional, in that their content is interpretable in the light of some theory of linguistic functions – of a functional theory of language, in other words. He has no structures, but that is immaterial; he is not yet using structure as a mechanism for his expression. The time will come, fairly soon, when he will have to build up structures, so as to be able to integrate different functions of language into a single utterance – in order to be able to do more than one thing at once, so to speak, since that is what structure is for. But the functional basis of his language will remain.

Our conception of language has for a long time – for too long, I think – been dominated by the notion of structure. This has penetrated into the classroom, so that the English class has become a time for drawing trees on the blackboard, the tree being now well established as the diagrammatic representation of a linguistic structure.

Unfortunately linguists, and some teachers, seem to get so bemused by trees that they can no longer see the wood. A tree could almost be defined, nowadays, as that which a linguist cannot see the wood for. The tree, or more generally the notion of structure, is certainly appropriate as a means of revealing some of the internal workings of language. But in an educational context, where our concern is surely with the meanings that can be expressed, and only secondarily with the mechanics of their expression, one aspect of language that need not be at the centre of attention is the structural one.

The study of the language of a very young child is of interest here not merely because it shows us language without structure, and very effective language at that, but also for the more positive reason that it gives us an insight into linguistic function. Because of its relative simplicity – the choices are few, and each one is fairly uncomplicated – we can see what the child achieves by the use of his language, what he makes it do for him; and we can set up a theoretical model of the functions of language on this basis. With the older child, or the adult, the meaning potential is immeasurably greater; but the functions which language serves for him, provided these are interpreted in the most general sense, as distinct from this or that particular condition of use, do not greatly differ. The main headings are those we have already had, or are closely related to them. In some respects, the set of functions may even contract: in how many of us, for example, does the imaginative function of language, that is so important to a young child, remain creative and alive in our maturer years?

If we are concerned with the learning of the mother tongue, and with the part the school plays in this process, our efforts are likely to be focused on the students' ability to use language successfully in a wide variety of functional contexts. For this purpose we need a functional approach to language; an approach in which structure, if we give it a place at all, will be a derived and dependent concept. We shall be interested in structure, in other words, because it is the means whereby language operates. Language is structured in the way it is because it has to express meanings that are functionally complex. If we find it of interest to explore linguistic structure in this light, well and good; but it is the functional basis of the language system that provides the context for doing so.

It was this that I had in mind when I suggested that, if we are taking language seriously, we need to put grammar in perspective. Nobody will come to any serious harm by being made to do some parsing, whether new-style or old. But he is not likely to gain much from it either, particularly if it is not enshrined in any context which gives it significance. The notion of the functions of language gives us a reason for looking into linguistic structure if we want to do so. This is, first and foremost, because it can help to explain why language has structure in the first place.

Language is as it is because of what we make it do for us. Language serves certain very concrete functions, as the child is aware early in his life: he soon internalizes the fact that language is meaningful behaviour that marks him off from, and at the same time relates him to, his environment. As the meanings he learns to express become more complex, and in particular as each utterance comes to serve more that

43

one function at once, he has to develop a grammar to match these requirements. The form the grammar takes – the fact that it includes a level of linguistic structure, and even the properties of the tree such as they are – seems to reflect fairly closely the functional origins of the linguistic system. If we wanted to return to the musical analogy, we could say that linguistic structure is polyphonic: it consists of a number of melodies unfolding simultaneously and, within limits, overlapping at their boundaries. We normally keep more than one tune going at a time.

If we look at grammar in this perspective, in the context of some integrated view of the function of language, then even if we start from an interest in linguistic structure for its own sake, we shall inevitably find ourselves involved in considerations of language in use. But from an educational point of view, our concern in the first place is surely with language in use, since success in the mother tongue – and this is the only significant goal of our efforts – is the same thing as success in its use. It is no accident that the materials prepared by our programme for teachers of English in secondary schools finally came to have just this title; they are called, simply, *Language in Use*. They are materials written for the teacher, who is invited to guide the student in a free-ranging yet systematic exploration of language as human, social potential; and hence, of the relation of language to social structure, to human institutions (such as the school itself), to the structure of knowledge, and so on. I should like to try to give some indication here of what these materials are. *Language in Use*

[*Language in Use*] consists of 110 individual units, each one of which provides an outline for a sequence of lessons. Each outline is built around a particular facet of the way we use language. There is a head-note to each unit which describes this topic and indicates what a class might achieve by exploring it. The units are grouped together in ten themes, each of which is concerned with one major aspect of language in use. In turn, these themes are drawn together into three broad divisions: the nature and function of language, its place in the lives of individuals, and its role in making human society possible. These three divisions provide the basis for the three parts of the volume. [Introduction]

The ten themes are: A, using language to convey information; B, using language expressively; C, sound and symbol; D, pattern in language; E, language and reality; F, language and culture; G, language and experience; H, language in individual relationships; J, language in social relationships; K, language in social organizations. Examples of unit titles are: "words and actions" (A.1), "formal and informal" (B.1), "order in sentences" (D.2), "man's job/woman's work" (F.2), "playing many parts" (H.3).

No specialist knowledge of linguistics is required on the part of the teacher who is using these materials, nor is the student expected to operate within a technical framework or to master complex analytical procedures. (But there is nothing to prevent teacher and student from launching into explicit technical linguistics if they wish to do so; the units provide an excellent launching pad, as those who have used them in colleges of education have observed.)

> [Language in Use] is concerned with the relationship between pupils and their language. This relationship has two major aspects: what pupils should know about the nature and function of language, and how they can extend their command of their own language in both speaking and writing. The units aim to develop in pupils and students awareness of what language is and how it is used, and, at the same time, to extend their competence in handling the language. [Introduction]

The most important fact about the student in his role as a member of the English class is that he already knows a great deal of English, and he knows it not as a system in abstraction from reality but as a dynamic potential, a mode of being and doing in concrete functional contexts.

> Pupils bring to the classroom a native speaker's knowledge of, and intuitions about, language and its place in human society. In this sense, the task of the English teacher is not to impart a body of knowledge, but to work upon, develop, refine and clarify the knowledge and intuitions that his pupils already possess. Consequently, he is interested in language as it affects the lives of individuals and the fabric of society. [Introduction]

In other words, the balance of emphasis is different from that of the specialist in linguistics, whose central concern is likely to be "the explicit, formal and analytical description of the patterns of a language" (ibid.). This leads us back to the notion of a linguistic sense of proportion; and to 'language study' as the theoretical background, which includes all the kinds of enquiry that lead to an understanding of language, and so allows us to adjust the perspective in accordance with the particular task in hand.

This is not to say that the conception of language study is in conflict with the goals of linguistics. On the contrary, "language study" is simply another name for linguistics when this is defined in its widest sense, as many linguists would already define it. The work that is being done here in Toronto at York University, by Professor Michael Gregory and his colleagues (including your present president), on varieties and styles of English is an excellent example of the kind of language study that is most directly relevant to the teacher of English, one of whose main concerns is likely to be with the way language varies in different contexts of use. A number of the units in *Language in Use* are in fact built around just this theme.

As an accompaniment to *Language in Use* there will be a separate volume by the same authors entitled *Exploring Language*. This is intended as an introduction to language study, for teachers of English who want to pursue further their own linguistic interests and to extend their acquaintance with the intellectual background to *Language in Use*. *Exploring Language* contains five parts: I, Language and the teacher; II, The individual context of language; III, The social context of language; IV, The diversity of language; V, Command of a language; together with a glossary, and an appendix showing how the various parts of the two books relate to each other.

I shall not attempt here to describe the materials produced for learning to read and write, *Breakthrough to Literacy*. These were produced by other members of the same team, and came out early in 1970. Much of what I have said about *Language in Use* would apply, *mutatis mutandis*, to *Breakthrough to Literacy*. As I tried to show in describing it to the 1971 Claremont Reading Conference, *Breakthrough to Literacy* also embodies a "linguistic approach", provided again that this is understood in the broad sense that I have outlined. In particular, it is based on the view that becoming literate is a natural stage in the process of learning one's first language – natural in the sense that it is functionally motivated: there comes a time in the life of the individual (as in the history of mankind) when what one wants to do with language demands a move into a new medium. The spoken channel no longer suffices for all the parts that language has to play. Hence the approach is one in which learning to read and write is placed squarely in the context of mastery of the mother tongue, and not treated as a separate and rather esoteric exercise as it so often is in our own schools.

I hope I have been able to give some indication of what I meant by 'taking language seriously', and also of the sense in which we have been attempting to develop a "linguistic approach" to the teaching of English in schools. It is perhaps unwise to try to sum up, but there are three points which, together, represent the perspective I have wanted to convey.

First, language is not treated as a phenomenon in and of itself, in isolation from the individual and from society. But neither is it viewed exclusively from just one external standpoint. For many linguists today the study of language is closely tied to the study of the human organism, particularly the investigation of the nature of the human mind. But this is only one of many angles, and it is almost certainly not the one that is most significant for the teacher of English. In *Language in Use* we have tried to give due weight to each of what seem to us to be the three significant perspectives on language: language as a system, language and the individual, and language and society.

Second, the study of the mother tongue in school is not interpreted to mean the acquisition of a body of knowledge, or pedagogical content, in the form of rules of language and facts about language, knowledge that has first to be acquired and then applied, if at all, consciously and mechanically in composition exercises and the like. It is treated as the exploration of a human potential, a potential that is extended in the explorer as he explores it. In *Language in Use* we have tried to follow through the implications of this uniquely human ability, the ability to mean, and in so doing to lead the student to develop this ability as fully as possible in himself.

Finally, a language is not treated as an inventory of structures, however "deep" these are supposed to be. Instead, what we achieve through language is regarded as more important than the mechanisms by which it is achieved. In *Language in Use* we have tried to give some insight into the functions that language serves in the life of man, and of the extraordinary demands that we make, day in and day out, on the resources of our mother tongue. (It does let us down sometimes, of course, but surprisingly seldom, and usually through our own fault.) The fact that language effectively serves such a variety of intents, without our even being aware of what these are unless perhaps we are students of rhetoric, is good reason for emphasizing its functional character as a basis for our understanding and appreciation of language.

I referred earlier to an aspect of the broad ideological context in which we are now working, one which has changed markedly in the course of the last two decades. Fifteen or twenty years ago, although few people were complacent about the present, the atmosphere was essentially one of confidence in the future: as educational opportunities increased, so illiteracy and other forms of failure would disappear. Now the feeling is very different. We are conscious that there is a dangerous level of almost total educational failure in our urban population, in Britain, the USA and to a lesser extent in other countries as well. I do not know whether this is a significant problem in Canada or not, but I have no doubt that teachers and educators are alerted to its existence elsewhere. In Britain my colleague Basil Bernstein, of the London University Institute of Education, has done more than anyone to uncover the nature and causes of this failure. His work has shown that, at one level, educational failure is largely language failure: failure to achieve one's potential in the mother tongue.

Of course, as Bernstein points out, this is not an ultimate cause; there are social factors underlying language failure, and these too are gradually becoming clearer. But as far as the school is concerned, the remedy has to be found at least partly in language. The school cannot influence the underlying social factors — it cannot, for example, affect the pattern of communication in the family, the linguistic means whereby the child is initiated into the society — or it can do so only indirectly, and in the very long run. But it can offer the opportunities that are needed at the next stage of the child's development. These are, first and foremost, opportunities for realizing the vast potential that every individual has in his mother tongue. I do not think that we are yet offering to our children the best linguistic chance in life. But if we can learn to take language seriously, we shall be removing some of the artificial barriers that stand in their way.

Chapter Three

SOME THOUGHTS ON LANGUAGE IN THE MIDDLE SCHOOL YEARS★ (1977)

The notion of the 'middle school years' suggests a stage that is in between: one that is neither a beginning nor an end, but is in some sense transitional – and yet (since we are giving it a name) one that has some special features of its own, distinct from what precedes it and what follows. The question that often arises, in discussions of language education, is whether the middle school years can be recognized as a definable stage in a child's development of language.

It would be helpful, no doubt, to be able to give a definite answer one way or the other, but as in so many critical issues, we have to hedge. There is a great deal that is not yet known about language development at this stage; but even if we knew much more, there might still be no very clear-cut answer. Instead of approaching the question in this way, let us suggest some of the features that seem to be characteristic of children's language in the middle school years.

Obviously, children of this age range already have an extensive command of the resources of their mother tongue. First, they can understand and express a wide range of *meanings*, putting the meanings into appropriate *wordings* and the wordings into appropriate *sounds*. In other words, they have some mastery of the language as a *system*.

Second, they can perceive how the language varies, along the lines of *dialect* (geographical and social differences) and of *register* (differences of context and purpose), and can to some extent vary their own language

---

★ This chapter puts together in an abridged form material from two public lectures, "Language in adolescence" (English Teachers' Association of New South Wales, May 1976) and "Language in the middle school years" (Victorian Association of Teachers of English, March 1977).

according to its use. In other words, they have some mastery of the language as an ***institution***. At the same time they still have much to learn, and we can identify some of the areas in which their language potential will be continuing to develop during this period.

The language as a system

Sounds (phonology):

Children of 8–9 already effectively control the sound system of their mother tongue, in its family, neighbourhood and primary school versions (all of which may vary in minor ways). They have built up the patterns of (i) intonation, (ii) rhythm and (iii) articulation (vowels and consonants). If they are learning new speech sounds at this stage this is likely to be because they are learning another dialect – perhaps some form of standard English that is different from what they spoke before.

Wordings (lexicogrammar):

(i) They are extending their grammatical resources into new areas. An example is the construction of complex sentences involving non–finite clauses, such as *Not knowing where to go, they lay down under a tree to rest*. (ii) They are learning new vocabulary, much of it through extending their use of language into new registers. As an example, consider the instructions issued with model-making kits, which often contain rare words and complex collocations.

Written language:

By contrast with their ability in speaking and listening, they are likely to be relatively uncertain in their control of the written language, in two particular respects: (i) they will still find it more difficult to express themselves in writing, and (ii) although they may read fluently, they will still find it harder to **learn** from reading than from listening.

Reading and writing are a part of a child's language development. But written language is not just spoken language written down; it has its own styles of meaning and of wording. In part these are purely conventional, like the convention of using expanded forms such as *do not, will not*, instead of the *don't, won't* of speech. In part they are motivated by the difference in the nature of the two media; spoken language – provided it is spontaneous – is planned by the speaker as he goes along, and processed rapidly once through by the listener, whereas written language, especially that of children, is planned and processed deliberately, and can be worked over more than once. Consider these examples:

Spoken:

You know, the extraordinary thing about going in for these jobs is that what you don't realize, because you don't get told, is that all this long period of waiting, when you're kept hanging about while various officials stride up and down, wearing fancy uniforms and looking full of serious purpose, is actually something they make you go through deliberately so the people who are going to interview you get a chance to observe the way you behave when you're up against this kind of stress.

Written:

Before the interview there is an inordinately long delay, during which uniformed officials stride purposefully up and down. Unknown to the candidate, the delay is deliberately contrived so that the panel can observe his behaviour under conditions of stress.

So, as these examples show, spoken language tends to have a more complicated grammar than written language, and a simpler, less closely packed vocabulary: the sentences may contain many interlocked phrases and clauses, but with the content words spread out more thinly among them. Conversely, in writing, while the grammar may by simpler, the lexical structure is very dense; a great deal of information is packed into each structural unit. This may be a further reason, quite apart from the difficulty of coping with the medium itself, why there is often a fairly big gap, at this age, between what a child can do with speaking and what he can do with writing.

The language as an institution

Children in the middle school years are often very adept at dialect switching; they can hear and recognize the differences among different regional dialects, such as Australian, English, Irish and American, and among different social dialects, such as urban and rural, old and young, middle-class and working-class; and they can often imitate and caricature a fair range of these. Many city children regularly switch dialects between home and neighborhood, or between home and school. But it is not until adolescence, around the age range 13–18, that they learn the social significance of dialect variation: the way in which adults use language as an index of social background, level of formality, and so on. It is in adolescence, too, that they take over the attitudes and prejudices towards language that are a feature of the adult world; and although we could not insulate them from these prejudices, even if we wanted to, as teachers we have to be able to stand far enough back from the scene so as to help them to retain some objectivity and tolerance in their attitudes towards the speech of others.

Dialects are, in principle, different ways of saying the same thing. Registers are ways of saying different things: using language in different contexts, for different purposes – serious or frivolous, ordinary or specialized, organized or haphazard. Language in school involves a wide range of register variation; English in the maths class is not the same as English in the history class, let alone English in the drama class or in the playground. Children in the middle school age group are beginning to build up a register range, and one of the encouraging trends in the last decade has been the broadening of language experience in the classroom, as teachers have become more willing to take account of the various different registers of writing and of speech.

Finally, under the second heading, children in this age range are becoming interested in verbal contest and display. The use of language for purposes of contest and display is something that will continue and flourish throughout the years of adolescence. In its detailed manifestations it differs very much among different cultures and sub-cultures; but in most populations, teasing, showing off, competing, putting others down, duelling with the opposite sex and suchlike rhetorical skills are highly valued functions of language, and excelling at these is fully comparable, in the status it confers on the individual, with excelling in other, non-verbal, forms of prowess. Such skills are typically acquired outside the classroom; within the school context, they are sanctioned in such forms as that of the debate, a practice that is nowadays rather out of favour but can be extremely valuable as a means of expanding linguistic resourcefulness. These is obviously a limit to the extent to which verbal contest and display can become school activities, if only because they are in one of their aspects a form of verbal resistance to the educational process. But the more literary types of contest and display, ranging from parody and satire, through improvised versifying, to capping other people's stories, are not so entirely remote from the realms of rhetoric and composition that they could not have some place in a middle school English programme.

People concerned with language education are moving more towards a conception of language development as a continuous process, one that begins in the pre-school years – at birth, in fact – and goes on throughout the years of primary and secondary schooling. This is a positive and forward-looking approach. By the time a child comes to school he already has a considerable experience of language behind him – of language in the home and language in the neighborhood. The family and the young children's "peer group" are the first two of what sociologists call the "primary socializing agencies", the interpersonal environments in which a child builds up his picture of the world that is around him and inside him.

These are the two groups of people with whom a young child spends most of his time. From a linguistic point of view, they are the ones with whom he exchanges meanings – we might think of them as his "meaning groups". Of course, they are not totally separate from each other; there are often other young children in the family who are also part of the neighborhood network. But the two tend to make rather different demands on a child's language – on his meaning potential, as I have called it. He first learns to speak in the family, an environment that, despite the presence of other children in it, is essentially adult-oriented. Here his use of language tends to be directed towards such things as:

- definition of the 'self' by reference to 'others': 'I'm me, because (i) I'm not you and (ii) I interact with you'
- inclusion and exclusion, including 'getting back in' when rejected
- controlling behaviour and 'social manners'
- learning by seeking to understand: parents as source of explanation and instruction
- relaxation: not having to be at one's best all the time
- moral judgment: good and bad ('naughty')
- imagining: play and pretending; story, song and rhyme

When the child comes to mix with other children, the emphasis changes. The peer group is child-oriented; it has no adults in it, and language has to function for the child in new ways:

- solidarity: group identity, with the individual defined by the group: 'I'm me because I'm one of us'
- group interests: hierarchy and conformity
- competition and cooperation: self-reliance, but also mutual assistance, as twin themes
- boasting, insults, humour: verbal contest and display
- oaths, secrets, alliances: concepts of 'face', of friendship, of winning and losing
- laws, rights and obligations; 'fair' and 'unfair'
- games; turns and rituals

At this point the school comes into the picture, and once again new demands are made on language. The school is child-centred but adult-oriented:

- institutionalized norms and success criteria: 'I'm me because I succeed'
- controlled competition; competitive evaluation of performance: good and bad in new meanings
- organization of knowledge ('classification') and of exchange of information ('framing')
- 'strategic' conception of learning (= being taught); ritualized instruction
- stratification; chains of command and transmission
- organized play; controlled exercise of imagination

By the time they are in school most children have been developing their language not only quantitatively, by enlarging the total potential, but also qualitatively, by learning to use language in new ways – in the service of different realities, so to speak. There is nothing by itself that is problematical about adding a third scheme of things – the world of the school – to the pre-existing worlds of family and peer group; children quite happily tolerate any number of different realities provided the tension that is set up among them is not excessive. The point is, of course, that while a bilingual child may have a different language for different realities, with a one-language child all realities are coded in the same language, using the same semantic potential.

How does a child build up his picture of the world around him? One thing stands out: that at one and the same time he is both learning language and learning **through** language. This does not imply, of course, that he is learning by instruction; by far the greater part of the learning that takes place in the home and in the neighborhood is learning without being taught. In the micro-encounters of daily life are contained all the essential meanings of the culture. His mother says: "Leave that stick outside; stop teasing the cat; and go and wash your hands. It's time for tea." There is a wealth of cultural information lurking in that innocent sentence: about boundaries, and what goes where; about the regularity and predictability of the events of daily life; about humanity and near-humanity; about norms and rules of behaviour. Taken by itself, one single speech event is of little significance; but events like this are going on all the time – a child is surrounded by them, either addressed to him or spoken within his hearing – and it is from these that he builds up a picture of what life is like.

The process is a **creative** one, but not an **individual** one. It is worth stressing this, perhaps, in view of the tendency among both educators and linguists to confuse these two conceptions of language development. I have referred to language development as a process which has two sides to it, learning language and learning **through** language – in other words, every child is at the same time both learning language and using language to learn. Both these aspects can truly be called 'creative': the child is creating his language, and also using his language to create his model of reality. A more appropriate term for this creating would perhaps be *construing*, since construal gives the appropriate sense of a mental construct; but we can retain the more familiar term creation which is readily understood in this sense, provided we recognize that this kind of creation does not and cannot take place within the individual. A child is not an island. When he construes a language and when he uses that language to construe a 'reality' – a social order and a personal identity for himself within it, he can do so only because others are joining in. The process is not individual but social. It has been aptly called by some psychologists an *intersubjective* one.

We can see this in its clearest form in the very first year of life. Soon after he is born, a child begins to exchange attention with his mother; as soon as she addresses him and talks to him he becomes animated, moving his face and the whole of his body in harmony with her sounds and smiles and gestures. Very soon these exchanges evolve into a symbolic mode, the exchange of meanings through vocal and gestural symbols; and this is the beginning of language. At this stage it is not yet the mother tongue; it is a child tongue, a protolanguage, that the child is creating for the purpose of interacting with his mother and any others – father, perhaps, and a small number of other adults or children – who are in regular, intimate contact with him. These others share in the language-creating process. They 'track' the child's language – not in the superficial sense of imitating his own sounds and feeding them back to him (this is something a child usually rejects; it is not what he wants, and it suggests to him that his efforts are not being taken seriously) – but in the sense of understanding what he is trying to mean to them and responding to him with meanings of their own. At any given stage in his development, the mother has his language also inside her head, side by side with her own. This tracking process is entirely unconscious; she does not know she is doing it, and could not bring it to the surface and say what a particular sound or gesture means: 'When he says "Oh!" it means "go on playing with me!" ' Yet she engages in ongoing interaction with the child that makes it abundantly clear to anyone who is observing that she does in fact interpret his sounds and gestures; she knows what he means, because she shares the language with him. This sharing of his language by at least one other person – typically in this very early stage his mother – is a prerequisite for his successful language development and therefore for his development as a whole; without it he cannot learn. Creating language, and creating through language, are essentially interactive processes; they can never take place inside one individual's skin.

When the child starts going to school, the part that a teacher can play in his subsequent language development is in a direct line of continuity with his early experience. This does not mean that the teacher takes on the role of a parent, since by this time the conditions of learning have radically changed. With children of this age the general pattern of 'learning language, learning through language' is well established; they are quite accustomed to using language to learn. Moreover, they have taken in, subconsciously, the fact that every use of language has a twofold significance: it both relates to their experience of reality, having to do with the things and happenings of the real world, and carries forward their interaction with other people, expressing their own personal 'angle' and what they expect of whoever they are addressing. In other words, they have discovered that language is at once a mode of reflection and a mode of action. Since language is *experiential* in function, it enables a child not only to reflect on his experiences but also to extend them, and since it is *interpersonal*, it enables him not only to enact his relationships with others but also to enrich them: and so his language becomes extended and enriched in its turn. The teacher is faced with the task of expanding the child's horizons, which means adding to the experiential and interpersonal demands that are made on his language; in order to do this effectively the teacher has to introduce a new dimension of structure into the learning situation, related to the concept of 'what is learnt in school' and to the very different environment in which the learning takes place. At the same time the child is still the same child; he can learn more only by building on what he has learnt already, and nowhere is this continuity more important than in the development of his powers of language.

Many teachers have felt that, within the whole period that children spend in school, the middle school years are the ones in which they are most naturally predisposed to explore language itself. This has traditionally been the time at which formal grammar was begun; children were introduced to the "parts of speech" (an absurd term that derives from the mistranslation of a classical Greek expression meaning 'parts of the sentence') and were taught how to parse. Generations of children have grumbled at the tediousness of school grammar, but until recently it continued to flourish, partly though the inertia of educational practice and partly because of a vague conviction that, though dull, it was useful – it helped the children to become more literate and more articulate.

But in the absence of any firm evidence for this latter view, formal grammar has increasingly come under attack, both from teachers and from linguists, though each for different reasons: teachers because they found it just as dull as the children did, linguists because they saw it as negative in its effects. This was not so much because it was 'wrong' – it is, after all, just a way of looking at things – as because it distracted attention from what was important in language, leaving each generation of school-children with an image of language that was about as remote from the real thing as was the image of history based on the dates of the kings and queens of England. And like this kind of history, grammar became simply an occasion for facile moral judgments: King John was a bad king; *It's me!* is a bad sentence. Unfortunately, whereas the response of history teachers was to try and devise better history, English teachers (who had a much harder task in this respect) tended to react by abandoning language altogether. This coincided with the emergence of what I have referred to elsewhere as the 'benevolent inertia' concept of education, according to which, provided the teacher does not actively interfere to prevent it, learning will somehow take place, so anything as drily professional as language study was out of favour.

Actually, the exploration of language can be the most exciting pursuit in the whole curriculum. This even applies to formal grammar; I have watched junior high school children in the USA actively wrestling with parsing problems with enthusiasm and total involvement. But I doubt that this had any direct bearing on their own subsequent use of language. Rather than seeing grammar as dull but useful, I am inclined to think of it, at this level of education at least, as exciting but useless. At any rate, there are many other ways of exploring language in the middle school, which have a greater relevance to the developing language of the children themselves.

In the Schools Council (originally Nuffield) Programme in Linguistics and English Teaching, which I directed at University College London in 1964–70, we attempted to work towards some approach to language that would be more relevant to the deeper concerns of language in education. Two sets of materials were produced, written in each case by teachers at the level in question. In the initial literacy materials, *Breakthrough to Literacy*, the main purpose was already clear:

enabling children to become literate. But this was not just a matter of 'reading and writing', treated as they so often are as if they were something totally separate from language; it was a matter of extending each child's existing language potential in new directions in response to new kinds of demand; and the *Teacher's Manual* (of which a new and revised edition has just now gone to press) focused on the tasks of learning to read and write as linguistic processes located squarely within the context of language development as a whole. At the other end of the scale, the materials devised for secondary schools, *Language in Use*, were designed to suggest ways of exploring different aspects of language as a resource – language in individual and social relationships, varieties of language (registers and dialects), speech and writing, language in expressive and informative functions, language and experience, and so on. The original background book for *Language in Use* was *Exploring Language*; this has since been followed up by a number of others brought together under the series title *Explorations in Language Study*, which deal with various aspects of linguistics, applied linguistics, psycholinguistics and sociolinguistics, from the point of view of teachers who want to take language seriously as a field of educational endeavour.

During the last phase of the programme, work was begun on a third series of materials for use in the middle school age range. These were not able to be completed within the timespan of the project, but the teachers involved have subsequently developed their ideas and carried them through to publication, and the materials have recently appeared under the title of *Language and Communication*. The authors take the view that children of this age are ready and keen to explore the nature of language, and that to do so is not only a valuable educational experience but may also contribute significantly to their own linguistic development.

The topics that they consider may serve as a way in to the exploration of language include such things as: animal communication systems, and how far they are resembled by human language; the nature and evolution of different kinds of writing, and so on. As with the older students, it is quite possible to work on language at this level without focusing attention on grammar, or on the nature of language as a system. But there are also many ways of exploring the system of a language along lines which are somewhat different from the traditional apparatus of subject, verb and object. For example, one can explore the melody and rhythm of the language, how English uses intonation and stress to convey meanings of various kinds; or its sound symbolism, the way words of Anglo-Saxon origin often carry a semantic signal in their phonological makeup. One can explore the word-creating resources of English: the strategies by which the language meets the never-ending demand for new names of things, and how these strategies tend to vary over time and over different functions of language. One can investigate the grammatical principles that lie behind dialogue, and the ways in which speakers use language as a means of exchange, exchanging either information or goods and services. And one can look at any of these topics with the focus either on the system as it is when fully developed, or on how it is built up from infancy by a child. These are examples of the kinds of question that can be taken up by a teacher who wants to direct attention on to the meanings, wordings and sounds of the language in a systematic programme of exploration.

In explorations of this kind, the teacher is leading the way; and while the teacher may also at first be exploring new ground and discovering things that had not come his way before, the facts that emerge are not themselves new facts. But it is also true that with children of this age the classroom can be a centre of linguistic research, in which teacher and pupils working together find out things that are not already known. Language is almost infinitely variable, and there is unlimited scope for investigation and interpretation in such areas as neighborhood speech patterns, functions of language in the young children's peer group, communication in the family, and so on; there are also techniques, such as keeping language diaries, that can be used in a variety of different forms according to the age of the children and the particular features of the community in which they live. (I have discussed some of these in *Language and Social Man.*)

I make no apology for presenting this section in terms of the concept of 'exploring' language. Part of the difficulty that many children had with working on language in the old way was that learning about nouns and verbs was a classificatory exercise that had no real function or context for them, since it corresponded to nothing that they could recognize as a quest (let alone as a problem to be solved); it was a set of answers without any questions. I am not saying that there must be an immediate and practical payoff for linguistic work in school; this of course there cannot be, and most of the study of language is bound to appear, like much else the children are doing at this stage, as knowledge that is, for the time being at least, for its own sake. But the only context that was usually offered for studying grammar was that of the correction of grammatical errors, in which rules of behaviour were set up for certain marginal features of language, but nothing was done which could lead a child to feel that he had in any way increased his resources for meaning.

59

As I see it, from the point of view of the student the main purposes of studying language in school, particularly in the middle school years, are really twofold: to develop an understanding and appreciation of language in general, and of one's own particular language or languages; and to develop the potential for using language in all the contexts, in and out of school, that are relevant to someone growing up in the community. Pursued with sympathy and insight, these two purposes will support and reinforce each other. For example, teachers who have explored variation in language have found that the students begin to ask for explanations of why language varies in certain ways, and this has led naturally into discussions of the nature of language, and so into the heart of the system, which is grammar. In this way the teacher may move, not 'back' to grammar, because it is not grammar as it used to be presented, but forward to grammar. It is now up to the linguists to go further towards interpreting grammar in a way that will have a more direct bearing on language in an educational context.

One thing that can be said with emphasis about language study in school is that it should embody the basic notion of language as a **resource**. Language is the most important instrument of human consciousness, as well as being the principal means by which we learn, whether we are thinking of commonsense knowledge or of the knowledge that is taught in school. But for many teachers in the past – and hence also for their pupils – the dominant image of language has been one not of language as a resource but of language as a set of rules. The most influential trend in linguistics from the 1940s onwards was the formal one represented by American structuralism, which seeks to reduce language to considerations of structure; at first the approach was operational, based on the principle of 'find out what goes with what', but when this line of approach reached its limits it was superseded by an attempt to represent language in terms of formal rules. This later version happened to chime in with the traditional view of language transmitted in the schools, which was also expressed in terms of rules, although these always tended to degenerate into rules of socially acceptable verbal behaviour.

Linguists who describe language in this way do so for a particular purpose, that of interpreting language as a formal system; the ideological framework is one in which linguistics is part of philosophy and grammar is part of logic. These linguists do not usually claim that what they are doing has any significance for language education. In fact there is good reason for thinking that a much greater relevance for educational concerns is to be found in the other main tradition in Western linguistics, one that is functional rather than formal in its orientation; according to this view, language is a social and cultural phenomenon, a potential for meaning rather than an edifice of structures, and grammar, if it is part of anything, is associated with rhetoric rather than with logic. In this tradition language has been viewed primarily as a resource; in an educational context, this implies a resource that a child constructs for himself in interaction with those around him, rather than a set of structures or of structure-forming rules that he has to acquire.

If we see language as a resource, we are less inclined to 'idealize' it, to reduce it to a set of norms that define what is "grammatical" and what is "ungrammatical"; we are more concerned with what people actually say and write. This is sometimes taken to imply an insistance that 'anything goes', that everyone should be allowed to speak or write in any way they like. It is true that there is a great value in being able to stand back from the firing line of public debate on 'good English' and look objectively at the linguistic rules that people make for themselves (and more especially for others); a file of newspaper cuttings showing people's attitudes to the 'rights and wrongs' of grammar should be part of every language teacher's backroom equipment. But to take a functional standpoint does not mean disregarding the issue of whether or not someone is using language successfully. Rather the contrary; it means being concerned with the effective functioning of language in the many and varied contexts in which it is used – with the demands that people make on their language, and how it can best be developed to meet those demands.

This is what language education is about. If we take seriously the responsibility of the school towards children's language development, we need clearly thought out, professional approaches to language in the classroom, based on teachers' understanding of how language functions, of how its internal form relates to the way it functions, and of how children come to learn it. This can ensure that there is continuity with children's pre-school and out-of-school language development; that literacy is treated as part of language development, not as something largely unrelated to it; and that children's explorations of language in school have some bearing on the functions that language has and will have in their lives – including the functions that it has in other school contexts, a concern that is embodied in the formulation "language across the curriculum", which voices the growing awareness of the part played by language in all learning activity.

Not the least important aspect of language in the middle school years is one that has not been touched on up to this point: the place of foreign languages in language education. This is beyond the scope of the present discussion, but it should be stressed that the conception of language as resource refers to the total language ability of the individual, and therefore includes his learning of a foreign language and, in a situation where he is being taught in a medium that is not his mother tongue, his learning **through** a foreign language also. Many of those involved in the teaching of foreign languages in primary schools are keen on exploring the use of one such language as a medium of instruction, and it is interesting to note that this is simply applying to the foreign language the principle that operates in the learning of the mother tongue, namely that learning language and learning through language are different facets of the same creative process.

We are a long way from even adequately defining the fundamental problems of language education, let alone from solving them. But the level of discussion has risen considerably over the past few years, and this reflects a readiness to take language seriously – which means taking seriously the language of the children we are teaching, since this is the foundation on which all their learning has been based, even if we think that as it stands it is inadequate to their needs. It is not easy to listen to a person's language; many people go through life without ever really learning to do it. The middle school years are a time when children are potentially very aware of language, and receptive to new ways of exploring and exploiting it. How far they are able to realize this potential will depend partly on our finding out more about this critical stage of language development, and partly on our incorporating what we already know into the design and practice of language education.

Chapter Four

DIFFERENCES BETWEEN SPOKEN AND WRITTEN LANGUAGE: SOME IMPLICATIONS FOR LITERACY TEACHING (1979)

It was said of the great Chinese lyric poet Po Chü-yi, of the Tang Dynasty, that he wanted his poems to be intelligible to everyone, including the illiterate, and that he used to read them aloud to an old peasant woman – if there was anything she couldn't understand, he would change it until she could. Po Chü-yi believed in the unity of poetry and the everyday language, although the one was written, self-conscious and lasting, the other spoken, spontaneous and transitory. A thousand years later, Wordsworth was espousing the same cause, and likewise putting it into practice in his verses – with results that varied from the sublime wording of *Tintern Abbey* to the lines from *The Thorn* that Coleridge, at least, considered ridiculous:

> I've measured it from side to side
> 'Tis three feet long and two feet wide.

What Coleridge is objecting to is Wordsworth's claim that (in Coleridge's words) "the proper diction for poetry in general consists altogether in a language taken, with due exceptions, from the mouths of men in real life, a language which actually constitutes the natural conversation of men under the influence of natural feelings" (*Biographia Literaria*: 189). In a footnote Coleridge refers to Wordsworth's own wording, from the advertisement to *Lyrical Ballads* (first edition, 1798): "the language of conversation in the middle and lower classes of society". (In the preface to the editions of 1800 and 1802 this is replaced by "a selection of the real language of men in a state of vivid sensation".) Coleridge objects on three grounds:

(i) He objects "to an equivocation in the use of the word *real*", pointing out that "every man's language varies", having "first its

63

individualities; secondly, the common properties of the class to which he belongs; and thirdly, words and phrases of universal use".

(ii) He protests at Wordsworth's choice of "low and rustic life" as the model, noting that the results of his own experience, as well as that of country clergymen he knew, "would engender more than scepticism concerning the desirable influences of low and rustic life in and for itself"; nor can he accept that "from the objects with which the rustic hourly communicates the best part of language is formed".

(iii) Finally, in relation to Wordsworth's assertion that "there neither is or can be any essential difference between the language of prose and metrical composition", Coleridge considers that "prose itself, at least in all argumentative and consecutive works, differs, and ought to differ, from the language of conversation; even as reading ought to differ from talking" (*Biographia Literaria*: 189–203).

I return to the last point below.

It is with reference to the language of poetry, and "poetic diction", that controversy about the relation of written language to spoken has been most explicit. But the issue is a much wider one, and views have ranged all the way between two extremes – that writing and speech should be as close as possible, and that they should be kept as far as possible apart. In the history of literate societies we see both tendencies at work. In origin, written forms are derived from spoken ones, and inevitably in its early stages writing reflects fairly closely the spoken language of the community (though not necessarily that of spontaneous conversation – other registers are likely to need writing down first). But since writing is a conscious process, written language is on the whole conservative, whereas speech is spontaneous and so spoken language tends to be innovative. And where writing is associated with a recognized form, as in many genres of poetry, the tendency to conservatism is increased; the lyric form that Po Chü-yi had used, the *shi*, became within the next two centuries so conventionalized and rigid, the poems themselves so stilted and stylized, that the Sung poets rejected it and evolved a new, freer lyric form, the *ci* – which itself went through the same cycle in the course of a few generations. On a broader scale, an entire written language may persist long after its spoken version has evolved into something quite different. Sanskrit, classical Arabic, classical Chinese, Latin in medieval Europe – all these are examples of languages surviving for writing for hundreds of years after they have ceased to be spoken. (Or rather, for hundreds of years after they have ceased to be anybody's mother tongue; they may continue to be learnt and spoken as a second language.)

Once people become literate, an interesting thing happens. Because writing is a conscious process, they become conscious of language – but only of language in its written form. So for literate people – and even, it seems, for illiterate people in a literate community – language **is** written language. We tend to think of written language as the norm; as real language; as, indeed, all that there is. Language for us is made of paragraphs and sentences and words and letters, instead of melodic units, rhythmic units, syllables and sounds. The imagery we use is visual rather than auditory: a 'long sentence' is one that takes up a lot of lines on the page, a 'long word' is one with a lot of letters in it, and so on. If we think of speech at all, we envisage it as a kind of debased and distorted copy of written language. We forget that men and women talked for a million years before they wrote.

This gave rise to the mode of thought that used to be dominant in the theory and practice of education: language in school means written language. In this perspective, there is no need to take spoken language very seriously. The three R's are reading, 'riting and 'rithmetic. No doubt this arises in part because we have got to concentrate on the teaching of reading, as the first major development step that is going to be taken in school as part of the process of being educated. But it is easy to be misled into assuming, as I think teachers often have assumed even in the primary school, that once a person is literate, from then on all his learning is going to take place through written language – by writing and reading. This is not so, at any rate for the majority of children. Most of us go on, through school and even through life, learning by listening and talking at least as much as by reading and writing.

In the late nineteenth century, the two most prominent grammarians in Britain were Henry Sweet, from Oxford, and Alexander Bain, from Aberdeen. Sweet, as well as being a distinguished grammarian, was one of the founders of modern phonetics; he was also a great practical phonetician, and was the original of Henry Higgins in Shaw's *Pygmalion*, later filmed as *My Fair Lady*. Sweet constantly stressed the importance of the study of the contemporary (including the spoken) language – "living philology", as he called it – by contrast with the study of dead languages that was characteristic of the linguistics of his time (referred to subsequently as "morbid linguistics").

If Sweet had a lasting influence on linguistics, Alexander Bain had a much greater influence on education. He wrote the successful two-volume textbook *English Composition and Rhetoric*. Rhetoric, in ancient

Greece, meant the use of the spoken language; rhetorical skill meant skill in verbal debate, argument and persuasion. With Bain, however, rhetoric meant the functions of the written language, a meaning derived from the Renaissance; and especially poetic functions – nearly all Bain's examples are drawn from verse. This emphasis reinforced still further the view of language in school as, essentially, written language. It was writing that was evaluated: writing that was good or bad, elegant or awkward; writing that conveyed ideas, emotions, imagination. Speech simply did not come into the picture. And this view, although it has been considerably modified, is still very widespread today.

There was another factor, one perhaps slightly outside the scope of our discussions but which is nevertheless not without interest: this was the very strong tradition of orthoepy and spelling reform in English linguistic studies. Ever since Timothy Bright published the first short-hand in 1588, English and Scottish linguists had been concerned, indeed obsessed, with the inconsistencies in English spelling. David Abercrombie writes: "A very reasonable theory has been put forward that phonetics started in England owing to the striking discrepancies between the way English is spelt and the way it is spoken: a new speculative approach to problems of pronunciation was forced on us because of the inadequacy of the traditional approach, derived from the classical grammarians" (*Studies in Phonetics and Linguistics*: 61). There are three main reasons for the discrepancies between spelling and pronunciation in English. One is the paucity of the Roman alphabet, which simply has not enough letters in it (because Latin had a very simple sound system and did not need any more); so we have to write compound symbols such as *sh* and *th* and *ng* representing single sounds. (We did originally have symbols for the two sounds now written *th*, as in *then* and in *thin*, but the Norman scribes were too lazy to learn to use them.) The second is the far-reaching sound changes that took place in Middle English, around Chaucer's time (loss of final vowels, changes in vowel quality, and so on), which radically altered the whole English sound system. The third was the introduction of Greek and Latin vocabulary on a large scale; these words brought into English a secondary sound system that had some very complicated alternations in it, as in the words *telephone, telephony, telephonic* – these words sound very different, but the differences are regular, and the spelling preserves their unity. So the spelling system had moved far from its original Old English simplicity; and there arose a tradition of reformed spelling, in which whole new alphabets were devised, often with very detailed phonetic analysis lying behind them. None of these systems or modifications was ever adopted; English adults are no more disposed than those of any other literate community to take a decision by which they would render themselves illiterate overnight. Nevertheless the thinking that lies behind these schemes is reflected in our attitude towards the existing orthography. We treat spelling as an enemy, a monster to be placated; and we see the child who is just becoming literate as an innocent victim of its arbitrary tyranny.

One consequence of all this has been that our school readers, or primers, have traditionally made little concession to the spoken language. *See Spot run. Run, Spot, run!* – this was the road to literacy. There was no feeling that the language used in learning to read need have any particular connection with speech, with the spoken language the children already had; in fact we often behaved as if they came into school with no previous language at all, so there was nothing there for the language of the primer to have a connection with. Furthermore, seeing that the spelling system of English was, according to the general opinion, so very difficult to master, then spelling considerations alone should determine the nature and sequence of the material presented for learning to read and write. The result of this was an artificial kind of "primer language" that made no real contact with the child's previous linguistic experience.

Twentieth-century linguists took Henry Sweet's dictum about living language very much to heart, and under the combined influence of British phonetics and American anthropological linguistics the spoken language came well to the fore. The changes that took place in foreign language teaching with the coming of the "direct method" in the 1910s were all part of a new concern with the spoken word. This found its strongest expression in structuralist linguistics, with some linguists arguing as if written language was not really language at all, although they always used written language to say so. In this they had been anticipated by the Scottish linguist James Burnet, Lord Monboddo, who wrote at the end of the eighteenth century that "language spoken may be said to be *living language*, compared with written language, which may be called *the dead letter*, being altogether *inanimate*, and nothing more than the marks or signs of language" (*The Origin and Progress of Language*, 6 vols, Edinburgh, 1773–92: Vol. IV p. 170, quoted in Abercrombie, op. cit., p. 37 n. 3). It is important that we should be able to look at this question dispassionately, and to recognize the different values that speech and writing have in our lives.

It took a long time for the interest in the spoken language to be reflected in the teaching of reading, largely I imagine because there was no widespread concern about illiteracy until some decades later. I suspect that in Britain at least it was mainly the education units of the armed services, in the two world wars, who were most alert to the real level of illiteracy among the adult population: there were many recruits who could not read the small-arms manuals. But this would be put down to poverty, ill health and a lack of opportunity for schooling, rather than to any failure in the teaching process. It was only from the late 1950s that educational failure became a public issue, and it was in this context that reading schemes came under criticism, for trying to teach the children a new language, under the guise of teaching them a new medium for representing the language they already had. In the terms of James Britton's model, children were being expected to learn not only a new medium but also at the same time new functional codes, or registers, instead of first learning to write the form of language they already knew and then extending their linguistic resources, spoken and written, into new functional contexts.

So the slogan became 'write as you speak'. First learn to read and write in language that is familiar, then go on to read and write – and also to listen and speak – in language that is new. I think most of us who have worked in developmental linguistics – the study of how children learn their first language – would happily assent to this. There is little doubt that some of the failure in reading and writing of which we are all so conscious nowadays has been due at least in part to children failing to make the conceptual leap that relates writing to speech, never co-ordinating the new behaviour with an ability they already possess, the ability to speak and listen. The new experience never clicks into place alongside the old.

In the 1960s, in London, I directed the Schools Council programme that produced *Breakthrough to Literacy*, and there we tried to address ourselves to this problem by devising a scheme that had no pre-existing input, no readymade language at all. There are no primers. Children build up their own reading material by constructing written discourse, first using the sentence-maker in which the words are readymade, and subsequently using the word-maker so that they are also constructing the words. The teacher guides them step by step into the correct word order and spelling, but the language is the children's own. The *Teacher's Manual*, written by David Mackay together with his primary colleagues in the programme, carefully sets out all the things a child cannot be expected to know in advance: what is a beginning and an ending (where does a line or page of writing 'begin' and 'end'?), how writing differs from drawing, and so on. In selecting the words for the sentence-maker we used a small-scale word-frequency count of children's language that had been carried out at the University of Birmingham. The recent work by the Mount Gravatt team, directed by Norman Hart and now taken over by Richard Walker, has taken this principle further, with extensive research into the spoken language of children aged 6, 8 and 10; the results of this survey, which covers the children's grammar as well as their vocabulary, are then built into a programme which is more than a reading scheme and comes closer towards realizing the *Breakthrough* conception of an integrated programme for language in the primary school.

To say that a child is helped if his earliest experience of written language is closely related to his speech is not to suggest, however, that all writing is speech written down, or that the injunction to 'write as you speak' is a universal educational principle. The 'write as you speak' concept is helpful as a bridging device for the initial stages, in which the child is grasping the principle of reading and writing and gaining familiarity with the process. As Abercrombie puts it, "writing is a medium for language in its own right, and though it is, in the last analysis, constructed on the basis of spoken language, the aim of writing is not, usually, to represent actual spoken utterances which have occurred" (p. 36). Children seem perfectly well aware of this; once they have learnt to write well enough to express themselves in writing they see it as having different functions from speech, and sense that what is written down is not exactly the same as what is said. No doubt many children have by that time already experienced what Abercrombie, following Coleridge's distinction, calls "spoken prose" – for example, having had read aloud to them stories composed in writing. Perhaps, also, it is just so difficult to write as you speak that it simply never occurs to them to try.

If children have this awareness of the difference between spoken and written language, and especially if they have it as a result of their experience of the difference between conversation and spoken prose, having unconsciously taken in the fact that the two are distinct, then it should be possible to say what the differences are. It is not easy to find any general descriptions of the difference between speech and writing – partly because linguists have usually concentrated their efforts on describing the linguistic system that lies behind both of them, and partly because until recently they have neglected the study of one fundamental aspect of language, that of discourse, or connected passages of language in actual use, whether spoken or written, and this is where many of the differences lie. But I should like to suggest one or two general features in respect of which written language differs from spoken, features that seem to me to be particularly significant in relation to reading and writing as ways of learning – to the part played by written language in extending and organizing our experience.

Perhaps the most obvious feature that marks off written language is that it is not anchored in the here-and-now, not tied to the environment in which it is produced in the way that conversation is. Every language contains numerous words and expressions that signal this relationship of the text to the environment, elements that depend for their interpretation on knowing when and where the text was produced, and who it was produced by: things such as *I* and *you*; *here* and *there*; *yesterday, today* and *tomorrow*; *has done, is going to do*; tag questions, speaker comments, and so on. If there are such signals in a written text, they have to be resolvable within the text; a written text must create its own context in which they can be understood. So there has to be a point of reference for them (for example, as dialogue embedded in a narrative), and if we don't find one, as often happens with children's writing, we consider the text to be faulty.

So texts such as (1) and (2) clearly belong to the spoken language:

(1) I was going to say, did you take your food, or did you buy some on the way, or what?
(2) Don't drop it, otherwise I'll have to pay for it.
   – But we have paid for it.
   – No we haven't. You only pay for the juice, not the glass.
   – Why don't you pay for the glass?
   – Well you give it back, you don't keep it.
   – Then you shouldn't have to pay for the juice.
   – Oh no, you have to pay for the juice.
   – But there's no point in paying for the juice, 'cause you drink it.

(The second is a discussion between Nigel, aged 6, and his mother in a snack bar). On the other hand texts such as (3) and (4), which have no such deictic elements, may just as well belong to the written language (and there are other indications that in fact they do):

(3) Every other trip had emphasized reducing weight as much as possible.
(4) Its use unquestionably leads to safer and faster train running in the most adverse weather conditions.

Not that these sentences are complete in themselves; they both contain items needing to be resolved from elsewhere (*other, its*). But the resolution is to be found in the preceding text: 'trips other than the one I am recounting in this letter', 'the use of Automatic Train Control'.

70

Differences of this kind, reflecting the nature and extent of the inter-dependence of language and situation, are predictable from the different functions of speech and writing and the different contexts in which they come into being.

Because written language is less a product of the moment, writing systems tend to omit certain features of language that typically express this involvement with the context of situation. In Abercrombie's words, "The whole object of written language is to be *free* of any immediate context, whether personal or situational, and that is why it dispenses with systematic indication of intonation and rhythm, only giving the vaguest of hints in the form of question marks, commas and so on" (p. 43). Let me give another example from earlier times. In 1775 another English linguist, Joshua Steele, published a book called *An Essay towards Establishing the Melody and Measure of Speech, to be Expressed and Perpetuated by Peculiar Symbols* (it was reissued in 1779 with a rather shorter title, *Prosodia Rationalis*). Steele knew the famous Shakes-pearean actor David Garrick, and he used his 'peculiar symbols' to give an accurate account of how Garrick recited the Hamlet soliloquy beginning 'To be or not to be'. This is the most faithful record of any human voice that had ever been made before the invention of the gramophone.

Steele was well aware that the English writing system gives no indica-tion of what he called the "melody and measure" of speech – in modern terminology, of intonation and rhythm. He had a most remarkable insight into both of these, and had analysed the intonational and rhythmic patterns of the English of his day with great care and with a profound understanding of the nature of spoken language.

It is a fact that most writing systems leave out intonation and rhythm, no doubt for the reasons put forward by David Abercrombie. But this means, of course, that they take a lot of the personality out of language – they have no way of showing how different actors speak the same lines. Many of us are accustomed to making up this deficiency, in personal kinds of writing such as intimate letters or diary entries, by scattering our own peculiar symbols around the page – underlinings, capitals, series of exclamation marks or anything else we can think of. If we want children to write expressively we should perhaps encourage them to do the same. But additionally, there are times when not only the interpersonal meanings but also the texture, the internal fabric of the text, is expressed by rhythm and intonation. Consider examples (5) and (6), which are both taken from books written for children, roughly 5-year-olds and 13-year-olds:

(5) This was the first railway engine. Steam made it go.

(6) A further complication was the 650-ton creeper cranes poised above the end of each 825-ft arm; these had been used to lift from lighters in the harbour the various steel sections as they were built into the arch. It was the firm of Dorman Long that carried this amazing task to a successful conclusion.

It is hard enough for a child to build focus (tonic prominence) into his reading. But he soon learns a simple principle: put it at the end. Writing doesn't show focus, so one proceeds on the assumption that the focus is the end unless there is some linguistic indication to the contrary. In (5) there is none; so the natural reading is "Steam made it **GO**". This doesn't make sense; all that the writer need have done was to write *it went by steam*, which would then have been read as "It went by **STEAM**", a structure that would probably in any case be easier for a child to understand than the causative with inanimate agent. Now notice what happens in (6). Supposing the author had written *The firm of Dorman Long carried this amazing task to a successful conclusion*. It would now have been interpreted, and read, as "the firm of Dorman Long carried this amazing task to a successful **CONCLUSION**". But the author wanted the focus on *Dorman Long*, so he used a structure that forces you to say it that way. In similar fashion the author of (5) could have written *It was steam that made it go*, which would have located the focus on *steam* ("it was **STEAM** that made it go"), while retaining the causative structure that he preferred.

A further interesting contrast is illustrated in (7) and (8). In recounting a cycling holiday to a friend, the speaker said:

(7) And as it turned out it worked really well, because nine people can carry a lot of things.

The last part of this was spoken as follows:

//4 ∧ because / nine / **PEOPLE** can / carry a // 1 lot of / **THINGS** //

(Tone 1 is falling, tone 4 is falling-rising.) But when the same person wrote a letter about the same holiday, then in order to get the focus on *nine people* he switched it to the end:

(8) I had no idea how easily great amounts of food and extras can be carried by nine people.

This is a very good instance of what is the typical function of the passive in English: to distribute the balance of information the way the speaker wants it to go. I am not suggesting, of course, that these things are done consciously; on the contrary, to know a language means to control its resources at a level below that of conscious awareness. (It is the linguist whose unpopular task it is to bring them to consciousness.)

These variants are not, of course, unique to written language; all occur a great deal in speech, especially informal spontaneous speech, because they interact with the rhythmic and intonational patterns and in so doing reinforce and add further subtleties to the rhetorical structure of the discourse. What the writer does is to use them as structural signals to indicate how the text is to be read. Here is one more example of a spoken text showing how the varied intonation and rhythm gives a dynamic meaning to the discourse as it unfolds, with each part building on what has gone before. Nigel, age 7, is talking to his father:

(9) How come you can see the sun in the day and the stars in the **NIGHT**?
   - The **STARS** are there all the **TIME**. You can't **SEE** them in the −
   - (interrupting) I mean I thought the **SUN** was a star, so **IT** should be at **NIGHT**.
   - **RIGHT**. But the **SUN** is a **SPECIAL** star. It's the **SUN** that **MAKES** it day; and it makes it so **BRIGHT** you can't **SEE** the stars.
   - Which is the **BIGGEST** star? Which is the **NEAREST** star?
   - The **SUN** is the **NEAREST**.
   - **HEY** − guess what they said in the **PLANETARIUM**? − that **SIRIUS** was the nearest star to us!

My third heading is lexical density. Here is a typical sentence from a written text:

(10) In bridging river valleys, the early engineers built many notable masonry viaducts of numerous arches.

Notice how the content is packed into that single sentence. We have to take in all the following facts: that there are valleys, with rivers in them; you can put a bridge across them; engineers often did this, in the early days; they did it by building viaducts; the viaducts are very famous; they are made of masonry; and they have lots of arches in them. At least nine distinct and quite substantial pieces of information are squashed into that one sentence.

In order to read it aloud, you have to break it up into a number of separate tone groups, something like the following:

// ^ in / bridging / river / **VALLEYS** // ^ the / early / **ENGIN-
EERS** // built /many / notable / masonry / **VIADUCTS** // ^ of
/ numerous / **ARCHES** //

This is the same technique that radio announcers use to cope with the
news bulletins they are given to read, for example:

// ^ the / prime / **MINISTER** has ac//cepted an / **INVI/TATION**
to // visit /**LONDON** for pre//liminary / **TALKS** on the
Aust//ralian **PRO/POSALS** for // inter/national **CON/TROL** of
the pro//duction and / marketing of /**BEAN CURD**//

This very high lexical density is characteristic of written language.
What this means is that there are a large number of lexical items, content
words, often including quite difficult words, of fairly low frequency,
packed closely together; and typically, packed into what is a rather
simple grammatical structure. Spoken language has a lower lexical
density than written language; and among the different kinds of spoken
language, 'language-in-action' – language that forms an integral part of
some ongoing activity, like a sport, or a task with constantly changing
conditions, where the talk is a necessary element in the process,
determining who does what, what happens next and so on – has the
lowest lexical density of all. An example of this kind of language would
be (11):

(11) O.K. Now put it over there by the board, just where you're
     standing.
     – Here?
     – Right. Now hold it there.
     – I think it might be a bit too high.
     – No, it's all right. But you've got to make sure it doesn't slip.
       Er – have you got a peg? Well put a peg in there, just a little
       way to the right, will you, and that'll hold it in place. Right.
       That'll do the trick.

But there is a corollary to this. Contrary to what many people think,
spoken language is on the whole more complex than written language in
its grammar, and informal spontaneous conversation, especially sustained
and rather rapid conversation, is the most grammatically complex of all.
The more unselfconscious the language, the more complex it is liable to
become. Here are some examples from tape-recorded conversations.
Rendering them into print, of course, destroys their characteristic of
being spoken language, and one cannot reproduce their spontaneity in

74

reading them aloud. But it is possible to imagine something of how they sounded. To give a developmental flavour, I have arranged them in order corresponding to the ages of the speakers – but backwards: (12) is a girl in her twenties, (13) are male students around 20, (14) is a 16-year-old girl, (15) are three 9-year-old girls, (16) to (18) are Nigel at ages 6 years 4 months, 4 years 3 months and 2 years 7 months.

(12) This does bring up the point that was one of the things I was interested in last night, and that was this question of the word "conversation". In fact we use this word "conversation" to cover many types of activity – it's very interesting because it fairly soon is established when you're meeting with somebody what kind of conversation you're having: for example you may know and tune in pretty quickly to the fact that you're there as the support, perhaps, in the listening capacity – that you're there in fact to help the other person sort their ideas; and therefore your remarks in that particular type of conversation are aimed at drawing out the other person, at in some way assisting them by reflecting them to draw their ideas out; and you may tune in to this, or you may be given this role and refuse it – refuse to accept it, which may again alter the nature of your conversation.

(13) And you get a penalty for that, do you, the other side?
      – Depending on whether it's kicking or passing forward. Passing forward, no; it's a scrum. If you kick it forward, and somebody else picks it up, that will be a penalty.
      – And if not, if the other side picks –
      – If the other side picks it up that's all right; but the trouble is, this is in fact tactics again, because you don't want to put the ball into the hands of the other side if you can avoid it because it's the side that has possession, as in most games of course, is at an advantage.

(14) . . . you do basically the same thing, but it is a bit more involved through all the years you stay at school; like, from kindergarten to sixth form you do basically all the same work in maths, and in English you do a bit more, but, like, unless you want to be an English teacher you don't need verbs and that.

(15) Well if it's just – if you don't know what it is I think you ought to call it "it", because you don't know whether you're calling it a boy or a girl, and if it gets on and if you start calling it "she" then you find out that it's a boy you can't stop yourself, 'cause you've got so used to calling it "she".

75

  - Um – Mrs Symmonds says that if – if some neighbour has a new baby next door and you don't know whether it's a he or a she, if you referred to it as "it" well then the neighbour will be very offended.
  - Well if it's in your family I think you should call it either "he" or "she", or else the poor thing when it grows up won't know what it is.

(16) When we ride on a train in the railway museum it's an old-fashioned train but we call it a new-fashioned train though it's old-fashioned because it's newer than the trains that have only got one.
  - One what?
  - One driving wheel. But when we ride on a Deltic not in a museum we call it an old-fashioned train.

(17) Isn't it funny? if something liquid is inside another thing liquid and you've got it too much in then it makes the other thing go up.

Isn't it funny? if something is big it can land on something big but if something is small it can land on something big and small.

(18) Want Daddy to go away into the other room and look at the old American steam train book and find the train that has fallen off the bridge and say "poor train!"

Shall Mummy tell you the river in Providence again in which there were lots and lots of tiny fishes and they were dead?

These examples show something of the richness of the grammar of natural speech. Even with the very young it is already beginning to be apparent; with adults the sentence structure of spontaneous conversation can reach a remarkable degree of complexity, such as is rarely attained in writing and indeed is difficult to follow when written down. At first sight this seems surprising, since we are accustomed to thinking of written language as having the more complex syntax of the two. But it is not really surprising when one takes into account the nature of the two media. Writing is a deliberate and, even with modern technology, a relatively slow process; the text is created as an object, and is perceived by the reader as an object – it exists. Spoken text does not exist; it happens. The text is created, and is perceived by the listener, as a process. Its reference points are constantly shifting; the speaker keeps on going, and the listener cannot pause and hold up the text for contemplation – he is carried along with it, tracking the process as it happens. The reader, of course, also has to keep moving; but in this case it is he and not the writer who determines the pace. So, while speech and writing can both be very complex, the complexities tend to be of different kinds. The complexity of speech is choreographic – an intricacy of movement. That of writing is crystalline – a denseness of matter. In linguistic terms, spoken language is characterized by complex sentence structures with low lexical density (more clauses, but fewer high content words per clause); written language by simple sentence structures with high lexical density (more high content words per clause, but fewer clauses). We could express this even more briefly, though at the cost of distorting it somewhat, by saying that speech has complex sentences with simple words, while writing has complex words in simple sentences.

In real life it is hard to find a pair of texts which match in all respects except that one is written and the other spoken. The texts from which (7) and (8) above were taken came fairly close to this, if taken as wholes; but they would be too long to consider here. So I have made up two short texts, both accounts of the same experience (waiting to be interviewed), one in written language (19) and the other in spoken language (20):

(19) Before the interview there is a lengthy period of delay, and uniformed officials stride purposefully to and fro. Unknown to the candidate, the delay is deliberately contrived. This enables prospective employers to observe the candidate's behaviour under conditions of stress and loss of self-confidence.

(20) And what you don't realize, because you don't get told about it, is that all this time you're hanging about waiting to be interviewed while people wearing fancy clothes stride up and down looking as if they have serious business to attend to, you're actually being kept waiting on purpose so that the people you're going to work for can watch you without your knowing it, to see how you react when you're put in a position where you're likely to feel tense or uncertain of yourself.

The difference, it should be said very clearly, is one of degree; I am far from wishing to suggest that spoken and written language are separate, discrete phenomena. They are both manifestations of the same underlying system. We all know speakers, and writers, who manage to achieve both kinds of complexity at once! What I have been illustrating are general tendencies; and I have chosen examples which display rather clearly the differences I have been discussing. Most texts lie some way in between. Nevertheless the tendencies are very real ones, and if we are presented with any typical passage of discourse we can usually tell in which medium it was originally produced.

Of course the distinction we are looking at is not simply one of written versus spoken. The features I have described relate closely to the degree of spontaneity of the text; I am using "spoken language" in the sense of the 'most spoken' kind, natural free conversation that is unself-conscious and unmonitored – the speaker is not listening to himself as he goes along. A great deal of spoken language is far from spontaneous; it is 'spoken prose', in which the speaker is either reading aloud from a written text or at least consciously constructing and attending to his own speech. And there are kinds of written language that are more like speech. Some people can actually compose simulated conversation, but this is rare: most attempts turn out to be simply written discourse interspersed with expressions such as *you know* and *like* to give it credence. Dramatic dialogue is very far from spontaneous speech – fortunately, or most theatrical entertainment would be extremely boring. Texts such as tourist guides and written sets of instructions often resemble speech in having deictic elements that relate them to the situation in which they are functioning; but in other respects they are not like speech at all.

The difference between speech and writing is actually an instance of a more general phenomenon of variation in language, that of register. Language varies according to its use, according to the functions it is made to serve; and there are many other variables – rhetorical mode, degree of 'openness' or unpredictability, level of technicality, conventionality, and so on. Much of secondary education consists in becoming sensitive to this kind of register variation and learning to control it – this was the main thrust of the second set of materials put out by the Schools Council project I referred to earlier, namely *Language in Use*. There is always a danger in the educational context of downgrading this kind of variation to the level of good manners, of knowing how to behave appropriately in particular social situations; but it is really not like that at all. We are not talking about some ideal norm that the adolescent has to learn to conform to; we are interpreting what actually happens in real life, whenever people speak and listen or read and write. The language they use varies according to what they are doing with it. Some of this variation, it is true, is merely conventional, such as the rule that we write *is not, do not, I have, he will*, whereas we say *isn't, don't, I've, he'll*; this is just linguistic table-manners. But most of it is not. Most of the variation is motivated; there is some good reason why the language associated with a particular function should have the special properties that it has.

But while there is a great variety in the demands that are made on language in the secondary school, and in fact already in upper primary, in the earlier stages of education it is the written language/spoken language distinction that is the critical one. A child who is learning to read and write already knows language in its spoken form; but he does not know he knows it – as Asher Cashdan expressed it in his paper, "children use complex language quite early on, but they are not aware of the parameters of the language they are using". They have just put in three or four years of hard work learning to talk and listen; they have internalized the system, and now they are being required to bring it up to the level of consciousness again. They have to think about the processes of production and reception while at the same time still operating with it as living language, getting meaning from it and putting meaning into it. This is quite a considerable achievement.

It is in this context that we can see the value of the notion 'write as you speak'. As I have stressed all along, it is not to be taken literally. Writing is not, and cannot be, an exact copy of speech. Children have to move towards specifically written modes of discourse, learning them as they go along. This is why we teach reading and writing when we do: from reasons not so much of psychological maturation as of social maturation – they need to use language, both in and out of school, in functions that require the written medium. The principle is a familiar one: relate what the child is learning to his own previous experience. We repeat this slogan all the time, but we often forget that, in the case of learning to read and write, it means above all relating it to his previous **linguistic** experience. This is the real significance of the 'write as you speak' injunction. The modes of expression, and the styles of meaning, or "semantic styles", as they are called, that go with written language are bound to be different, but there is no reason why the written language that a child first encounters should not be such as to make sense to him in terms of what he knows of language already. In this connection it is worth repeating the point made by John Elkins in his paper: "Children are brought up on a diet of narrative – can't we vary the functions they meet in the written mode?" I always appreciate classrooms that are surrounded by written texts of heterogeneous kinds: road signs, labels from toys and food packages, cartoons, maps, advertisements, newspaper cuttings – all the things that give an idea of the diversity of what we use writing for.

It is useful to be reminded, as we have been, that there is much we still do not know about learning to read and write. We need to be aware of our limitations. At the same time, those who are now charged with responsibilities in this area know more about it than their parents and grandparents did. The same point could be made about theoretical and applied linguistics. There is a great deal we do not know about language and language development. But we are finding out more all the time, including some things that have not yet begun to be reflected in educational theory and practice. So we should be wary of demands for going 'back to' things, suggestive of some glorious golden age gone by. I do not believe in golden ages in the past – nor, I see, does the Queensland Institute for Educational Research in its recent report on literacy. I do not believe in utopias round the corner either. But if we can coordinate our efforts in the whole field of language education, in its three aspects of learning language, learning through language and learning about language, recognizing that while there are a number of specific educational tasks to be done there is also much that is common to all, I see no reason why we should not continue to move forward – which is really the only worthwhile direction.

Chapter Five

LANGUAGE AND SOCIALIZATION: HOME AND SCHOOL (1988)

The theme for this workshop has been defined as "Language and Social-ization: Home and School". As an opening speaker I have just one regret, and that is that it is me standing up here and not the person that it should be, Basil Bernstein. I think the orientation of the work-shop was suggesting that the foundation for whatever understanding we have of these issues is very much to be found in Bernstein's work. So I'm sure there will be constant reference to his work during the discussions.

I would like to start off by talking a little bit about the early part, and still the best-known part, of his own contribution, which is really the work that he and his team did at the Sociological Research Unit at the University of London largely during the 1960s. Like most highly original thinkers, Bernstein was widely misunderstood, and the fact that he went on learning and thinking and developing his own ideas, and was not afraid to change his mind when he thought he had been wrong before, only helped people to add to their other criticisms the particularly moronic accusation that he was not consistent.

One of the problems with Bernstein was that he never fitted people's stereotypes, their readymade categories into which all thinkers are supposed to fit. So the left branded him as right wing and the right wing branded him as left wing. He was in a sense a bit like the various creatures that Mary Douglas showed us to be taboo in all cultures because they do not belong to pure categories, like the cassowary, which is a bird but can't fly, and the pangolin, which has scales but climbs trees, or the pig, which has a cloven hoof but doesn't chew the cud. So everyone meeting Bernstein cried 'unclean' whenever they couldn't understand his ideas. His ideas are, of course, not simple, because the things that he was trying to explain are not simple, and he didn't distort them by pretending that they were.

So anyone's attempt to expound Bernstein's ideas briefly is in danger of oversimplifying; but nevertheless I want to try. I think that we are making progress by building on Bernstein's achievements. But, of course, we can't do that unless we recognize what they are.

I've known Basil Bernstein personally for 25 years, and for the first ten of these, when he was doing his major research throughout the 1960s. I often discussed and argued with him. These discussions began on a particular day in Edinburgh in 1961 or 1962, when we at Edinburgh invited Bernstein to give a seminar in the Linguistics Department. At that time he was just trying to organize his ideas in the form of a hypothesis about language. He was trying to look at what people actually say. He had his famous recorded discussions by secondary school students on capital punishment; he had just begun to use them as a source, and we were about the only linguists of the time who were studying discourse in our own work. We encouraged Bernstein to formulate his ideas in linguistic terms. (He might have felt the word "encourage" was a bit misleading – what we did, I remember, was to corner him in the bar in the staff club and attack him for about four hours for his very naïve assertions about language. He took it very well.) We suggested that the kind of linguistic theory that Firth had been developing could offer an interpretation of language that would be compatible both ideologically and methodologically with his developing ideas as we understand them.

Now let me just recall to you how Bernstein started. He himself was a teacher in a working-class area of London, and he had a very deep personal concern for children who faced the high probability of failure in school. Now this educational failure was just at that time, about the late 1950s, being shown experimentally to be class-linked; in other words, Bernstein's work began just at the time when studies had shown that the discrepancy between the measurements of verbal IQ and non-verbal IQ was a function of social class. In the working class the verbal IQ scores were way below the non-verbal IQ scores; furthermore, the discrepancy between non-verbal and verbal IQ scores widened, became greater, as the age of the pupils increased.

These were two significant findings. Bernstein had started trying to explain them in terms of a theory of modes of perception; in his 'Sociological determinants of perception', "a sensitivity to content versus a sensitivity to structure" was one of his early formulations. But the studies suggested that the critical variable was language. So he started to try to focus on language, and the first distinction that he tried to make was in terms of what he called "modes of language use". He distinguished between a "public" language to which working-class children were oriented, and a "formal" language as orientation of the middle class. The public language as he defined it was characterized by what he called a highly expressive symbolism in which feelings were communicated but with very few personal qualifications. They were not individually distinguished. In the formal language, there was a clear orientation to certain generalized social values, but the child was individually differentiated within them, so that there were a great many personal qualifications added. The public language of Bernstein's formulations was a concrete descriptive mode with the 'here and now' as strongly determining. It was characterized by fragmentation, by logical simplicity and by leaving implicit notions of causality, and so on. The formal language embodied generalizations of experience removed from, not dependent on, the immediate context of the 'here and now' and was characterized by an explicit formulation of relations of space, time and cause as well as social relationships. In many ways this anticipates the sorts of things that Katherine Nelson was talking about 15 years later in her developmental studies, where she distinguishes between expressive and referential modes of learning.

Bernstein's point was that the working-class child is typically confined to the public language, while the middle-class child was capable of manipulating both. And as he said the public language was unsuited to the school, was disvalued by the educational process. So the theory was that the working-class child faced a cultural discontinuity. The teacher and pupils disvalued each other: no personal relationship is set up between them, and there is no recognition of the underlying principles of what they are trying to achieve. This contrasts with the continuity of the middle class child's experience. Note that Bernstein was saying **nothing** here about intelligence.

Now in the following years, the early 1960s, Bernstein tried to make his concepts explicit and testable in linguistic terms. He tried to do this around two basic notions, which we might call "predictability" and "complexity". The public language was defined as being more predictable; and that in turn Bernstein explained as offering a narrower range of syntactic and/or lexical choices. (I say 'and/or' because at one stage he suggested two sub-varieties of it: one in which the syntax was more predictable, one in which the lexis was more predictable. It was a kind of on-the-road hypothesis that he later discarded.) So, more predictable; but also, second, less complex – in the sense of less elaborated, with a less explicit elaboration of semantic relationships. And at this point he came to rename the two, public and formal language, in the terms that became familiar to all of us in those discussions, namely "restricted code" and "elaborated code". Here is an example from one of the formulations that Bernstein gave of this linguistic hypothesis. He said "elaborated code tends to have more subordination, more complex nominal and verbal groups, and more use of conjunction; and to be characterized by egocentric rather than sociocentric sequences". He also went into more detailed interpretation of the use of the pronouns: the 'I's' against the 'we's', and so on. Various hypotheses were then set up on the basis of this kind of inventory that were tested or partially tested at the time. There was also, Bernstein said, a great deal more verbal planning associated with elaborated code; so you got more hesitation (hesitation phenomena were being extensively studied at the time by Frieda Goldman-Eisler, and Bernstein worked on these with her). There was more use of modality and other expressions of uncertainty in the elaborated code, while the restricted code tended to be less hesitant, more fluent, and more explicit.

Why did these distinctions arise? Bernstein said that the restricted code tended to be used in conditions where there was a common set of closely shared identifications, interests and experiences. There was no need in these conditions to verbalize the subjective intent of the participants and make it explicit, because it was simply taken for granted. Then, in turn, the use of a highly implicit code of this kind reinforces the forms of the social relationship that engenders it. Elaborated code, on the other hand, was associated with conditions where not everything is shared, where the intent of the speakers who are interacting can not be taken for granted. So the elaborated code is explicit and expresses what he called universalistic meanings; that is, meanings that are context free in the sense that they could be interpreted in the absence of any specific immediate contextual conditions. Now, it's obvious that written language is typically to be encountered in this elaborated code; and if you look at Chafe's lists of the features of the written language, drawn up in 1982, nearly 20 years later, they look very like Bernstein's early attempts to characterize elaborated code.

Bernstein, as I said, was looking for some linguistic model that would enable him to carry out his work. Apart from a brief and abortive flirtation with some of Chomsky's ideas, he found his insights in the functional linguistic tradition. He was already well aware of the work of Sapir and Whorf, and he came to know that of Malinowski and Firth. By then he and I were talking fairly often together. Now at that time in systemic theory – it didn't yet have that name; one might call it proto-systemic – we had some sort of general model of lexicogrammar, and a notion of context of situation developed by Firth out of Malinowski and my own representation of this in terms of field, tenor and mode. And we had some sense of the way in which the system and the text were related. We had as yet no clear concept of semantics as interface, to bring together the lexicogrammar with the context of situation. I was convinced myself that we had to start with partial representations: with what I called "situation-specific semantics". In other words, there was no point in trying to think in terms of 'a semantics of English' in the way one could think of 'a grammar (or lexicogrammar) of English'. We were working towards the notion of sociosemantics; and Bernstein's researchers, for example Geoffrey Turner, used this notion to produce sociosemantic networks, which represented the meaning options that were available to the interactants in different social contexts. In this way we tried to work towards a semantics that would function as an interface between the lexicogrammar and the context of situation, so that via these sociosemantic networks we could get from the semantic choices associated with a given context to the lexicogrammar – that is, to the realization of these choices in the form of wording. But at the same time these sociosemantic networks were motivated from the other end, in terms of Bernstein's social theories. So the features in the sociosemantic networks had to face both ways. In other words, a semantic network has to be interpretable 'from below' in terms of the forms and functions of the grammar so that the grammar is seen as the realization of these choices in meaning. But it also has to be motivated 'from above' in terms of some coherent theory of whatever it is that is conceived of as the environment of language – in this case clearly some model of the social system and of social processes.

Hence the sort of notions that are familiar from Bernstein's *Class, Codes and Control, Volume 2*, where, for example, questions are asked about what strategies for regulating and controlling a child's behaviour are used by parents in certain types of situation. These strategies are modelled as sociosemantic options. Meantime, Bernstein's theory itself was of course changing and developing. It was no longer conceived of just as an explanation of educational failure through cultural discontinuity; it was becoming, in Bernstein's own terms, a general theory of cultural transmissions – of how the forms of the social order are transmitted to each generation of children. To quote from Bernstein himself: "As the child learns his speech or, in the terms used here, learns specific codes which regulate his verbal acts, he learns the requirements of the social structure" (1971a: 124). And again: "Clearly one code is not better than another; each possesses its own aesthetic, its own possibilities. Society, however, may place different values on the orders of experience elicited . . . through the different coding systems" (Bernstein 1971a: 135). This being the case, we may need to change the social structure and social practices of educational institutions. Until we can do that, a child who is limited to restricted code will continue to be disadvantaged.

Who are the children who are limited to restricted code? These are mainly to be found, Bernstein says, among the children of the lower working class. But "social class is an extremely crude index for the codes . . . It is possible to locate the two codes . . . more precisely by considering the orientation of the family-role system, the mode of social control and the resultant linguistic relations" (Bernstein 1971a: 135–6).

So Bernstein distinguished two family role systems, the "personal" and the "positional". The positional family role system is one in which the structural organization of the family group is based on ascribed status, in the sense that the role of any member in the family is determined by that person's family position. You are the mother, or the father, or the elder sister or whatever, and that fact determines your status and the part you play in such things as decision-making in the family, in negotiations of various kinds. On the other hand, the personal type of role system is based on achieved status, where family role depends much more on the personality, the psychological qualities of the individual member. As Bernstein says, a typical family will embody some kind of mixture of the two. There will be elements of a personal-type role relationship and there will be elements of a positional type. But there are families that are based on a strongly positional role system, and these will be mainly found in the lower working class. (They are also to be found in the remnants of the feudal aristocracy, but there aren't many of these latter left around.) Now it is the positional form of the role relationship that engenders restricted code. That's the chain of reasoning, therefore, that Bernstein presents in the second half of the period I have been considering.

Now typically, as an individual goes through life, he or she has to enter into four major role sets: three in childhood, those of the family, the peer group and the school, and then subsequently one more, that of the work group. Those of childhood – family, peer group and school – in turn provide the basic contexts in which socialization takes place. These "critical socializing contexts", as Bernstein calls them, are four: the regulative or control context, the instructional context, the imaginative or innovating context and the interpersonal context. If these were put in systemic terms we would refer to them as generalized situation types:

that is to say, general types of context of situation defined by what is going on between parent and child. So in the regulative context the parent is primarily regulating the child's behaviour. In the instructional one, obviously, the parent is teaching the child. In the imaginative or innovative context they are together exploring some realm of experience, perhaps through stories or imaginative literature of one kind or another. In the interpersonal they are exploring and enacting personal relationships, often in some context where there is a need for sympathy and understanding.

In the final phase of his ten-year project, Bernstein set out to explore each of these contexts in turn. These studies, many of them reported in *Class, Codes and Control, Volume 2* and subsequent volumes in the series, found that mothers from different social classes typically took up different options in these critical socializing contexts. These differences were not usually categorical; rather, they were in the relative frequency with which different options were selected. So, for example, in control or regulative situations working-class mothers tended to emphasize positional explanations. In other words, when they were giving an explanation for why the child should or should not do something, this tended to be related to positional factors – the child's place in the family: children shouldn't behave like this, boys don't do that sort of thing. The middle-class mothers, on the other hand, when they were giving rules, tended to operate more with personal explanations. A second example from instructional contexts, when the mother is helping the child to do something. Dorothy Henderson, who carried out this study, made the distinction between what she called "person area" instructions and "skill area" instructions. She found that the middle-class mothers tended to emphasize the person area instructions, instructions that could be tied to personal characteristics: whereas the working class tended to emphasize skill area instructions – how to do something. And within the skill area there was also a statistically significant difference between the two classes, in that middle-class mothers tended to emphasize general skills and to encode these in terms of general principles, whereas working-class mothers tended to emphasize the mastery of particular skills.

In these ways Bernstein suggested that the social class structure limits the access that children have to the elaborated code and therefore to universalistic orders of meaning which they need for education. So the codes become, as Bernstein renamed them in the final phase of this part of the work, "sociolinguistic coding orientations". That is, they are tendencies to take up certain semantic options, to explore certain orders of meaning in certain contexts of situation. See Ruqaiya Hasan's discussion of 'Code, register and social dialect' in *Class, Codes and Control, Volume 2* for a clear account of code in contradistinction to these other related concepts.

So according to this view children are socialized, through language, into particular cultural and semiotic practices, which in turn constrain their access to education, and hence to the power basis of society. This in very summary form is the socialization model that came from the Sociological Research Unit at the University of London Institute of Education, which Bernstein directed throughout this period of ten years and more. However, much as we can now refine, modify and build upon this work, I think it is important to realize how far it forms the basis of all our further understanding.

I now pass to the second half of my presentation, which is a commentary on and elaboration of some of these issues. Let me first note two major strengths of Bernstein's theory in relation to the history of sociological thought. First, Bernstein gives a place to language in his theory. It is not uncommon in sociological literature to find a sentence saying how important it is to recognize the significance of language. And there it rests: language is never referred to again throughout the work. Bernstein is the first sociologist to give a place to language in his chain of explanations, and by doing so he offers an explanation of how culture is transmitted. Since this obviously is largely a linguistic process, he is able to interpret the mechanism of primary socialization in a way that is in principle general to all cultures and subcultures. Second, in so doing Bernstein offers a model that can accommodate both persistence and change. As he himself points out, referring to Durkheim on the one hand and to Marx on the other, one of the problems of classical sociology was that the theory either showed how society could stay the way it always had been, as in Durkheim, or showed how society could change from one state to another, as in Marx, but there was no way to put the two together. It was impossible to explain under the same rubric both factors of persistence and factors of change. Bernstein doesn't claim to have solved this problem; but he has interpreted an important aspect of it (his "cultural transmissions") in terms that do address both these phenomena as one.

We can, I think, criticize his methodology, which was defective in a way that was characteristic of the period. His studies are not based on natural data; they are based on experimental data in which the situation has been set up – and set up not as a situation but as a hypothesis. So mothers are asked to say what they would do if a certain thing happened; hence the answer is their perception of what they would do if such a situation arose, rather than what they actually do in real-life contexts. That doesn't invalidate the results, but it does constrain the way in which we would have to interpret them. Similarly, with the study of the mothers' orientation in instructional contexts, the question that is asked by Dorothy Henderson could be paraphrased as "if you were helping the child in each of the following tasks" – and here 11 tasks are given – "how much more difficult would this task become if you didn't have language with which to do it?" So it's an intellectual, hypothetical question that the mothers are being asked to answer. But it is also true that, while there has been a lot of theoretical discussion of Bernstein's work in the 15 years since this research took place, there haven't been any comparable fact-finding research projects – at least not until Ruqaiya Hasan's project at Macquarie University. Hasan's research does show the possibility of finally providing an adequate data base for examining Bernstein's hypotheses.

Now let me probe a little more closely the notions of language and socialization. Children are said to be "socialized", and this means presumably that they learn to participate actively in the semiotic processes that constitute a culture. But this notion of socialization presents a number of problems. I'll mention one now, and come to the others towards the end. Most immediately, "socialization" has exactly the same problems that we find with "language acquisition". Like acquisition, socialization is a flawed metaphor. Both these terms tell us that there is something 'out there' that pre-exists, called society or language: by implication, an unchanging something to which children are gradually moulded until they conform. But society and language are not unchanging. Even in the most static periods of human societies there is variation. After all, those in different kinship groups or different castes or in different social classes are not insulated from each other. In our own societies there is a great deal of such variation based on class, generation, sex, provenance, and so on. The child's socialization, if we are going to use this metaphor, has to take account of the fact that he is aware of all this variation and also participates in it. We are indebted to Labov for an understanding of how this variation works linguistically. This makes it all the more ironic that Labov himself was one of the most vicious and persistent misrepresenters of Bernstein's ideas. The irony lies in the fact that it is only through Bernstein's work that Labov's linguistic findings have any significant social interpretation at all.

This kind of variation is what Mathesius referred to many years ago as "static oscillation". To recognize static oscillation is to say that the something out there that is implied in terms such as socialization and language acquisition is not a homogeneous unity to which all have to conform. It is a complex structure full of divisions and discontinuities. On the linguistic side, it has its dialects and its registers. It has subcultural distinctions that lie behind the dialects, and divisions of labour that lie behind the registers. At the very least, 'being socialized' means entering into and mastering a large number of different discourses. Some of these may be sharply distinct from and indeed in conflict with each other. The different socializing agencies, the home, the neighbourhood and the school, may of course present discontinuities of this type; that is the point of Bernstein's discussion of home and school. They have somehow to be reconciled or at least transcended. Now since Bernstein's early work there has tended to be a change, a change in which he himself has participated, in the metaphors used for exploring all these issues. Largely under the influence of European scholars such as Foucault, we've come to interpret social processes as forms of discourse; so that the language of interpretation, the metadiscourse, has once again shifted to linguistics rather than sociology or psychology. I say "once again" shifted to linguistics because if we look over the whole history of ideas in the West it's quite remarkable how often the major political, ideological and intellectual issues have been encoded and fought over in linguistic terms. I think there is a very good reason for this: language is the only phenomenon that partakes in all the realms of human experience – natural, biological, social, and so on. So the metadiscourse is now located within linguistics.

There are certain dangers inherent in this position. The notion of representing everything in discursive terms – all aspects of a culture as modes of discourse, all learning as the learning of discourse – can lead into an extreme form of idealism, and this is something we may need to watch. At the same time, it is a way of talking that we can put to positive use; and we can do this in a number of different ways at once – see Terry Threadgold's introduction to *Semiotics, Ideology, Language* for an excellent interpretative background.

First, by using the metaphor of discourse we put language back in the centre of the picture; and this, for us here, means in the centre of the picture of learning. Learning becomes something that we can interpret in linguistic terms. I've remarked before on the efforts that we had to make as linguists, back in the 1960s, to get the concept of 'language' into educational discourse at all. It wasn't there. There was no place for language in learning. It wasn't mentioned in syllabuses; learning to read and write was seen as having nothing to do with any other linguistic abilities; and there was no concept of language development.

Today, not only do we think of language development as something that runs throughout all education; we also use it to link school learning with that of the home – to bring together commonsense knowledge and educational knowledge. So, for example, Clare Painter is investigating the development of discourse abilities by pre-school children and its relevance to their subsequent experiences of learning in school. The notion of knowledge as discourse helps to break down the conceptual barriers that separate one form of knowledge and one form of experience from another. And this in turn leads to what I see as a second advantage: it will provide the foundation on which we can build a general language-based theory of learning. In the first place, such a theory cannot be other than a theory of language **and society**: "socio-linguistic" in the deep sense of that term. In 1959 Bernstein said that "the semantic function of a language is the social structure" (1971a: 54). Mary Douglas wrote, "if we ask of any form of communication the simple question what is being communicated? the answer is: information from the social system" (1971: 389). What the discursive metaphor does for us is enable us to use linguistics to interpret knowledge as a social construction and to interpret learning as the social process of which knowledge is a product. In the second place, if learning is seen as a semiotic process, a form of "languaging", we can use our understanding of language to model the processes of learning; and in the course of learning, we can hope in turn to increase our still very partial under-standing of language itself.

The third line of enquiry that social semiotic concepts open up is that of exploring the nature of education, since they allow us to interpret education also as a complex of discursive processes. This is what Martin and Rothery set out to do with their studies of children writing in the early 1980s; what Frances Christie is doing with her study of curriculum genres; what Jim Martin, Suzanne Eggins and Peter Wignell are doing with their investigation of the language of the disciplines in secondary schools. It is this perspective that Gunther Kress, Ruqaiya Hasan, Cate Poynton, David Butt, Michael Christie and others are exploring in their contributions to the Deakin University *Language in Education* series – and that all of us in different ways are adopting towards these workshops. We are treating educational processes as being in a fundamental sense processes of discourse.

In this context, learning a subject is being interpreted as learning the discourse of the subject, and hence we can use linguistic methods to interpret that discourse – to interpret its construction of technical terminologies, its use of grammatical metaphor, its forms of intertextual reference, and so on. If we can do this we shall have a powerful tool for helping to make these processes more accessible to those who are learning.

And fourth, the discursive model enables us – in fact forces us – to use language itself as a means of understanding the world. This is a complex point, which I shan't try to develop in detail here. But I would like to refer to just three aspects of it.

1 The grammar of every language is at once a theory of experience and a theory of personal and social relationships. Now in relation to this word "grammar" I have to warn you of a possible confusion here, brought about by the English language. We distinguish terminologically between "language", the phenomenon, and "linguistics", the study of that phenomenon. But we don't make a comparable distinction with the word "grammar", which is made to do duty for both: both the phenomenon – that is, grammar as a part, or level, of language; and grammar as the study of that phenomenon – which I propose to refer to here as ***grammatics***. In saying that grammar is a theory of experience, I mean grammar, not grammatics. Grammatics is a theory of grammar; but grammar – that is, the form of every language – is a theory of experience, and also a theory of personal and social relationships. It is an entirely unconscious theory, of course – but all the more powerful for that. So a child who is becoming a grammatical being by learning his first language is in that very process construing the world he or she lives in. We can then use our grammatics, particularly our functional theories of grammar, to work towards an understanding of these processes.

2 Following the work of Jay Lemke, we recognize that language, being a human social system, belongs to the wider class we call "dynamic open systems" – systems which remain in existence because they are constantly changing, in interaction with their environment. Since we know something – not a lot, but perhaps more than with other social systems – about how this dynamic exchange with the environment happens in language, we can use our knowledge of language to help us understand society, since all other social systems are essentially of this same kind.

3 At the most abstract level, even the physicists now tell us that the universe is made of language. Instead of the cause and effect models of classical physics, it is now recognized that fundamental physical processes have to be seen in terms of the exchange of information. My colleague Brian McCusker has said that the universe should be seen as one, whole, indivisible and conscious. I would like to rewrite this – cautiously, as I haven't yet consulted him – by saying that the universe should be seen as one, whole, indivisible and communicative. I suggest that it is not so much psychology, as McCusker suggested, but rather linguistics that has to supplement physics as the science of science.

So starting with static oscillation, that concept introduced by Mathesius, we have moved on to the 'dynamic open system', which is what we understand by social semiotics. For more on the social semiotic let me refer you to important recent papers by Paul Thibault and Bruce McKellar.

So this leads me back to language and socialization in home and school. We needed to take apart the concept of socialization – as has been done by the sociologists themselves; but looking at it rather more linguistically. To return, then, to the crypto-grammatical features of the term: one problem with the metaphor of "socialization" is that it ends with –*ization*. This means 'being acted upon so as to become something'; thus *hybridization* means 'being acted upon so as to become a hybrid'. So socialization means being acted upon so as to become – become **what**? Social, presumably; so as to become a social being, a member of society.

But this, of course, is a highly ideologically loaded construct. A child is not in fact moulded so as to fit some prearranged pattern. He or she construes society. Furthermore what we mean here by society, or social reality, or the social system, is not some ready-made object but a meaning potential made up of a complex of semiotic systems, having ideational and interpersonal components – that is, a domain of understanding and a domain of action. It is a complex way of thinking about and acting on the environment. So in our kind of social semiotic model, becoming a member is not 'being semioticized'. In interpreting the social as a social semiotic we do not take over the notion of socialization and say that what's going on is a passive process of 'semioticization'. Rather it is 'becoming a communicator'. This is what is happening with a child – one who is learning how to mean.

I'd like to end up with a few observations on what this implies, observations which build very directly on Bernstein's work. Let me come back to the notions of the system and the text. The child is becoming a communicator, becoming a semiotic being; and what this means is learning to construe the system from text and text from the system. This is a multilevel process; but we will think of it for the moment as having just two levels: the social and the linguistic. At each of these levels we have at one end the system, that is to say the underlying potential; the social system, and the linguistic system. At the other end we have the instance, which in language of course means text, bits of discourse, things that people actually say and write; in society it means (what linguists call) situation.

93

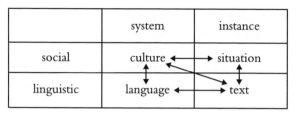

Figure 5.1 System and instance in society and language

The two top boxes, when considered as environments of text, correspond to Malinowski's notions of context of culture and context of situation. For a child, learning to become a semiotic being means filling in this entire box complex, with all of the arrows, across, up and down, and diagonally. The diagonal arrow is particularly important, because what it means is that you use the linguistic instance for constructing the social system. It's not merely that you construct the social semiotic out of instances of social processes and the linguistic semiotic out of instances of linguistic processes, and each whole level out of the other. You also make a diagonal link by using instances of the language to construct the model of social processes, the social system. (This is what makes Bernstein's researches possible.) And the social system in this sense incorporates all domains of knowledge, including those that we recognize as educational knowledge. This is the outer context in which the concept of educational knowledge has to be interpreted.

But in contextualizing educational knowledge in this way we also problematize the distinction between educational and commonsense knowledge. This distinction is an important one which Bernstein had to make for explanatory purposes; and it is a real distinction in the sense that the two do tend to be differently represented – they are presented to us in different shapes. Commonsense knowledge is typically transmitted in the home; it tends to be spoken, non-technical, informal, without boundaries, and with room for discretion on the part of the child learner, who can take it or leave it. Educational knowledge usually comes packaged by the school; and it differs in these five ways: it is written, technical, formal, with strong boundaries and with much less discretion on the part of the learner. These two last points are covered in Bernstein's notions of classification and framing. So there is a difference in the typical forms in which these two kinds of knowledge are presented to us.

But our linguistic approach should also enable us to neutralize these distinctions. Let us take a political stand here and say that by acting on language we can change the nature of knowledge – and therefore, the nature of learning and of education as well. But we can do this only if we understand – in particular, only if we first understand why educational knowledge came to be packaged as it is. For this we need to go back to the time of Newton and his colleagues in the early days of the Royal Society in England and their contemporaries in other countries. There were very good reasons why the language of scientific knowledge took the forms that it did; and while one may be critical of much modern scientific discourse this is of little use if one fails to understand why it evolved in this way in the first place.

We are now in a period of history where the changes in the forms of discourse are at least as vast as those that were taking place in the seventeenth century. New forms of language are appearing constantly, and this is the time for a reappraisal of the semiotic distance between home and school. There is in fact no need why knowledge should be packaged in these two very different ways, largely insulated one from the other. One thing that must be emphasized here is that informal spoken language is every bit as systematic as formal written language; the two are simply organized in different ways. Spoken language is not at all the way it is being represented in the linguistic press as a hodge-podge of unstructured fragments and meaningless little asides. Spoken discourse is highly systematic; and the way commonsense knowledge is represented in speech is no less meaningful than the way any other kind of knowledge is represented in writing. When we look carefully – and linguistically – at children's real learning experiences, we find that there is clear register-type variation of the kind we mentioned, with these two typical formations or packagings of knowledge: casual speech, and formal writing. But at the same time, the child is learning through many different registers, spoken and written, all at once. There are no registers that are **not** used for learning.

So when Robert Borel de Bitche sets out to investigate the nature of the transition from primary to secondary school, he finds he needs to look at teacher talk, teacher–pupil talk, teachers' notes and handouts, textbooks, pupils' class notes and reports, library work, homework, and talk with parents, including parents answering their children's questions. All of these collectively define the processes of learning, and also what is learnt. So 'learning science', for example, is seen to be a complex process in which the concept of science itself has in turn to be problematized. One way to approach this is through the teaching–learning processes themselves; I have remarked before that the various teaching–learning modes have different, and complementary, functions, in that some aspects of a subject are more effectively learnt through the teacher's

95

spoken exposition, some through reading the textbook, some through pupils' peer group talk, and so on. To put this in terms of register theory, there is a strong association between mode and field, and this is no accident – it reflects the complex nature of knowledge itself, with its systems, structures, processes, tendencies, analogies, disjunctions and complementarities. It is not surprising that this complex and sometimes contradictory mass of knowledge needs different modes of discourse with which to construe it. Lemke has remarked that meaning is created at the intersection of the material and the discursive – where discourse is made to confront experience, we could say. Meaning is also created at the intersection of different modes within the discursive: when the different discourses that constitute "learning science" come together – and sometimes conflict – then people are able to learn. It is important, of course, that they should be recognized, and valued, as all having a part in making meaning.

So "socialization" means constructing, through discourse, a social reality that is itself 'discursive': not in the sense that it is 'made of' discourse (that is a separate issue, which I alluded to briefly before), but in the sense that discourse is what turns our experience into knowledge. In saying this, therefore, let me not overprivilege the discursive, at the expense of those kinds of learning which are not mediated through language. Once we have language, of course, we tend to assume that there is nothing which is not – or at least nothing which could not be – represented in linguistic form, as meanings realized in wordings: if we can't say a thing, then we don't know it. I see no reason to assume that this is so. But whether it is or not, in an age that is somewhat obsessed with the concept of discourse I think it is important to end on a contrary note. I strongly believe – otherwise I would not have spent most of my life working for it – that the concept of language education, and of learning as primarily a linguistic process, will for as far ahead as we can see be the best way we have of understanding, and therefore of intervening in, the directions and practices of education. But I would want to be able to recognize at what point language becomes 'language', discourse becomes 'discourse' – that is, when they are metaphors for other, non-linguistic forms of knowledge and other, non-discursive ways of learning.

Chapter Six

LITERACY AND LINGUISTICS: A FUNCTIONAL PERSPECTIVE* (1996)

1 A linguistic view of literacy

In this chapter I shall try to explore the concept of literacy from a linguistic point of view. By "linguistic" here I mean two things: (1) treating literacy as something that has to do with language; and (2) using the conceptual framework of linguistics – the theoretical study of language – as a way of understanding it. More specifically, the framework is that of functional linguistics, since I think that literacy needs to be understood in functional terms.

The term "literacy" has come to be used in recent years in ways that are very different from its traditional sense of learning and knowing how to read and write. It no longer has a single accepted definition. One leading writer on literacy, Harvey Graff, has attempted to define it in a unified way – although his own practice shows that he feels the need either to narrow the definition or to extend it.[1] It is now almost 25 years since we launched our "initial literacy" programme *Breakthrough to Literacy* (Mackay, Thompson and Schaub 1970a) from the Programme in Linguistics and English Teaching at University College London.[2] When we used that title, people assumed we were boasting; they thought we were saying that here at last was a programme that broke through, that for the first time enabled children to succeed in becoming literate. What we actually had in mind was that becoming literate was itself a breakthrough. The only double meaning we had intended was the obvious one, in the grammar, whereby *breakthrough* could be read either as a process (a verb, perhaps in the imperative) or, by grammatical metaphor, as the result of such a process (as in *you've made a breakthrough*). No doubt by using the learned term *literacy*, instead of just *reading and writing*, we were signalling that this was a breakthrough to a higher mode of meaning: that, in becoming literate, you take over the more elaborated forms of language that are used in writing – and the system of social values that goes with them. (We might even feel that the tension set up between the Anglo-Saxon word *breakthrough* and the Latin word *literacy* represents what today would be seen as 'impacting of the material and the discursive', so helping us to locate literacy in the overall context of the social semiotic.)

In the generation or so since *Breakthrough* first appeared, literacy has come to mean many different things. The concept of literacy is incorporated into the framework of various disciplines: psychology, sociology, history, politics, economics – and these new senses of literacy are sometimes contrasted with a 'traditional, purely linguistic' conception. But I would argue that in fact literacy seldom has been seriously investigated as a linguistic phenomenon. It has not typically been interpreted, in the terms of a theory of language, as a process that needs to be contextualized on various linguistic levels, in ways which bring out something of the complex dialectic relations within and between them. To cite one piece of evidence for this, it is my impression that in university linguistics courses, if literacy is dealt with at all then the level of **conscious** understanding that is brought to the discussion of it is below even the level of **unconscious** understanding that must have been reached when language was first written down, some 200 generations ago. And while the "literacy debate" has moved on to higher, more rarefied levels, it tends to be forgotten that reading and writing are activities constructed in language. Yet it is impossible to explain these activities, no matter how we relate them to other theoretical concerns, without reference to language as the source from which they derive their meaning and their significance.

In many instances the term *literacy* has come to be dissociated from reading and writing, and written language, altogether, and generalized so as to cover all forms of discourse, spoken as well as written. In this way it comes to refer to effective participation of any kind in social processes.[3]

Having argued for much of my working life that we still do not properly value spoken language, or even properly describe it, I naturally sympathize with those who use the term in this way, to the extent that they are by implication raising the status of speaking, of the spoken language, and of the discourse of so-called "oral cultures". The problem is that if we call all these things literacy, then we shall have to find another term for what we called literacy before, because it is still necessary to distinguish reading and writing practices from listening and speaking practices. Neither is superior to the other, but they are different; and, more importantly, the interaction between them is one of the friction points at which new meanings are created.[4] So here I shall use literacy throughout to refer specifically to writing as distinct from speech: to reading and writing practices, and to the forms of language, and ways of meaning, that are typically associated with them.

2 The written medium

At this first level, then, literacy means writing language down; and to be literate means to write it and to read it. We tend to use expressions such as 'to know how to' read and write, but I think it is more helpful to conceive of literacy as activity rather than as knowledge.[5]

When you write, your body engages with the material environment. You make marks in sand, or arrange wooden shapes, or move a pointed stick across a surface so that it leaves a mark. (As a small child, I had a magnificent set of large wooden letters; but since they were letters, I posted them. After that I made letter shapes out of any suitably inert sinuous material, such as wet string, or my father's watch chain.) Or, if you use *Breakthrough to Literacy*, you arrange printed cards on a stand; in this way you can be engaging with the written symbols without being required first to master the material processes of constructing them.

The nature of the material environment, and the way our bodies were able to create patterns in it, opened up the possibility of writing, and also circumscribed the forms that writing took.[6] (I will come back in the next section to the question of how this actually came to happen.) In the process, a whole variety of new **things** came into being. The patterns of writing create systemic properties which are then named as abstract objects, like the ***beginning*** and ***end*** of a page or a line, ***spaces*** between ***words***, and ***letters***, ***capital*** (or ***big***) and ***small***. The different kinds of letter have their own names: they are called ***ey***, ***bee***, ***sea*** and so on; and there are other symbols called ***comma***, ***question mark***, ***full stop*** (or ***period***). Children learn that ***writing*** is different from ***drawing***; and that while 'what I have drawn' is named with reference to my world of experience, such as a cat or a house, 'what I have written' is of a different order of reality: either it has its own name, as an object created in the act of writing ('you've written a "c"'), or it is named with reference to another symbol – to an element of the language, usually a phoneme or a word ('you've written /k/'; 'you've written *cat*'). This last is, of course, very complex, since it is a symbol standing for a symbol.

Names, however, do not occur as lexical items in isolation; they function as elements in lexicogrammatical formations, like *What shall I do? – Go and read your book*. These clause, phrase and group structures construe the relationships among writer, reader and text, with wordings such as

> The capital letter goes at the beginning of the sentence.
> You must put two ells in *silly*.
> I've written a letter [where *letter* is ambiguous; contrast *I've written you a letter*, where it is not].
> *Hippopotamus* – that's a very long word.
> You say it, and I'll write it down.

If we analyse expressions such as these grammatically, in terms of the processes and participant roles in the clauses, and the experiential structures of the nominal groups and prepositional phrases, we gain interesting insights into the nature of writing, at this level of the written medium.

At this level, then, to talk about literacy in social processes means that these are being enacted, at least in part, by language in the written medium; and being literate means engaging with language in its written form: distinguishing what is writing from what is not writing, and producing and recognizing graphic patterns. These patterns include the symbols themselves, and their arrangements relative to each other and to the frame. They also take into account the many variants of these forms and arrangements, such as typeface, printing style and layout, including, today, all the innovations coming in the wake of the new technology – but those will take us up to another level. Meanwhile the next link in our chain of linguistic interpretation will be to consider the nature of writing systems.

3 Writing systems

It would be wrong to suggest that, historically, writing began as language written down: that writing simply grew out of speaking when certain people began devising a new means of expression. That is not likely to be how it happened. People came to write not by constructing a new medium of expression for language, but by mapping on to language another semiotic they already had. Writing arose out of the impact between talking and drawing (i.e., forms of visual representation).

If you create a certain outline, and say it represents a horse (the object), you have 'drawn a horse'. If you say it represents *horse* (the word), you have 'written *horse*'. It may be exactly the same outline, in both cases. But in the first case it cannot be 'read', whereas in the second it can. When you can read the outline, and match it to a **typically unambiguous** wording, it is writing. This process seems to have been initiated successfully only three or perhaps four times in human history, and then to have spread around – although the line between doing something yourself and copying someone else is not as clearly marked as that formulation suggests. In the course of this process, however, there evolved various different kinds of writing system: that is, different ways in which the visual, non-linguistic semiotic came to be mapped on to the (hitherto only spoken) linguistic one.

The significant variable here is: at what point do the written symbols interface with the language? – at the level of lexicogrammar, or at the level of phonology? In other words, do the symbols stand for elements of *wording*, or for elements of *sound*? If the written symbols interface with the wording (a writing system of this kind is called a "charactery"), then they will stand for *morphemes*, which are the smallest units at the lexicogrammatical level. In principle they might also stand for *words*; but in practice that would not work, because there are too many words in a language. The number of morphemes in a language is typically of the order of magnitude of 10,000; the number of words will always be considerably higher.[7] If the written symbols interface with the sound, on the other hand, then they may stand either for syllables (a "syllabary") or for phonemes (an "alphabet"), or for something in between the two – depending on the phonological system of the language in question.

A writing system may be relatively homogeneous, belonging clearly to one type, such as Chinese (morphemic) or Italian (phonemic); or it may be much more mixed, such as Japanese or English. In Japanese, two systems interact – one purely syllabic, the other in principle morphemic – while English is in principle phonemic but contains various sub-systems and is modified in the direction of the morphemic.[8] The differences among different writing systems lie not in the **form** of the symbols but in their **function** relative to the language concerned; specifically, what linguistic elements, identified at what level, the symbols represent.

Like sound systems (phonologies), writing systems (or "graphologies") usually contain prosodic and paralinguistic features over and above their inventories of elementary symbols. These are patterns extending over longer stretches, affecting more than minimal segments; some of them construct systems (these are the "prosodic" features), while others (the "paralinguistic") do not. In phonology, intonation and rhythm are typically prosodic features, while voice quality is typically paralinguistic; but again it is the function rather than the form that determines their significance. In writing, some of the features referred to briefly in the previous section are of this kind: punctuation symbols function prosodically, while typeface (roman, italic, bold, etc.) and graphic design (indentation, line spacing, and so on) function paralinguistically – although all paralinguistic features are available as potential resources for constructing further systems.

If we talk about literacy in the context of this level of the interpretation, we would mean operating with a writing system of a particular kind. Literacy in this sense has a great deal of effect on cross-linguistic movements of one kind or another: for example, patterns of borrowing between languages, and the maintenance of personal identity under the transformation of proper names. It also affects internal processes such as the creation of technical vocabulary, as well as the intersection of written text with other, non-linguistic semiotic systems.[9] For a person to be literate, in this sense, means to use the writing system with facility, and also to have some understanding of how it works, so as to be able to extend it when the need arises (e.g. in inventing brand names for products, or new personal names for one's unfortunate children). Some people achieve this understanding of a writing system at an unconscious level, without going through the process of knowing it consciously, but others don't, and for certain purposes one may need to have access to it as conscious knowledge, for example as a teacher coping with children's – or adults' – problems in learning. To be literate is also to reflect on what writing is **not**: it is not pictures of things, or representations of ideas (the terms "pictograph", "ideograph" refer to the origins of symbolic **forms**; as functional terms they are simply self-contradictory). It is also to reflect on the limits or a writing system – can everything that is said also be written down? in what ways is it transformed, or deformed, in the process? – and on how writing systems interact with other visual semiotics such as maps, plans, figures and charts (which will take us up to another level).[10] Meanwhile, to investigate questions that are raised by our exploration of writing systems, we need to look into the nature of written language.

4 Written language

As a writing system evolves, people use it; and they use it in constructing new forms of social action, new contexts which are different from those of speech. These contexts in turn both engender and are engendered by new lexicogrammatical patterns that evolve in the language itself. If we reflect on the lexicogrammar of written English, for example, we soon recognize features that are particularly associated with language in its written mode.

A great deal has been written, since the early 1970s, on spoken and written language; much of it purports to show that written language is more logical, more highly structured and more systematically organized than speech. This is the popular image of it, and it is very largely untrue – although you can readily see how such a picture came to be constructed. If you compare tape-recorded speech, with all its backtracking, rewording and periods of intermittent silence, with the highly edited, final form of a written text from which all such side-effects of the drafting have been eliminated; if you regard the overt intrusion of 'I' and 'you' into the text as making it less logical and less systematic; and if you then analyse both varieties in the terms of a logic and a grammar that they were constructed out of, and for the purposes of, written language in the first place – you will have guaranteed in advance that written language will appear more orderly and more elaborately structured than spoken. And you will also have obscured the very real and significant differences between the two.

It is true, of course, that first and second person are much less used in written than in spoken texts. The system of person in the grammar construes a context that is typically dialogic, with constant exchange of roles between speaker and listener; this is not the pattern of written language, which is typically monologic and, except in a genre such as informal correspondence, does not accommodate a personalized reader as co-author of the text. (This is not to deny the role of the reader as an active participant in discourse, but the reader reconstitutes the text rather than sharing in its construction.) Hence there is less of a place for personal forms when making meaning in writing. And interpersonal meaning is made less salient in other ways besides; for example, there is much less variation from the unmarked choice of mood – most writing is declarative, except for compendia of instructions where the unmarked mood is imperative. The discursive relationship between writer and readers tends to be preset for the text as a whole. But it would be wrong to conclude from the absence of 'I' and 'you', and of interrogative clauses, that the writer is not present in the lexicogrammar of the written text. The writer is present in the attitudinal features of the lexis, in words which signal 'what I approve/disapprove of '; and, most conspicuously, in the network of interpersonal systems that make up modality. Modalities in language – expressions of probability, obligation and the like – are the grammar's way of expressing the speaker's or writer's judgment, without making the first person 'I' explicit; for example, *that practice must be stopped* means "I insist that that practice is stopped", *it couldn't possibly make any difference* means "I am certain that it doesn't make any difference". Modalities never express the judgment of some third party. They may be presented as depersonalized, or objectified, especially in written language (e.g., *it seems that, there is a necessity that*); but all are ultimately manifestations of what "I think". The account given so far assumes that the clause is declarative. If, however, it is interrogative, the onus of judgment is simply shifted on to the listener: *could it possibly make any difference?* means "do you think it possible that it makes some difference?"

However, a more significant feature of written language is the way its ideational meanings are organized. If we compare written with spoken English we find that written English typically shows a much denser pattern of lexicalized content. Lexical density has sometimes been measured as the ratio of content words to function words: higher in writing, lower in speech (Taylor 1979). But if we put it this way, we tie it too closely to English. In a language such as Russian, where the "function" elements more typically combine with the "content" lexeme to form a single inflected word, such a measure would not easily apply. We can, however, formulate the content of lexical density in a more general way, so that it can be applied to (probably) all languages. In this formulation, lexical density is the number of lexicalized elements (lexemes) in the clause. Here is a sentence taken from a newspaper article, with the lexical elements in italics:

> Obviously the *government* is *frightened* of *union reaction* to its *move* to *impose proper behaviour* on *unions*.

There are nine lexemes, all in the one clause – lexical density 9. If we reword this in a rather more spoken form we might get the following:

> ||| Obviously the *government* is *frightened* || how the *unions* will *react* || if it tries to make them *behave properly* |||

There are now three clauses, and the number of lexemes has gone down to six – lexical density $6/3 = 2$.[11]

Needless to say, we will find passages of varying lexical density both in speech and in writing, with particular instances showing a range of values from zero to something over twenty. To say that written texts have a higher lexical density than spoken texts is like saying that men are taller than women: the pattern appears over a large population, so that given any text, the denser it is the more likely it is to be in writing rather than in speech. This explains the clear sense we have that a passage in one medium may be in the language of the other: someone is 'talking like a book', or 'writing in a colloquial style'.

How does the difference come about? It is not so much that when we reword something from a written into a spoken form the number of lexemes goes down; rather, the number of clauses goes up. Looking at this from the other end we can say that spoken language tends to have more clauses. But if one lexically dense clause in writing corresponds to two or more less dense clauses in speech, the latter are not simply unrelated to each other; they form hypotactic and/or paratactic clause complexes. Thus the spoken language tends to accommodate more clauses in its "sentences"; in other words, to be less lexically dense, but more grammatically intricate. This may not emerge from averaging over large samples, because spoken dialogue also tends to contain some very short turns, and these consist mainly of one clause each. But given any instance of a clause complex, the more clauses it has in it the more likely it is to be found occurring in speech.

Most of the lexical material in any clause is located within nominal constructions: nominal groups or nominalized clauses. Thus in the example

> The *separable* or *external soul* is a *magical stratagem* generally *employed* by *supernatural wizards* or *giants*.

there are two nominal groups, *the separable or external soul* and *a magical stratagem generally employed by supernatural wizards or giants;* and all nine lexemes fall within one or the other. But what makes this possible is the phenomenon of grammatical metaphor, whereby some semantic component is construed in the grammar in a form **other than** that which is prototypical; there are many types of grammatical metaphor, but the most productive types all contribute towards this pattern of nominalization. What happens is this. Some process or property, which in spoken language would typically appear as a verb or an adjective, is construed instead as a noun, functioning as Head/Thing in a nominal group; and other elements then accrue to it, often also by grammatical metaphor, as Classifier or Epithet or inside an embedded clause or phrase. In the following example the two head nouns, *variations* and *upheaval*, are both metaphorical in this way:

> These small variations of age-old formulas heralded a short but violent upheaval in Egyptian art.

How do we decide that one of the two variants is metaphorical? If they are viewed synoptically, each of the two is metaphorical from the standpoint of the other; given an agnate pair such as *her acceptance was followed by applause* and *when she accepted, people applauded*, we can say only that there is a relationship of grammatical metaphor between *her acceptance* and *she accepted*, but not – at least in any obvious respect – that one is metaphorical and the other not, or less so. If they are viewed dynamically, however, one form does turn out to be the unmarked one. Thus, in instances of this type, there are three distinct histories in which 'accept' is construed as a verb **before** it is construed as a noun:

1. diachronically, in the history of the language;
2. developmentally, in the history of the individual; and
3. instantially, in the history of the text.

Thus (1) the noun is usually derived from the verb, rather than the other way round (the derivation may have taken place in ancient Latin or Greek, but that does not affect the point); (2) children usually learn the verbal form significantly earlier than the nominal one; (3) in a text, the writer usually proceeds from verb to noun rather than the other way round, e.g.,

> She accepted the commission. Her acceptance was followed by applause.

In all these histories, the process starts life as a verb and is then metaphorized into a noun.[12]

One of the reasons why these nominalizing metaphors appeared in written language may be that writing was associated from the start with non-propositional (and hence non-clausal) registers: for example, tabulation of goods for trading purposes, lists of names (kings, heroes, genealogies), inventories of property and the like. But another impetus came from the development of science and mathematics, originating in ancient Greece, as far as the European tradition is concerned. To pursue these further we shall have to move 'up' one level, so as to take account of the contexts in which writing and written language evolve (see section 8 below). Meanwhile, we have now reached a third step in our linguistic interpretation of literacy: literacy as 'having mastery of a written language'. In this sense, if we say that someone is literate it means that they are effectively using the lexicogrammatical patterns that are associated with written text. As I said earlier, this does not imply that they are consciously aware of doing so, or that they could analyse these patterns in grammatical terms. But it does imply that they can understand and use the written wordings, differentiate them from the typical patterns of spoken language, and recognize their functions and their value in the culture.

I am not suggesting that written language is some kind of uniform, homogeneous 'style'. On the contrary, writing covers a wide range of different discursive practices, in which the patterns of language use are remarkably varied. But the fact that such practices are effective, and that such variation is meaningful, is precisely because certain 'syndromes' of lexicogrammatical features regularly appear as a typical characteristic of text that is produced in writing. This means, of course, that there are other combinations of features that do not appear, or appear only seldom, even though they would not be devoid of meaning: for example, we do not usually combine technical or commercial reports with expressions of personal feeling. But we could do; such gaps, or "disjunctions", are not forced on us by the language, and with new developments in language technology there are already signs of change (see section 6 below).[13] By thinking about what does not usually occur, we become more aware of the regularities, of what is common to the varied forms of written discourse.

The value of having some explicit knowledge of the grammar of written language is that you can use this knowledge not only to analyse the texts, but as a critical resource for asking questions about them: why is the grammar organized as it is? why has written language evolved in this way? what is its place in the construction of knowledge, the maintenance of bureaucratic and technocratic power structures, the design and practice of education? You can explore disjunctions and exploit their potential for creating new combinations of meanings. The question then arises: are the spoken and written forms of a language simply variants, different ways of 'saying the same thing'? or are they saying rather different things? This takes us to the next link in our exploratory chain.

5 The written world

I referred in the last section to the way in which metaphorical patterns of nominalization are built up in the course of a text. The example referred to in note 12 was a paper entitled 'The fracturing of glass', in *Scientific American* (December 1987); it contains the following expressions, listed here in the order in which they occur (in different locations spaced throughout the text):

1. the question of how glass cracks
2. the stress needed to crack glass
3. the mechanism by which glass cracks
4. as a crack grows
5. the crack has advanced
6. will make slow cracks grow
7. speed up the rate at which cracks grow
8. the rate of crack growth
9. we can decrease the crack growth rate 1,000 times.

Note how the metaphorical object *crack growth rate* is built up step by step beginning from the most congruent (least metaphorical) form *how glass cracks*.

To see why this happens, let us focus more sharply on one particular step:

> ... we have found that both chemicals [ammonia and methanol] speed up the rate at which cracks grow in silica. . . . The rate of crack growth depends not only on the chemical environment but also on the magnitude of the applied stress. (p. 81)

This shows that there are good reasons **in the discourse** (in the *textual* metafunction, in systemic terms). In carrying the argument forward it is often necessary to refer to what has already been established – but to do so in a way which backgrounds it as the point of departure for what is coming next. This is achieved in the grammar by thematizing it: the relevant matter becomes the Theme of the clause. Here the Theme, *the rate of crack growth*, 'packages' a large part of the preceding argument so that it serves as the rhetorical foundation for what follows.

When we look into the grammar of scientific writings we find that this motif recurs all the time. The clause begins with a nominal group, typically embodying a number of instances of grammatical metaphor: this summarizes the stage that has now been reached in the argument and uses it as the taking-off point for the next step. Very often, this next step consists in relating the first nominal to a second one that is similarly packaged in a logical semantic relationship of identity, cause, proof and the like. Thus a typical instance of this clause pattern would be the following:

> The sequential appearance of index-minerals reflected steadily increasing temperature across the area.

Here is a condensed version of the context in which this is built up.

[Barrow] recognized a definite and consistent order of appearance or disappearance of particular metamorphic minerals (index minerals), across the area. . . . the differences in mineralogy observed by Barrow could not be due to chemical differences because the rocks all have similar bulk chemical compositions. The most likely explanation . . . is that the sequential appearance of index minerals reflected steadily increasing temperature across the area. (Clark and Cook 1986: 239)

In a study of the evolution of the grammar of scientific English from Chaucer to the present day (reference in note 13 above), I found that this clause pattern is already operational in Newton's writing (the English text of the *Opticks*), becomes well established during the eighteenth century, and has become the favourite clause type by the early years of the nineteenth century. Since this kind of nominalization is frequently objected to by stylists, it is valid to point out that, however much it may become ritualized and co-opted for use in contexts of prestige and power, it is clearly discourse-functional in origin.

However, while these nominalizing metaphors may have been motivated initially by textual considerations, their effect in the written language – perhaps because they arose first in the language of science – has been to construct an alternative model of human experience. Spoken language is organized around the clause, in the sense that most of the experiential content is laid down in the transitivity system, and in other systems having the clause as point of origin; and this – since the clause construes reality as processes (actions, events, mental processes, relations) – creates a world of movement and flux, or rather a world that is moving and flowing, continuous, elastic and indeterminate. By the same token the written language is organized around the nominal group; and this – since the nominal group construes reality as entities (objects, including institutional and abstract objects, and their quantities, qualities and types) – creates a world of things and structures, discontinuous, rigid, and determinate. Here experience is being interpreted synoptically rather than dynamically (Martin 1991).

This is the same complementarity as we find between the two different media. Spoken language is language in flux: language realized as movement and continuous flow, of our bodily organs and of sound waves travelling through air. Written language is language in fix: language realized as an object that is stable and bounded – as text in material form on stone or wood or paper. Thus the complementarity appears at both the interfaces where the discursive connects with the material (both in the meaning and in the expression); and both are significant for the social-semiotic functioning of language. If we use David Olson's distinction between communicative and archival functions (Olson 1989), spoken discourse is typically communicative, and becomes archival only under special conditions (e.g., a priesthood transmitting sacred oral texts); whereas written discourse is typically archival, a form of record-keeping, and hence can accumulate knowledge by constant accretion, a necessary condition for advancing technology and science.[14] And on the other hand, those who are constructing scientific knowledge experimentally need to hold the world still – to stop it wriggling, so to speak – in order to observe and to study it; and this is what the grammar of written language does for them.

Thus the written world is a world of things. Its symbols are things, its texts are things, and its grammar constructs a discourse of things, with which readers and writers construe experience. Or rather, with which they reconstrue experience, because all have been speakers and listeners first, so that the written world is their secondary socialization. This is critical for our understanding of the educational experience. Despite our conviction that we as conscious subjects have one 'store of knowledge' rather than two, we also have the sense that educational knowledge is somehow different from 'mere' commonsense knowledge; not surprisingly, since it is construed in a different semiotic mode. The language of the school is written language.

But, of course, educational knowledge is **not** constructed solely out of written language. While our primary, commonsense knowledge is – in this respect – homoglossic, in that it is construed solely out of the clausal grammar of the spoken language, our secondary, educational knowledge is heteroglossic: it is construed out of the dialectic between the spoken and the written, the clausal and the nominal modes. Even though the scientific textbook may be overwhelmingly in nominal style, provided we are reasonably lucky our total educational experience will be multimodal, with input from teachers, parents and peers, from classroom, library, teachers' notes and handouts, all of which presents us with a mix of the spoken and the written worlds. At its worst, this is a chaos, but it does offer the potential for more effective participation in social-semiotic practices than either of the two modes can offer by itself.

Literacy, then, in this context, is the construction of an "objectified" world through the grammar of the written language. This means that in at least some social practices where meanings are made in writing, including educational ones, the discourse will actively participate in an ideological construction which is in principle contradictory to that derived from everyday experience. To be literate is, of course, to engage in these practices, for example as a teacher, and to construe from them a working model to live with, one that does not deny the experience of common sense. Again, I would observe that, in order to turn the coin – to resist the mystique and the seductive appeal of a world consisting entirely of metaphorical objects – it is helpful to have a *grammatics*, a way of using the grammar consciously as a tool for thinking with. It seems to me that, as David Bohm (1980) suggested with his demand for a return to the "rheomode",[15] the two worlds have been pushed about as far apart as they can go, and in the next period of our history they are bound to move together again. I think, in fact, they are already starting to do so, under the impact of the new forms of technology which are deconstructing the whole opposition of speech and writing. This is the topic we have to take up next, as the next link in the interpretative chain. But in doing so, we are back where we started, concerned once again with the nature of the written medium.

6 The technology of literacy

The critical step in the history of writing technology is usually taken to be the invention of printing with movable type. The significance of this from our present point of view is that it created maximum distance between written and spoken text. A written text now not only existed in material form, it could be cloned – it had become a book. Books existed in lots of copies; they were located in libraries, from which they could be borrowed for variable periods of time;[16] they could be possessed, and bought and sold, as property. Producing books was a form of labour, and created value: printing, publishing, bookbinding were ways of earning a living. The book became an institution (the book of words, book of rules), without thereby losing its material character; note the expression *they threw the book at me* 'quoted the authority of the written word'. With printing, language in its written form became maximally objectified; and this extreme dichotomy between speech and writing was a dominant feature of the 500 years of 'modern Europe' from about 1450 to 1950.

We have seen how this object-like status of the written word is enacted metaphorically by the nominalizing grammar of the written language. Meanwhile, however, the technology has turned itself around. Within one lifetime our personal printing press, the typewriter, from being manual became first electric then electronic; and from its marriage with the computer was born the word processor. With this, in hardly any time, the gap between spoken and written text has been largely eliminated. On the one hand, while as in the printing era the written text passed out of the writer's control in being transmitted, we now once again control our own written discourse; and since we have our own private means of transmission, the communicative function of writing has come to the fore, as people write to each other by electronic mail. And as the functional gap has lessened, so also the material gap has lessened, and from both ends. With a tape recorder, speech becomes an object: it is on the tape; can be 'played' over and over again (so listening becomes like reading); can be multiply copied; and can be stored (and so used for archiving functions). With a word processor, writing becomes a happening; it can be scrolled up the screen so that it unfolds in time, like speech. The tape recorder made speech more like writing; the word processor has made writing more like speech.

We have seen the effects of this in education. Teachers who favour "process writing" are emphasizing the activity of writing as well as – and sometimes at the expense of – the object that results from it.[17] Children who learn to write using a word processor tend to compose their written discourse in a manner that is more like talking than like traditional writing exercises (Anderson 1985). What is happening here is that the consciousness barrier is disappearing. When the material conditions of speaking and writing are most distinct, the consciousness gap is greatest: speaking is unselfconscious, proceeding as it were from the gut, while writing is selfconscious, designed and produced in the head. (This is why the writing of a 6-year-old typically regresses to resemble the spoken language of age 3.) Although writing and reading will always be more readily accessible to conscious reflection than speaking and listening, **relatively** we now have more occasions for being selfconscious when we speak (international phone calls, talkback shows, interviews, committees, and so on), and more chances of remaining unselfconscious when we write.

This suggests that the spoken and the written **language** will probably come closer together, and there are signs that this is already beginning to happen. Not only textbook writers but also public servants, bankers, lawyers, insurers and others are notably uneasy about the "communication gap"; they are even turning to linguists to help them communicate – note the success of the Plain English movement towards greater reader friendliness in written documents.[18] I have referred already to the scientists wanting a discourse of continuity and flow, and suggested that the way to achieve this is to make their technical writing more like speech, so that they are not cut off from the commonsense construction of experience. But we need to think grammatically about this. To the extent that written discourse is **technical**, to that extent it probably has to objectify, since most technical constructs are metaphorical objects, organized in paradigms and taxonomies.[19] Even non-technical writing has numerous functions for which a nominal mode seems called for. So it is not, I think, a question of neutralizing the difference between written language and spoken. What the technology is doing is creating the material conditions for interaction between the two, from which some new forms of discourse will emerge. Again, the effects are likely to be felt at both the material interfaces of language: new forms of publication, on the one hand, with (say) print and figures on paper combining with moving text and graphics on the screen; and on the other hand new ways of meaning which construe experience in more complex, and hence more 'realistic', ways arising out of the complementarities of the spoken and the written modes. Such a construction of experience would seem to call once again for the poet-scientist, in the tradition of Lucretius; I think Butt (1988a, 1988b) would say that Wallace Stevens is the first such figure in our own times, at least among those writing in English, but there are also scientists with the semantic prosodies of poetry, such as Stephen Hawking. And if science is to technology as poetry is to prose, then the marriage, or perhaps *de facto* relationship, has already been arranged: in the post-industrial, information society the real professional is the semiotician-technician, for whom the world is made of discourse/ information and the same meta-grammar is needed to construe both the grammar of language on the one hand, and the "grammar" of the teleport, on the other.[20]

At this fifth level, then, literacy is a technological construct; it means using the current technology of writing to participate in social processes, including the new social processes that the technology brings into being. A person who is literate is one who effectively engages in this activity (we already refer to people as "computer-literate", a concept that is now much closer to literacy in its traditional sense than it was when coined). But – the other side of the coin again – I think that here, too, and perhaps especially in this context, we need the concept of literacy as informed defence. To be literate is not only to **participate** in the discourse of an information society, it is also to resist it, to defend oneself – and others – against the anti-democratic 'technologizing' of that discourse. And here more than ever one needs to understand how language works, how the grammar (in its systemic sense of lexicogrammar) interacts with the technology to achieve these effects. If you hope to engage successfully in discursive contest, you have first to learn how to engage with discourse.

7 The frontiers of literacy

We were able to define writing, historically, as the mapping of non-linguistic visual communication practices on to language. This, as I have tried to suggest in the foregoing sections, was an important move in the history of *semogenesis*, the potential for producing meaning – comparable in many ways to the shift in the potential for material production that took place along with settlement.[21] We now need to take this one level up, and in doing so we shall perhaps reveal the counter-tendencies that always existed and are now coming to be foregrounded once again. What is happening today is not a loosening of the bond between the written symbol and the language (that could be achieved only by destroying the writing system altogether, and this has never happened)[22] but the creation of new systems of visual semiotic that are not themselves forms of writing – that have no (in principle) unique mapping on to lexicogrammatical or phonological elements – yet are used in conjunction with written text.

Take a mathematical expression as an example. Mathematics is not, of course, a form of visual semiotic, but it is expressed in symbols that look like, and in some cases are borrowings of, written symbols. The simplest of all such expressions would be something like $2 + 2 = 4$. This is not writing; we cannot read it, because it has no exact representation in wording. We can, of course, **verbalize** it – that is, find semantically equivalent wordings, such as *two and two make four, two plus two equal(s) four, two added to two comes to four, four is the sum of two plus two*, and so on. But each of these has its own written form (I have just written them here); and, of course, they are all different – although they are all equivalent mathematically, they are certainly not synonymous. Linguistically they mean different things, as the grammar can readily show.

I am not saying that the boundary between what is and what is not writing is absolute, clearcut and determinate. We saw above that readers are presented with a lot of visual symbols that are on the fringes of writing: the prosodic and paralinguistic features referred to in section 3. But they are also presented, nowadays, with a great deal of visual information that is clearly not writing, and yet has to be processed along with a written text: maps, charts, line graphs, bar graphs, system networks, diagrams and figures of all kinds. None of these can be read aloud; they have no unique implication of wording, even though again they can often be verbalized: for example, a feature on a weather map could be verbalized as *a cold front is moving in a northeasterly direction across the Tasman Sea.*

So although these are not made of language, they are semiotic systems whose texts can be translated into language, and that offer alternative resources for organizing and presenting information. Reporting on his research in Vancouver, Mohan (1986) explores this potential in an educational context in his work with English as a second language students in primary school. It is exploited in artificial intelligence in text generation systems, which use non-linguistic representations (e.g., maps) as the source of information to be presented in text form. These can also now be incorporated into the text itself, and obviously the graphics capabilities of personal computers will encourage writers more and more to integrate non-verbal material into their writing.

In the context of a discussion of literacy, the critical feature of these non-verbal texts is that referred to above: that they can be translated into natural language. This means that they can be interpreted semantically – they can be construed into meaningful wordings even though always with a fair amount of semantic 'play'. We tend to assume that such semiotic systems are from a linguistic viewpoint metafunctionally incomplete: that they construct ideational meanings (experiential and logical) but not interpersonal ones. (What this means is that we assume all the interpersonal choices are unmarked: declarative or imperative mood, according to the semiotic function; non-modalized; attitudinally neutral, and so on.) But if we think about these texts grammatically, we find that the situation is more complex. There are interpersonal devices, some of them very subtle; the problem is that it is here that the distance from language is probably greatest, so these meanings are the hardest to 'read aloud'.[23] On the other hand, the ideational meanings may be very indeterminate and ambiguous, and the textual meanings are notoriously hard to retrieve: texts are usually presented in the context of other textual material which **is** in language, but this, while it may solve some problems, often creates another one – namely, that we do not know how the verbal and the non-verbal information is supposed to be related.[24]

Somewhere in this region lie the frontiers of literacy as traditionally understood. But it would be foolish to try to define these frontiers exactly. What is relevant is that, in social processes in which writing is implicated, we typically find it associated with a variety of non-linguistic visual semiotics, which accompany it or in some cases substitute for it (like the – often totally opaque – signs displayed for passengers at international airports). Being literate means being able to verbalize the texts generated by these systems: 'reading' the weather charts, stock exchange bulletins and share prices, street maps and timetables, pictorial instructions for kit assembly and the like. (Perhaps we should include here the filling in of forms; these are, in principle, made of language, but I suspect that in coming to terms with them we rely heavily on their non-verbal properties!) Being literate might also include, finally, knowing what meanings have been lost, and what new meanings imposed, when there is translation between the verbal and the non-verbal; and exploring the semiotic potential that lies at their intersection – the new meanings that can be opened up when writing impacts on other visual systems that lie outside (but not too far outside) the frontiers of language.

8 The contexts of literacy

These other systems of visual semiotic, referred to in the last section, could be thought of as the contexts for a **writing system**. The contexts of a **written language**, on the other hand, are the systems and processes of the culture – the various contexts of situation that engender written language and are engendered by it.

Writing does not simply duplicate the functions of speech. It did not originate, or develop, as a new way of doing old things. Writing has always been a way of using language to do something different from what is done by talking. This is what children expect, when they learn to read and write; as Hammond (1990) pointed out, in explaining why a class of children who had just been talking about a recent experience in very complex terms regressed to more or less infantile language when asked to write about it, it made no sense to them to go over the same task again in writing. They expect what we can call a "functional complementarity" between speech and writing.

Historically, as already implied, writing evolved with settlement; and if we think about it historically, we can construct the metaphor linking writing with its contexts in other social processes. Under certain conditions, people settle down: they take to producing their food, rather than gathering it wherever it grows or hunting it wherever it roams. Instead of moving continuously through space-time, these people locate themselves in a defined space, marked out into smaller spaces with boundaries in between. (We can notice how this unity of people and place becomes lexicalized, in terms such as *village, homestead, quarter.*)

These people create surplus value: they produce and exchange durable objects – goods and property. The language that accompanies these practices is similarly transformed: it becomes durable, spatially defined, and marked with boundaries – it settles down. This is writing. In the process it also becomes an object, capable of being owned and exchanged like other objects (written text and books).

The meanings construed by this language-as-object are themselves typically 'objects' (inventories, bills of lading, etc.) rather than processes. Meanings as things split off from meanings as events; the nominal group replaces the clause as the primary meaning-producing, or *semogenic*, agent in the grammar. This is written language. The nominal group then functions to construe other phenomena into objects (nominalization), thus 'objectifying' more complex forms of social organization (noun as institution) and their ideological formations (noun as abstraction).

Production processes are technologized; objects are created by transformation out of events (e.g., heating). The nominalizing power of the grammar transforms events into objects, and their participants into properties of those objects (grammatical metaphor). These transformed 'objects' become the technical concepts of mathematics and science.

All experience can now be objectified, as the written language construes the world synoptically – in its own image (writing is language synoptically construed). Writing is itself technologized (printing). The flux of the commonsense environment, reduced to order, is experimented with and theorized. Writing and speech are maximally differentiated; written knowledge is a form of commodity (education), spoken knowledge is denied even to exist.

What I am trying to show, in this highly idealized account (of processes that are in fact messy, sporadic and evolving, not tidy, continuous and designed), is that our material practices and our linguistic practices – not forgetting the material interfaces of the linguistic practices – collectively and interactively constitute the human condition. They therefore also change it. In our present era, when information is replacing goods and services as the primary form of productive activity, it seems certain that the split between speech and writing will become severely dysfunctional. But it is still with us, and throughout this long period of history writing has had contexts different from those of speech. In some ways these are complementary; in other ways they are contradictory and conflicting.

Malinowski gave us the concepts of 'context of situation' and 'context of culture'; we can interpret the context of situation as the environment of the text and the context of culture as the environment of the linguistic system. The various types of social process can be described in linguistic terms as contexts of language use. The principle of functional complementarity means that we can talk of the contexts of written discourse.

Certain contexts of writing are largely transparent: if we represent them in terms of field, tenor and mode then there is a fairly direct link from these to the grammar of the text. Such relatively homogeneous forms of discourse, like weather reports, sets of instructions (e.g., recipes), shopping lists and other written agendas, and some institutional discourses, can be specified so that we can construe them in either direction: given the context, we can construe the features of the text, and given the text we can construe the features of the context. To be literate implies construing in both directions, hence constructing a relationship between text and context that is systematic and not random.

Other written texts are not like this; they present a more or less discordant mix of multiple voices. These are texts whose context embodies internal contradictions and conflicts. As an example, one large class of such texts consists of those designed to persuade people to part with their money. The goods and services offered have to display all desirable qualities, even where these conflict with one another, as they often do; and to combine these with a price-figure that is in fact in conflict with their claimed value, and has to be presented as such but with the inconsistency explained away ('you'd never believe that we could offer . . . but our lease has expired and we must dispose of all stock', etc.). In the following example the text has to reconcile the 'desirable building land' with the fact that it is on a site that should never have been built on; the linguistic unease is obvious:

> . . . is a high quality, bushland, residential estate which retains environmental integrity similar to a wildlife reserve.

Such features need, of course, to be demonstrated with full length texts.[25]

Another example is technocratic discourse, which, as Lemke (1990b) and Thibault (1991b) have shown, intersects the technical-scientific with the bureaucratic – the authority of knowledge with the authority of power – to create a contradictory motif of 'we live in an informed society, so here is explicit evidence; but the issues are too complex for you to understand, so leave the decision-making to us'; they go on to 'prove' that children who are failing in school do not benefit from having more money spent on them, or that the environment is not under serious threat. Reproduced below, however, is an example of a different kind (though not unrelated to these last). It is a party invitation addressed to tenants in a prestigious "executive residence" (name withheld).

Dear tenant
IF YOU JUST WANNA HAVE FUN . . .
Come to your MOONCAKE NITE THEME PARTY next Saturday.
That's September 20 – from 7.30 p.m. until the wee hours!!

A sneak preview of the exciting line-up of activities includes:

* Mr/Ms   Tenant Contest
* Find <u>Your</u> Mooncake Partner
* Pass the Lantern Game
* Bottoms Up Contest
* Blow the Lantern Game
* Moonwalking Contest
* DANCING
* PLUS MORE! MORE! MORE!

For even greater fun, design and wear your original Mooncake creation, and bring your self-made lantern passport!
But don't despair if you can't because this party is <u>FOR</u> you!
Lantern passports can be bought at the door.
Just c'mon and grab this opportunity to chat up your neighbour.
Call yours truly on <u>ext. 137</u> NOW! Confirm you really wanna have fun!! Why – September 20's next Saturday.
See you!
Public Relations Officer
P.S. Bring your camera to 'capture' the fun!

In the cacophony of voices that constitute this text, we can recognize a number of oppositions: child and adult, work and leisure, 'naughty' and 'nice', professional and commercial – constructed by the lexicogrammar in cahoots with the prosody and paralanguage. But this mixture of bureaucratic routine, comics-style graphic effects, masculine aggression, childism and condescension, straight commercialism, conspiratorialism and hype adds up to something that we recognize: late capitalist English in the Disneyland register. Presumably there are institutions in southern California where people who are being trained to 'service' business executives learn to construct this kind of discourse. The context is the Disneyfication of Western man (I say "man" advisedly), whereby the off-duty executive reverts semiotically to childhood while retaining the material make-up of an adult.

Literacy today includes many contexts of this contorted kind, where the functions of the written text have to be sorted out at various levels. To be literate is to operate in such complex, multiple contexts: to write with many voices, still ending up with a text, and to read such texts with kaleidoscopic eyes. Once again, the grammatics will help: it is the point about conscious knowledge again. And once again there is the other side of the coin, literacy as active defence: resisting the Disneyfication, as well as more ominous pressures; probing the disjunctions and extending the semogenic potential of the culture. This leads into the final heading, section 9 below.

9 The ideology of literacy

There is of course no final step; but this is as far as I shall try to go. In using the term 'ideology' here I do not mean it in the classical Marxist sense where it is by definition false consciousness; nor am I implying that it is a coherent, ordered system of hidden beliefs that are taken over by the oppressed from the dominant group that is oppressing them. I use it as Martin (1986), Hasan (1986) and others have used it – though not as an explicitly stratal construct.[26] If we conceive ideology in this way, I think we have to take seriously Gramsci's point that it is not so much a coherent system of beliefs as a chaos of meaning-making practices, within and among which there is incoherence, disjunction and conflict – which is why it always contains within itself the conditions for its own transformation into something else (Thibault 1991a). But in agreeing that ideological constructions are typically anything but consistent, I would add that there is a certain mystique at present about the opposition between order and chaos. In foregrounding chaos – as end-of-millennium postmodernist thinkers do, whether in physics or in semiotics – people have tended to reify the dichotomy, that is, to treat it as a property of the phenomena under study, whereas I see it more as the standpoint of the observer. Anything we can contemplate is bound to be a mixture of order and chaos, and either can be made to figure against the grounding of the other. Rather than arguing that one or other is correct – at least in relation to semiotic practices – I would ask what we can learn about them by interpreting them one way and then the other.

The dominant ideological aspect of literacy is obviously the authority of the written word. Consider this in relation to school textbooks. If they are to function effectively, the readers they are addressed to must believe in what they say. Luke, Castell and Luke (1989: 245ff), as also Olson (1989: 233ff), raise the question of how textbooks derive and maintain their authority. They show that textbooks sanctify "authorized (educational) knowledge" simply by authorizing it – what is in the text-book is thereby defined as knowledge – and textbooks maintain this authority by various means such as claiming objectivity and creating distance between performer and reader, and so come to be accepted as 'beyond criticism'. They then go on to point out that textbooks strive for clarity, explicitness and an unambiguous presentation of the facts;

they seek to "delimit possible interpretations". I think they do strive for these things; but I also think they often fail to achieve them. Consider these examples:

1. In many algebra books you will see numerals such as "– –6". This means, of course, the *opposite of* 6, that is, the opposite of positive 6. Thus – –6 is exactly the same number as negative six or –6.

2. Your completed table should help you to see what happens to the risk of getting lung cancer as smoking increases. Lung cancer death rates are clearly associated with increased smoking.

3. In the years since 1850, more and more factories were built in northern England. The soot from the factory smoke-stacks gradually blackened the light-coloured stones and tree trunks. Scientists continued to study the pepper moth during this time. They noticed the dark-coloured moth was becoming more common. By 1950, the dark moths were much more common than the light-coloured ones. However, strong anti-pollution laws over the last twenty years have resulted in cleaner factories, cleaner countryside and an increase in the number of light-coloured pepper moths.

I have commented on texts such as these elsewhere;[27] they can be obscure, ambiguous or even misleading to someone who does not already know what it is they are trying to say.

Looked at from the point of view of order, such 'failures' are highly dysfunctional: the passages in question fail to give an unambiguous message. But from the point of view of chaos, they are positively functional, because not only do they admit of multiple interpretations, but they can also be used to explore such multiple interpretations – to consider alternative readings and argue about which to accept. For example, in *lung cancer death rates are clearly associated with increased smoking* it is the grammar that reveals that there are other ways of interpreting the statistics on smoking; it also shows what the alternatives are: does *are associated with* mean 'are caused by' or 'cause' (cf. *means* in *higher productivity means more supporting services*)? Are *lung cancer death rates* 'how many people die of lung cancer' or 'how quickly people with lung cancer die'? Looking at them in this light we might conclude that literacy is the ability **not** to retrieve a single, fixed and correct meaning from the text. Similarly, with the pepper moths, the grammar offers interesting alternatives to a Darwinian explanation!

To say that a textbook authorizes and sanctifies knowledge means that it derives its authority from its function in the educational context. But what is it that sanctifies the written text? It is not simply the high status that is accorded to the social contexts of writing; it is equally the written words themselves, and most of all, perhaps, the interaction between the two. In other words, the authority of the text rests ultimately on the perceived resonance of form and function: the "fit" between its linguistic properties (especially its lexicogrammar and discourse semantics) and the sociocultural processes by which its value and scope of action are defined.

From this point of view, to be literate is not just to have mastered the written registers (the generic structures and associated modes of meaning and wording, as described in section 8 above), but to be aware of their ideological force: to be aware, in other words, of how society is constructed out of discourse – or rather, out of the dialectic between the discursive and the material.[28] There is a vigorous debate on this issue among educators in Australia, between those who favour explicit teaching of the linguistic resources and those who consider that such teaching is unnecessary and can even be harmful. Essentially, this is an ideological debate about the nature of literacy itself: does literacy enable, or does it constrain? Is control over the linguistic resources with which educational knowledge is constructed a liberating or enslaving force? The former group sees it as enabling, admits the (often arbitrary) authority of the written genres, but insists that all members of society should have the right of access to them, as the gateway to becoming educated: children should be taught to master the structures of the genres the school requires and the grammatical resources by which these structures are put in place. The latter group sees it as constraining, con- sidering that any acceptance of formal structure limits the freedom and creativity of the individual; ideologically, this is the motif of individual autonomy and salvation that derives from liberal protestant romanticism. In this view, children should **not** be taught these structures, but instead should be ideologically armed so they can defend themselves against them.[29] (As far as I am aware, these same principles have not been thought to apply to numeracy, the most highly structured activity of all.)

This motif of literacy as both 'access to' and 'defence against' has recurred several times throughout my chapter. My comment on this debate is that defence will be effective only if it is **informed** defence – a point made also by Hasan (1996); to me it seems dangerously quixotic to say 'go out and fight against those who control the meanings; but you need not try to master their discourse yourselves'. What both sides agree on, however, is that literacy means being able to participate effectively in social processes by working with written language. They are concerned with literacy at this highest level – with what Hasan, in the context just referred to, calls "reflection literacy". Hasan embraces within this concept the ability to understand how systems of value, and patterns of power and prestige, are construed and maintained in language (typically, in varieties of written language); and to use that understanding in bringing about social change, or in resisting those changes that are socially divisive and corrupt.

But if we are adopting a linguistic perspective, we cannot isolate 'using written language' from 'using language' in general. It is true that written language has these special features of its own, its distinctive registers and genres. But everyone who writes and speaks, and our understanding of written language, derives ultimately from our understanding of speech, and from written language in contexts that are defined by speaking. Our construction of experience comes from the interplay between the clausal and the nominal in the grammar – between reality as happening and reality as things. Our modes of discourse range from the clearly structured genres typical of conscious writing to the unbounded flow of casual conversation (still structured, but in a rather different way). So as well as separate concepts of literacy and oracy, we need a unified notion of **articulacy**, as the making of meaning in language, in whatever medium. If literacy is redefined so as to include all this and more besides, so be it; but then, as I said at the start, if we want to understand it fully, we shall still need some way of talking about it in its specific sense, of living in a world of writing.

10 Conclusion

I have tried to trace a course through what Graff called the labyrinth of literacy, while interpreting literacy in linguistic terms. The route has led through a number of stages, which could be summarized as follows:

1. **The written medium**
    engaging with the material environment to produce abstract symbolic objects called "writing".
2. **Writing systems**
    mapping these symbols on to elements of language and constructing them into written text.
3. **Written language**
    construing meaning through lexicogrammar in written text: lexical density, nominalization, grammatical metaphor.

4. **The written world**

  construing experience through semantics in written language: the world objectified as the basis of systematic knowledge.

5. **The technology of literacy: (1) revisited**

  from books to computers: refining the medium, realigning writing and speech, technologizing discourse.

6. **The frontiers of literacy: (2) revisited**

  from writing to other systems of visual semiotic: expanding the potential for meaning.

7. **The contexts of literacy: (3) revisited**

  from text to context: locating written language in its socio-cultural environment.

8. **The ideology of literacy: (4) revisited**

  from the construction of experience to participation in the social–semiotic process.

This suggests a kind of helical progression, as set out in Figure 6.1.

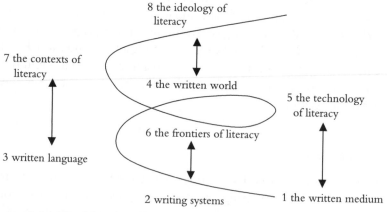

Figure 6.1 The labyrinth of literacy

This recalls Bruner's well-known helical model of learning. I should stress, however, that this is not to be taken as a linear sequence of learning steps. Although there is, broadly, a developmental progression in the ordering of these motifs, such that each implies some engagement with the one before, they are analytic constructs and not pedagogic practices. Leaving aside considerations of maturity, an adult moving into the literate world could operate from the start with concepts from any stage. This principle is clearly enshrined in Hasan's discussion of 'levels' of literacy in the model she has presented in her work.

We are all familiar with the claim that linguistics has nothing useful to say on the subject of literacy. But it always seems to be a kind of linguistics very remote from life that is cited to justify the argument. It is a pity, because to reject linguistic insights seals off an important avenue of understanding. What I have tried to suggest here is that a functional linguistic perspective provides a valuable complementarity to the view from sociology and the philosophy of education.

Notes

* This is a revision of a paper presented at the Inaugural Australian Systemic Functional Conference, Deakin University, 1990 and appearing in Frances Christie (ed.), *Literacy in Social Processes*, Centre for Studies of Language in Education, Northern Territory University.

1. Graff (1987: 18–19) writes that 'literacy is above all *a technology or set of techniques for communication and for decoding and reproducing written or printed materials*: it cannot be taken as anything more or less' [his italics]. Compare this with his formulation 'the skills of literacy: *the basic abilities to read and write*' [his italics].

2. See especially the revised and illustrated edition of the *Teacher's Manual* (Mackay, Thompson and Schaub 1978). For an account of the programme, see Pearce, Thornton and Mackay (1989).

3. The following is taken from *Australia Post*'s description of International Literacy Year 1990: 'Literacy involves the integration of listening, speaking, reading, writing and critical thinking; it incorporates numeracy. Literacy also includes the cultural knowledge which enables a speaker, writer or reader to recognize and use language appropriate to different social situations' (*Australian Stamp Bulletin* No. 203, January–March 1990: 10).

4. The situation is similar to that which arises with the term *language*. If we want to extend it to mathematics, music and other semiotic systems, in order to emphasize their similarities of form or function or value in the culture, then we have to find another term for language. The expression *natural language* arose in response to just this kind of pressure. I am not aware of any comparable term for literacy in its canonical sense.

5. Graff (1987: 23) quotes the following from Lewis (1953: 16): 'The only literacy that matters is the literacy that is in use. Potential literacy is empty, a void.'

6. See Thibault (1991a) on how these "meaning making practices" are enabled and constrained by the material (and other) conditions in which they take place.

7. I put it this way for simplicity; the actual situation is obviously much more complex. The number of words in a language is open-ended – new ones

can always be constructed; whereas morphemes, unless borrowed, form a closed set. Moreover, in many languages it is hard to decide what a word is, or whether one word is the same as another (e.g., different inflectional variants of the same stem). But it is a reasonable approximation to say that a language has too many words to be able to afford a separate symbol for each. For an excellent account of writing systems, see Mountford (1990). See also Halliday (1985b).

8. For an excellent brief account of the English writing system see Albrow (1972/1981). Albrow's account reveals the various sub-systems that co-exist in the writing system of English, thus distinguishing clearly between what are simply irregularities and what are systematic variations.

9. For example: a language written in a strongly phonemic script will not only 'rephonologize' but also 'regraphologize' borrowed words; hence Italian and Czech *filosofia* (not *ph-*). A language written morphemically will tend to calque (translate the component parts) rather than borrow; for example, Chinese *xiangguang* 'facing light' = phototropic (but this is part of an extended linguistic syndrome in Chinese, including other features such as syllable structure). Writing English personal names in Chinese, and Chinese personal names in English, creates real problems of identity (which deserve a paper to themselves!). Constructing new technical meanings might seem to be the same in all languages, but it is also shaped by the writing system, especially where the lexical resources are drawn from outside the language, as in English (Graeco-Romance) and Japanese (Chinese, English); at the same time the writing system in its turn is shaped by these semogenic processes. It would take too long to illustrate these points in detail; but consider the relationship of graphology to phonology in series such as *analyse, analysis, analytic, analyticity* in English (where each of the four words is accented on a different syllable); or the use of *kanji, hiragana* and *katakana* in creating new meanings in written Japanese.

10. For a discussion of some of these issues with special reference to maps in geography texts, see van Leeuwen and Humphrey (1996).

11. There are of course many possible rewordings. We might, for example, keep the word *move* and end with *if it moves so as to make the unions behave properly*; this adds two lexemes, *move* and *unions*, but it also adds one clause, a hypotactic clause of purpose, giving a ratio of 8/4, still = 2. Other variants would alter the lexical density, but it would be difficult to find a convincing 'spoken' version in which it was not significantly lower than in the written one.

12. For an instance of how grammatical metaphor is built up in the course of a text, see Halliday (1988).

13. See Lemke (1984) who introduces the notion of 'disjunctions' in the context of a general theory of language as a dynamic open system which provides an essential component of the present interpretation.

14. Note the apparent paradox that, in the archival function, written language becomes the dynamic member of the pair. The spoken archive (canon of sacred texts, traditional narrative and song, etc.) can **change** in the course of transmission, but it cannot grow – it cannot become a library of knowledge.

15. See especially Chapter 2. Bohm is expressing his dissatisfaction with the "fragmentation" imposed by language on the world, and seeking "*a new mode* of language" [his italics] which would represent continuity and flux. His suggestions are linguistically naïve; but the interesting point is that he is trapped in the confines of written language – in particular the meta-language of his own science, physics – and does not see (or rather hear) the "rheomode" that is all around him.

16. According to *The Return of Heroic Failures*, by Stephen Pile (Penguin Books, 1988), the most overdue book in the history of the lending library was borrowed from Somerset County Records Office, in England, by the Bishop of Winchester in 1650, and returned to the library by the Church Commissioners 335 years later, in 1985. The book in question was, appropriately, the *Book of Fines*.

17. This issue has been foregrounded in the "genre debate" in Australia; see for example, Painter and Martin (1987) and also Moore (1990).

18. See for example, *Plain English and the Law, Report and Appendices 1–8*, published by the Law Reform Commission of Victoria (for which Robert Eagleson was Commissioner-in-Charge of the Plain English Division), 1987.

19. Martin (1990) has argued convincingly that the technicalization of discourse must depend on nominalization and grammatical metaphor. On the other hand, Whorf pointed out that the technical terms of Hopi metaphysics were typically verbs. (But probably not taxonomized?)

20. For an overview of the development and present state of information technology see Jack Meadows (1989).

21. There are striking homologies, both phylogenetic and ontogenetic, between semiotic and material 'histories' (e.g., it seems that infants begin to use symbols along with reaching and grasping, to use protolanguage along with crawling, and to use language along with walking). In human history, people began to write when they settled down (even here we might detect an ontogenetic parallel!); that is, when they moved from hunting and gathering to husbandry and agriculture. Whether these new practices improved the human condition is open to question (I happen to think they did); what is not open to question is that they changed it.

22. The nearest example I can think of is one where a writing system was replaced by another one, leading to the 'de-mapping' of the first, which then remained in existence as an art form – Chinese characters as used by Vietnamese painters, for example.

23. Since I am addicted to maps, let me use the map as an example. Obviously,

there is the matter of projection: on a world map, the projection defines the mapmaker's orientation towards the subject-matter (compare projection in the sense in which we use it in systemic grammar); but also towards the user, who is being treated more as an equal with conical projection, whereas Mercator is for outsiders (compare the projection of mood in report and in free indirect discourse). But there are many directly inter-personal signals: choice of colouring (there is one atlas where the colour is so strident it is difficult to read the print), size and variety of typeface, pictorial representations of various kinds, not to mention all the modern descendants of the old-fashioned ships and sea monsters. At the least, such things indicate degrees of concern for the user; but some are more specific, for example using special symbols to indicate that the mapmaker is only guessing (probability), or that some feature is present only some of the time (like rivers in Australia – usuality). Note in this connection O'Toole's use of systemic metafunctions in interpreting the semiotics of visual art (O'Toole 1990, 1994).

24. There is a case to be made for defining "writing" in such a way that it includes these other forms of visual semiotic. If the semantic system is part of language (as I think all functional linguists would agree, even if they would interpret its relationship to the lexicogrammar in different ways), then by that token visual systems which can be verbalized, and thus shown to represent language at the semantic level, could be considered to be writing systems. Against this are the following considerations: (1) they are all domain-specific and therefore partial, whereas a writing system repre-sents the whole of a language; (2) they are language-neutral, a 'universal character' rather than a writing system; (3) some, at least, cannot be decoded out of their context – that is, you cannot construe the context from the text.

25. For detailed treatment of a fund-raising text, approached by various lin-guists from different angles, see Mann and Thompson (1992).

26. Martin (e.g., 1992) stratifies the context into three levels, or **strata**, those of register, genre and ideology, and shows that these can be networked, as systems of paradigmatic relations, like the lexicogrammar and the discourse semantics.

27. See Halliday (1989). It should be pointed out that almost any clause in English can be shown to be in many ways ambiguous in its grammar, but most interpretations are too far-fetched to pose real problems to a reader. I am not talking about these. The examples I am talking about are those that are problematic for the readers for whom they are intended (e.g. because of the kinds of grammatical metaphor they are using). It is after one has recognized them as problematic that the grammatics can be brought in to explain the problem – and also to suggest how it might be avoided.

28. See Hasan (1995, 1996).

29. See the original project reports by Martin and Rothery (1980–81); the critique by Sawyer and Watson (1987); the reply to this critique (Martin, Christie and Rothery 1985); see also Reid (1987), and Threadgold (1988a, 1989).

PART TWO

SECOND-LANGUAGE LEARNING

EDITOR'S INTRODUCTION

It is in fulfilling its main task of describing language that general linguistics can contribute most to language teaching, provided that description takes meaning into account. While formal, linguistic criteria have their place in such descriptions, nevertheless, as noted in Chapter Seven, 'General Linguistics and Its Application to Language Teaching' (1960), "what we cannot accept is this dichotomy between form and function, for it is a false opposition". Moreover, by observing language in use, the linguist can describe language in context.

The title of Chapter Eight poses the question, 'Is Learning a Second Language like Learning a First Language All Over Again?' (1978). In this keynote, given at the first Congress of the Applied Linguistics Association of Australia, Professor Halliday compares language learning under natural conditions with what he calls 'induced' language learning, or that kind of learning which typically takes place when learning a second language under institutional conditions. While the means can never be the same – "whatever we do to approximate to the natural, it will always be contrived", nevertheless both first and second language learners share a similar ambition to succeed. But, as Professor Halliday points out, "success will always be a relative matter; in a second language we may be aiming for success in quite specific areas, not necessarily restricting our ultimate aims but at least ordering our priorities".

Chapter Nine, 'Learning Asian Languages' (1986) continues on this theme of success in second language learning as Professor Halliday takes up the subject of learning Asian languages as second languages in Australia – particularly by Australians of non-Asian background. "Learning a language," as defined by Professor Halliday, "means learning to think with it and to act with it in one and the same operation." The

difficulty in achieving this with Asian languages in Australia is complicated by the lack of a context in which Australians "can get a sense of
what they have achieved". In analysing the problem, Professor Halliday
looks at three major factors: the social context of the language learning,
the cultural distance to be bridged, and the linguistic problem to be
faced. Far from being negative about the prospects for learning Asian
languages in Australia, however, Professor Halliday argues that "a learner
should feel that he has succeeded if he has explored, and exploited, some
of the riches of an Asian language, every one of which is not only the
vehicle of a living culture, thus embodying meanings out of the past, but
also, like every language, a semiotic powerhouse, out of which will come
the new meanings, and the new cultures, that we can expect to arise in
the future."

Chapter Seven

GENERAL LINGUISTICS AND ITS APPLICATION TO LANGUAGE TEACHING (1960)

There are already so many definitions of language that it seems a pity to add to their number still further. Rather than attempting to define language, we can adopt an alternative approach and begin by specifying those properties of language which are relevant to the subject under discussion. Our starting point here, then, could be the observation that language is organized noise.

Linguistics and phonetics are the two disciplines whose purpose it is to account for language. Phonetics studies the noise, linguistics the organization. This explains both the similarity and the difference between the theories and methods of these two disciplines: they study different aspects of the same observable phenomenon. Various other disciplines also take account of language in one way or another; what distinguishes linguistics and phonetics from the rest is that the former study language in order to throw light on language, whereas other subjects such as literary criticism, psychology, logic and anthropology study language in order to throw light on something else. Linguistics and phonetics can thus be appropriately called 'the linguistic sciences'.

Both these subjects have their various subdivisions or branches. In linguistics what is usually recognized to be the primary division is that into descriptive (or synchronic) linguistics and historical (or diachronic) linguistics. In descriptive linguistics we are interested in the operation of language: how does a given language work? In historical linguistics, clearly, we are interested in the history of language: how does a given language come to be what it is? The main branches of phonetics, on the other hand, are concerned with the different stages in the speech event: production by the speaker, transmission through the air and perception by the hearer. To these correspond articulatory phonetics, acoustic phonetics and perceptual phonetics; the first and last are physiological studies, or physiological and psychological, while the second is physical.

These and the many other branches and divisions of each subject are united and controlled by the overall theories known as "general linguistics" and "general phonetics". Since these two are in turn closely inter-linked they are often subsumed under the single name "general linguistics". In this chapter I shall use the term "general linguistics" to refer to the whole body of theory, linguistic and phonetic, that lies behind the study of language. Since the branch of linguistics that is most relevant to language teaching is descriptive linguistics, I shall be concerned with that area of general linguistic theory which bears on the description of languages. Here both phonetics and linguistics play an essential part: neither will suffice without the other. But their roles are different, and need separate discussion; in what follows I shall concentrate mainly on the role of linguistics. In other words I shall be dealing with the linguistics side of that part of general linguistic theory that enables us to describe effectively how a language works.

"General linguistics" implies a general theory of language, and this in turn implies that we can identify the properties that are common to all languages and distinguish these from the features that are specific to a given language. Many features often assumed to be universal, in the sense of 'common to all languages', are not in fact universals at all: concepts like *verb, phrase* and *syllable* are not linguistic constants and must to a certain extent be redefined for each language. The syllable in French, for example, has a very different status from the syllable in English; in some languages we do not find anything which we should want to call a "verb" because there is nothing that displays enough of the properties of what are called "verbs" in the languages to which this term was first applied. To find what is common to all languages we must invoke more abstract concepts than these. It is rather as if we said that all human beings must drink, and therefore all societies have some means of drinking; but not all societies use cups, and sometimes we are doubtful whether a particular vessel should be called a "cup" or not.

The understanding of what are the inherent properties of language as such is extremely important, since it provides a framework of categories for a powerful and accurate description of any language. We will not find a *verb* in every language, so "verb" will have no place in a general theory; but we shall find the category of which verb is a special instance, namely the category of *class*. All languages have classes, and the "class", appropriately defined, does have a place in a general theory of language. General linguistics is necessary if we seek to explain how language works. In fact all description of languages, however elementary, presupposes some theory or other; but the more adequate the theory, the simpler, more comprehensive and more exact the description will be.

Descriptive linguistics has other applications besides language teaching, although language teaching is certainly one of the most important. In all such applications the first essential is a good description of the language or languages concerned. For language teaching purposes we also need to compare languages; the methods are those of comparative descriptive linguistics, sometimes known also as "contrastive linguistics". The principal contribution of general linguistics to language teaching is thus that it makes possible the provision of adequate descriptions and comparisons of languages. A secondary but still important contribution is that it shows how a description may take different forms according to the aim that is in view.

1 The description of a language

The basic principle of description is to analyse the language according to its various kinds of patterning: to break it down into what we call *levels*. Language, as said above, can be thought of as organized noise. To this we can add: 'used in situations', actual social situations. Organized noise used in social situations, or in other words 'contextualized systematic sounds'. I shall be concerned here mainly with spoken language; not that I wish to suggest that written language is unimportant, but merely so as to avoid complicating some of the formulations. With this as a starting-point I should like to consider in outline one possible approach to the description of a language.

Language, whether spoken or written, has a substance: this is the material aspect of language. The substance may be phonic or graphic, but for the moment we will consider only the phonic. The noise, then, is the substance. Language also has a form: this is the organization. In language, therefore, we recognize a level of *substance* and a level of *form*. Now the organization of language, its form, is meaningful: that is, linguistic activity participates in situations alongside man's other creative activities. Thus for a complete description of language one has to account for the form, the substance and the relationship between the form and the situation. The study of this relationship could be called the *semantic* level; but since it involves an approach to meaning rather different from that normally implied by "semantics" we may refer to this as the *contextual* level, the "context" here being the non-linguistic environment.

There is thus a resemblance between "context" as used here and "meaning" in its non-technical sense. But what is generally understood by "meaning" is perhaps too limited to be adequate for linguistics, being confined almost entirely to referents or concepts. For the linguist any consideration and any description of language, be it formal or contextual, is concerned with meaning: this is inevitable, for language is meaningful activity. It is often said that "structural linguistics" represented an attempt to describe a language without reference to its meaning; whether or not this is so, we would rather insist that the aim of a description is to elucidate linguistic meaning at its various levels. At the same time it should be stressed that we are concerned here with linguistics and not philosophy. What "meaning" means to a philosopher may be a rather different question.

The domain of the linguistic sciences, as far as the description of language is concerned, can be illustrated as follows:

LINGUISTIC SCIENCES				
	Phonetics			
		Linguistics		
SUBSTANCE		FORM		SITUATION (environment)
phonic	phonology	{grammar/lexis}	context	extra-textual features

Language, by its nature as contextualized systematic sound, presupposes substance (phonic substance), form and situation, the last being the associated non-linguistic factors. Under "form", however, we must make a further distinction between **grammar** and **lexis** (vocabulary), a distinction likewise made necessary by the nature of language. In every language the formal patterns are of two kinds, merging into one another in the middle but distinct enough at the extremes: those of grammar and those of vocabulary (or, to use a technical term, of lexis). I shall come back later to the criteria on which the distinction between grammar and lexis depends.

The link between form and phonic substance is provided by phonology: this is the meaningful distribution of speech sounds. It is here that phonetics and linguistics overlap. Phonetics covers the study of phonic substance and also of phonology from the standpoint of phonic

138

substance. Linguistics covers the study of form and also of phonology from the standpoint of form. Linguistics also extends to the right of the diagram so far as to take in the study, not of the non-linguistic features themselves, but of the relation between these non-linguistic features and linguistic form: that is what we are here calling the study of context.

These then are what we call the "levels of analysis" of descriptive linguistics: phonic, phonological, grammatical, lexical and contextual. For the written language, matters are a little more complicated: one cannot simply replace "phonological" and "phonic" by "graphological" and "graphic", for in most languages the orthography represents the linguistic forms not directly but via the phonology: we must therefore add the study of the relations between the two.

The levels of analysis are derived in the first place by a process of abstraction from our observations of the language material. We observe, to start with, the linguistic events we call "utterances", in which we find regular patterns of partial likeness between events. Then we generalize from these observations, grouping elements together according to the likenesses. Afterwards we make abstractions: we set up categories of language and so construct a theory, with hypotheses depending on the theory, to explain the facts observed. Finally we present our description, made in terms of the categories so established.

Observation, generalization, theory, presentation: this, one might perhaps say, is the scientific method of description. The facts of language are such that we must proceed by a set of abstractions at several levels at once, all constantly interrelated but each level having its own categories. These categories enable us to arrange systematically the mass of events constituting a language.

2 Grammar

What do we mean by grammar? The most fruitful criterion seems to be this: when we are dealing with a *closed system* we are concerned with grammar. A *closed system* is a series of terms with the following characteristics:

1. the list of terms is exhaustive – it contains (say) *a, b, c* and no more;
2. each term excludes all the others – if *a*, then not *b* and not *c*;
3. one cannot create new terms – if *a, b, c*, then one cannot add a *d*.

To be more exact, as one can always imagine the creation of new terms and their integration into a grammatical system, the third condition should rather be formulated thus: (3) if a new term is added, at least one of the previous terms undergoes a change of meaning, so that in effect a new system replaces the old.

To take an example: the cases of the noun substantive in Latin form a closed system. No speaker of Latin could borrow a new case from another language or create one himself. The Latin case system is a flexional system: the exponents of the cases are bound morphemes (as distinct from free morphemes), which have not themselves the status of words. But one can also have a closed system whose members are free morphemes, for example the definite article in French. Let us suppose – however improbably – that French were to borrow the nominal category 'dual' from Samoyedic as a third term in the number system of the definite article; this would change the meaning of the word *les*: instead of as at present 'two or more' it would become 'three or more'. This change would be both formal and contextual. There would also be a change in the formal, but not the contextual, meaning of *le* and *la*, since *le/la* would be opposed not to one term in the system but to two, and this would lead to a redistribution of information. Thus 'information', in the sense it has in information theory, is in linguistics the **formal** meaning of an item or category.

Let us take by way of contrast a series of lexical items: the names of various means of locomotion, for example *train, car, bus, taxi, motorcycle, bicycle*. One day a new kind of vehicle appears: the *monorail*, let us say. This word is absorbed into the vehicular series without any change of meaning in any of the other words. My bicycle is still a bicycle. In this case we are in the domain of lexis, not grammar. We readily accept that there are grammars on the one hand and dictionaries on the other, but often without asking ourselves where the difference between them lies. It is sometimes stated as follows: a dictionary deals with words, a grammar with the construction of words in sentences (one should add at least 'and of morphemes in words'). But this is not enough to distinguish grammar from lexis: does the classification of words, for instance, belong to grammar or to lexis? The real difference consists in the relations between the items. The dictionary – or rather lexicology, since there are other ways of describing lexis than by writing a dictionary – lexicology is concerned with *open relations*, whereas grammar studies *closed relations*. In other words where, in linguistic form, there is a choice among a fixed number of possibilities, this is the realm of grammar.

Grammatical relations are not, of course, confined to flexions (bound morphemes), nor even to relations below the rank of the word (morphemes in general). It is a characteristic of language that patterns occur

140

over stretches of varying extent. In discussing a grammatical item or category one may thus ask at what **unit** it is operating: where in the language is this particular choice made? The stretches that carry the grammatical patterns are what I am calling "units". The unit is the first of the general grammatical categories that I should like to discuss, and it is a technical term in the description. In this sense every language will have at least two grammatical units: indeed this is perhaps one universal feature of languages. We might go so far as to say this: 'All languages have at least two grammatical units: a larger one which is the unit of contextual meaning, the one with which the language operates in situations, and this we call the **sentence**; and a smaller one which is the unit that also mainly enters into lexical relations, and this we call the **word**.' For our purposes it is enough to take it as established that the sentence and the word are two universal units of grammar.

It is doubtful whether any language operates solely with these two units. There are other units in between the sentence and the word, and in many cases there is also one below the word. Those between the sentence and the word are in many cases complex and often lend themselves to very confused interpretations. English grammar needs two such: the clause and the group. Textbooks generally treat these at length, giving a great many negative rules (what one must not say or write), but they rarely explain what a clause or group is. Obviously one does not expect definitions of these terms such as are found in dictionaries: scientific technical terms cannot be defined in this way, for each category is defined by its relations to all the others. It is only when the whole grammar of the language has been described that you can know what a clause is, and at the same time you will know what a sentence, a group, a word and a morpheme are. But in most textbooks such information is difficult to extract when one needs it.

In general the units of a language are related to each other in a hierarchy based on the notion of constituency; each is composed of one or of several members of the unit next below. The term **rank** is used for the position of the unit in the hierarchy. In English, for example, there are five grammatical units: sentence, clause, group, word, morpheme. A sentence is thus one complete clause or several complete clauses. A clause is made up of one or more than one complete group; and so on. It may of course happen that a given sentence consists of one clause consisting of one group consisting of one word consisting of one morpheme, for example the sentence *Yes.* or *Pardon.* or *Run.* French grammar in this respect is similar to English; in describing French it is most convenient to operate with these same five units. For example, the sentence *le* *concert commence très tard* is a sentence consisting of one clause (a "simple" sentence); the clause consists of three groups which are made up of two, one and two words respectively. Unit boundaries may be indicated as follows:

‖‖	between	sentences
‖	"	clauses
|	"	groups
(space)	"	words
+	"	morphemes

Each boundary of course implies a boundary at all lower ranks. Thus:

‖‖ le concert | commence | très tard ‖‖

The substitution of *commencera* for *commence* would give a compound instead of a simple word, the rest remaining unaltered:

‖‖ le concert | commenc + er + a | très tard ‖‖

If we substitute *a commencé*, we have:

‖‖ le concert | a commenc + é | très tard ‖‖

This time it is a compound group that has been substituted for the simple one. The clause in each instance consists of three groups.

The formulation used above was that 'it is most convenient' to operate with five units, and not 'one must'. It should be stressed that linguistic descriptions are not, so to speak, monovalent. A description is not simply 'right' or 'wrong' in itself (it may be wrong, of course, if it does not conform to the facts); it is better thought of as more useful or less. Some facts are quite evident and not open to question: we do not need very advanced general linguistics to tell us that French nouns are either masculine or feminine. But there are many linguistic facts which are much less simple. For example, the analysis of English compound ("phrasal") verbs: the differences in their patterning are extraordinarily complex, and it is difficult to decide whether they form one class or twenty or a hundred classes. The various pronouns and pronominal adjectives in French are likewise extremely complicated. The distinction between 'in French there are . . .' and 'in describing French it is useful to recognize . . .' is a very delicate one. One should beware of statements such as 'in French there are 36 phonemes'. The phoneme is a phonological abstraction (I shall return to it later) and there are several ways of regarding it. There might be no question of there being 10 or 90

142

phonemes in a given language, but different analyses yielding 20 or 30 or 40 might all be possible. The aim is to find the simplest description that will account for all the facts, and one often has to have described a considerable area of the language before being able to judge which of two possibilities is the simpler.

Each unit, then, is made up out of combinations of the unit next below it in rank. In this respect orthography serves as a model for grammar. In the construction of a written text each paragraph consists of (orthographic) sentences which consist of sub-sentences which consist of (orthographic) words which consist of letters; and we may have a one-to-one relation all the way, as when *I.* occurs, in answer to a question, as a complete paragraph in English. We do not say that the paragraph consists of one letter, in any meaningful sense, because it would be absurd to analyse the structure of a paragraph as a sequence of letters; nor do we deny that *I* is a word merely because it consists of one letter, or that it is a sentence because it consists of only one word. Grammatically, sentences in English do not consist of words in this strict sense; they consist of clauses, which in turn consist of groups, and these groups consist of words. To analyse a sentence grammatically as a string of words or morphemes is like trying to describe the patterns of a written paragraph by treating it as a string of letters.

In grammar however there are two complications to this relation of rank. In the first place, the boundaries between units are by no means always clearcut. Sometimes they are, with one item, say a group, beginning just where the previous one ends. Sometimes, however, they may be discontinuous, with for example one clause in the middle of another; or they may be fused, as when for example a word is made up of two morphemes but not in such a way that it can be split into two segments. An example of the latter is the English word *took*, which we can regard as consisting of two morphemes *take* and 'past tense'; unlike *walked*, it cannot be split into two segments, and indeed the morpheme 'past tense' has no recognizable item corresponding to it at all: nevertheless this morpheme is present in the word *took*. The French word *commence* above could (here is an instance of a choice in description) be analysed as two morphemes, *commence* plus '(third person) singular'; we might then write it *commenc + e*, but this would be merely a notational device and there would be no separate item corresponding to the morpheme 'singular'. All inflexional paradigms provide instances of fused morphemes.

The second complication is the phenomenon known as **rankshift** (or **downgrading**). Here an item of one rank is as it were shifted down the scale of rank to form part of an item either of lower rank than itself or of equal rank to itself: a clause within a group, for example, or a group within a group. English *the man who came to dinner* has a rankshifted clause *who came to dinner* inside the group *the man who came to dinner; the railway company's property* has the group *railway company's* inside the group *the railway company's property.* Many, if not all, languages display this phenomenon of rankshift in their grammar.

This then is the relation among the grammatical units of a language: for each given unit, every item of that rank is made up of one or more items (or perhaps rather **instances**, since in the case of fusion the 'items' may be pure abstractions) which will be either of the rank immediately below or, with rankshift, of equal or higher rank. But, as is readily observable, there are restrictions on the ways in which such items may operate, both alone and in combination, to form an item of next higher rank: it is not true, for example, that any group can go anywhere and play any part in any clause. In other words, each unit displays a limited set of possible **structures**.

Structure is the second of the general categories of grammar. It is an abstract category, of course, like the others: in the clause *the old man is sitting in the garden* the elements of structure are not *the, old, man, is* and so on, nor even *the old man, is sitting* and so on. The structural elements of the clause are abstract functions established to enable us to give a precise account of what can be said or written at the rank of the clause. In English clause structure four primary elements are needed: subject, predicator, complement and adjunct. English grammarians normally distinguish between complement and object; this distinction is borrowed from Latin, but in English it belongs rather to a different stage of the analysis, as also in French. If we confine ourselves to these four elements, this means that all clauses in English are made up of combinations of them. Using the capital letters S P C A to symbolize them, we allow for SPC, SAPA, ASP and so forth, specifying that every item operating in every clause is an exponent of S, P, C or A.

Here two observations are called for. First, elements like subject are not best defined in conceptual terms such as these: 'the subject is the person or thing that performs a given action or is in a given state'; 'the object is the person or thing that undergoes the action'; 'the infinitive is the form of the verb that expresses the idea of the verb and nothing else'. Definitions of this kind are neither precise nor practical. In *my son likes potatoes* (SPC: || my son | like + s | potato + es ||) what is the state my son is in or the action he is performing? What action do the potatoes undergo? The conceptual or notional categories of traditional grammars are not incorrect but irrelevant at this point. It is because of its value in the structure of the clause that *my son* has the status of subject.

Second, it should be noted that sequence is sometimes a structural feature, sometimes not. Or, to put it in other terms, it sometimes happens in a language that to change the sequence of the constituents destroys (or changes) the structure; in other cases a change of sequence has no effect on the primary structure. In French, sequence generally has structural value. *Le bateau a quitté le quai* cannot be replaced (at least in modern French) by *a quitté le bateau le quai*, which would not be understood, nor by *le quai a quitté le bateau*, which is possible but differs as to which of the formal items of the original fill which places in the structure. The description should show whether or not the sequence is, wholly or partly, determined by the structure, indicating here that it is an essential feature of this structure that the elements occur in a fixed sequence. This condition is very rare in Latin and Russian, where sequence carries more delicate distinctions (still structural, but not determining primary categories like subject); frequent but by no means universal in English and French; normal, though still not without exception, in Chinese and Vietnamese. The French *il y a des fraises dans le jardin* can be changed into *dans le jardin il y a des fraises*; it is only the sequence of *il y a* and *des fraises* that is fixed, and this restriction has no contrastive function since the items are not interchangeable. I would not suggest that there is no difference between the two versions of the French clause: almost every linguistic variation is meaningful, so that where there is a formal distinction there is almost always contextual differentiation. But this distinction represents a more delicate structural difference: the primary grammatical relations between the elements of structure are the same.

We need now to consider the status of the forms which function in the structure of each unit. These are not unrelated items, considered as words or sequences of sounds, but rather sets of possible items that have the status of the unit below: in the structure of the clause, for example, the components are groups. It is clear that the choice of group, that is the possibility of choosing a given group, depends on the structure of the clause: in the clause *the old man is sitting in the garden*, the group *the old man* could be replaced by *the stationmaster* but not by *will go*. Similarly, the choice of word depends on the structure of the groups, and so on. Thus we can classify the items, and the important point here is that we do so according to their function in the structure of the unit above. This gives us *classes*: clause, group, word and morpheme classes. The third of the general categories of grammar is, then, the class. If we consider once

145

more the group in French, there seem to be three main classes: the verbal group (which operates as predicator), the nominal group (subject and complement) and the adverbial group (adjunct). These have their more delicate subdivisions: active verbal group, passive verbal group, and so on; here it should be stressed in passing that it is the verbal **group** that is active or passive and not the verb, which is a class of word.

The class then is a grouping of the members of a given unit that have the same potentiality of occurrence. Moreover each class is assignable to one unit: different units may have different classes. The class is that set of items which operate in the same way, playing the same role in the structure of the unit next above, There will, of course, be classes and sub-classes and sub-sub-classes, each more delicately differentiated as one takes into account more and more delicate distinctions of structure. For example, at the first degree of **delicacy** *the old man is sitting in the garden* and *the old man is served by the gardener* have the same structure SPA: subject, predicator, adjunct. Analysing more delicately, we distinguish the structures of the two clauses, so that *is sitting* and *is served* belong to different sub-classes of the verbal group, *in the garden* and *by the gardener* to different sub-classes of the adverbial group. We first display the likeness between them, and then the unlikeness.

Before passing to the fourth of the general categories, it may be helpful to consider the way classes are established. The class, it was suggested, is determined according to function in the structure of the unit above; that is, the unit immediately above. The relation is thus one of **downward** determination: it is the unit above that provides the basis for classes of the unit below. Upward analysis, giving groupings derived from below (that is, sets of items alike in their own structure), does not by itself produce classes – not, that is, unless the two groupings coincide.

There are of course many cases where the criteria of downward analysis and those of upward analysis do agree: so much the better. But when they do not, as is frequently the case, it is the criterion of downward analysis that is decisive. Consider the words *venait, venons, venant, venu*. In their own structure, they are parallel: the same bound lexical morpheme *ven* together with a grammatical morpheme which is related to it in structure, and which is also bound. These words form a paradigm in the same way as *vieux-vieille* or *cheval-chevaux*: they should, it might seem, belong to the same class. But *venait* and *venons* represent in themselves finite verbal groups: for example in *nous autres venons plus tard*. On the other hand, *venant* and *venu* can never be the only element of a finite verbal group: *venu* requires *suis, est* (*je suis venu*) whereas *venant* never functions in the predicator of an independent clause. *Venait, venons, venant, venu* are members of the same *paradigm*, "paradigm" being the name of the grouping determined by upward analysis; they will however (at some stage) be assigned to different classes.

There are two technical terms which in their traditional sense have insufficient generality, and which we can thus generalize to refer respectively to downward and upward analysis: namely "syntax" and "morphology". In the traditional meaning of these terms, at least in English, syntax is concerned with units larger than the word, morphology with units smaller. What is the origin of this distinction? It was recognized that the classical languages, Latin and Greek, tended to display one type of structural relation above the word, in the combination of words in higher units; and a structural relation of a different type below the word. The difference is between *free* forms and **bound** forms, which is a useful opposition in the classification of linguistic elements. A bound form is one that cannot be an exponent of the unit above (a morpheme that cannot stand alone as a word, and so on), whereas a free form is one that is able to operate at the rank of the unit above. In general, items below the word (morphemes) in Latin are all bound, while higher elements tend to be free. Hence the distinction between *morphology*, the formation of words out of bound forms, and *syntax*, the formation of clauses and sentences out of free forms.

A distinction on these lines is a feature of certain languages only, and there is no need to take it into account in describing other languages than these. To say of Chinese or English that distinction 'does not exist' there is not the point, which is rather that there is a misplacing of emphasis if the distinction is drawn in this way. The same considerations apply also to French. We can however use the terms "syntax" and "morphology" to refer to an important and in fact closely related, but more general, distinction that is of methodological value. It seems reasonable to use "syntax" to refer to downward analysis, from sentence down to morpheme, and "morphology" for upward analysis, from morpheme to sentence. Hence one could say: the class is determined by syntactical and not by morphological considerations; in a word, classes are syntactical.

Finally we come to the fourth and last of the general grammatical categories, which we have already mentioned in discussing the criteria for determining what grammar is: this is the *system*. Consider the verbal group *ont été choisis* in *les délégués ont été choisis*. In the selection of this as opposed to other possible verbal groups, various choices have been made. In voice, it is passive; it could have been active: *ont choisi*. In tense, it is past in present; it could have been simple present, simple future, past in future, present in past or past in present in past: *sont choisis, seront choisis, auront été choisis, étaient choisis* or *avaient été choisis*. In polarity, it is positive; it could have been negative: *n'ont (pas) été choisis*. All these choices are closed; there are no possibilities other than those listed. Wherever, at a particular place in structure (in this example, at P in the clause), we face a choice among a closed set of possibilities, we have a system: for example the system of *polarity*, whose terms are *positive* and *negative*.

If however we consider the set of items from which *choisir* was chosen, we find that it is uncircumscribable. It includes all the members of a large sub-class of the class of verb in the French language, a class that moreover is constantly having new items added to it. We can never say that *choisir* can be defined by excluding all the other possible items, as positive can be defined by excluding negative. *Choisir*, then, is not a term in any system: it is a member of an open grammatical class. Similarly in *celui du général, celui* represents a closed choice (*ceux, celle, celles*), *général* an open one; in *elle me regarde, me* represents a closed choice (*te le la se nous vous les*), *regarde* an open one.

The system, then, is the last of our postulated general categories of grammar. At every place in the structure of every unit, one or more choices are made. When the choice is closed, we have a system. When the choice is open, we are dealing with a lexical selection, not a grammatical one. All that can be said about the choice of *choisir* is that there must here be some word belonging to a sub-class of the class "verb"; the choice from among the members of this sub-class is a purely lexical matter. Where there is a system, the choice among the terms of the system is strictly grammatical, and the distinctions belong not to the dictionary but to the grammar. In such cases we can always define each term in the choice negatively as well as positively: in the finite verb "not first or second person" gives exactly the same information as "third person". There is no way, on the other hand, of describing a lexical item negatively.

There are, of course, borderline cases: we are not always certain whether we are dealing with a closed system or not. But this does not affect the principle: it is merely one more illustration of the complexity of language. An example of a borderline case is to be found in the personal pronouns of several languages, including French. The question, basically, is this: do they constitute a whole class in themselves or do they form part of a larger class, the class of substantives, for example, or of an intermediate sub-class? The French conjunct personal pronouns, together with *y* and *en*, form a distinct class: they enter into the structure of the verbal group and may be considered as "verbal pronouns"; this is a completely grammatical system. As for the disjunct pronouns, the nominal pronouns, it is difficult to decide whether they form a system or not. In fact, considered as a sub-class of the nominal group, they do make up a system; but this sub-class is fairly delicate and has certain features in common with the sub-class of personal names. From a syntactic point of view, there is some resemblance between *moi* and *Pierre*.

These four categories – unit, structure, class and system – provide the framework for the grammatical description. They are bound up with the general linguistic theory. One does not arrive at them inductively from an examination of the facts. They are established as primitive categories of the theory and retained because they enable us to give a fairly simple account of all the facts, as simple as we could expect considering that we are dealing with such complex material as language.

Let me not give the impression that such a view of the description of languages is revolutionary. There is no need to be revolutionary, to cast away all the work of our precursors. Linguistics, with mathematics and astronomy, is one of the oldest of sciences. It flourished in ancient China, in India, Greece and Rome. Twenty-five centuries ago, Indian grammarians were making extremely elegant descriptions of Sanskrit: rigorous, integrated and exact to a degree never surpassed before the twentieth century. It is this tradition, perhaps more than that of the last four centuries in Europe, that modern descriptive linguistics has inherited. Unfortunately for the modern language teacher many descriptions of languages written in recent years, and still current today, are not sufficiently rigorous, integrated or exact. In many cases they do not show the difference – nor, therefore, the connection – between formal and contextual relations; nor do they distinguish between particular description (looking at each language in its own light) and transfer description (looking at one language in the light of another).

How did these confusions, between form and context, and between one-language description and inter-language comparison, come about? The Greek and Latin grammarians studied and described their own languages; indeed for them other languages had no reason to be thought worthy of study. They took their languages as given. The Greeks naturally had no preconceived idea of an ideal language; they set about discovering the categories of Greek such as they really were, and then described them. Except perhaps for assumptions about language and logic – the belief that relations in language derived from those of some external logic – their theory and practice were exemplary. The Romans based their grammars on those of Greek; this could have been disastrous, but as it happens the structure of Latin is very like that of Greek: they were able to superimpose the categories of Greek on to the Latin ones, and by chance this worked fairly well. However, when the national languages of modern Europe came to be studied from the sixteenth century onwards, the grammars of Greek and Latin were used as models, and this time it **was** disastrous. It was assumed that all languages were like Latin; or, if they were not, they should be. As a result particular description tended to be replaced by comparative description of the type known as "transfer". Grammarians were saying, as it were, not so much 'this is what happens in French', but rather 'this is how we can make French what it should be: a reflection, albeit imperfect, of Latin'. Fortunately we no longer find extreme examples of this attitude, such as the imputation of a category of case to the noun in French or English. But the attitude is still reflected in many grammars, including those used for teaching English abroad. For example, one sees the subjunctive in English treated as though it was a general category of the verb used in contrast to the indicative, whereas in fact it is a largely non-contrastive variant, mainly limited to the verb *to be* and to certain specific structures.

How did language come to be looked upon in such a way, almost as a form of behaviour ruled by the canons of good manners – manners, moreover, measured by the standards of another language and another civilization? To understand this, we must come back to the first of the distinctions mentioned above, that between linguistic form and context. This can be illustrated by an example. The noun substantive in Latin has a declension, the cases being formally distinct: the difference between the nominative and the accusative can, in general, be heard (or seen). Thus, in order to identify the elements of structure of the Latin clause, the subject and object are defined as follows: the subject is the noun which is in the nominative case, the object is that which is in the accusative. (There are of course complications of detail, but these do not affect the reasoning.) Now the noun in English and French does not show case, and to arrive at a definition of subject and object other criteria must be found. But instead of asking what in fact happens in these language, what true linguistic difference there is between subject and object, grammarians abandoned the formal linguistic criteria and replaced them by conceptual criteria such as those quoted above. The subject, for example, became 'a noun or pronoun indicating what person or thing performs the action or is in the state expressed by the verb'. Definitions of this kind were, originally, attempts to explain the **contextual** meaning of what had been **identified** on **formal** criteria, and as such they were not unsuitable: at least there **were** facts to be explained. But the use of such concepts as criteria for defining linguistic categories is doomed to failure from the start. When one looks at or hears a Latin noun, one often knows whether it is nominative: the case is directly identifiable, by its *exponent* or manifestation in substance. It is impossible to tell by looking at a French or English substantive whether the noun is 'performing an action' or is 'in a state'.

The same thing happened with word classes, or what are termed "parts of speech". The Greeks knew what a noun was: it was something that could be inflected for case and number but not for gender. As a secondary statement, to explain its contextual meaning, they added that a noun was the name of a person or thing. How should one describe it in French? From a linguistic point of view, the noun substantive in French is the class of words having a certain value, filling a certain place, in the structure of the nominal group, which in turn has a certain value in the structure of the clause. But the noun substantive is clearly marked; admittedly it has no declension, but it has, at least in the written language, distinct forms for the singular and plural and it may be accompanied by the definite article. This is not a definition, for every class is defined syntactically; it is however a most useful formal indication, very much more useful than saying that 'nouns are the names of persons and things'. How can one expect a schoolchild to know that the word *soustraction* is the name of a person or thing whereas the word *celui* is not?

It is a principle of general linguistics that defining criteria should be formal and particular. "Formal" implies first stating the linguistic relations and the items acting as terms in these relations; one then tries to state the contextual meanings, which however are never given as principal criteria. "Particular" implies that categories are derived first from the language to be described: we can then go on to compare this with another language if this is useful to our purpose. Formal meaning is necessary to an understanding of contextual meaning, because the first is internal to language while the second concerns its external relations. One of the most insufficient of the very many definitions of language is the one according to which language is the expression of thought. This is significant for the psychologist, who is concerned with thought processes. But in linguistics, whether 'general' or 'applied', it is difficult to operate with a thought, which can be neither seen nor heard, nor systematically related to another thought. The linguist operates with language and text, the latter referring to all linguistic material, spoken or written, which we observe in order to study language. The linguist's object of study is the language and his object of observation is the text: he describes language, and relates it to the situations in which it is operating. Thoughts do not figure in the process, since we cannot describe them.

3 Lexis

Many of the same principles apply to lexicology as to grammar. The relation between lexis and grammar might be put as follows: if one analyses the grammatical units of a language, one will find that there is one unit, below the sentence, many of whose members enter into a different sort relation with each other in addition to their relations in grammar. It is this unit we call the *word*. The word is a grammatical unit like all the others, with its own classes and structures; but it is distinguished from the other grammatical units in that, after it has been treated exhaustively in the grammar, there always remains much to be said about it. A grammar can state that the word *train* is a noun. A more *delicate* grammar might add that it is a noun of sub-class, say, F.22. But even this will not distinguish it from *car, bus, bicycle* or *taxi*. Grammar has no way of distinguishing them, because they do not form a closed system. They are part of an open lexical set, and it is the task of lexicology to account for them.

Traditionally, lexicology is approached via lexicography: that is, the making of dictionaries. For the particular description of a language, a monolingual dictionary is normally prepared in which each article is composed of two main parts: definition and citation. In most dictionaries there are also of course additional pieces of information: word class (grammar), etymology (historical linguistics), pronunciation (phonetics or phonology, according to the dictionary); but these are as it were extraneous, not part of lexicology proper. The definition is the contextual description, the citation the formal description. In lexis as in grammar, the items have a contextual and a formal meaning: the definition aims at relating the lexical item, which is a linguistic item, to extra-linguistic phenomena. For this it is necessary to use other words: all sciences use words, but the special problem of linguistics is that it is, as has been said, language turned back on itself. However, just as in mathematics one can define the number five as 'four plus one' but not 'one times five' (the concept *five* may not be used in the definition of five), so the word x must not occur in the definition of the word x. This sometimes results in strange definitions, when a word of high frequency is defined by means of a string of words some of which are much rarer, rather as though one were to define *five* as 'one hundred and thirty-two minus one hundred and twenty-seven'. For example, the definition of *cut* in the *Shorter Oxford Dictionary* reads *to penetrate so as to sever the continuity of with an edged instrument; to make incision in; to gash, slash*. This is not much help to the student. Such definitions represent an important attempt to generalize about the function of the item in the language; the technique of definition has, however, clear limitations as a practical measure.

On the other hand, the citations are purely formal: they describe a word in relation to its linguistic environment. This relation between one word (or rather **lexical item**, since a lexical item is often more than one grammatical word, as for example *pomme de terre*) and another with which it is associated is called ***collocation***. The collocation of words is the basic formal relation in lexis. It is extremely important for the study of the language of poetry, since poets, and writers in general, draw their effects in part from the interaction of familiar with new collocations; and the creation of new collocations, interacting with other linguistic features, is a highly effective stylistic device. Collocation is outside grammar: it has no connection with the classes of the word. It is the lexical item, without reference to grammar, that enters into collocations. We can say *open the window*, or *an open window*, or *the opening of the window*; it is in each case the same collocation of the item *window* with the item *open*.

The relation of collocation enables us to group items into ***lexical sets***. The lexical set is formally defined as a grouping of words having approximately the same range of collocations. *Train, car, taxi* and so on frequently collocate with *take, drive, passenger, engine* and others. Contextually, the set is a grouping of words having the same contextual range, functioning in the same situation types. In a similar way the criterion of *disponibilité*, or "availability", has a formal and contextual aspect: "having a wide range of collocations" and "operating in a wide range of situations". In general formal and contextual criteria yield the same groupings; but the two are distinct from a methodological point of view, since they represent different ways of approaching the facts.

The dictionary provides of course an excellent framework for presenting the items of the lexis, especially when it gives citations. It is, however, not the only possible means. Note that in a dictionary the order of the lemmata, or articles, is, from a linguistic point of view, almost irrelevant to their meaning. Alphabetical order is an indexing device, by which each word has its place where it can be found without difficulty; but this place has no linguistic value and tells us nothing of the word's meaning. There is another method in which, this time, the order of words is meaningful: the place of each word is part of the description of the word. This is the ***thesaurus***, a number of which have been produced such as *Roget's Thesaurus* for English and the Duden volumes for French and certain other languages. For the foreign language student, the thesaurus can be very useful, and would be more so if it included citations.

153

The principle underlying the way words are grouped in a thesaurus is basically that of the lexical set. Brought together in one place are all the items that can be used under similar formal or contextual conditions. The lexical set is thus the closest analogy to the grammatical system. The latter is in effect a set of possible terms available for choice under the same grammatical conditions: this means that where any one term in the system may be chosen, so may all the others, and it is this fact that gives its meaning to the one that is in fact chosen. In grammar the choice is limited: the *a* of *il y a* may be replaced by *avait, aura, aurait* and a few compound forms, but that is all. In lexis the choice is not limited: there are words that are more or less probable, which gives a continuous scale of probabilities. For example, the names of fruits, such as *apple, orange, pear, peach*, form a lexical set. They frequently collocate with *dessert, eat, sweet, fruit* and so on. In a large number of utterances containing the word *orange*, the word *apple* could occur in its place: *I don't like oranges when they're too sweet*, for example. The probability of the word *apple* (that is, the probability of its being able to replace *orange* in a given utterance) is higher than that of the word *coffee*; but *coffee* is by no means impossible: instead of *orange-coloured* I could say *coffee-coloured*. *Orange* and *coffee* both collocate with the item *colour*. Words like *disagreeableness* or *carburettor* are extremely improbable in such environments, but not altogether impossible. Nothing is wholly impossible in lexis, and one could construct ad hoc contexts to substantiate this. The thesaurus would therefore list the words *orange, apple, pear* in the same set and give citations for them: examples of sentences in which all the words of the set could operate.

Here it might perhaps be appropriate to say a word about the categories of "idiom" and "cliché". These give a great deal of trouble to language teachers and even more to students. They should be considered, I feel, from the point of view of formal relations, especially those of lexis. It is often assumed that with the idiom one gives up all attempts at explanation, telling the pupil that it is 'an expression' and has to be learnt by heart as such. And it must be admitted that linguists too have often given up, saying in effect 'we don't know what an idiom is', or perhaps 'an idiom in the language being described is anything for which no equivalent is found in the mother tongue'. The teacher is doubtless right: it has to be learnt by heart. But at the same time he has the right to ask for a definition to enable him to recognize and classify phenomena of this kind. It may at least be possible here to observe and classify the facts. The question of naming the appropriate categories is secondary, although it is still important – it is said that linguists pay too little attention to matters of terminology. First, there are "fixed" collocations of lexical items, which are of high probability and without grammatical restrictions, for example *danger de mort* and *danger mortel*; there are several example of this type where one of the words thus collocated is never found except in association with the second, giving a unique collocation like the English *in the nick of time*. Is the word *zeste*, for example, ever used other than in the group *zeste de citron* or *gousse* other than in *gousse d'ail*? Fixed collocations of this kind, including unique collocations, could be called "clichés".

Second, there may be one or more lexical items that are always tied to a particular grammatical structure; for example, the French expressions *le cas écheant* or *en (avoir) plein le dos*, or the English *let the cat out of the bag*. You cannot say *le cas échoit, est échu* or *the cat is in the bag*. This category may be called "idioms".

Third, there are the so-called "compound words", which I would prefer to call "compound lexical items": items such as *pomme de terre* and *pèse-lettres* (letter balance), which collocate as single units. The list of probable collocations of *pomme de terre* is different from that of *pomme* or of *terre* and is certainly not the sum of the two.

Here it should be noted that orthographic criteria cannot, strictly speaking, be used to define or delimit grammatical or lexical units. Most European languages have their conventional rules of orthography: the use of the full stop, the space, capital letters and so forth. Some of these rules are generally considered as decisive for grammar. There exist, as is well known, hundreds of definitions of the word and the sentence; but for most people the sentence, if one thinks about it, or perhaps if one does not think about it, is 'what in orthography would have begun with a capital letter and ended with a full stop', while a word is 'what is found between two spaces or between a space and a hyphen'.

This custom has its practical usefulness, and rather than abandon it some would seek to reform the orthography. But it should not be forgotten that orthographic usage is often deceptive. French of course has not only been codified orthographically, but has also an academy to give rulings on spelling and other features; as a result it has a fairly coherent orthography, more obviously systematic than that of English. Yet French too is not without its contradictions. These contradictions are difficult to resolve precisely because they are due to the complexity of language; to return for a moment to our *pomme de terre*, given that *pomme, terre* and *pomme de terre* are three different lexical items, how can one achieve orthographic consistency? Perhaps one could standardize the use of the hyphen as in *pèse-lettres*. We should need it in English to distinguish between, for example, *run up* as two lexical items, in *he ran up the hill*, and *run + up* as a single lexical item, in *he ran-up a bill*.

The reason why it is important to be aware of the conventions of orthography is that different levels are involved, and these should not be confused. We have distinguished lexis from grammar: not that there is no relation between them – on the contrary they are very closely linked – but because they involve different items and relations and consequently require different methods and categories of description. The same applies to the two varieties of substance, phonic and graphic. In the nineteenth century the spoken language was rather neglected, and even considered unworthy of study, so that at the beginning of the twentieth century some linguists tended to reverse the situation, concentrating exclusively on the spoken language. Now, perhaps, attitudes have become more balanced: speech and writing are recognized to be equally important. From a historical and logical standpoint, speech is primary, writing being derived. But linguistic documents, the records of language in action, include both spoken and written texts; and as far as language teaching is concerned the student wants to learn how to read as well as to listen, to write as well as to speak. One should thus recognize the two kinds of substance and know wherein lies the difference, so that one can clarify the relation between substance and form.

I should now like to turn for a few moments to a consideration of this relation. I shall confine myself to phonic substance, since it is here that the special problems of phonology come into focus. The treatment of the problems raised by orthography, although they are by no means simple, has not demanded a parallel body of specialized theory.

4 Phonology

Other than in cases of lexical or structural ambiguity, a change of form involves a change of substance. If it is accepted for example that singular and plural are different terms in the grammatical system of a particular language, then it follows that there must somewhere be differentiated sounds to manifest or **expound** this system. (It may be noted in passing that **one** of the factors which suggest that the number system in modern French should be attributed to the nominal group, and not to the noun word, is that its exponence for the most part involves the article.) However, we do not relate the formal distinctions directly to the phonetic data. In describing for example the difference between the two forms *je chante* and *je chantais*, we do not say that it consists in the addition, after the voiceless unaspirated apico-dental plosive, of a half-open unrounded front oral vowel; we say rather than an /ε/ is added.

What is this element /ε/? Formally, in grammar, it is the fused exponent of the categories of numbers, person and tense (first, second and third person singular, and third person plural of the imperfect). As for its nature as phonic substance, it is perfectly true that it is a half-open unrounded front oral vowel. In grammar, and lexis, we account for the meaningful contrasts in the language. In phonetics we account for the nature and production of the sounds. What is needed finally is a discipline that can state which are the sounds used in the particular language as exponents of all such contrasts; one, that is, that can link substance to form. This discipline is phonology. Languages exploit their phonic resources in ways that are too complex to allow us to match phonetic statements directly to grammatical and lexical statements; the bridge is provided by phonology. This is why phonology is where linguistics and phonetics meet.

The variations in the sounds of language, though not infinite, can be infinitely subdivided or graduated. Acoustically, there is variation in fundamental frequency, harmonic frequency, amplitude and duration; to these correspond (in total, but not one to one) what are perceived as pitch, quality, loudness and length. It is not surprising that no two languages use these various resources in the same way. It often happens that a difference in sound which counts in one language (which realizes, or expounds, a formal distinction) does not count in another (does not expound any formal distinction); and it regularly happens that a phonetic distinction is used in one way in one language and in a quite different way in a second language. For example, in French, **vowel** nasality is generally distinctive: *presse* is distinct from *prince*. In English it is found only as a by-product and is nowhere distinctive: *man* is pronounced [mæn] or [mæ̃n] without any formal change. But, on the other hand, **consonant** nasality is distinctive in English as in French and, moreover, also in certain structural positions where it is not found in French: *pat* is distinct from *pant*. The two languages use the contrast between nasal and non-nasal articulation in different ways. Phonology is concerned with the phonetic resources as they are used in the given language. Here we can recognize a second series of units: phonological units. These, like grammatical units, carry patterns; but this time the patterns lie in the distinctive sounds. The units naturally differ from language to language just as the phonetic features vary; but there are general tendencies, since human beings are all very much alike from a physiological point of view.

For each language we recognize one which is the smallest of the phonological units: the minimal contrastive segment of speech sound. This is the well-known **phoneme**. Normally contrastive at this rank are the articulatory features which shape the consonants and vowels. What the English or French speaker as a rule recognizes as a 'sound', a vowel or consonant, is a phoneme; we may note in passing that this is not true of the Chinese, who in general are conscious of the syllable but not of the phoneme: the latter plays a different part in their language. Above the phoneme, it is said that every language has the unit **syllable**; but even in the role of this there is considerable variation. In Japanese as in Chinese, the syllable is usually felt to be the basic phonological unit; yet the Japanese syllable is totally different from that of Chinese, being indeed much more like that of French. The syllable often carries stress contrasts and thus enters into rhythmic patterns; yet there are languages, such as Vietnamese and Cantonese, where the syllable carries pitch. In English, above the syllable we have the foot and above this the tone group; the former carries the rhythm and the latter the intonation system. The impression is that in most languages the phonetic resources are organized into three or four phonological units.

Once the phonological patterns have been stated they are brought into relation with the formal levels: we need to show what formal contrasts are realized by what phonological distinctions. In English, where pitch is distinctive at the rank of the tone group, the intonation system expounds, at the level of form, a grammatical system, or rather a number of grammatical systems. In Cantonese, on the other hand, where the syllable is the unit that carries pitch contrasts, the intonation system is the exponent of distinctions at the lexical and not (with two exceptions) at the grammatical level. Cantonese syllables ending in a stop have three "tones" (three tonic possibilities), those not ending in a stop have eight; in each case the value of the terms in the tone system is like that of the features of articulation: variation produces different lexical items (e.g., ˉyat 'one', _yat 'day'; _yan 'to print', ˏyan 'man', ˌyan 'to lead'). The phonological system is closed, but the formal contrasts expounded by it belong to open sets.

In the same way, languages differ as regards the relation between their phonological and grammatical units, and in the extent to which there is regular correspondence between the two. In Cantonese the correspondence between the syllable (a phonological unit) and the morpheme (a grammatical unit) is almost absolute: one syllable, one morpheme. Such a regular correspondence is not met with in the Indo-European languages: the English tone group, for example, often coincides with a clause, but we also commonly find the tone group covering a whole compound sentence (two or three clauses) or, on the other hand, concentrated as it were on a (grammatical) group or even a single word.

Phonology, like grammar, deals with closed systems: no doubt the number of contrastive sounds that can be produced and identified at a particular moment in the chain of speech is very limited. A speaker may have at his disposal an infinite variety of consonantal sounds but he has only a small set of consonant phonemes. For example, in French a plosive is voiced or voiceless: we may have either *bas* or *pas*, and there is no third possibility for a bilabial plosive. If then an Englishman speaking French produces an English [b], which is different from either of the normal French plosives, a Frenchman has to identify it with one or other of the two possible phonemes. The number of possibilities may be further reduced by restrictions as to position. In Cantonese, for example, there are 19 consonant phonemes that may occur in syllable-initial position, but in syllable-final only six. We treat the positional distribution of phonemes in the syllable, or that of syllables in the unit next above, whatever it happens to be, by methods parallel to those of grammar: that is, by recognizing structures. The elements of structure of the syllable may be simply the places where consonant and vowel phonemes occur, say C and V. Every language has a certain number of possible structures at syllable rank: in Japanese, for example, the only permitted structures are V and CV, giving *a i u e o ka ki ku ke ko* and so on. In Cantonese we find CV, CVC or CVVC. Some languages, such as the Slavonic group, allow complex consonant clusters in syllable-initial position; even in English we find such forms as CCVCCCC *glimpsed*. In French, syllable structure is much more restricted.

For each of these structures there is a system of exponents for every element: an English syllable beginning with CCC can have only /s/ as its first element. As far as language teaching is concerned, one importance of phonological structure is that it conditions the phonetic realization of the elements entering into it. For example, in English syllables beginning with a single stop consonant, such as /p/ in *pan*, there is an opposition between voiced and voiceless: between *pan* and *ban*. On the other hand, where the syllable begins with CC, the first being the phoneme /s/ and the second a plosive, there is no longer any opposition between voiced and voiceless: one only is possible. We find a syllable written *span*, but with no contrasting form such as might be written *sban*. There is thus no need here for the /p/ to be distinguished from a /b/. Now in cases where /p/ and /b/ are distinguished, they differ from each other in

159

respect of two phonetic features, voicing and aspiration: the /p/ is voiceless and (lightly) aspirated, the /b/ voiced and unaspirated. After /s/ there is only one possibility, and it is phonetically identical with neither /p/ nor /b/. It is in a sense a sort of mixture of the two: voiceless but unaspirated. In orthography it is always represented by the letters standing for the voiceless consonant phonemes: p t k/c, never b d g; but this is an accident as far as the language as such is concerned. It is idle to ask the question: 'is the /p/ of *span* a /p/ or a /b/?', since different elements in the structure of the syllable are involved.

These phonological categories derive, of course, from a process of abstraction from the linguistic material, just as do the categories of grammar. Speech does not consist of a succession of discrete units: we do not finish pronouncing one syllable and then retire to regroup for an assault on the next one. A phonetic feature may persist across several phonemes: some, such as pitch contour, always do, while others may or may not. In the French word *néanmoins*, for example, nasality is usually present throughout. This is an isolated example; but if such a thing happens as a regular pattern in the language the feature is abstracted as a **prosodic** feature and assigned to a segment larger than the phoneme. Some modern linguists have developed very fully the concept of prosodic features; their work in this field is sometimes referred to as "prosodic phonology". It is important always to recognize that speech, and in fact language itself, since a spoken language is a set of actual and potential speech events, is a form of activity. One breaks it down in order the better to understand it and to talk about it; but the reality remains in the whole, not in the segments such as the phoneme or the morpheme.

I have cast here only a rapid glance at the theories and methods of the formal description of a language. It is not, of course, possible in so short a space to explore all the corners of the linguistic landscape. I have not been able to touch on statistical linguistics, a subject likely to be of importance to the language teacher if it treats not only of statistics but also of linguistics. I have left aside the level of context; not only for the sake of brevity but also because it is less systematized and more controversial. Much of the theoretical work in the next ten years may well be devoted to the search for generalized semantic categories and to the systematic description of the relation between linguistic and situational features. Up until recently work in semantics has tended to remain somewhat unintegrated with descriptive linguistics as a whole; the integration of the two, and the development of "contextual" semantics, is of importance not only for linguistic theory but especially, perhaps, for its pedagogical applications. Meanwhile it is useful to remember that as

160

soon as one gives informative labels to a grammatical system and its terms; for example, "system of number; terms: singular and plural", one is already making observations, however approximate, about contextual meaning.

5 The comparison of languages

In touching on the formal levels of descriptive linguistics and also a little on the level of phonology, which links form and substance, I have tried to show that just as the sounds of a language may be described, with the help of phonetic methods, in such a way as to be of benefit to the student, so a description of the form of language, if based on general linguistic theory, can provide language teachers with a useful and efficient tool. Needless to say, it is not phonetics and linguistics as such that are relevant to the language student, but the results of phonetic and linguistic analysis. I have devoted the major part of this chapter to this topic because the description of the language concerned is in my opinion the main task for which general linguistics can be applied to language teaching.

But there remains another aspect to be considered: the comparison of languages, and, in particular, the comparison of the foreign language with the mother tongue. There are different points of view on this question. Some teachers are convinced that one should pay no attention to the learner's mother tongue; that one should keep one's gaze firmly on the foreign language throughout. There are of course cases where no use can be made of the mother tongue; for example, if one has a class of 20 students with 20 different native languages; such instances are clearly outside the discussion. This point of view is no doubt partly a reaction against some former methods that were not perhaps very useful: the translation of isolated uncontextualized sentences, the learning of word-lists with translation equivalents, and so on. And if the native language itself is not well described, it is difficult to use it effectively. However, given the right conditions one can make positive use of the student's mother tongue; and in such cases to neglect it may be to throw away one of the tools best adapted to the task in hand.

The question is one of priorities. Sooner or later the time comes when one wants to explain to the English student the tenses of the French verbal group. By making a comparison with the English tense system, bringing out both the similarities and the differences, we can take advantage of the adult student's ability to make generalizations and abstractions, which is one of his greatest assets.

It is impossible to specify at what stage the native language comes in; the answer depends on the pedagogical principles adopted. On the one hand, one might attempt to make an overall comparison of the grammatical structure of the foreign and native languages; on the other hand, one might take account only of cases of equivalence, cases where there is a high probability that an item in the native language will always be translated by one and the same item in the foreign language. In any case, whatever the stage of teaching at which it is proposed to use the mother tongue, valid methods of comparison will be needed, and these methods too depend on general linguistic theory.

What is the nature of the equivalence between two languages? We take it for granted that there can be such an equivalence; that in some sense at least, and despite the Italian proverb "traduttore – traditore", an utterance in language₁ may be *translated* into language₂. If we take two texts in different languages, one being a translation of the other, at what rank (among the grammatical units) would we be prepared to recognize "equivalence"? In general, this would be at the rank of the sentence, this being the contextual unit of language; it is the sentence that operates in situations. In other words, as could be expected from what is said about the way language works, it is generally the case that (1) a single sentence in language₁ may be represented by a single sentence in language₂: if we have an English text consisting of 47 sentences, the French translation could also consist of 47 sentences, divided at the same points; and (2) a particular sentence in language₁ can always be represented by one and the same sentence in language₂.

But this equivalence of units and of items is lost as soon as we go below the sentence; and the further down the rank scale we go, the less is left of the equivalence. Once we reach the smallest unit, the morpheme, most vestige of equivalence disappears. The morpheme is untranslatable; the word a little less so, but it is nevertheless very rarely that we can say that a particular word in language₁ may always be translated by one and the same word in language ₂ – this being condition (2) above; even condition (1) is not always fulfilled for the word, since one word in language₁ is often the equivalent of part of word, or of several words, in language₂. The nearer we come to the sentence, the greater becomes the probability of equivalence; yet it remains true to say that the basic unit of translation is the sentence.

As an illustration, here is an example of a sentence in French translated *rank by rank* into English. First, each of the French morphemes is translated into English, by what as far as one can say would be the most probable equivalent (if one can be found) for that item irrespective of its environment. The translation is incomprehensible and meaningless. Next the same process is repeated at word rank: this shows more meaning but is still not English. Then in turn at group, clause and sentence rank. What is for some reason called "literal translation" is translation at, roughly, the rank of the group.[1]

				la	jeune	fille		avait + +		raison		je	vais	+	lui	demand	+er	pardon	
M	X	young	daughter	have	X	X	reason	X	go	X	X	ask for	X	pardon
W	the	young	daughter	had			reason	I	am going	him	to ask for			pardon
G	the girl			had			reason	I am going to ask him for						pardon
C	the girl was right							I am going to apologize to him						
S	The girl was right; I am going to apologize to her.													

        X= grammatical morpheme
        += fused morpheme (e.g. *avait* consists of three fused morphemes)
        M= morpheme equivalents
        W= word equivalents
        G= group equivalents
        C= clause equivalents
        S= sentence equivalent

It may be useful here briefly to comment on the process of translation from a theoretical point of view: the theory of translation is an important, if somewhat neglected, aspect of general linguistics. Translation can, I think, be divided into three stages. This does not mean, of course, that the human translator carries out these three operations in a fixed order, or even that he separates them from each other. Note, however, that in machine translation they might have to be separated: the basic problem of machine translation could be said to be to devise categories drawn from certain aspects of general linguistic theory (description, comparison and translation) whose exponents are such that a machine can be programmed to recognize them. The three stages of the translation process are distinct, rather, from a logical point of view.

In the first stage, for every item at each of the units (every morpheme, every word and so on) there is one equivalent in language₂ that is the most probable: the equivalent which, were one able to amass a large enough sample, would be the most frequent. For example, the French verbal group *ont été choisis* probably has as its most frequent English equivalent *were chosen*. But under certain given conditions other equivalents will be found, such as *have been chosen*; and similarly in the move from English to French there will be a number of equivalents, one being the most probable. The human translator has, as it were, a scale of probabilities recorded in his brain. In the second stage, the choice of equivalent is reconsidered in the light of the linguistic environment: we examine the units above, going as far up the scale as the complete sentence. For example, in the clause *les délégués ont été choisis hier soir,* we would keep in English the most probable equivalent *were chosen,* whereas in the clause *les délégués ont été déjà choisis,* it must be replaced by *have been chosen.* To take another example: the most frequent French equivalent of the English word *head* is *tête,* but if the nominal group in English was *head of the department* we should have to translate by *chef de section.* Here again it is the unit immediately above that provides the necessary information. In the third stage we take account of the internal grammatical and lexical features of language$_2$: of grammatical concord (of gender, number, etc.), verbal tense sequence, fixed collocations, idioms and the like. It is interesting to note that in this stage language$_1$ no longer provides any information; it is only the features of the language into which we are translating that count.

A translation is, then, the final product of these three stages in the process. We may add in passing that the second stage, where we take account of the linguistic environment, extends in fact to a consideration of the situation. It is the stage where we examine the entire environment, formal and contextual. If we are translating a written text, the environment is purely formal: the linguistic entities surrounding the given item. A spoken text, on the other hand, is already contextualized: that is, it is operating in a situation, and this is part of the environment we consider with a view to determining the choice of equivalent. But as soon as the spoken text is recorded on tape, there is no longer a situation; it becomes decontextualized, just like a written text. Hence the usefulness of filmstrips in language teaching; they enable us to recontextualize the spoken text.

This brief outline of the nature of translation is not unrelated to the problem of the comparison of languages. The type of comparison with which we are concerned is, of course, descriptive and in no way historical. This means that no historical relationship is implied between the languages under comparison. Any language at all may be compared with any other. If one is teaching French to a Vietnamese one can compare, from a purely descriptive standpoint, Vietnamese and French. The aim of such comparison is to bring out their similarities and their differences. We cannot give any reason for similarities and differences between languages. One of the great problems of linguistic typology is to know why it so often happens that languages belonging to the same region, and spoken by communities showing similar patterns of culture, have resemblances in their structures, without there being any lexical correspondences or other evidence of historical relationship.

When we undertake a comparative description of two languages, we have as it were two kinds of evidence at our disposal. The first is translation equivalence; the second is formal comparison. The translation equivalents are linked to the category of grammatical unit, and they enable us to say that each particular item or category in language$_2$ is the normal (that is, most probable) equivalent of an item or category in language$_1$; this means, or at least suggests, that the two items or categories are comparable. The **possibility** of translation equivalence is, of course, a prerequisite of comparison: if two items can never translate each other, it is of no interest to compare them. Translation can thus be considered as a contextual comparison: if we say that an item $a(_1)$ in language$_1$ can be translated by an item $a(_2)$ in language$_2$, this means that the two items would have the same role in the situation. But we need to complete this observation by a formal comparison: we must know not only that the two items are the equivalent of each other in their contextual meaning, but also whether or not they operate in the same way in the formal structure of the two languages: whether or not they have the same formal meaning (which is also, as I have throughout tried to emphasize, part of the total linguistic meaning).

We must, then, compare the position of the items within the framework of the categories of the grammar: units, structures, classes and systems. One might ask here whether the two languages have a comparable set of units. If not, if for example language$_1$ does not distinguish between word and morpheme while language$_2$ does, the student's problem will be greatest at word rank, for the words of his own language will have two sorts of equivalents. Suppose, on the other hand, the two languages have the same set of units, as French and English have: then is **one** French clause translated by **one** English clause, and so on? *le médecin est venu, the doctor has come*; in both languages we have here one clause, which consists moreover of two groups || *le médecin* | *est venu* ||, || *the doctor* | *has come* ||; they are identical as far as the category of unit is concerned. Consider now *le médecin de campagne*, in English *the country doctor*. They are both nominal groups. But in English the group is made up merely of words, whereas in French there is a rankshifted adverbial group *de campagne* functioning as qualifier in the structure of the nominal group. The important thing from the student's point of view is that English also has nominal groups with the structure: head (noun) plus qualifier (rankshifted adverbial group), for example *the doctor at the* *hospital*, but that this structure is not used in *the country doctor* and similar cases.

This non-equivalence in the structure of the nominal group in the two languages is quite normal; and therefore it should be handled systematically. Similarly the nominal and verbal groups in *le médecin est venu* and *the doctor has come* have the same structure, yet *ce matin* added to the French clause would produce a change of structure in the English verbal group: *has come* would have to be replaced by *came*. Now the two **clauses** have the same structure SPA: it is important to note that the clause structure remains the same in the two languages; but the two verbal **groups** are different: we have a simple group in English, a compound one in French. None of this is at all new; it merely serves to show that descriptive theory provides a way of establishing precisely what is identical and what is different in the utterances to be compared.

The same applies to lexis. The conventional method of comparing the lexis of two languages is the bilingual dictionary: equivalence is shown by translation, that is by contextual comparison. To say that the French word *venir* is translated in English by *come* means that in a context where a Frenchman uses *venir* an Englishman would have used *come*. In a bilingual dictionary the translation replaces the definition of the monolingual dictionary. But note that we have here translation **at word rank** which, as we have already seen, is very far from translation proper; this is why a comprehensive dictionary may offer us up to 50 equivalents for a single word. It goes without saying that the part played by the citation is here even more essential, if this is possible, than in a monolingual dictionary: not only is the range of contextual meaning of words radically different from one language to another, but so too is their collocational spread. Take for example the translation of a French word in a French–English dictionary, the word *relever*: one well-known dictionary offers us the following list: *raise again; set up again; restore; raise; take up; pick up; lift up; draw up; turn up; curl up; twirl up; heighten; enhance; relieve; set off; adorn; give a relish to; extol; exalt; revive; notice; point out; criticize; reply to; take up; free; release; absolve; collect (letters); clear (letterboxes); remove (a dish); recover; depend, be dependent (on); (law) be amenable (to); step high;* and some others. If one then translated English clauses containing these words into French one would find oneself saying for example: *je vais (me) relever (=m'installer, me pelotonner: curl up) dans un coin avec mon livre, ca a relevé (=occupé: took up) tout l'après-midi, on est en train de relever (=re-construire: restore) le château, je relevais le service (=me plaignais du service: was criticizing the service) de ce restaurant.* All these examples represent normal usage of the English words; they are not idioms. It is clear that, for showing the meaning, formal or contextual, of the French word, translations without citations are of limited use.

Another problem in lexical comparison arises from the fact that the relations between words forming a lexical set are very varied. Let us return to what I called the vehicular set:

FRENCH	ENGLISH	CHINESE
train	train	huoche
auto	car	qiche
autobus	bus	gonggongqiche
taxi	taxi	sirenqiche
bicyclette	bicycle	zixingche
"tram"	tram	dianche

In Chinese, however, there is another term *che*, corresponding in some degree to the French word *voiture* but without any equivalent in English. The word *che* is the neutral term in the set, and is used in situations where the object in question is obvious or unimportant. If the bus stops in front of you, you would not say *kuai shang gonggongqiche ba*! 'hurry up and get on the bus'), which would be too specific, but *kuai shang che ba*! In English there is no choice: in this set we have only specific words, no general or "neutral" term. In French there is the word *voiture* which is partly general, but partly specific: one says *voici l'autobus qui arrive* rather than *voici la voiture qui arrive*. The important point to note in this respect is that this is a systematic feature of one section of the lexis of Chinese: many sets of items are related in this way, most of them being grammatically nouns. With verbs, in fact, the comparative situation tends to be exactly the reverse. English has a word *cut*, French the corresponding *couper*; Chinese has as equivalents some 15 terms – to cut with a knife, with scissors, with an axe, with a scythe and so on – but no non-specific word *cut*. To oversimplify, in English, generally speaking, sets of items that are verbs tend more often to have a non-specific member than do those made up of nouns, whereas in Chinese it is the other way round. French seems to have more non-specific nouns than English: thus lexically Chinese seems to resemble French more than it does English or the other Indo-European languages, although in its grammar it seems closer to English.

As a last example of comparison, I should like to consider the personal pronouns of French, English, Chinese and Italian:

CONTEXTUAL COMPARISON

I Principal system: reference to participant(s) in situation

	FRENCH	ENGLISH	CHINESE	ITALIAN
I	moi	I	wo	io
2	toi/vous	you	ni/nin	tu/Lei
22	vous	,,	nimen	voi/Loro
3	lui/elle	he/she	ta	lui/lei
I2(2)	nous	we	zamen	noi
I(2(2))3(3)	,,	,,	women	,,
33	eux/elles	they	tamen	loro

I = speaker
2 = addressee
3 = other participant
22 = two or more addressees
33 = two or more other participants
( ) optional

II Sub-systems:

A *sex of participant(s)*

	FRENCH		ENGLISH		ITALIAN
	3	33	3		3
M	lui	eux	he		lui
F	elle	elles	she		lei

M = male, including mixed company if more than one
F = female

B *social relationship of participant(s) to speaker*

	FRENCH		CHINESE	ITALIAN	
	2		2	2	22
I	toi		ni	tu	voi
E	vous		nin	Lei	Loro

I = interior to social group
E = exterior to social group

FORMAL COMPARISON

Number of different systems:

	FRENCH	ENGLISH	CHINESE	ITALIAN
verbal	3			3
nominal	1	2	1	2
total	4	2	1	5

A Verbal systems: personal pronoun as (bound) word in structure of verbal group (exemplified by forms for 1 and 3M)

	FRENCH			ITALIAN	
	1	3M		1	3M
(a)	je	il			
(b)	me	le		mi	lo
(c) } (cd)	} (me	lui {		mi	gli
(d)				me	glie-

(a) = verbal subject
(b) = verbal direct complement
(c) = verbal indirect complement (independent)
(d) = verbal indirect complement (dependent)

In French there is only one system (cd), but this incorporates a sub-system (cd★) operating in the structure in which the personal pronoun follows the verb. Examples:

il le lui présentera   je te le donne   donne-le-moi
a b cd   a cd b   b cd★
lo conosco   gli parlo   glielo presento   dammelo
b   c   d b   d b

B Nominal systems: personal pronoun as nominal group, operating as subject or complement in clause or as complement in adverbial group (exemplified by forms for $_1$ and $_3$M)

	FRENCH		ENGLISH		CHINESE		ITALIAN	
	1	3M	1	3M	1	3M	1	3M
(x) (y) } (xy)	} moi	lui {	I me	he him	} wo	ta {	io me	lui lui

(x) = clause subject
(y) = clause complement or adverbial group complement

French and Chinese have only one system (xy); in French, pronouns of this system operating as clause subject or clause complement under most conditions require a verbal pronoun in concord. Examples:

moi je sais bien	je le connais, lui	c'est moi	c'est à lui
xy a	b	xy	xy
	xy		

In Italian, pronouns of system (y) operating as clause complement may be accompanied by a verbal pronoun in concord. Examples:

io non so	non so, io	l'ho visto, lui	e lui	e per me
x	x	b y	x	y

For the sake of simplicity the reflexive pronouns of Italian and French have been omitted, as also the Italian forms *egli, ella*, etc. (which are rare in the spoken language). The non-personal pronouns of French, English and Italian have likewise been left out of consideration, as these require partially separate treatment.

The distinction in Italian between *lei* and *Lei, loro* and *Loro* is purely orthographic. The now somewhat rare use of *Voi* as 2E ("polite second person singular") has been ignored.

In the comparison of languages we may take advantage of the fact that, as mentioned above, there are always several different ways of describing the same linguistic phenomenon; it is thus possible to adapt the description of one language to that of another. The aim of this *transfer comparison* is to draw attention to the resemblances between the two languages. For example, Chinese has no word class corresponding to the preposition in French and English; to translate into Chinese adverbial groups of structure "preposition – complement" such as *into the garden, on the table* (*dao huayuan li, zai zhuoz shang*) we must use one or both of two sub-classes, of the verb and the noun respectively. But the contextual equivalence to English prepositions is so exact that in teaching Chinese to English students one can combine them both into a single distinct class, subdivided of course, and call it the class of prepositions, thus emphasizing the regularity of the equivalence we find in translating from English into Chinese. Transfer comparison is an example of the description of a language made with a specific aim in view, namely foreign-language teaching.

6 Conclusion

Most of the first part of this chapter was devoted to discussing the description of language at the formal levels. In the last section, speaking of the comparison of languages, I have devoted more time to contextual considerations, since comparison presupposes contextual equivalence, which can be established by translation. At the same time effective comparison depends on description, so that linguistic form cannot be neglected here either. Whether we are concerned with linguistic theory or with its application to language teaching, the foundations of the linguistic study of language will involve grammatical and lexical theory.

It is important here to avoid the impression that the "formal" study of language is something mechanical or lifeless. It is perhaps unfortunate that the word "formal" should have been chosen, for it may carry a connotation of devitalization, as though one were dealing only with the skeleton of language. Nothing could be more untrue. The grammatical and lexical study of English poetry, for example, in the light of general linguistic theory, can, it seems to me, be successful in throwing some light on the problem of how poetry, or rather a particular poem, achieves its effects so that it is recognized as a work of art. The analysis of linguistic form is an integral part of stylistics which, far from impairing the aesthetic appreciation of literature, can contribute positively towards it. This is not to imply that we can replace literary criticism by linguistic description. On the contrary, the critic himself, starting from the linguistic analysis of a work, finds his own field of action enlarged, since he has more material on which to base his judgments and the comparisons he makes between literary works.

We must admit, however, that general linguistics has sometimes given the impression of dehydrating language; the fault perhaps lies with our own interpretation of those who sought, understandably, to free themselves from the tyranny of mentalism and of ideas, from the demand that "the ideas behind" language, rather than language itself, should be described, and thus attempted to exclude considerations of meaning. They said in effect: 'Our predecessors failed to solve the problems involved in describing a language because they based their categories on conceptual criteria; if we are to avoid making the same mistakes, we must exclude concepts, exclude all consideration of the "meaning" of language, all reference to non-linguistic facts; our analysis will be rigorously formal.' But, as I have tried to show, the formal analysis of language is itself a study of meaning. It is impossible to describe language without taking into account the meaning. We entirely agree with those linguists in demanding formal – that is, linguistic – criteria for linguistic categories; but what we cannot accept is this dichotomy between form and meaning, for it is a false opposition. It can I think fairly be claimed that linguists such as J. R. Firth and others have avoided both these extremes; they have rejected the principle that as soon as one begins to speak of linguistic form, one is no longer concerned with meaning. This is why, although making a structural (or rather structural-systemic) analysis of language, Firth never admitted the designation "structuralist".

But if we speak of the views of particular linguists, we should add a word of explanation in case of misunderstanding. I would certainly not want to give the impression that linguistic theory has a fragmented character. There are, of course, as in all sciences, especially when they are expanding, different approaches. In the recent history of linguistics, the Prague linguists, the Saussurian group at Geneva, Hjelmslev and the Copenhagen circle, those who followed Bloomfield and Sapir, in America, Daniel Jones, Firth and their colleagues in London, and many others have all contributed to the development of ideas. There are still, certainly, differences of approach; but the point has already been reached where what is held in common by linguists everywhere is much more fundamental than what they disagree about. In those parts of the theory where there are important divergences of opinion I have represented here my own views keeping in mind the question of relevance to language teaching. I have attempted to avoid both the so-called "mechanism" of some structural linguistics, with its emphasis on "procedures of description" rather than on a comprehensive theory of language, and on the other hand the more rarefied atmosphere of the Copenhagen circle, whose methods are somewhat difficult to apply to the practical description of a given language. At the same time it is their work no less than that of other linguists that has contributed to an overall theory of language that is both valid from the point of view of contemporary scientific thought and at the same time capable of being applied, not only in the description of any particular language but also in the use of a description for important practical or educational needs such as modern language teaching. A description of a language, if it is to be of practical use, must be based on a general theory; a theory of language, if it is to remain in touch with reality, must be tested in the description of languages. There is no cleavage between the pure and the applied in linguistics; on the contrary, each flourishes only where the other is also flourishing.

Note

1. The description of French grammar that forms the basis of this illustration, as well as of other examples cited in this chapter, is the work of R. D. Huddleston.

    This chapter was first presented in French at the Centre International de Linguistique Appliquée, University of Besançon, and published in *Etudes de linguistique appliquée*, Vol. 1. The English version appeared in Angus McIntosh and M. A. K. Halliday, *Patterns of Language*, published by Longman in 1966.

Chapter Eight

IS LEARNING A SECOND LANGUAGE LIKE LEARNING A FIRST LANGUAGE ALL OVER AGAIN? (1978)

It is a pleasure and a privilege for me to be asked to be a keynote speaker at this first Congress of the Applied Linguistics Association of Australia. I consider the creation of this Association to be an event of major importance, and I am delighted to be in at the start. But privileges, of course, entail responsibilities; and I recognize that being a keynote speaker carries certain special kinds of responsibility of its own.

In planning this address I was reminded of an occasion some years ago when I sent to the BBC a script for a talk which I was proposing to give on the Third Programme. My script was rejected, and with it came a little note from the producer which said that the responsibility of the Third Programme was to stimulate, not to inform.

Clearly I had committed the major sin of trying to tell people things. With this lesson in mind I ought perhaps to assume that the responsibility of a keynote speaker is likewise to stimulate and not to inform. In which case, it may be rather rash to offer a title which asks a question, since questions demand to be answered. However, the question it asks is one which seems to me is bound to be raised in a great many of the deliberations that take place in meetings of a group such as this: namely the perennial question of the similarities and dissimilarities between first- and second-language learning.

In one sense, of course, the question is very simple to answer. If it is put like that, "Is learning a second language like learning a first language all over again?" the answer is obviously 'no' – if only in the sense that everybody learns a first language, while by no means everybody learns a second language, and those who do have learnt a first one first. However, we should not be asking the question if there was not a great deal more to it than that. The issue is a real one, as can be gathered from a

174

reading of the papers on language learning psychology presented at the Second International Congress of Applied Linguistics in Cambridge in 1969, brought together in the volume edited by Pimsleur and Quinn. Over the past few years, many writers in the applied linguistics field have stressed the similarities between first- and second-language learning rather than the differences. Pit Corder, for example, envisages the adult language learner having a built-in strategy or 'syllabus' for language learning, which he is inclined to regard as being essentially the same as that of a child.

The notion that the two are essentially alike is by no means new. David Reibel, in a paper on adult language learning, refers to this point having been made already by Henry Sweet in 1899, in his book *The Practical Study of Languages*, and by Otto Jespersen in 1904, both these linguists stressing the similarities between second-language learning and first-language learning; and again in 1922 by Harold Palmer, advocating the aural/oral method of teaching languages, and relating this to the learning of the mother tongue. Traditional language teaching **practice**, of course, as enshrined in the "grammar–translation method", ran directly counter to this view; this was one of the reasons why many linguists objected to the practice and tried to change it. Theoretical justification for treating the two as different came mainly from the direction of psychology, although some linguists have attempted to capture the difference by referring it to a particular model of language, an example being McNeill's suggestion, made in 1965, that while the child learning a first language tends to proceed from deep structure to surface structure, the adult language learner tends to proceed from surface structure to deep structure.

In work published during the past ten years various findings have been put forward as evidence of similarity between first- and second-language learning. One type of evidence that is widely cited is that which is drawn from the study of language errors. In the earlier discussions it was usually assumed that, if there was any general principle underlying both mother-tongue errors and foreign-language errors, this was simply the use of analogy, and nothing more specific than that. More recently, however, it has been maintained that many second-language errors are actually the same as the errors made by mother-tongue learners. This is in part a reaction against the view that lay behind the main efforts in language teaching of the 1950s and 1960s, which is implicit in the approach through contrastive analysis, that foreign-language errors were to be explained, and could in principle be predicted, by reference to interference from the mother tongue. In the collected papers by Gerhard Nickel from the Third International Congress of Applied Linguistics, held in Copenhagen in 1972, the discussion of contrastive analysis centres largely around this point; one could gather the impression that the unique function of contrastive analysis is to predict the errors that foreign-language students are going to make. I am not sure that it does this very well, although I do think there are other good reasons for undertaking it.

I doubt whether anyone ever thought that **all** second-language errors were the result of mother-tongue interference. Most people would probably accept the sort of perspective given by Ravem, in a paper cited as evidence by Susan Ervin-Tripp. Ravem observed his 6-year-old Norwegian-speaking son learn English in Scotland, and found that in using the English verb the little boy regularly made mistakes in negatives and in interrogatives. The errors that he made in the interrogative were typical interference errors; his interrogatives were like those of Norwegian and not like those of English mother-tongue learners – for instance, he said *Like you ice cream?* and *Drive you car yesterday?* His negatives, on the other hand, were like those of some English mother-tongue learners, and quite unlike anything found in Norwegian outside certain special contexts; for example – *I not like that. I not sitting on my chair.*

Here within the same grammatical system there were two very clearly differentiated types of error, one that could be explained as interference from the mother tongue, the other that could not. An example of a general statement of the position is the observation made by Lance, in his study of Spanish-speakers learning English, that "From one third to two thirds of the deviant features of the foreign students' speech could not be traced to identifiable features of Spanish". Here again the role of interference is played down.

Susan Ervin-Tripp, who quotes Lance, tends to emphasize the similarities, and it is interesting that in her own work she started off as a specialist in first-language learning, studying her own and other children in some depth; the family then happened to go to live in Geneva for a while, and she began to study the way in which her own children were learning French. It soon struck her how similar some of the learning processes seemed to be. She reports her finding that "In this respect first language and second language learning must be quite alike"; and if we look to see what this refers to, we read that "The learner actively reorganizes, makes generalizations and simplifies." Her context for saying this is the assertion that learning is an active process. The child "actively reorganizes" the language he is exposed to. In other words she is not

176

really claiming much more than in both first- and second-language learning that there is what she calls "selective processing" by the learner: "One way of looking at second language learning is to assume that the first encounters with a second language will be handled by the apparatus of structure and process already available." By "already available" she means apparatus that has already been brought to bear in the process of learning the first language.

The most clear-cut cases of similarity would be those of the current learning of two languages by bilingual children, true "coordinate bilingualism", in the terms of Ervin–Tripp and Osgood, where a child is learning both languages from the start. Even when the second language is learnt some time later than the first, it may still be the case that, in Susan Ervin-Tripp's words, "some prior processes and structures will be employed", but we may expect to find rather greater differences. But if we are looking for the more dramatic differences in learning conditions, these will be determined not so much by whether the language being learnt is first or second, as by whether the learning is natural or induced. Is it natural language learning or is it classroom language learning? Once the second-language learning becomes induced as opposed to natural – once it becomes applied linguistics – then the similarities with first-language learning may tend to evaporate.

We have to remind ourselves, of course, that first-language learning is also partly induced. I am not talking about what may happen in a home, with anxious parents, but about what happens when the child comes into the educational process, and particularly when he starts to become literate. Presumably we shall find that there are similarities between induced second-language learning and those aspects of first-language learning which are also in some sense institutionalized, in particular learning to read and write. Kenneth Goodman, discussing misconceptions that are current in the teaching of literacy, refers to the misconception that meaning may be derived only from spoken language and therefore that reading involves recoding graphic input as phonic input before it is decoded. This, he says, may be done by some learners in the early stages of learning to read and write, but that is all. He goes on: "An analogy can be found in the early stages of learning a second language. The learner may be going through a process of continuous translation into his first language before he decodes, but eventually he must be able to derive meaning directly from the second language with no recourse to the first." In learning to read and write, the goal is to derive meaning directly from the written text without translating it into the spoken medium; and since spoken and written language differ very sharply in

177

their functions and their relation to the context, reading and listening will employ variant psycholinguistic strategies to cope with the variant characteristics of the two forms. When we come to first language and second language, we will not find them differing in their relation to the context in the sense that reading and writing do; but we will find them differing in their functions, particularly in cases of so-called coordinate bilingualism.

Bringing up the question of learning to read and write reminds us of the comment by the primary-school teacher who remarked "It's lucky we're not responsible for teaching them to **talk**. If we were they'd never learn that either." Nevertheless, a surprising number of people do become literate, mostly through being taught; and in the same way, perhaps, a surprising number of people do succeed in learning second languages. Some people would say that, given that we are in some form of classroom situation, this success is achieved to the extent to which we can minimize the difference between the two conditions, to the extent to which we can make the process of induced language learning resemble that of natural language learning.

If we look through the applied linguistics literature we find models of second-language learning which clearly do not make this assumption. A well-known example is Carroll's learning model of 1963, in which mastery of a task is seen as a function of five factors, two of them being instructional factors: (i) presentation of material, text, teaching, and so on and (ii) time allowed for learning; the other three being student factors, (iii) general intelligence, glossed as ability to follow instructions, (iv) motivation, or degree of perseverance, and (v) aptitude, the time needed for learning. This calls to mind a comment made some years later by Peter Strevens, that after all his experience in applied linguistics and language teaching he was inclined to the conclusion that the only significant variable in the whole process was the time of exposure, the time the student actually spent on the task. Another model of this kind is Larry Selinker's, stating the four processes that establish the knowledge that underlies inter-language behaviour, namely language transfer, transfer of training, strategies of communication, and overgeneralization of linguistic material (which means analogy). So there is no lack of interpretations of the language learning process which are based on the assumption that it will not be naturalized, but will remain very much a consciously induced process.

But there is also a long history of what we might call naturalistic theories of second-language learning and teaching, theories concerned with the attempt to simulate conditions of first-language learning in the organization and teaching of the second language. These go back at least to François Gouin, one of the pioneers of language teaching theory in the nineteenth century. Gouin had studied German in Paris for eight years. He then went to Berlin to study, and was distressed to find that not only could he not follow a word of what was said in the lectures but he couldn't even order himself a cup of coffee. (Failure is not a new phenomenon.)

So Gouin became interested in the problems of second-language learning and teaching, and wrote a very interesting book in which he put forward certain ideas attempting to simulate in the second-language situation that aspect of first-language learning in which the child is organizing, categorizing and interpreting reality. Gouin indeed expressed the hope that, if adequate materials were devised for representing in the target language all those events, processes, qualities, objects, and so on of daily life that language served to encode, the teaching programme and the materials could "exhaust the phenomena of the objective world". A noble aim, and one that is implicitly shared by many language teachers today, although in general, I shall suggest, we have moved forward from that position.

Materials deriving from Gouin have appeared at various times and places; I was in fact taught Chinese with materials of this kind, devised by Walter Simon and C.H. Lu. Each lesson described in great detail all the small processes that take place when for example you take one step forward, or open a door. It took 30 sentences to complete the process of going out of a building. "I rise from my chair. I walk towards the door. I reach (arrive in front of) the door. I stretch out my right hand. I grasp the handle (with my hand)", and so on.

Gouin's ideas had a strong influence on the development of the direct method, which was the modern way in which teachers were trained to teach languages in England in the 1910s. No written materials were to be used and no word or morpheme uttered in the mother tongue. The direct method was a conscious attempt to simulate natural conditions of language learning.

Among more recent developments along these lines, the one I find most interesting is the approach we might call "listen-but-keep-quiet".

Sorensen refers to an area of the Upper Amazon, on the borders of Colombia and Brazil, where a number of tribes are in regular contact and every adult typically speaks three or four distinct languages. The members are aware of the patterns of use and of the conditions that enable them to become plurilingual, although no explicit language instruction is given. It appears from his account that they learn by listening. In most cases it is only after they reach adolescence that they have the opportunity to hear the languages they need to learn; but when the time comes they are able to listen in to a large amount of speech without being required to participate in the conversation. The success rate appears to be remarkably high. I have the impression of having read somewhere of a community in which the process is even more orderly, where the young men of marriageable age go and sit outside the entrance to the village which is the home of their future wives. The language is quite different from their own; but after a few months of listening to the passers-by, they can not only understand it but also speak it with a fair degree of competence. Unfortunately I have not been able to trace the reference to this, although I believe it to be authentic.

There is an unfortunate legacy from the ideas of the previous decade, one that derives from transformational theory in linguistics, according to which after the maturational threshold that is reached about the ages of 9 to 11 it becomes impossible to learn a second language with native-born competence. This I think is quite untrue. It may become more difficult, but it does not become impossible. There are many parts of the world where it is quite normal for adults to learn a second and even a third and a fourth language and to achieve native-like competence in the process.

How widespread the use of "listen-but-keep-quiet" technique is in these informal language-learning situations I do not know. But it has been proposed as a method in language teaching. To quote from a paper on this topic by Annie Mear: "The acquisition of a receptive repertoire prior to the introduction of the productive component of the language would constitute a most powerful advantage for the acquisition of adequate expressive behaviour" – which means if you want to learn to talk, first listen. This idea has been built into certain language-teaching programmes.

The simplest form that it takes is the use of Skinnerian concept of "mands": giving instructions which the learner can carry out without having to verbalize any response. He is required to move around, to hand objects across, to point out certain things, to put on and take off clothing, and so forth, without saying anything himself. There is a variety of instructions that the teacher can give that demand no verbal expression on the part of the learner.

Nevertheless their range is very limited, and it is clear that if we are going to restrict our language teaching material to items of this kind we shall not get very far in simulating the functions of the first language. Clearly something with much more content is needed, if the programme is to be anything like a real-life language-learning situation. In fact, programmes of this kind have been devised; an example is that developed by Harris Winitz and James Reeds at the University of Missouri, Kansas City, which includes materials for teaching German, Japanese and Hebrew along these lines. These materials are not limited to imperative, or "mands" of any kind; they include both narrative and dialogue, and various techniques are being explored for presenting language in different functions in such a way that the learner is not required to perform at all for some considerable time. Active participation by the student can be introduced at different times and in a number of different ways. As in all foreign-language learning, there are no simple measures of success; I know no way of evaluating the results in terms that are quantifiable and still significant. But the approach is an extremely interesting one, and it is based on the proposition that, if we take seriously the notion that learning a second language is or ought to be in some respects like learning the first language, then we should take note of what actually goes on when one learns one's first language, one important characteristic of which is that the infant from birth onwards can be there and listen without having to produce responses. A baby never has to do what the unfortunate student in the language class has to do, namely spend all his time and mental energy thinking about what he's going to say next, thereby being prevented from ever really listening to what others are saying now.

This emphasis on listening is one of two developments in the last ten years that I find particularly interesting. The other one is something very different, and that is the move towards teaching languages for special purposes (see the CILT Conference report under that title edited by George Perren). This practice is derived from register theory, from the notion that all use of language, including the mother tongue, is to be explained by reference to the contexts in which language functions (see Halliday 1973; Ellis and Ure; and Ure and Ellis). Language is essentially a variable system, and one aspect of its variability is that different areas of "meaning potential" are typically associated with different types of social context; hence the context will tend to determine which semantic systems are more readily 'accessed' by a speaker and listener. But this is another topic, which I shall not have time to go into here.

Obviously the central problem for an approach to second-language learning based on first-language learning, in which one is attempting to simulate natural processes, is that one has to have a clear idea of what learning the first language is like. This may not be easy, because there have been shifting patterns in the interpretation of the learning of the mother tongue, with many changes of emphasis over the last 25 years. If one goes back a quarter of a century or so the main emphasis among those who were studying the way a child learns his first language was on phonology and morphology, which are the most obvious aspects of the linguistic system: how does a child learn speech sounds? how does a child learn word construction? By the end of the 1950s the attention had begun to shift away from phonology and morphology on to syntax. Since then we have been through various stages in quick succession; Maris Rodgon, in her recent book on one-word sentences, talks about the syntactic, the semantic, the cognitive and the communicative explanations of language acquisition. During the 1960s, which have been labelled the syntactic age, the learning of the mother tongue did tend to be interpreted, mainly under the influence of Chomskyan theory, as the acquisition of syntax; and here we should note not only the word *syntax* but also the word *acquisition*. The prevailing metaphor for talking about the learning of the mother tongue in the 1960s was the metaphor of 'acquisition', suggesting that language is some type of commodity that the child has to acquire. One shouldn't make too much of such metaphors; but it is noticeable how much of the work of this period is affected by the notion that language exists independently of people speaking and understanding; that there is an object called a set of rules which constitutes adult language, and it is the task of the child to acquire this ready-made object.

By the end of the decade linguists were moving away from this view and beginning to pay attention to the learning of meanings, proposing semantic rather than syntactic models of first-language learning. The syntactic age was giving way to a semantic age. In fact, however, there has never been a semantic age, at least in the field of child language studies, because at the same time as shifting the emphasis from syntax to semantics those concerned with interpreting first-language learning, or language development as it is now more appropriately called, were trying to look even beyond semantics into whatever it was that the semantics was being seen as the encoding of. The reasoning was that, if a child is learning to mean, this is not because meaning is an activity in and of itself. It is because meaning is a mode of action that has some further context from which it derives its value and significance. There are essentially two directions in which one can look beyond the meaning system: the cognitive and the social. I would call it "social" rather than "communicative". We can consider a child learning to mean against the background of his development of a cognitive system as part of learning to think; or we can consider it against the background of his social development as part of learning to interact. The former implies some theory of individual learning and cognitive development; the latter implies some theory of social learning – of socialization and the social construction of reality.

Many of the basic ideas in developmental psycholinguistics have been derived from the work of Piaget, although since Piaget sees all linguistic processes as secondary it is not easy to interpret his thinking in linguistic terms. Hermine Sinclair has developed some of Piaget's ideas in explicit linguistic form, so that one can evaluate them in relation to what actually happens when children learn language. The basic notions are familiar; we can cite just one example. Piaget at one point postulated four stages in cognitive development – the sensory-motor stage, the pre-operational stage, the stage of concrete operations and the stage of formal operations – and he claims that the learning of language, and hence the learning of meaning, is constrained by the stage of cognitive development that the child has reached. One standard example of a concept belonging to the stage of concrete operations is that of conservation, the conservation of a liquid or plastic substance under transformations of shape. If a child can interpret what happens when he pours a quantity of liquid from a container of one shape into a container of another shape, as he does in his mathematics class, he must have a certain conceptual framework involving serial ordering (bigger than, longer than, etc.) and recognition of contrasting properties (short but fat, etc.)

These are concepts deriving from the stage of concrete operations which Piaget associates typically with the age range 7 to 11, although his age assessments tend to be a bit late because they are based on experimental rather than natural behaviour. Inhelder and Sinclair have shown that children who have acquired the concepts of conservation and seriation can do three things with language which children who have not acquired these concepts cannot do. (1) They can use comparative forms correctly: 'one thing has or is more than another'. (2) They can express differentiated properties in co-ordinated descriptions: not just 'this is large', but 'this is long and this is fat'. (3) They can express contrasting notions like 'this one has less in it but it is bigger'. Inhelder and Sinclair say that children who have not yet reached the stage of mastering the concepts of conservation and seriation will not naturally control these semantic systems. They then go on to ask whether these semantic patterns are teachable, whether children who are not yet conservers and serializers can be made to learn them; and they come out with three different answers. They say that children who have not got to this stage can readily be taught differentiated terms, like separating out the concept of 'big' into its component concepts of 'long', 'fat' and so forth; that they can less easily be taught to use comparatives; and that it is practically impossible to teach them the use of coordinated and contrastive descriptions.

Now I must comment on this as a linguist. Part of the problem is that what children do linguistically under experimental conditions is very little guide to what they are doing naturally, and it is necessary to back up the vast amount of experimental psycholinguistic studies of children's language with a substantial number of language diaries of individual children. Intensive observation of this kind gives an insight into the total meaning potential that the child has in real-life situations at a certain age. And this may be very different from anything that can be brought out under experimental conditions.

Another aspect of the problem is that experiments based on categories of cognitive development fail to take account of the semantic **system**, and so do not place the particular items under investigation in their significant context, which is the totality of what the child can mean. Maris Rodgon has been studying the development of certain particular semantic patterns, namely possession, location and transitivity; she comments that she finds no clear cognitive or sensory-motor correlates to these. She also says, referring to the earlier stage, that Hermine Sinclair's claim that completion of sensory-motor development is necessary for the development of representational intelligence in the form of combinatorial speech – that is, for the development of certain syntactic and semantic structures – is not supported by her own findings, although not clearly refuted either.

So one major thrust of language development research, with which one of those particularly associated was Lois Bloom, has been towards an interpretation in terms of some theory of cognitive development. The most comprehensive and elaborated ideas in this field were those of Piaget; but not everyone is committed to a Piagetian philosophy, and recent work by Colwyn Trevarthen is providing an alternative framework which seems in many respects to allow a more satisfactory interpretation of how a child learns how to mean.

The other direction in which these studies have been moving is towards an interpretation in social or "communicative" terms. Here one is looking at the development of the semantic system not as an aspect of cognitive development but rather as an aspect of social development or socialization. One step in this direction that was taken within the acquisition model was to describe language development as the acquisition of communicative competence. I am inclined to see this notion of communicative competence as a rather misguided attempt to rescue the Chomskyan notion of competence, by applying it in an area to which it is in fact quite inappropriate. This view will certainly be disputed. But the difficulty with communicative competence as a model of language acquisition is that is does tend to degenerate into a sort of 'good manners' view of language learning, interpreting it as learning how to behave linguistically in social situations; it is noticeable how often the examples used are of the acquisition of socially appropriate language behaviour, such as forms of greeting and leave-taking. There is no need, of course, to limit the notion in this way.

A more recent step has been the attempt to apply the notion of speech acts, now widely used in linguistics. John Dore has suggested interpreting language development as the acquisition of speech acts. We might characterize speech act theory as a belated attempt on the part of philosophers of language to take account of the fact that people talk to each other. This is an important discovery; but the theory presents certain problems. One is that it is somewhat static in its conception of the speech process, not leaving much room for the dynamic unfolding of dialogue. The other is that is tends to operate with logical concepts rather than with semantic ones. It would I think be likely to throw more light on language development if its basic concepts were derived from the semantic system that underlies the process of dialogue, starting from the meanings that are actually coded in the language rather than presuppositions about the hearer's state of mind.

Still in this same general direction is the interpretation of language development in terms of the concept of socialization.

Here the leading figure is Bernstein, whose theoretical ideas have been translated into linguistic terms by Geoffrey Turner and applied to the study of the meaning potential developed by children of early school years in certain "critical socializing contexts". Again the socialization model embodies a metaphor, that of child 'being socialized', which could lead one to think that there is something readymade 'out there', that the child has to be made to conform to. It is important I think to look at the socialization process not as one of moulding the child to some pre-existing scheme of things but as a process of intersubjective development in which the child is actively involved together with the 'significant others' in creating both a language and the social reality behind it.

Common to all these approaches is a renewal of interest in the functions of language, in the part played by language in the life of the speaker and the demands he constantly makes on it. We cannot really hope to interpret the learning of the mother tongue except by asking what the child is learning language for, what he is doing with it, and what the underlying functions are from which he derives his own acts of meaning and his understanding of the meanings of others.

Katherine Nelson in some recent work suggests that very young children in the first stages of language learning tend to be differentially oriented towards different types of linguistic function. She finds two functional groups, which she calls the referential children and the expressive children. The group she calls referential tends to be oriented towards interpreting and classifying the real world. These are the children who are interested primarily in language as a means of categorizing reality and imposing pattern on their experience. The second group, which she calls the expressive, are those who are oriented towards the interpersonal functions of language, language as a means of interaction between people. One of the questions that interests her is whether there are any social correlates to these two groups.

Functional semantic interpretations of child language, among which I would include my own study *Learning How to Mean*, make it possible to identify acts of meaning long before a child has any recognizable syntax; before even the appearance of the one-word sentence. In the syntactic age one typically measured the stage the child had reached by reference to the mean length of utterance (MLU), counting words or, in a sophisticated version, counting morphemes. Behind this lay various assumptions: first of all that there are such things as words and morphemes in children's language at this stage, which is quite problematic; second that one can identify them, which is even more problematic; and third that the number of such items in an utterance is a significant measure of something other than itself. This is not to deny, of course, that a great deal of important work was done along these lines; the profound insights displayed in Roger Brown's work show the positive value of a lexico-grammatical approach and of a conception of syntactic complexity. But concentration on the length of utterance led to the assumption that language development began only at the point when the MLU was greater than one; in other words that language learning begins with structure, when the child produces a sentence – a sentence being something with (at least) two elements in it.

But it is impossible to ignore the fact that there is a great deal of meaning in a one-word sentence. Whether one claims that there is also structure is likely to depend on whether one subscribes to the syntacticist notion that structure is necessary to meaning. An interesting structural interpretation of the one-word sentence is that by Greenfield and Smith. Maris Rodgon, who I mentioned before, is also mainly concerned to offer interpretations of one-word sentences; but her approach is in functional-semantic terms.

The one-word sentence, or "holophrase" (to give it its technical name), is a regular feature of infant speech from around 16 months – though I would comment in passing that it is a mistake to attach too much importance to it, since its developmental status is very variable: some children like to stay in the one-word stage for a very long time, whereas others skip through it in a couple of weeks. Not every one-word utterance is a holophrase; Maris Rodgon recognizes three different categories: (1) repetition, where the one word is an attempt to imitate adult speech; (2) naming, where the one word is an attempt to label some phenomenon of the real world; and (3) the holophrase, which she defines as "the use of a single word to convey meaning that is typically expressed in an adult by more than one-word structure". Among the one-word sentences of the children she was studying she finds instances of all three; and she attempts to relate these to Katherine Nelson's ideas about children's orientation towards different functions.

Once we move out beyond purely linguistic interpretations, we can conceive of theories of language development not only in terms of syntax or even semantics but also in terms of the cognitive and social processes that in some sense lie behind the semantic system. This is the direction in which we have to look if we are taking seriously the question of the extent to which second-language learning resembles first-language learning. In this way first- and second-language learning may be more readily relatable not merely to each other but also to learning theory in general. In what senses is language learning like, or unlike, learning of other kinds; and what does it mean to say that language learning is a problem-solving activity, or that language learning is information processing, or that language learning involves a number of language-processing strategies? What do these concepts (strategies, problem solving, information processing – all of which have been used to characterize language learning) mean in terms of a general learning theory by reference to which language learning is being explained?

Also in relation to learning theory, how are learning processes related to the use and understanding of language?

In particular, when does hearing become learning? What implications do we derive from our interpretation of the processes of reception and decoding of language? In Kenneth Goodman's formulation, "the efficient language user takes the most direct route and touches the fewest bases necessary to get to his goal", and he does this by sampling, by predicting, by testing and confirming. If these are processes involved in hearing, in the decoding of language, what is their relation to the learning strategies that we say are involved?

We must be prepared, I think, to admit anecdotal evidence in applied linguistics, as in many other respectable fields of activity. There are very many facts relevant to language learning that have not yet been codified and written up in academic papers. One example that sticks in my mind is from that delightful book by Gerald Durrell, *My Family and Other Animals*.

Gerald Durrell grew up in England until he was 10 years old, when his mother, looking out of the window one morning and seeing that it was raining, said to her four children 'Let's go and live in Corfu'. So they went, knowing no Greek at all; and Gerald Durrell describes how he used to lean over the wall of the house where they were living and listen to the people talking to each other in the fields. One morning he went to lean on the wall as usual, and discovered that he knew Greek. This is what I would call the "click" phenomenon.

We need to understand this phenomenon and bring together different kinds of evidence that have a bearing on the experience. It has happened to me only once; but the way in which it happened is interesting because I had not had the advantage of learning a second language under natural conditions. I had been taught Chinese for military service, starting at the age of 17, and when the war finished I went to China to study. One day after a few months in Peking I suddenly realized that I knew Mandarin phonology. As far as the speech sounds were concerned, I was now the equivalent of a native speaker. I had got a native-like command of the phonology of that form of Chinese. Not that I was never going to make any mistakes; but from then on they would be native-like mistakes, slips of the tongue.

I had a clear sensation that something had clicked. But unlike Gerald Durrell, for whom the whole system had clicked, with me it was only the phonology; and that is as far as it ever got. I was living and working quite competently in Chinese, listening to lectures, writing essays in Chinese, and so on; but the rest of the language never clicked. I never became a native speaker in the lexicogrammar, still less in the semantics; and I never shall. I count myself lucky to have experienced this phenomenon once, even in that partial sense. But this may well be a difference between the adult and the child. I am not altogether surprised that with me, as an adult, this phenomenon was specific to one particular component of the linguistic system, namely the speech sounds, and that it did not go beyond there. With a child, perhaps, it happens all at once.

188

One psychologist who has done some most interesting work in the field of language processing is Ruth Day. She has found a bi-modal distribution, another way of dividing the human race into two classes, along the lines of what she calls the "language-bound" and the "stimulus-bound". What this means is that there are essentially two different ways of listening; and in her experiments almost every subject belongs clearly to one type or the other. Some of us are "language-bound", which means that when we hear language we only listen to the meaning. We do not shift our attention up and down the system, switching it on to the wording, the grammar and vocabulary, or on to the sound, the phonology and phonetics. Others of us are "stimulus-bound", which means that when we are listening our attention wanders all the way up and down the system; we may switch off the semantics and start attending to the grammar or the phonology. Ruth Day has done some nice experiments which bring this out. For example, she gives her subjects the task of transposing sounds, substituting [l] for [r] and [r] for [l], so that given the word *bramble* they are required to respond with [blæmbr] (i.e., an imaginary word *blamber*, as it would be pronounced in American English). For one group the task is so simple and obvious that they can't see what the problem is; they just do it. The other group not only cannot do it; they often cannot understand what it is they are being asked to do. The latter group are the language-bound; they are so taken up with the content of language that they find it difficult to tune in to anything else. The former are the stimulus-bound; they can tune in to any aspect of the coding, but are likely to be correspondingly less rigorous in their commitment to the content.

The labels are misleading; the phenomenon is one of orientation rather than bondage, and the two might be better named "content-oriented" and "code-oriented". But from her findings there do appear to be these clearly differentiated groups; and if this is so, then we would expect to find somewhat different strategies among language learners, including (if the difference appears early enough) among young children learning the mother tongue, according to which of these two groups they belong to.

In my own recent work on the learning of the first language I have been paying particular attention to what goes on **before** the learning of the mother tongue. The notion that one need not start listening to what goes on until the child is using words that one can recognize as those of English, or whatever the mother tongue is, is simply not valid. We have to recognize that behind a child's first use of words at the age of, say, 14 to 18 months is a long period of language development, and that in many instances before beginning to use the mother tongue the child has created for himself, in interaction with those around him, some kind of proto-language, a linguistic system through which he can exchange meanings with his mother and probably a small group of significant others, constituting his 'meaning group', and which has a functional semantic system of its own, something that is not derived from, although it will be ongoingly modified by, the semantic system of the mother tongue. Even within this general pattern, of course, we will find tremendous differences among individual children as regards the strategies they adopt – and again, common to all of them will be certain universals of human development. Fashions change; there are times at which one is looking more for universals, there are times at which one is looking for cultural or other systematic variations. We have to try to keep our focus on both. It is just this issue that arises in the second-language learning situation; if we have a group of 30 students in front of us we are faced with different learning styles. Those designing materials usually assume that, because we cannot accommodate all the individual variation, we have to treat all learners as alike. But there are probably a small number of very general learning styles, in part at least relatable to social factors in the broadest sense; and it seems reasonable to suggest that our language teaching effort should try to get to grips with these.

If we are interested in the relation between the natural condition of language learning and that which I have called "induced", which involves learning a second language under some sort of institutional conditions, then a difference must be made here between the means and the goal. The means cannot be those of natural language learning, in the sense that whatever we do to approximate to the natural, it will always be contrived. That does not imply that it's not a good thing to do, but that we are deceiving ourselves if we think that the avenue of approach to the second language in the induced situation can ever be the same as the avenue of approach to the first language.

But while saying that we should not lose sight of the equally important fact that the goals are essentially alike. The goal of the language learner, whether of first language or second language, will always be a goal of the same kind; the difference is a matter of degree. In other words, what we are aiming for in a second-language situation is the same kind of thing as we were aiming for in our first-language situation, namely success. But success will always be a relative matter; in a second language we may be aiming for success in quite specific areas, not necessarily restricting our ultimate aims but at least ordering our priorities. This is where I favour the notion of "languages for special purposes". Even in the mother tongue, however, there is a limit to what is within our scope; none of us will ever control our mother tongue in all the possible functions for which it is used. So here too there is only a difference of degree. Whether in first- or in second-language learning the aim is to succeed; and it is success rather than perfection that I think we need to emphasize. Perfection is a goal that goes with a conception of 'language as rule'; it implies following the rules, getting things right and free of errors. But our language is never error-free, and I think there is too much emphasis on the avoidance of linguistic errors. Success goes with a conception of 'language as a resource'; it is a native-like concept, which highlights the similarities, not in the **process** of first- and second-language learning but in the nature of the achievement and in our evaluation of what has been achieved.

I would like to end with two points made in an anecdotal vein. The first concerns my own experience in Chinese. When I was leaving China, I wanted to bring away various books and other objects of value with me, and this was subject to certain export restrictions. When I went to apply for a permit, I discovered that instead of there being a form to fill in, the applicant had to write a letter setting out exactly what it was he wanted to do. I was in rather a hurry, having moved out from where I was living, and said I would like to write it on the spot. The official looked rather surprised, but gave me a piece of paper, and I wrote out a letter in documentary Chinese applying for an export permit and giving all the details about the books and other things I wanted to export.

The letter was undoubtedly not free from errors. But documentary Chinese is a very special form of Chinese, not like literary and not like colloquial, and I had never before had to write anything in that variety of the language. Nor had I ever studied it systematically. If I had been given a classroom exercise requiring me to write something in documentary Chinese, I would not have known where to start. I had no notion that I knew that language; but under this pressure, when I had to write something quickly, I wrote it right off without the slightest hesitation. This illustrates for me the fact that it is unreal to assume that the classroom situation can be in any sense like real life, because one cannot bring about these conditions in any kind of organized teaching situation.

As a learner of foreign languages, I am about average, somewhere around the middle of the scale both in experience and in ability. But the particular problems I have are ones that never seem to get into the literature at all. I have no trouble with grammar; I can learn the grammar of any language in a few days, and although of course I make mistakes, they are ones which don't matter – they don't affect communication.

And without too much trouble I can work up an intelligible and inoffensive pronunciation.

But I have one immense difficulty in foreign-language learning, and that is lexical memory. Where has this been seriously discussed? I can find references to the fact that learning vocabulary is **not** a problem, and I wish I could be convinced by them. But to me it is almost the only problem. I can look up a word in a dictionary a hundred times and the hundred and first time I meet it I still don't know it and I've got to look it up again. The only way I can learn a word is by hearing it, and then using it myself in a living context of speech.

As I have stressed all along, not everyone learns in the same way. But I do not believe that I am unique; there must be other people like me who have this same problem. Is anything being done to help up solve it?

I have another minor problem, and this is one that a few people, such as John Oller, have begun to talk about, namely that in a foreign language I don't know what to say. This applies as much to learning a second dialect as it does to learning a second language. People say different things and one has to learn the semantic styles. You have to recognize that in some way or other, as Joan Maw remarks, when you are learning a new language you are learning a new reality. We can refer to this by the metaphor of being resocialized; what it means is that the foreign-language learning is constructing a new reality, a reality in which people exchange different meanings, and he has to learn both the relevant contexts of situation, together with how to identify them, and the particular meanings that are likely to be exchanged in any type of situation he may encounter.

I do not mean to suggest that an association for applied linguistics should devote its efforts to solving my own particular problems in language learning. So let me end with an example of a typical human problem of a kind needing to be approached through applied linguistics. In 1974 there was held in Nairobi a UNESCO Symposium on Interactions between Linguistics and Mathematical Education, in which linguists and mathematics educators came together to look into the linguistic problems associated with the teaching of mathematics, with particular reference to various countries of Africa, including some in which the normal medium of instruction is English and others in which it is an African language, for example Swahili or Yoruba. Some of the problems are of an institutional-linguistic kind (in Trevor Hill's sense), relating to language policy and planning, creation of terminology, and so on. Others relate more closely to the topic I have been discussing: for example, it is likely to be easier for a Luo speaker to learn Swahili than to learn English because, although neither language is related to his own, Swahili belongs to the same culture area and therefore largely shares the same meaning styles; but for the mathematics learner much of this advantage may be thrown away if the Swahili mathematics textbooks are simply translated from English, since the mathematical concepts will be introduced and interrelated in ways that reflect the meaning styles and folk mathematics of European languages instead of those of East Africa. This is an example of a fundamental problem in applied linguistics; and it is something which has immense importance for the lives of large numbers of people in the world today. It is also an example of the sort of problem to which I very much hope that the efforts and energies of an association such as this will come to be directed.

Chapter Nine

LEARNING ASIAN LANGUAGES (1986)

It is a privilege to be asked to give this year's Annual Lecture to the Centre for Asian Studies. This has been, and continues to be, a very active year for the Centre, with a programme extending across many different fields of study. In this context in particular, I welcome the opportunity to bring up for discussion the question of the learning of Asian languages. I am not – let me make it clear from the start – going to take up time arguing a case for learning Asian languages; I shall take this position for granted. In other words, my concern will be not with why people should make the attempt but rather with whether and how they might hope to succeed.

Perhaps you will allow me to begin on an autobiographical note. I was recalling earlier this year, when I spoke at the International Seminar on Language Across the Curriculum held at the Regional Language Centre in Singapore, that it was then exactly 40 years since I had given my first language class. I was a very junior officer in the British army, and I was assigned to teach Chinese to a class of RAF officers vastly my senior in age and rank – one of them was already a Group Captain. Germany had just surrendered, and there stretched ahead of us, or so we all thought, a long-drawn-out war in the Pacific Region with a growing need for personnel trained in key Asian languages. The war soon came to an end; but the potential being built up in this way was felt to be a valuable national resource, and the programmes and the new recruits were already in place. So the classes continued; I taught Chinese in that setting for two years, to about a dozen groups from navy, army and air force, and I have always been grateful for that early encounter with the learner's problems seen from the teacher's end.

That first class I taught was, I remember, a dictation – a very useful, if now rather neglected, teaching device. The materials that we worked with had been prepared by the director of the programme, who had also been my own teacher, Dr Walter Simon, then Reader in and later Professor of Chinese in the University of London. Simon had been somewhat influenced by François Gouin, one of the late nineteenth-century pioneers in what today would be called applied linguistics. Gouin had studied chemistry in his own country, France, and was going on to complete his studies where the best science education was then to be obtained, namely in Germany. He had studied six years of German in secondary school, but found, when he got to Berlin, that he could neither understand the chemistry lectures nor even, what was worse, order himself a glass of wine and a snack in a German bar. Reflecting on this sad state of affairs, he came to feel that what the language learner needed to do was to analyse his experiences of daily life down to their smallest components and then learn to describe these in the target language. So one of the lessons in our first Chinese textbook (Simon and Lu 1942: 149), based on this principle, went (giving English translation) as follows:

I GO OUT OF MY ROOM

1 My room is on the third floor.
2 I intend to go out (having (some) business).
3 I must first go out of my room.
4 I rise from my chair.
5 I walk towards the door.
6 I reach (arrive in front of) the door.
7 I stretch out my right hand.
8 I grasp the handle (with my hand).
9 I open the door by turning (the handle).
10 I pull the door open.
11 I step over the threshold.
12 I walk out.
13 I turn round.
14 I stretch out my hand again and grip the outside door handle.
15 I pull the door to (or: close the door).

In this way, Gouin claimed, one could "exhaust the phenomena of the objective world" (Gouin 1880/1893).

Put like that, of course, it sounds laughable; we all know that the phenomena of the objective world are inexhaustible. And yet that is just what a language does; it renders them exhaustible. That is what language is for – or at least it is one of the things language is for. A language is a means of semanticizing experience; that is, it enables us to construe experience – and this means the whole of the experience – into

195

constructions of meaning. The concept of 'mastering' a language, in its active sense (the standpoint of the speaker), means that there is nothing in our experience that we cannot encode in that language – even such aberrant experience as we have in dreams, which tend to stretch this mastery to its limits. Notice that this is true by definition of the mother tongue. We could in fact turn the whole thing round and define experience as "that which can be described in language". What we mean by a "native speaker" of a particular language is that that is the language through which his experience has been construed, and which does therefore exhaust for him the phenomena of the objective world. (This leaves entirely open, of course, the possibility that one may have more than one native language.)

There is one other dimension to the picture, one that Gouin's formulation leaves out although his discussion shows he was aware of it. To parallel Gouin's expression we should add that the learner needs to master the controls of his subjective world: meaning by this not the expression of inner experience, how to talk about the phenomena of our own consciousness (these are just another aspect of the objective world, as far as language is concerned), but how to use language to get things done. Not only do we think with language: we also act with it. It enables us to win friends and influence people – to change the world, as well as reflecting on it. To master a language is also to master its rhetorical potential. And again this is part of what we recognize as a "mother tongue". If experience is 'that which we can reflect on in language', then personality is 'that which we can achieve through language'; to be a native speaker means, also, that this is the language through which one establishes and maintains one's interpersonal relationships – and hence the language with which one acts on the world as well as understanding it.

Clearly for François Gouin, despite six years of study in a French school, German served him in neither of these contexts: he could neither construe the world with it, nor use it to get things done. These two aspects are not, of course, distinct operations in life; rather they are different facets of every single act of meaning, such as ordering a glass of wine. To do this, you have to be able to act on, to influence, the wine bottle; and since bottles are not native speakers this means acting on the waiter or the barman. This is the active, interpersonal element in the language, encoded in the grammar as mood, together with various other systems associated with mood. But you also have to be able to **refer to** the wine, its quality, quantity and so on, and this requires the reflective, experiential element in the language, encoded in the grammar as transitivity, again with various other associated grammatical systems. Every act of meaning, with a few exceptions such as greeting and swearing, involves both these semantic components at once; learning a language means learning to think with it and to act with it in one and the same operation.

Now a child learning language at his mother's knee controls this principle by the end of the second year of life; and as a principle it does not have to be relearnt for another language, since it is equally valid for all languages. What the learner of a second language has to do is to hone this second language to the service of the same twofold function. But we have all forgotten how we did it, because once we have a language that construes all experience and all personal interaction into meanings we no longer have any way of reconstituting the world of our pre-semantic existence. Not that it would help much if we could; the second language learner has to arrive at this goal by a very different route. He cannot become an infans, a non-speaker, again; indeed the most important fact about the learner of a second language is that he already has a first one. His task is to use the second language to build up at least some of the same potential.

All this has nothing special to do with Asian languages – but it has a great deal to do with learning Asian languages in Australia. An Asian language is a language like any other; an Asian child learns his first language in exactly the same way as a European or an African or an Australian child learns his first language; and the criteria of success are no different whether you are speaking English or Arabic, Aranta or Chinese. It is, of course, marvellously impressive, and thoroughly chastening, to listen to 2-year-old children chattering fluently in Chinese – all those little Orientalists, if I may draw an image from Professor Worsley's talk last year – but they are, simply, being Chinese children; and now that we have some insight into how children learn their mother tongue, building up the kind of two-way functional potential I was talking about just now, we find they do it in very much the same way. This has been shown by one of our Chinese colleagues, Qiu Shijin, who has just completed a thesis on developmental linguistics in which she studied the development of the semantic and grammatical systems of small children learning to talk in Shanghai (Qiu 1984).

So from one point of view, all language learning is alike: a first language is a first language, and whatever language it is it has the same function in life; it is also construed as part of life, since a small child makes no difference between learning his language and using that language as the principal tool for learning everything else. Now, however, let us move to the other extreme, and suggest that no two language learning experiences are ever exactly the same. If we see a class of 20 Australian high-school pupils of English-speaking background studying Indonesian, we can recognize 20 different learning situations – they all have their own personalities, their own educational history, their own family background. This too may be a valid point of view; but the problem is that we can do nothing with it. What we need to do is to focus somewhere in between these two extremes, and ask what are the significant, typical features of the situation we are concerned with: the process of learning Asian languages, in Australia, as second languages – particularly by Australians of non-Asian background.

Let us look at three of the factors involved: the social context of the language learning, the cultural distance to be bridged and the linguistic problem to be faced.

Any Australian wanting to learn a second language has to struggle for the opportunity to do so: first with educational authorities and school principals, second with parents and with peers. There are whole districts, and not just in the countryside, where no foreign language is offered in the school curriculum. Eltis and Cooney (1983), in their valuable report on *Languages Other than English in the Senior Secondary Curriculum*, reported that school principals, when asked about the contribution of languages to a range of educational goals, tended to have a rather negative attitude, rating language among the least valuable subjects under all but two out of nine headings. This ideological bias was likely to be reinforced by the attitude of parents, who, while few of them said they were opposed to languages being taught, consistently ranked them in the lower half of a scale assessing the relative benefit to be derived from different high school subjects by those who study them. Eltis and Cooney remark (1983: 30): "This (result) suggests that parents will not be likely to urge their children to study a language because of the perceived importance of the subject". This in turn reflects the prevailing view that languages are there for maintenance; if you learn a language that is not your mother tongue, then it must be because it is your grandmother tongue. It is natural that ethnic communities should promote their languages as cultural heritage; but it is unfortunate that official policy sets up an artificial barrier between language maintenance and other language-learning contexts, thus reinforcing the stereotype that languages are for 'ethnics'. Hence except for the traditional school languages, which are Western European ones, there is no recognized status for languages in the community; and Asian languages fare worst, since they are based outside European culture. For John Smith, or Maria Schmidt, to persist with the study of Arabic or Japanese requires a degree of commitment that not everyone can be expected to possess.

And this leads into the second point, that of cultural distance. It is obvious that there is a greater cultural distance separating English and Indonesian than that which separates, say, English and Italian; the question is, what is the significance of this for the language learner. Here we need to distinguish between two points of entry of cultural factors into second-language learning. There are certain patterns that are built in to the core semantics of a language, that simply cannot be understood by a learner from a distant background without cultural explanation: for example, how to handle person ('I', 'you', etc.) in Indonesian or Japanese. Some basic discussion of social or religious values and beliefs is likely to have a place wherever the learner is above a certain age. At a more abstract level, an analysis such as that of implicit meanings in Urdu given by Ruqaiya Hasan in her 'Ways of saying: ways of meaning' (1984), is of immense significance for anyone learning an Indian language, although it demands some degree of sophistication in linguistics to be able to apply it. These are issues which inevitably arise the moment one makes contact with the languages at all.

There is another point of entry, however, which is very different from this; where cultural factors enter in by choice – that is, because it is considered that part of the purpose of teaching the language is that of using it to introduce the culture. Two weeks ago I attended a conference in China, the International Symposium on the Teaching of English in the Chinese Context (ISTEC) in Guangzhou, or Canton. There were about 20 of us from overseas, from four English-speaking countries, but the majority of the participants were Chinese teachers of English; they gave papers on applied linguistics apologizing earnestly for their inadequate mastery of the language, both the apology and the paper itself being delivered in English – an English of remarkably high standard. The title of the conference referred to 'the Chinese context'; but one of the main points was that English is taught in China in a variety of very different contexts, from those, at one end, where the students want English as an international language for a very specific purpose, such as technical English for translating engineering reports, to those at the other end where the students are going to be honours graduates in English who want to understand Shakespeare, Pope and Sterne, or else Ernest Hemingway, William Golding or Patrick White. For the former group there is no cause to buy in to any of the English-speaking cultures, beyond the minimum that may be needed to understand their own specialized field (which might include exotic things like mortgages) and some general patterns such as personal names and titles. For the latter, obviously, the situation is very different. They are likely to be involved from an early stage with problem areas of English culture, such things as the concept of privacy (try translating into Chinese this example from a letter to the *Sydney Morning Herald*: "intrusions by the government into the legitimate privacy of non-government schools"); and learning about such matters will for them become an inseparable part of learning the English language.

What concerns us here is the principle of choice. It is wrong to assume that every Australian attempting an Asian language necessarily also wants to explore the culture of those who speak it. Anyone proposing to take a degree in the language presumably does, or so it may reasonably be expected. But a nurse working in a hospital with a large number of Arabic-speaking patients might simply want to be able to interact with them, and reassure them, in their own language. There is a wide range of purposes behind the learning of an Asian language for which very little cultural knowledge is required; and it is important to insist on this point, because in many learning contexts time is extremely precious, and it is simply not necessary to spend it in discussing the tea ceremony. Learning a language is hard and intensive work, and it is sheer self-deception to think you are teaching students Japanese when you are describing how to get around the Tokyo underground system – and describing it in English.

Let me come now to my third factor, the special linguistic problems of learning an Asian language. The fact that the language being learnt is an Asian language does not make it intrinsically either more or less difficult than a language of any other continent on the earth's surface. In themselves, as languages, Chinese or Arabic or Indonesian are neither more nor less difficult than French or Russian. There may be some languages that are objectively easier or harder than others – we have no way of measuring these things; but if so it has nothing to do with the language being an Asian language. By and large, however, all languages seem to display a similar overall complexity; they are just complicated in different ways, at different points in their systems. Table 9.1 sets out a few of the features that learners, especially English-speaking learners, are likely to find difficult in some major Asian languages (with French and Russian included for comparison). They are not features of any great theoretical significance; they are rather low-level, concrete aspects of the language design – but important for the language learner. For a teacher of any

Table 9.1 Some examples of linguistic features typically found difficult by English-speaking learners

		Non-Asian languages		Asian languages				
		French	Russian	Arabic	Hindi/Urdu	Chinese	Japanese	Malay/Indonesian
pronunciation	prosodic	rhythm			rhythm	syllabic tone	rhythm; tension	
	articulatory	nasal vowels	palatalization	pharyngealization post-velars	voicing/aspiration	palatoalveolars; apicals		
grammar and vocabulary	morphology	irregular verbs	general inflexional complexity	affixation/vowel variation	verb morphology; gender marking		verb morphology	(affixation)
	syntax	conjunct pronouns; prepositional constructions	aspect	verbal categories	transitivity; aspect	phase; indefinites	theme; logical connectives	aspect; transitivity/voice
vocabulary:	choice			derivation; collocation	collocation	generality; collocation	collocation	compounding; collocation
	learned source	(classical Latin/Greek)	classical Slavonic; (Latin/Greek)	classical	classical Sanskrit/Persian	classical	Chinese	Arabic; (Sanskrit)
writing symbols:	quantity					charactery	charactery	
	shape					characters	characters;	
	use	spelling	(letters)	"letters"	"letters"		syllabics	
culture	variation			dialectal and sociolectal marked	dialectal and sociolectal marked	dialectal	sociolectal	sociolectal
	distance	(slight)	(noticeable)	marked	marked	marked	very marked	very marked

given language, of course, it is important to have a deeper and more comprehensive picture of the features that are likely to be problematic. At the same time, it should be stressed that these are excrescences on the general language-learning task. In other words, the main difficulty is simply that of learning a second language; no more than a small fraction of the problem is caused by special features of this kind.

With one exception; and at this point I would like to discuss one example in a little more detail. I shall use for the purpose Chinese, since it is a language I taught, for about ten years altogether, and since it does exemplify in a rather strong form what is perhaps the one significant exception to the principle I enunciated above.

Chinese, then, presents some problems to the English-speaking learner, problems such as every language displays: in the case of Chinese, the tones, one or two features of articulation (apical vowels, palato-alveolar and retroflex consonants, late voice onset time), some syntactic features (e.g., indefinite nominals, phase and aspect in the verb), plus the usual semantic problems that come from cultural distance – one has to learn to make the right predictions about what people are going to say next. But it has in an extreme form the special problem that is presented by most Asian languages – all the major ones except Turkish, Indonesian and Tagalog: namely the script.

There is a great deal of mythology about the Chinese script, including among the Chinese themselves; in the West, since it first became known in the late-sixteenth century, it has been very widely misinterpreted (a notable exception was Timothy Bright, an early English specialist in shorthands and writing systems, who wrote about the Chinese script in a work appearing in 1588 and seems to have understood its nature remarkably accurately). It is often said to be ideographic, and regarded as a rather primitive kind of writing system; whereas in fact it is not ideographic but logographic, and it is not primitive either – it is simply of a special kind that happens to be well suited to the form of the Chinese language.

The Chinese script is not difficult to use – to read or write – once you have learnt it; but it is difficult to learn, because of the large number of symbols. Now for the Chinese, this is not a severe problem, because they know the language already before they learn to write it. Provided you know the language first, the script is manageable. But to try to learn the script at the same time as learning the language imposes a virtually impossible burden; the learner cannot cope with sound, sense and sight all being new at once (cf. Simon and Lu 1942: 19). So for the foreigner it is a major obstacle; and the only way to cope with it is to become fluent in the language before starting to learn the charactery. In the course on which I first studied, we had a year's intensive instruction in the language, using a romanized script, before embarking on Chinese characters; as a result, when we did come to learn the characters we were able to proceed rather quickly.

When Chinese is taught in our high schools, however, the pupil is confronted with characters more or less from the beginning; he is trying to learn both the language and the very complex writing system from scratch at one and the same time, with the result that each gets in the way of the other and both become unattainable. The operation becomes an elaborate farce, with the student straining his eyes to decode unfamiliar symbols (the so-called 'simplified characters' now used in China, which again work very well for those who know the language, have made this operation even more stressful by removing much of their previous redundancy); it bears about the same relation to learning a language as reading a musical score does to learning to play the violin. A minimal step forward would be to remove all characters from the first three years of study of the language, so that the student had the chance to learn some Chinese first; those going on to Higher School Certificate could then take up the characters in Year 11. Judging by my experience as a teacher of Chinese, they would know more characters at the end of those two years than they do now after five years in which they have had to cope with characters from the start.

What is needed for this purpose is a large amount of reading material in romanized transcription; and this could be produced very quickly and cheaply. The present system of romanization, Hanyu Pinyin, is not a bad one; indeed for the purposes for which the Chinese designed it it is highly effective. But they did not design it for foreigners, so it is not as good for studying Chinese as a foreign language as the one we learnt from in London in the 1940s – just as with the simplified characters, so also the romanized Pinyin spellings are underdifferentiated. Once the learner has become familiar with its conventions, however, it could be perfectly adequate for the purpose. The proper use of romanization as a learning tool would at least give the learner some more than minimal chances of success.

I have dwelt on this example at some length because I want to make explicit one central point, which is this: when we do teach Asian languages in our schools, we do it in such a way that those who learn them are virtually assured of failure. I do not mean by that that they will never pass their examinations; on the contrary, those who teach them are conscientious, highly motivated and anxious to ensure that they do –

that they will not suffer from having chosen to study an exotic language. But they fail in the way that François Gouin failed – and no doubt he too had passed all his examinations. They have achieved no power **over** the language, and hence they have achieved no power **with** the language. They cannot do with it any of the things that a language is really for, which is not to pass examinations but, as we saw at the beginning, to know things with and to do things with. They could not use it to buy an ice cream, or the latest piece of software; to argue politics, watch the news or learn about anything that interests them. Nor could they interpret with it if their services were suddenly needed.

The reasons are not far to seek. If one had to pick the worst possible period in the life of a human being for him to start learning a second language, it would be the beginning of adolescence, say age 13 or 14; so that is when they start. The task needs very intensive study for concentrated periods of time; so we give him four 40-minute periods a week strung out over two or three school years. It needs real-life contexts of language use, especially spoken language; so we turn the language into another classroom subject, put it between the covers of a book, and con it. Then, if it is an Asian language, we reify the script, as yet another thing-to-be-learnt; so that instead of being what it is, a vehicle for extending the functional range of the language once the language itself has been mastered, it becomes an additional barrier to prevent such mastery from ever being achieved.

Let me quote two short passages from a recent article in *Applied Linguistics* by Patsy Lightbown of Concordia University in Canada, a country where some of the most important language education research has been carried out:

2.8. One cannot achieve native-like (or near native-like) command of a second language in one hour a day. No-one knows how much time it takes, but it is quite clear that it cannot be done exclusively in a classroom – even in a classroom where the perfect magical balance between form and function, structure and communication, has been struck. The most successful 'acquirers', young first-language learners, may conservatively be estimated by the age of six to have spent some 12,000 to 15,000 hours 'acquiring' language. The child in a French immersion program (sc. in Canada) might be estimated to have received 4,000 hours of contact with French by Grade 6. In most school programs, the total number of hours after six years of study (for approximately five hours per week) would not reach 1,000.

2.9 The learner's task is enormous because language is enormously complex. And neither linguist nor teacher nor textbook-writer can really pre-digest the language sufficiently to make the task easy. What the learner has ultimately to learn goes far beyond what the textbook contains, beyond what the teacher can explain, and even beyond what the linguist has described. The studies based on the linguistic theories of universals and markedness are particularly helpful in illustrating the complexity of the learner's task and the inadequacy of the best pedagogical grammar to deal with it. (Lightbown 1985: 179)

There have now been some decades of applied linguistic research into different aspects of language learning and language teaching. The greater part of this research, and of its application in teaching practice, has been in the teaching of English to the speakers of other languages, including English to migrants, English in the context of a national language policy as in Singapore, and English in its international and foreign language functions. It has also figured prominently in the teaching of other European languages in particular situations: for example, French in Canada, which is one of the major success stories, French as a national and international language, and German and Swedish to guest workers. In the teaching of foreign languages in English-speaking countries this work has until recently had rather little impact; it has been made use of in teaching languages to the armed services, especially in the United States, and it is now beginning to be applied in teaching the language of the EEC in schools in the British Isles. But there is still hardly any applied linguistic research in the teaching of Asian languages, although both the Chinese and the Japanese are now starting to devise special programmes for training teachers of these languages to learners from overseas.

Applied linguistics is not a set of answers, or a toolkit for turning out successful performers. There are immense gaps in what we know about learning second languages – to take one example, we know virtually nothing about the processes whereby conscious study of a language is turned into the unconscious control that constitutes its mastery. But there are also some important findings; and a body of rather solid experience. As in all human endeavour, we have seen a succession of fads and fashions; in English language teaching we have had structural, audio-lingual, situational, cognitive code and functional-notional approaches – to say nothing of a number of others that Peter Strevens classifies under his "mystique-dominated paradigm": The Silent Way, Suggestopaedia, Counselling Learning, Neurolinguistic Programming and Total Physical Response – usually labelled by their practitioners as "holistic" (Strevens 1985). (One should add that all of these embody some good ideas and often work well in certain specific situations; it is as general panaceas that they fail.) At the same time Strevens recognizes considerable achievements in the mainstream "teaching–learning paradigm", achievements in what he considers to be the four "fundamental actions of teaching that bear on the learning process of the learner", namely "shaping the input, encouraging the intention to learn, managing the learning process, and promoting practice and use of the language" (ibid.: 5). These have, in his view, led to

> a marvellous array of teaching methods and techniques and materials, a highly professional force of informed teachers, a growing research effort geared to improving teaching and learning, a sophisticated intellectual base in applied linguistics – and a great deal of effective learning. (ibid: 17)

This is a far cry from Strevens' own observation, made in 1965 or thereabouts, when he said that the only significant variable in the learning of a second language was the total amount of time that the learner devoted to it.

Some of the effect has come from the application in teaching practice of ideas derived from theoretical concepts in linguistics – although the first time round these tend to be misinterpreted, or rather to be interpreted in a somewhat superficial and undigested form. For example, "situational English" in Australia was a very positive application of the linguistic principle of situational meaning; but the notion of situation was interpreted as a kind of setting, which is not what it is, so we had a setting such as "at the post office" which was then used as the context for a ready-made dialogue (admittedly better than a ready-made dialogue without a context at all). Now that the same notion has been reinterpreted at a deeper level, as it is used in linguistics, more effective practices have been introduced under the label of functional or communicative language teaching, which are certainly part of Strevens' "marvellous array". Another example of the same process is language for specific purposes, or "LSP". This began with the linguistic concept of a functional variety of a language, or "register": the meanings that are typically expressed in a given context of use (and therefore the forms that are produced to express them) are selectively called for by that context, and hence differ from one type of situation to another. A language learner often requires the language he is learning for use in certain types of context only; since he has a limited time available for learning it, it seems sensible to spend that time learning the functional varieties he needs rather than those he does not need. Here again there have been pitfalls; the register, or functional variety, was also at first tied too closely to ready-made texts, and then, when freed from that constraint, came to be interpreted as simply equivalent to subject matter, so we had technical varieties like chemical English and English for finance and banking. Now it has finally been recognized that the relevant notion is not that of subject matter, though this does come into the picture, but rather that of what is going on, such that those involved are engaged in some pattern of activity in which the language is playing a critical part. From this arises some very successful language teaching practice, for example, English for tertiary studies where the student learns to listen to lectures, take notes, interact with a tutor, look up references and write various kinds of assignment – the staff of our own Language Study Centre are doing excellent work along these lines.

The importance of developments such as these is that they make teaching a more effective aid to learning. Of all subjects in the curriculum, it is in languages that the role of the teacher, in relation to the learner, is the most complex and obscure. Once the language teaching takes on a more functional orientation, as has happened with these shifts of emphasis in TESOL, the teacher's part becomes a much more positive one: instead of appearing purely in a prophylactic role, as a preventer of errors, the teacher becomes an enabler, one who is helping the student extend his powers. Not surprisingly, therefore, a number of smaller but significant changes of attitude have been taking place in association with these developments. To mention just two of these: first, errors are no longer looked on as pathological, but rather as inevitable and in fact functional stepping stones in the learner's progression into the language. Second, serious attention has been being paid to the strategies adopted by people learning a second language (see for example Chesterfield and Chesterfield 1985), both communication strategies and learning strategies; these too are recognized to play an essential part in the complex process by which the learner internalizes the system of the new language and also puts it to use. To learn a language successfully a student has to be able to use what is learnt and to learn from what is used, such that these are no longer two different things; and this can be helped or it can be hindered, according to the teacher's conception of what a language is and how it is learnt.

It has to be said that teachers of foreign languages, including Asian languages, have not been as ready as their colleagues in English language teaching to explore new methods and new ideas. That being said, however, it is important to understand why. They tend to be working under very different kinds of constraints. Eltis and Cooney, in the report I referred to earlier, make a number of points in defence of language teachers in school (1983: 149–50). They are too long to quote in full; but

207

they include such things as the lack of consultancy services and other forms of support, the fact that "they are **personally** required to justify **at every turn** the very 'raison d'être', the very purpose of languages in the curriculum. No other subject area has to do this"; the fact that, unlike in other subjects, "one dull language teacher affects the whole class range"; the fact that "there has been little or no change in the preservice training of (language) teachers". All these things reflect the low value that is placed on their own work and on the goals at which they are aiming. Not only do they have to "sell their subject" to attract students – a sharp contrast with the generally very high motivation of students in TESOL courses – but the real consumers, the community that is the ultimate arbiter of the student's achievement, has little appreciation of what that achievement means. It seems obvious to us that the purpose of learning a language is to be able to use it for effective communication in some contexts other than the classroom; and furthermore, that studying literature in that language is a context like any other, since you cannot appreciate Japanese literature in the original if you cannot communicate in spoken Japanese – it was after all written for people who can. (My wife first took up linguistics in despair because she found herself required to teach *Alice in Wonderland* to Pakistani students who could not string three words of English together.) Yet there are many in the community – and some in the university – who place very little value on a functional mastery of the language, because they fail to recognize that a language is a potential for meaning, and that only by developing that potential, and so gaining the semiotic power of thinking with it and acting with it, can the learner then go on to achieve any of the further goals, whether purely practical or purely academic or anything in between, that are accorded some value in our linguistically very naïve society.

Let me not seem to imply that an Australian high school student, setting out to learn an Asian language, can hope to achieve native-like command. To come back once again to the child learning a first language: if we express his experience of the language not in terms of hours but rather more concretely in terms of the number of clauses spoken in his hearing, the clause being the semantically critical unit in the grammar of a language, then over a period of five years that child will have heard something of the order of a quarter of a million of them, all of these relating to some real-life context of situation. By contrast, our typical second-language learner, within a similar period of five years, will be lucky to have heard ten thousand clauses in the language he is attempting to learn. And a significant proportion of these are likely to have had no context other than that of a language lesson.

Suppose the learner could start a little bit earlier in life. This would obviously have the advantage of giving him a longer time in which to learn. But it would have other consequences as well. As children mature, a change takes place in how they learn a second language. Up to the age of 8 to 10, they are still able to do this more or less as they learnt their first language; after puberty this is no longer possible. The exact nature of this change is not well understood, and it is much more complex than the way it is often presented; but it is true by and large that while an adolescent, like an adult, has to learn by conscious attention and process-ing, a child below, say, upper primary age can still learn by processing language unconsciously. This does not mean, as has sometimes been suggested, that he can learn a language with hardly any input; on the contrary, he is very much dependent on a rich environment such as the first language learner has. But it does mean that his experience of the language is much more readily turned into communicative control; the language will "click", so that – and this is fundamentally important – speakers of the language will recognize him as someone they can talk to. Not that he necessarily talks like one of them – that is largely irrelevant; but that he can cope, using the language for the purposes language is meant for.

So there is everything to be said for starting young; the younger the better. One of our Sydney graduates in Japanese, Alena Rada, who is also a graduate in linguistics, was well aware of this fact, and wanted her small son to learn a language in primary school. The principal's attitude was unhelpful; so she talked the matter over with parents, and the result is that she now directs a school, the Sydney Language School for Children, which teaches ten languages, five of them Asian languages, to children ranging from pre-school to Year 6. At present the school has 72 classes, in widely scattered parts of Sydney; the number could be considerably higher, given the demand, but for one problem: there are no teachers. There is no programme anywhere in New South Wales for training people to teach languages in primary school. The assumption is that if you can speak the language, and are trained as a primary teacher, then you can teach the language to the children; and this is a disastrous misconception reflecting the typically amateur status that is accorded to the language teacher's role. Being a native speaker of a language, as had to be attested by painful experience in the teaching of English around the world, is no qualification for teaching it; indeed an untrained native speaker is likely to be worse than an untrained non–native speaker, since while neither knows how to teach the latter does at least recognize the difficulties that are involved. And being a trained primary teacher does not mean you know how to teach a language. So there is an immediate task for us here, to gain recognition for the professional needs, and professional status, of "language teacher K–6"; a move which in turn would help to raise the professional standing of all language teachers including our colleagues in the secondary schools.

The Senate Standing Committee on Education and the Arts, in its report *A National Language Policy*, has this to say (1984: 139):

> Many submissions to the Inquiry argued that the optimum age to commence language learning occurs in the early primary years, or even during pre-school, when children are able to acquire a language naturally with minimum interference from their mother tongue.

It then obscured the issue by quoting at length from two individual submissions pointing out that there is no age at which one cannot learn a language, which is certainly true – but irrelevant to the question of what age is best. The Canadian immersion programmes have shown very clearly how successful primary language learning can be in that situation, when there is one language to be learnt by all – in that case French – and it is used as the medium of instruction for at least some of the subjects being studied in the school. But these conditions are very different from those here in Australia, where we have not got a single language to take priority over all the others. More relevant is the British experience of the 1960s, when various different languages were introduced on a trial basis into a number of primary schools, each school selecting one and teaching in that language for a small proportion of the time. But we also need to understand why that very successful experiment was given up – or rather, the pretext on which it was given up (the deeper reasons were economic and political), namely that it did not have the support of the secondary schools.

It was, of course (with hindsight), politically inept not to involve the secondary teacher from the start; as it was they found themselves faced with a Year 7 class some of whom were absolute beginners and some of whom not only had had experience of the language but could actually use it as a living thing, to play with and to learn with. It was not, however, the language of the secondary school textbooks; and it included no paradigms of irregular verbs. I leave the rest to your imagination – the point being that it is no use bringing about a language change in the primary schools except as part of an overall language education policy, in which the practices and goals of secondary language teaching are re-examined and proper provision is made for the teachers to develop the appropriate professional skills.

There is an interesting model being developed for this purpose in the context of the EEC. It is usually known as the "graded objectives" model; and it is based on the conception of levels of language attainment. A number of levels of attainment are recognized, from Level 1 to, say, Level 10; and these are defined in terms of the ability to use the language for an increasing variety of functions, ranging from simple greeting and exchange of names to those such as service encounters, reading the newspaper and interpreting in an office or a hospital. The assessment is thus, as it is expressed, "criterion-referenced rather than norm-referenced"; one is assessed according to what one can do with the language, not according to how well one approximates to a particular predetermined set of norms. The student can then move in at whatever level corresponds to his own current level of attainment; and this would more readily accommodate those pupils having previously studied a language in the primary school, not only in recognizing that they already know something of it but also in giving value and relevance to the kind of ability that they have, the ability to use it in real communicative contexts.

The graded objectives approach is now being explored in Australia by a project supported by the Curriculum Development Centre in South Australia, the Australian Language Levels project, known, naturally, by its acronym ALL. The work was described at this year's annual congress of the Applied Linguistics Association of Australia by the Director of one of the British projects, John Clark of the Scottish Education Department, and the National Project Manager of the Australian team, Dr Anne Martin. One other aspect of the graded objectives model that is relevant to our consideration here is that it helps to overcome the dichotomy between the native and the non-native learner. We tend to organize the teaching and examining of foreign languages on the assumption that there are two clearly distinct categories of learner, one for whom the language is the mother tongue and the other for whom it is a foreign language. In real life, especially in a country such as Australia, and not least in Asian languages, there is a continuum, with learners being ranged at all points along the scale. With a conception of language levels, a learner can be expected to increase his proficiency from whatever level is taken as the point of his departure; and progress from level 1 to level 5 carries the same evaluation as progress from level 3 to level 7, or from level 6 to level 10.

This approach does not impose any particular method on the language teacher; but it does imply a particular kind of attitude to language. It implies the perception that a language is a resource; it is not a

211

compendium of rules. It makes no difference, in this respect, whether the language is the learner's mother tongue or not; and this leads to the second implication, which is that learning a second language (or a third, or a fourth) should be seen as a natural component of an individual's overall language development, not as some kind of extraneous growth. I said at the beginning that every language is a means of knowing and a means of doing – you can observe this at the core of the semantic system, the meaning potential as I called it, through its manifestations in grammar and in vocabulary. Developing language is developing the power that consists in knowledge and in control; and learning a second language is adding to this power. So while this perspective does not impose any particular teaching method, there are some that it militates against: all those, in fact, which treat language learning as an exercise in good behaviour and conformity to rule.

I drew a parallel with learning a musical instrument. Like all analogies, it is partial; music is not language, and musical knowledge and control are concepts of a very different, metaphorical kind. But of all the activities in school, the closest to that of learning a language is learning to play an instrument. It requires fluency before accuracy (you can tidy up afterwards; but if you insist on accuracy from the start you will never become fluent at all). It requires a great amount of listening during which one is not being expected to perform. And it requires an ability both to reproduce ready-coded sequences of text in the appropriate context and to improvise, to construct new discourse that is functional and meaningful to those who hear it. If you never listened to music without feeling it might be your turn to be on next, if you were never allowed to complete a melodic line unless each note was perfect, and if you always had to play just what was on the staff, your progress would be painful to endure. And – to return to my earlier point – if the score was written in an unfamiliar notation, so that you had to spend more time conning it than playing from it, you might easily be forgiven for giving up in despair.

You may not be allowed in the orchestra until you can play reasonably well; and this is one of the problems for our learners of Asian languages. Most Asian communities are not accustomed to hearing their languages spoken badly. They may be accustomed to speakers of deviant dialects; but the mistakes a speaker of another dialect makes are quite different from those a foreigner makes. So you may face the frustration of finding yourself not understood; you look like a foreigner anyway, so you obviously can't speak our language. This is not an unsympathetic reaction; it is simply one of giving up on an unfamiliar situation. But if it

212

means that the learner of an Asian language has to try that much harder, it also means that it is that much more important for the teaching to focus on these communicative goals.

One might also add, perhaps, that it is that much more rewarding to succeed. Whatever level one has reached is, of course, a measure of one's success; one of the valuable features of the graded objectives approach is the way in which success is defined. But in the last resort it is the individual learner who sets his own criteria of success or failure. This is why it is so often said that languages are unique in the school curriculum, in being the only subject in which the learner is almost always going to end up by failing: no matter how many exams he passes, since he knows what language is for, he will have failed, in his own eyes, if he cannot do with the second language at least some of the things he does with his first one. So the learner will always remain aware of how little he has achieved – especially if then he is discouraged from going on, for reasons outside either his or the teacher's control.

What is lacking, for Australians learning Asian languages, is a context in which they can get a sense of what they have achieved. If you are not one of those who has had a rich multilingual experience as a child, you will always have to work hard at a language; and you may easily be discouraged from trying, if you feel you are only going to reach a low-lying plateau and stick there. Ideally, of course, you go and spend some time in the country where the language is spoken, and make yourself live at least some parts of your life in it. But for those who cannot do that (and even for those who can), there need to be created many more language contexts for Asian languages here at home. It would be a useful task for our Centre to explore the means of doing this, so that the experience of learning Asian languages in Australia became something that is rewarding in itself, carrying its own criteria of success for those who take part. There are many ways in which this can happen – people's motives are amazingly varied (I once knew someone whose hobby was translating Chinese lyric poetry into Welsh). But a learner should feel that he has succeeded if he has explored, and exploited, some of the riches of an Asian language, every one of which is not only the vehicle of a living culture, thus embodying meanings out of the past, but also, like every language, a semiotic powerhouse, out of which will come the new meanings, and the new cultures, that we can expect to arise in the future.

PART THREE

MULTILINGUAL SOCIETIES

EDITOR'S INTRODUCTION

Chapter Ten, 'National Language and Language Planning in a Multi-lingual Society' (1972), was first presented as a public lecture at the University of Nairobi in May 1972, when Professor Halliday was a City of Nairobi Fellow, and Visiting Professor in the Department of Linguistics and African Languages, University of Nairobi. While on the one hand, acknowledging how it might seem somewhat perverse to want to interfere with what he describes as that most natural and unplanned of human activities, language, still, as he points out, "people have always interfered with each other's language, or tried to; and language planning refers rather to the attempt to control this interference, so as to make it positive rather than negative, and relevant to people's practical needs". Likening the linguist to the civil engineer who implements rather than dictates policy, Professor Halliday sees the positive role linguists can play in "help[ing] to avoid some of the disasters and disappointments that occur when a language policy is adopted that has no possible chance of succeeding". For the linguist coming at the issue from a functional perspective, it "is not a question of 'which language, this or that?', but rather 'which roles, or functions, for this language, and which for that?'."

In Chapter Eleven, 'Some Reflections on Language Education in Multilingual Societies, as Seen from the Standpoint of Linguistics'(1979), Professor Halliday points out how a functional linguistic approach is not only necessary for language planning, but also for tackling issues related to language education, including language teaching and learning, materials development and production, and teacher training. If the goal is to help learners "build up a resource for coping effectively with the demands that are made on language in real life situations and tasks", then what are needed are descriptions of languages based on "a conception of language as a treasury of resources".

In today's rapidly globalizing world, what happens when languages meet, or as some might put it, when languages collide? In Chapter Twelve, 'Where Languages Meet: The Significance of the Hong Kong Experience' (1998), Professor Halliday acknowledges the complicated cultural and linguistic dynamics which are bound to occur in a globalized community like Hong Kong. On the one hand, he notes the concerns of some over 'coca-colonization', and the negative impact on a community from over exposure to "the English-based, media dominated culture of modern commercialism: the high-powered consumerist advertising, the mindless sex-and-violence of television entertainment, the constant evangelizing of a particular political ideology and the like", but on the other hand, counters with the alternative view: "I am not sure there is clear evidence that people who know more English are necessarily more at risk. It might even be that they are better equipped to resist."

Chapter Ten

NATIONAL LANGUAGE AND LANGUAGE PLANNING IN A MULTILINGUAL SOCIETY*
(1972)

In this chapter I have tried to raise a number of questions concerning language that would be relevant to the present situation and current developments in Kenya and elsewhere; and to examine them from the perspective of a linguist, from outside, in a way that might be complementary to the more usual approach, which is that of someone from inside the country who is directly involved. My profession is linguistics, which means simply the study of language; not this or that particular language, but language in general – just as sociology is the study of society, not this or that particular society but society in general. I am not a specialist in any Kenyan language or any of the languages of Africa. But I have some acquaintance with questions of language development and language planning in different parts of the world, and it is this that I shall be drawing on here.

We live in an age of planning, whether economic planning, town planning or family planning; and language has not escaped from the general trend. Language planning is affecting the lives of millions of people all over the world. Yet language is one of the most natural and unplanned of human activities, and it seems somewhat perverse for anyone to want to interfere in it.

The real point, however, is that people have always interfered with each other's language, or tried to; and language planning refers rather to the attempt to control this interference, so as to make it positive rather than negative, and relevant to people's practical needs.

There are essentially, it seems to me, two kinds of language planning. One we might call the linguistic or internal kind of language planning,

*This is the text of a public lecture given at the University of Nairobi on 24 May 1972.

the external or social kind. The first of these is concerned
...ipulating the language, the second with manipulating the
...et us consider the second, the external kind, first. It has I think
...ects to it: the political aspect, the educational aspect and the
... aspect.

I have sometimes been asked why it is that linguists, if they claim to be the professionals in this area, do not pronounce with due authority on matters of language policy. "You're a linguist; you should tell us what to do!" This can perhaps best be answered by an analogy. The linguist is like a civil engineer. One does not ask an engineer to decide on a national policy for road-building. This is a matter for the people and their government to decide. The engineer is told where a highway is to be built; and then he goes and builds it. We can of course go a little further and call in the engineer as a consultant to ask his advice: will this project take a very long time, how much will it cost, should there be a temporary road here first, and so on? But it is still for us to decide whether to take his advice or not.

These are essentially the ways in which linguists are involved in questions of language planning. They can help to carry out policy, and they can give reasonably informal opinions, as consultants, on the practical needs and the consequences of whatever is decided (contrary to popular belief, linguists are usually very practical people). In this way they can often help to avoid some of the disasters and disappointments that occur when a language policy is adopted that has no possible chances of succeeding. But it is not the linguists' task to say what should or should not be done.

Educational language planning means deciding about language in the schools, and this is a familiar aspect of life in most multilingual societies. The distinguishing feature of educational language planning is that it cannot be avoided. Societies, and governments, can avoid taking explicit political decisions about national languages and language policy; they can simply let things take their course. But somebody has to take conscious decisions about what is to happen in schools, at least as regards media and subjects of instruction. What language or languages are going to be used as the medium of instruction, in different regions, at different ages; and what language or languages shall be taught as subjects: these are matters requiring deliberate planning and organized action. There is, however, a third aspect of language in school, which is something the planners do not decide; namely, what language is going to be the medium of teacher–pupil interaction? What language do the teacher and the children actually use when they are talking to each other? Even in a school, there are some natural processes at work, affecting the way people

220

behave; and the best we can hope for is that we should know what these processes are, and take them into account in our planning.

The cultural aspect of language planning refers to the fostering and promoting of literature and drama in a particular language or dialect; and to the planned use of radio, the press, the cinema and other media to enhance and extend the role of the languages of the community as vehicles of national and local culture.

There are conflicting views on the efficacy of political language planning. There are some people, including some linguists, who would hold that it never works, and who would lay the blame for the linguistically inspired acts of violence – so-called "language riots" – that afflict many parts of the world from time to time, on misguided attempts at organizing people's language behaviour. Certainly there is an impressive record of failure in language planning which those who hold this view can point to as their evidence. Others would seem to believe that planning is the solution to all language problems, and to various other problems as well; and they point to successful instances such as the adoption of Hebrew in modern Israel. The latter is certainly a very striking success; on the other hand, it is the only one that is usually quoted in this connection.

Most linguists would probably find themselves somewhere in between these two extremes, and agree that language planning in the social or political sense has a good chance of success if two conditions are present: (1) that it is going with the current and not against it: following, and not seeking to reverse, the direction in which events are moving naturally; and (2) that it is not in too much of a hurry. In other words, language planning will probably work if its aim is to lubricate and speed up – but not to speed up too much – a process that is taking place anyway. It will probably not work, according to the evidence, if it is going against the natural trend of events, or (a more difficult thing for the planners to accept) if it tries to change things too quickly. It is also expensive, in real human terms: it needs the mobilization of a large reservoir of human resources. This does not mean a massive programme of PhDs in linguistics; although at the same time it is worth stressing, perhaps, that enthusiasm by itself cannot entirely substitute for knowledge and training.

The central issue in language policymaking is that of the national language, and one of the major factors affecting chances of success is whether or not there is in the community a clear candidate for the status of national language. Let us take two great nations as examples: China and India. In China there is, in India there is not. In China, there could be no serious doubt in anybody's mind that the national language is Chinese, and, among varieties of Chinese, that it is North Chinese, the dialect known as "Mandarin", with the Mandarin of Peking as the received or standard form. All that was needed as far as decision-making was concerned was to define the status of the national language and of other languages relative to it – the other dialects of Chinese, the 50-odd minority languages of China, and foreign languages such as English and Russian. Where effort was needed was in directing and furthering the spread of North Chinese so that it could become a real and effective national medium; and this included the reform of the writing system, which I shall return to below.

In India, unlike China, there is no such obvious choice. The outsider thinks first of all of Hindi, which is the most widely spoken language of northern India and the one whose name stands for the whole country and its people. But other languages can claim as great a cultural heritage, both those that are related to Hindi, such as Bengali, and those that are not, such as Tamil. Hindi has neither the advantage of being spoken by a majority of the population, nor that of being neutral with respect to some major line of division in the country. Hence it has so far failed to arouse much enthusiasm, and successive governmental decisions regarding its national status have had to be rescinded. Among the attempts to make it acceptable is the famous "three-language formula", according to which for the sake of parity every speaker of Hindi would be required to learn one of the other 14 major Indian languages, but this has so far made little headway. There has been a great deal of discussion, but there is no real consensus among the people, and the complexities are formidable.

Two countries which have made rather more headway with their language problems are Malaysia and Singapore. In Malaysia the national language is Malay, and this has been accepted by the non-Malay speakers, including the Chinese who make up almost half the mainland population and form a majority in most of the towns. In Singapore, where nine tenths of the population speak some form of Chinese as a mother tongue, the national languages are Mandarin Chinese and English, and official policy is one of universal bilingualism. Chinese has been a medium of education for some two thousand years longer that English has, so there is no problem in this respect; and Singapore has two universities, one Chinese-medium and one English-medium. Malay is a language with a background not unlike that of Swahili. Its history can be traced back over several centuries; the Malays are Moslems, with Islamic educational traditions; there is written literature from the eighteenth century onwards; and Malaysia had a colonial history and had inherited an English-based educational system. A great deal of effort is being put into the development of the Malay language, both in general and as a medium of education at primary and secondary levels – and no doubt eventually at tertiary or university level also. There is an Institute, the Dewan Bahasa dan Pustaka ("Institute of Language and Literature"), which is responsible for dictionary–making, coining of new terms and the like, and a Linguistics Department at the University which gives training in linguistics at undergraduate and postgraduate levels.

Mention of the work that is being done with respect to Malay leads us into a consideration of the second meaning of "language planning", that which refers to the internal or purely linguistic aspects of it: that is, to working on the language itself. Here we can distinguish two headings: recording the language, and developing the language.

Recording a language consists in compiling dictionaries and grammars, which linguists refer to as "descriptions" of the language. This step must come first; one cannot 'develop' a language if one has not first described it. Linguists would take the view, however, that in a multilingual society **every** language ought to be recorded and described, whether it is going to be developed or not, and no matter how 'small' it is, in terms of the number of speakers. This is not just for scientific purposes, although naturally it is important to us as linguists that every form of human speech should be fully explored – for every language has something unique to offer. It is also for practical reasons. If a language is not to be developed, in the foreseeable future, this means among other things that the children who speak that language will be being educated in some language other than their own; and this requires a deep understanding of the similarities and the differences between their language and the one they are required to use in school. I would add one more point: to me, at least, it seems a basic human right that every people, however few in number, should have their language documented and recorded for posterity.

From the point of view of strict scientific truth, describing a language is an endless task. There can never be a complete description of any language; it is a logical impossibility, and even English, about which more books and articles and PhD theses have been written than about any other language, is far from being fully described and interpreted. But for practical purposes a good description, which means a semantic analysis, a grammar and dictionary, a phonetic analysis and a set of recorded texts – stories, myths, dialogues, etc. – can be done by a trained linguist, preferably a native speaker of the language in question, given proper facilities, in from five to ten years.

'Developing' a language is a very different matter, and the first question is, what does it mean? Are there under-developed languages, like under-developed countries? If so, presumably we should be up-to-date and refer to them as "developing languages". Or is the concept of 'developing a language' more like that of developing a film, bringing out what is already latently there?

Let us give a clear answer on one point. There is no such thing as an undeveloped language. All languages are fully developed instruments of human communication. Human beings have had language ever since they became human beings, some hundreds of thousands of years ago; and during this long period, language has evolved into a marvellous instrument for serving all the needs of man as an individual and as a social being.

Now, many of the needs which language serves are universal human needs, common to all societies at all times. We all have the same bodies and brains, and we all live on the same planet. Hence we all need to understand and to control the processes and the objects that we see around us, and to express our thoughts, our feelings and our perceptions. Every language is a highly evolved and technically beautiful precision instrument designed for these purposes.

But at the same time there are deep and significant differences between different human cultures; and these are also enshrined in language. There are differences of material culture; we live in different physical and technological environments – agricultural, pastoral, industrial; desert, mountain, seaboard, and so on. There are differences of social structure: different family types, different forms of social hierarchy, with tribes, clans, castes, classes, and so on. And there are differences of ideology and religion, different sets of moral values and concepts of what is acceptable and proper and what is not. Each language is adapted to its own environment, in the sense of the daily activities, the personal relationships and the spiritual and intellectual concerns of its speakers.

The consequence of this is that any language, when taken out of its environment, will appear somewhat imperfect and inadequate. It will serve the biological functions of language, those which are universal to the human species; but it will fall down on the cultural functions, which are not. (We cannot of course separate these, in the actual use of language; they are woven together into the fabric of speech. But they represent different aspects of the total resources of a language.) This does not mean, however, that such a language is undeveloped. It means simply that it has been transposed out of its context, and it has to adjust itself to meet the new requirements. The language of Shakespeare was not

224

undeveloped; but it would have been quite inadequate and inept for describing the workings of the internal combustion engine. Less obviously, but no less significantly, it would have been inadequate for a television commercial, a job interview or a circular from the Ministry of Education. These last do not depend particularly on technical vocabulary. They do, on the other hand, depend on language; but on patterns of meaning and forms of expression that are much more intangible than the mere words of a language (which you can put on cards and sort in a machine), and that are perhaps also more significant at the deepest level.

In the year 1622, a London newsprinter began using the news-sheet to announce the offer of his books for sale; this was the beginning of mass media advertising in English. It was soon followed by advertisements for wares of all kinds, from property and shipping to coffee and toothpaste; and naturally the goods or services offered were described in terms of praise, for example

> the drink called *Coffee*, which is a very wholsom and Physical drink, having many excellent virtues, closes the Orifice of the Stomach, fortifies the heat within, helpeth Digestion, quickeneth the Spirits, maketh the heart lightsome . . .

and so on (quoted by Blanche Elliott, 1962: 39–40). This development opened up a whole new range of linguistic usage. No doubt traders had always boosted their wares in the spoken language, and will continue to do so until there are no more salesmen but only supermarkets. But the use of mass media – billboards, the press, radio, cinema and television – creates a new semantic orientation in the language, new habits of meaning which had not been there before. Changes of this kind may involve, among other things, coining some new words. But words are only part of the story, and there can be significant extensions to the potential of a language which do not necessarily call for any new words at all.

In those countries where there are programmes of planned language development, through national language institutes, terminology committees and the like, the emphasis is almost always on the creation of new terms; and little or no attention is paid to semantic styles – patterns of meaning, ways of looking at things. The result is a tendency towards literal translations, from English or whatever is the dominant second language. School textbooks, news broadcasts and so on tend to look and sound like English meanings expressed in the words of another language. East Africans will readily be able to think of examples of this from Swahili; the late Professor Whiteley quotes a number in his book *Swahili: The Rise of a National Language*. It is very much easier to proceed in this way, by means of a form of translation, than to create in the other language, because it is difficult to preserve the essential spirit of a language when it is being extended very rapidly into new contexts. Such a thing takes time; and the question is whether it is possible at all.

Some people would say that it is not possible; that one cannot avoid changing the spirit of the language when new meaning habits are introduced. They would point out that, like many human innovations, the mercantile and industrial revolution took place only once in the history of the world, and has spread since then by diffusion; it may be that the deeper linguistic habits that go with it must also be spread by diffusion, and be superimposed on, rather than growing naturally out of, the linguistic resources of each different culture. Others would say that modern science and technology took over the particular world view of the Western European languages, adapting it but still preserving its essential character; and that there is no reason why other languages should not continue to evolve likewise in their own natural ways. We must admit that we simply do not know. But this, it seems to me, is where the writers and poets come in. They are not constrained by the laws of technology and science (nor, if we are not being too idealistic, by the need to advertise); and they are the ones who can follow the genius of the language wherever it leads them. In this way they can give a lead to others, and perhaps throw some fresh light on the question whether, just as there are other forms of literary and aesthetic experience than the drama, the poetry and the novel of the West, so also there may be other forms of scientific experience. The other day I read a report by a British Member of Parliament on his recent trip to China, during which he had visited a hospital and watched operations being done with the use of acupuncture in place of anaesthetics. He reports:

> The Chinese make no pretence of knowing why or how acupuncture works . . . one [theory] is that it operates on the 'channel system' of the body (a concept rooted in traditional Chinese medicine), and the second that it operates directly on the nervous system.[1]

I do not know what the channel system means; but it is a concept that has apparently saved many lives. One should not be too ready to dismiss the traditional learning of other non-western cultures, embodied in their languages, as an approach route to scientific thinking. Modern English did evolve, after all, however slowly and gradually, out of the language of Chaucer and Shakespeare; and, as the great American linguist Whorf pointed out, our own English forms of expression sometimes prove seriously inadequate and misleading in the context of scientific work.

So we should not think of the development of a language as being just the creation of an inventory of new vocabulary. Many people seem to think that language is simply words, and developing a language therefore simply a matter of introducing new words into it. But words are only a means to an end; they serve to express meanings (and they only do a part of that), and language development is a question of introducing new meanings. Sometimes, these are meanings that could not have been expressed before, just as the meanings of many new words, such as *electronic, transistor, synapse* or *antibiotic*, could not have been expressed in the English of a century ago. But often what is needed is new semantic orientations, the opening up of new paths within the meaning potential that already exists in the language.

This may help to put in their perspective some of the issues that are often debated about **how** new terms are to be coined. Are they to be created from inside the language, using its own word stock, by the process known to linguists as calquing; or are they to be borrowed from outside, from English or French or Russian or Arabic or Sanskrit or whatever other source is available? In the last resort, this will be decided not by an institute or a committee but by the speakers of the language, according to its natural tendencies. Some languages are mainly borrowing languages, such as English and Japanese, each of which has borrowed a good half of its vocabulary from elsewhere; others, such as Chinese and Icelandic, are mainly calquing languages, and draw on their own lexical resources; and there are many that adopt both methods. Attempts have been made from time to time to force a language to go against its natural inclinations, usually because it is felt that there is something disreputable about borrowing, as if it reflected some deficiency in the language (although nothing could be further from the truth); but such attempts have not been very successful.

There is much to be learnt from studying how industrial terminology developed in the West, particularly in Britain and France. Those who worked in the early industries – the mines, the textile mills, the railways – were country people, whose language, while perfectly attuned to an agricultural way of life, was not adapted to the environment of towns and factories. They had no idea of how to refer to the new machines and all their parts, and often they would create their own names based on resemblance to things that were familiar to them, like the beaks and snouts of poultry and farm animals, or on other forms of rural imagery. Popular and learned names frequently existed side by side, and

227

sometimes do so to this day; and words such as *cockpit* and *pigeonhole* remain as examples of the transfer of everyday terms into a technical register.

Information is still seriously lacking about the similar processes that are taking place in languages outside the Western world. One very important investigation has been carried out by the Indian linguist Bh. Krishnamurti, of Osmania University in Hyderabad. He is concerned with the development of Telugu, a Dravidian language spoken by some 30 million people in south central India; and he wanted to find out how speakers of Telugu, when they were faced with new processes – new machines, production techniques and so on – set about coining new terms if left to themselves with no committee on terminology or language promotion society to tell them what to do. He has studied three different occupational groups: farmers, fishermen and textile workers; and the results will be of immense value to the development of the language, in guiding the efforts of those who are working on the vocabulary, writing textbooks, translation manuals, and the like. It sometimes happens that those whose task it is to further the development of a language have little or no idea of how it has developed in the past or how it would continue to develop if left to its own devices.

The question of **how** new terms are created, important as it is, is essentially a question of form, of the **mechanics** of language development. Borrowing is just one way of coining words, neither better nor worse than another way. But whether or not they borrow the words to express them, all languages borrow meanings. No human group lives in total isolation (with rare exceptions such as the Stone Age people recently "discovered" in the Philippines, as reported in the *Daily Nation* of 8 April 1972). Ideas are diffused, new objects and new institutions spread around; and in this way new meanings get incorporated into the semantic system of the languages of the people who take them over. In the long run it probably does not much matter how the meanings are expressed as long as they are fully domesticated, fitted snugly into the hearth and home of the borrowing language. It does not do to have too many rules about what dress the new meanings must wear before they are fit to be admitted into the family, especially if the rules are made without a deep understanding of the existing manners and customs of the language.

The development of a language is essentially a functional concept. It means extending the functions of a language, the range of uses to which it is put. It is impossible for any language to be adapted to all uses in all human cultures. English, for example, which is reasonably well adapted to Western science and modes of thought, is not well adapted to Indian philosophy or Chinese medical theory. It suits the needs of a Yorkshire farmer but not those of a Lake Rudolf fisherman. It is well tuned to the European conception of theatre, poetry and prose; but it is not well tuned to African poetry, as Okot p'Bitek recognizes when he writes about his *Song of Lawino* that it is "translated from the Acoli by the author who has thus clipped a bit of the eagle's wings and rendered the sharp edge of the warrior's sword rusty and blunt, and has also murdered rhythm and rhyme". English can **become** adapted to African literature, as it is doing through the work of African poets and novelists, because all languages are infinitely adaptable; but the process takes time. And at the end of this process, the language might be scarcely recognizable to an Englishman.

Let us not exaggerate this point, however. If we look at Elizabethan English, it seems odd to us; and it will still seem odd if we modernize all the old spellings and word formations. This is because the meanings expressed are different and the cultural contexts unfamiliar. There is quite a lot in it that we cannot understand; and there would be even more that Shakespeare could not understand if he were to look at the English of today. But people, and cultures, do not remain static. They may rest for a time, but in principle they are always on the move; and they take their language with them and adapt it to their new conditions of life. The problem of change facing a 'developing' language today is nothing new in human history. What is new is just the speed at which the changes are being expected to take place.

In English, the changes took place slowly. It is 350 years now since the London newsprinter started the trend for advertising in the press; it is 300 years since the founding of the Royal Society, and 200 years since the economic origins of the Industrial Revolution and the beginnings of industry in the modern sense. I come from Leeds, in the West Riding of Yorkshire, one of the first areas in the world to be industrialized; where country people crowded into the towns, and in the process gave up their local, rural speech and developed new patterns to suit their new environment. Their language was urbanized and standardized, apparently in about one generation. Yet they did not entirely lose their regional culture and language, and they still write poetry in it. Here is an example:

Little Miss Robot (Fred Brown)

> Ah went to t'Department
> To settle a bill

229

A young lass were vampin'
An ovver-sahzed till.
She passed back mi noate
An' change fer mi brass.
A near-human till –
A mechanized lass.

This is not rural verse, it is urban, and it has words like *department* and *mechanized* in it; but it is still the language of the region. The country people speak the original local dialect, which is quite difficult for others to understand; the townspeople have given this up, and they speak a form of English that is really a compromise, recognizable as the national language but with a markedly regional flavour. Or rather, they often speak **more** than one form of English; and this brings us back to the notion of multilingualism, because many English people are multilingual, not in the sense that they speak more than one language, but that they speak more than one dialect, and they use their different dialects on different kinds of occasion. In some situations, it is necessary to 'talk proper'; in others, it would be absurd to talk proper, and they will use the local dialect. The two – or sometimes more than two – are complementary to each other as regards the functions they serve.

This is exactly what happens in a multilingual community. It is typical of multilingual communities, as we know from many parts of the world, that the various languages spoken are complementary to each other in the way they are used; there is a division of labour among them. People who speak more than one language in their own community generally use each one in certain types of situation only; they do not use them all interchangeably, in all situations (see, for example, T. P. Gorman's study of the use of English, Swahili and the vernacular by educated speakers of eight of Kenya's major languages).

One of the difficulties with this observation, however, is that we have to have some idea of what is meant by "type of situation". Sometimes this is assumed to mean simply who is talking to whom, who are the *dramatis personae*, as it were: what language do you use when talking to your father, for example (cf. Gorman: "Swahili is characteristically used more frequently than English in conversations with fathers and less frequently in conversations with siblings, although there are exceptions . . ." (1971: p. 213)).

But as we all know, and as Gorman is well aware, we may not always talk to a father in the same language; so we could try looking at the question as one of topic, or subject matter: for example, we could ask a hospital doctor what language he uses to talk about medical matters. But here again we will probably get the answer: "It depends." He might well tell us that he converses with his patients about their ailments in Luiya, gives instructions to the nurses in Swahili and lectures to his students in English.

So we may combine both personalities and topics, as Gorman does when he asks the children questions such as "What language or languages do you speak to the following members of your family at home when talking about school?" These questions are typical of those that are used by 'sociolinguists' to build up "language profiles" of multilingual societies. They answer the question expressed in Fishman's words as "Who speaks what, when, and to whom?"

But there is one big gap in this formulation of the question. In order to be truly significant, the question to ask is rather 'Who speaks what, when, to whom, **and why**?' In other words, in his choice of language the speaker takes into account not just who he is speaking to and what about but also what is going on, what the nature and purpose of the exchange is, which way the situation is going as it were.

So the idea of a linguistic situation, which is a fundamental one if we are trying to understand and interpret the use of different languages in a multilingual society, really involves three distinct though related factors. The first is who is taking part, and what kind of relationship exists between the person speaking and the person or people he is speaking to. It is the role relationship that matters, rather than the identity of the individuals. The second is what is going on, in the sense not just of what is being talked about, but in the rather deeper sense of what is the speaker trying to achieve. This does not mean of course that there is some deeplaid plot or hidden motive being pursued every time we open our mouths; but we are always doing something when we talk, however innocent and casual this may be. The third is what part the language is playing in the total situation; whether we are talking or writing, and in what mode – narrative, didactic, poetic, humorous, persuasive or what. These three factors taken together will tend to determine which language out of the speaker's total repertoire is used on a given occasion.

This phenomenon, of moving from one language to another, selecting according to the situation, is known as code switching. It goes on in all societies where the individual members are multilingual. But code switching is not by any means restricted to communities where more than one language is spoken. It also occurs, very commonly, between different dialects of the same language. As in my own home country, so in many parts of the English-speaking world, including both Britain and the United States, a large number, and in some areas perhaps the majority of speakers, speak more than one variety of English; typically, one kind which is more standard, and another which is more dialectal, characteristic of a particular group within the community, regional, socioregional or ethnic. They switch between the two – or sometimes more than two – dialects of English in exactly the same way that multilinguals switch between their different languages. Dialects, of course, are not so clearly distinct as different languages, so that the switching may be more gradual with intermediate stages between the two extremes; but even this is not very different from the kind of language-mixing that multilingual speakers commonly indulge in, using sentences that are half in one language and half in another, as is so strongly objected to by linguistic purists. Whiteley gives some examples in his book *Swahili: The Rise of a National Language* (1969: 105).

This takes us to the question of dialect and standard language. The notion of 'language standardization' is a familiar one in linguistics, and, as the suffix *-ization* shows, this is also a type of planning, one which consists in creating a standard language; not out of nowhere, but out of one form of an existing language, with or without deliberate modifications. So we have Standard English, Standard Chinese, Standard Swahili. The process has something both of the internal and of the external aspects of language planning: internal because it involves selecting among, and sometimes modifying, forms of the language itself, its pronunciation, grammar and vocabulary; external, because it involves directing people's language habits, telling them how they should speak or write.

The emergence of a standard language is, again, a natural process that takes place in the course of history; and planning means interfering in the process and speeding it up. But this kind of language planning is by no means new; it has gone on in Europe in one form or another for many centuries. An example is the conscious development of standard Czech, for which the originator has his statue in a public park in Prague, the only statue of a linguist anywhere as far as I know. In France there is an academy that legislates on matters of linguistic form and style.

Of all aspects of language planning, standardization is the one that can provoke the strongest resistance. The fact that it is necessary to standard**ize** means that there is no accepted standard as yet, no consensus, and every speaker naturally thinks his own version of the language is superior. (And so it is, for him.) So, do we want the English of London or that of Edinburgh, the Italian of Rome or of Florence, the Swahili of Mombasa or of Zanzibar?

Part of the resistance to standardization is due to a natural assumption that 'standard' implies 'having prestige' which in turn implies 'the best'. If one variety of the language is selected as standard, it must be better than the others, and this constitutes a slight on those whose language is **not** 'chosen'. In fact this is quite untrue. Intrinsically, no language is better than any other language, and no one dialect of a language is better than any other dialect. One variety becomes 'standard' for reasons that have nothing to do with the nature of the language itself, but simply with its use. Again, it is a question of the functions for which it has developed. Pekingese Mandarin is accepted as standard Chinese, without question, for a number of reasons all of which are concerned with the history of its use: it is the language of the city which has been the political capital of China; it is the traditional language of the court and the administration; and it is the language in which the great popular (non-classical) literature has been written for the past six or seven centuries. But it is not intrinsically better or more beautiful or more rich in potential than the other dialects of Chinese.

Mention of China raises the question of the reform of the script, a subject that has recently come up again in China following a period of quiescence. In the early 1950s there was much talk of reforming the Chinese script; a governmental committee was working on it, and in a massive public relations operation they received more than ten thousand suggestions, including no fewer than 600 complete programmes of script reform. Then suddenly the question was shelved. A "romanized" orthography (that is, one using the same alphabet as English) was accepted and put to some marginal uses, but nothing more was done. Then recently the distinguished writer, scholar and politician Guo Moruo reopened the issue; and, following the political developments of the 1960s it seems not impossible that script reform might now be carried through. The traditional Chinese script had, in fact, already been simplified, the number of characters (written symbols) in current use being reduced from some 5,000 or 6,000 by about half, to somewhere around 3,000, of which about 2,000 will suffice for many purposes. Also, methods of teaching children, and adults, to read and write had been greatly improved, so that the Chinese could achieve universal literacy, which is their declared goal, without discarding their ancient script. Nevertheless it is in many ways cumbersome and expensive; and it is also a barrier to the spread of the standard language, since it makes it much harder for a dialect speaker to learn Standard Chinese. The roman alphabet, if less decorative, is more practical in that respect.

Standardization of a language does not usually involve the complete reform of the script; but there are often decisions to be made about how words are to be spelt. The notion of a 'standard orthography' is in fact very deep-rooted; most people assume that there must be just one correct way of writing a language, even though this is quite a recent idea in modern Europe – until the seventeenth century, one could spell English more or less as one liked. The corollary to this is that, once an orthography is standardized, it is very difficult to change it; people are conservative in these matters, and react to any suggestions for reforming the spelling rather as if they were being asked to walk on their hands instead of their feet.

There is one problem associated with standardization that is very often overlooked, which is this. If one adopts a standard language, one has to ensure that people have the means of learning it; and this is often the central issue facing a multilingual society, since if anyone is being required to learn a new set of language habits he has to have adequate opportunity for doing so. If this is true in a multidialectal situation, where the "standard" form to be learnt is merely another version of his own language, it is much more true in a multilingual situation, where the "standard" is a totally different language. In other words, if there is to be a national language (or more than one), which everyone is expected to know, at any rate to some degree, in order to be a full member of the community, then there must be some solid foundation for bringing about what linguists call a "stabilized bilingualism".

As William Mackey, the Canadian linguist who is one of the world's leading experts on bilingualism, points out at the beginning of his book on the subject, "bilingualism, far from being exceptional, is a problem which affects the majority of the world's population". This does not necessarily mean, of course, that the majority of the world's population can actually speak more than one language; it may mean merely that they are at a disadvantage if they do not. In Western Europe, for example, one needs to be able to speak English, French and German, both for cultural reasons and for purposes of communication with particular countries: by and large, English for Britain, Ireland, Holland and Scandinavia, French for France, Belgium and Italy, and German for Germany, Austria and Switzerland, as well as for the rest of Central Europe. But until a few years ago most people in Britain and most people in France were quite incapable of speaking and understanding any language but their own.

However, the great majority of Europeans, even if they learn other languages, are educated in their mother tongue, and their mother tongue continues to play the principal role throughout their lives. This is not without exceptions; there are minority peoples in Britain, France, Germany, Russia and elsewhere whose languages are not available for secondary or higher education (or in some cases for education at all), and do not serve many of the functions for which people need language in the course of their lives. And there are many countries, nearly all the smaller ones in fact, in which one is considerably handicapped without some control of at least one foreign language; as well as a few countries, like Belgium, Switzerland, Finland and Yugoslavia, which are **officially** bilingual in the sense that their populations fall into different linguistic groups each of which is supposed to learn the other's language, although it does not always work out that way.

Now I think we can say definitely that, **other things being equal**, the mother tongue always serves one best. In an ideal world, while everyone would certainly learn more than one language, he would not **have** to do so in order to be a full and educated citizen of his own country: education, and the other primary functions of language, would all be available to him in his mother tongue. As Shaaban Robert wrote, "mother's breast is sweet and no other satisfies" (he wrote it in Swahili, needless to say). But we do not live in an ideal world, and other things are not equal. At a rough guess, out of the 3,000 to 4,000 languages in the world, probably about one-tenth function as media of education; these, of course, include all the major languages, covering some 70 per cent of the world's population, but that still leaves something like one person in every three or four speaking as his mother tongue a language that is not recognized as an educational medium, and is unlikely to be in the foreseeable future.

In this category are included the majority of people in the complex multilingual societies of Africa. It is inevitable for a variety of reasons, economic, political and social, that in this situation priority should be given to the development of just one language, or at the most a small number of languages, as having "national language" status. Speakers of other languages have to be weaned from the forms of speech that were their mother's milk. Now it should be made clear that this weaning takes place anyway, in the sense that the language we speak as adults differs widely from what we learnt as infants, even if it is the same language; adult speech is very different from child speech. Only, if it is the same language, there is a continuity of experience that is lacking if we switch to another language for educational and other purposes. Therefore, we must take account of the fact that the discontinuity is very much less, the gap very much narrower, if the transfer is into another langrage of the same region.

This is because languages of the same region tend to have the same semantic structure: that is, they organize their meanings in the same way.

This may be because they are related; in the words of M.H. Abdulaziz, there is "a high degree of isomorphous semantic structuring which makes it easy for a speaker of one Bantu language to learn another language of this family, and even to develop a native speaker's competence in it" (1971: 161). But this is not only true of groups of **related** languages such as the Bantu languages. If languages have lived together for a long time, whether related or not, they grow alike, just as people do. So we could replace "Bantu" here by, say, "Kenyan". Kenya has languages from at least three and probably four totally unrelated families; yet they are substantially similar in the meanings they express, as can be seen from the fact that it is easy to translate from one to another. Hence it will always be easier, if one is moving away from the mother tongue, to grow up and to become educated in a language from nearby than in a language that is culturally and geographically remote. As Dr Joan Maw says, "we must face the fact that in moving from one language to another in an educational system we are not simply changing the medium through which facts about geography or arithmetic are conveyed; we are, however imperfectly, presenting a new Weltanschauung" (1971: 231). Let us stress that this is **not** just a matter of common myths and common religious beliefs, important as these may be; it is a matter of habits of meaning, such as I referred to earlier.

Let us try and give a brief example. In general this is a phenomenon that can be shown up clearly only by a detailed consideration of long passages in context; but we can perhaps gain some idea from a single English sentence.

> Despite all that has happened since, Gresley still personifies steam; the impact of the later Pacifics was very small in relation to their numbers, and the only really significant product of the post-1941 era was after all no more than an assembly of Gresley standard parts.

This is neither poetry nor abstract scientific theory. It is taken (slightly adapted) from a popular book about railway engines. It contains hardly any technical terms – "Pacific" is the name of a class of engine; in any case technical language is the easiest kind of language to translate once the terms are there. But it would be quite difficult to translate this into Chinese or Japanese, or I imagine into Swahili.

It would not be very difficult, however, to translate it into Welsh. Welsh is a language only very distantly related to English; but the two have existed side by side for 1,500 years and the cultures have interpenetrated. As Mackey points out (1967: 44), "In some areas of Wales . . . more than half the population changed their language [to English] in less than a generation because of the development of industrialization in that area"; the industrialization came from England, under English management, but the Welsh found no difficulty in moving from one language to the other. (For this reason, it is difficult for a language like Welsh to survive, because the speakers find it perfectly easy to express their culture in the dominant language, English. In fact, much of Welsh culture is still expressed largely in Welsh, and this is no doubt why the language does survive and flourish; in contrast to the other Celtic languages of the British Isles, Irish and Gaelic, which in spite of strong political support are fast dying out, largely because the cultural life of the Irish and Scottish peoples is lived almost exclusively in English).

This factor of "areal semantics", as it is known in linguistics, is clearly relevant to the national language question. It can fairly be claimed, in respect of Swahili, for example, that it is easier for a speaker of another Kenyan language, not only, say, Kikuyu, which is related to Swahili, but also Luo, which is not, to be educated and employed through the medium of Swahili than through the medium of English; and this reinforces the arguments of those who, for the many more immediately obvious reasons, pragmatic and symbolic, of national unity and cultural development, favour the spread of an indigenous language, such as Swahili in Kenya. At the same time, policymakers and members of the public often draw attention to the need for continuing with the use of an international language, such as English, for reasons of economic development, of international (including African) cooperation and the like; and they point to the fact that in many highly developed countries, such as Holland, Sweden and Czechoslovakia, a very fundamental status is accorded to an international language – much of the higher education takes place in English, or French, or German, or Russian, and nearly all learned and technical publications are in one or other of these languages. As I said at the beginning, it is not for the linguist to make policy; he would not be allowed to, anyway. But there is, I think, a valid contribution that he can make to the discussion of these issues, and it is this. As a linguist sees it (and he is not just trying to sit on the fence!) the issue, in a multilingual situation, is not "which language, this or that?" but rather "which roles, or functions, for this language, and which for that?" I have tried to stress all along the value of a functional approach to the problem; just as 'language development' is a functional concept, a matter of broadening the repertoire of uses of a language, so also the national language question can best be seen in a functional perspective, as a question of assigning to each of the languages concerned its most appropriate set of functions in the life of the community and the individual. The division of roles is likely to be shifting and flexible rather than rigid and hard and fast; but there is no reason at all why the various languages should not co-exist in a stable relationship in which they are complementary rather than conflicting, and in which the use of any one language strengthens rather than weakens the use of all the others.

As in so many areas, the key man is the teacher. He is the one who has to convey the riches and the uniqueness of the subject he is teaching; and this applies no less to the teacher of language. Every language is the best language in the world; the teacher needs to be able to bring out the special and unique qualities of the language he is teaching or using as a medium. I have taught three different languages in the course of my career, and in each case demonstrated that the language I was teaching was the finest ever created. We can be proud of the ability of a language to borrow freely from other languages; or, equally, of its ability to do without borrowing. We can be proud of its rhythm, its intonation, its vowels and consonants – because they are beautifully simple, or because they are richly complicated. We can be proud of its morphology and its grammatical structure. Most of all, we can be proud of its ability to mean, as shown not only in its elevated moments but also in its everyday uses; the sayings, the rhymes and verses, the humour that it brings to daily life. Every language is a monument to the human spirit.

In this discussion I have taken my examples from different parts of the world, rather than focusing attention exclusively on East Africa. This, I hope, needs no apology or explanation. However much one may be concerned with the practical problems of one's own country and people, it is valuable to take some account of what is happening elsewhere. No one nation has exactly the same language problems as another; the "language situation" in any country is always a unique combination of different features. But any one of these features is likely to turn up elsewhere in some form or other; and there are often useful lessons to be learnt, both negative lessons, from other people's mistakes, and also positive ones, from their successes.

Note

1   "A Churchill in China", Winston S. Churchill MP, *Observer Review*, 30 April 1972.

Chapter Eleven

SOME REFLECTIONS ON LANGUAGE EDUCATION IN MULTILINGUAL SOCIETIES, AS SEEN FROM THE STANDPOINT OF LINGUISTICS (1979)

The present seminar marks the beginning of a new series of seminars at what is now called the Regional Language Centre. It seems appropriate that this change of name, denoting that the Centre now includes within the sphere of its responsibilities languages other than English, should be accompanied by a new emphasis on linguistic and cultural diversity, in which diversity is seen not as a troublesome complication having to be tolerated but as a positive and significant feature in the life of a nation. In the "Aims of the Seminar" it is stated that "multilingualism together with cultural diversity offers a vast potential of resources"; and it is this perspective that provides the context for what I have to say.

By the term "language education" I understand not simply the teaching of languages but (to quote the "Aims" again) "such areas as teacher training, curriculum and syllabus construction, instructional language of the classroom and the socio-cultural aspects of language teaching". In other words, the seminar is concerned with every aspect of language and learning, and also with the functions of language, and the value that is placed on language, in the educational process.

Approaching the question of language education in multilingual societies from the standpoint of linguistics seems to imply considerations of two kinds: (1) practical tasks of educational linguistics, and (2) problems of interpretation, the deeper understanding of the processes that are taking place, without which the approach to the practical tasks may be uninformed and lacking in direction. It is important to face both ways, towards theory and towards practice, so that the two can reinforce each other: so that the theory is balanced and relevant, and the practical steps that are taken are based on understanding and insight.

To say that linguistic and cultural diversity is a positive feature of the community implies more than merely recognizing that it exists, more even than recognizing it and taking pride in it. It implies that this diversity has significance for the culture, that it is a significant aspect of people's lives. The fact that there are different modes of meaning in the community has now become part of the total environment within which meanings are exchanged. In this situation it is no longer possible to treat monolingual societies as the norm and to regard all others as special cases, as if they were somehow deviations from the norm.

To express this in the terms of linguistics, we invoke the concept of language variation. As linguists see it (although they have taken a long time to reach this point), language is a variable system; there is linguistic variation both in the life of the community and in the life of the individual. A totally homogeneous society, in which everyone speaks the same way as everyone else all the time, is as much a fiction as a totally heterogeneous society in which no two individuals speak alike. Constructs like these are idealizations; they are the opposite poles that it is useful to keep in mind because we know that reality lies somewhere in between.

In real life, it typically happens that an individual does not speak the same way as all other individuals. More than that, he does not always speak the same way as himself. He switches; and the switching takes two forms. He may switch among different languages, and he may switch among different registers. Let us look at each of these in turn.

1 The language a person uses depends on who he is: his geographical and social origins. Everyone is born into some micro-community, whose language he learns. Typically, the micro-community is a family, and the child learns the language that is the language of the family and of his parents, although even in the family there will often be two or more languages spoken. When he starts to meet members of other linguistic micro-communities, one party has to switch to the language of the other; or else both parties switch to some agreed third language that is known to both and accepted by them as appropriate for this purpose.

2 The register a person is using depends on what he is doing at the time: the particular social situation in which he finds himself, and the part that language is playing in that situation. This may be the informal, non-technical register of everyday conversation, spontaneous, lively and fluent; or any one of a variety of more formal or more technical registers, spoken or written, and ranging (as far as the part played by language is concerned) from situations of a more active kind, various forms of collaborative work and play in which the language used is confined to

brief exchanges of instructions and most of the activity is non-verbal, to contexts such as meetings and public lectures, where talk is almost the only thing that matters.

It is possible to translate between different languages. People generally assume that different languages consist of the same meanings, but with different means of expression. In real life we know that it is not quite as simple as this; we search for equivalences and often cannot find them. By and large, however, the assumption is valid. It is not normally possible, on the other hand, to translate between different registers, since registers consist of different meanings. Technical English cannot be translated into English gossip; the two are not different modes of expression but different modes of meaning. There are perhaps occasional instances where translation between registers is possible, when a special ritual style that has come to be associated with a particular purpose is replaced by a more informal popular style. Recently the leading motor car insurers in Australia brought out a new insurance policy which they called a "Plain English Policy"; this was a "translation" of a more formal document the public had found difficult to understand. But even this was objected to by a legal expert, who claimed that the meaning was no longer the same as in the original.

It is clearly possible to go through life using only one language; but it is scarcely possible to go through life using only one register. Typically all adults are multilingual in the 'register' sense: they use language in a variety of different ways, for a variety of different purposes, and hence they are constantly changing their speech styles. This ability to control different registers is a natural human ability; it is built up in adolescence, and school plays a significant part in it. It also seems to be a natural human ability to control different languages, given the right conditions for doing so. Not all adults, obviously, are multilingual in this other sense, of controlling different languages. But if we extend the notion of variation in language to include variation in dialect, we shall find that very many more adults are multilingual in this sense: they may not switch among different languages, but they do switch among different dialects of the same language. Some linguists have suggested terms that might be used to cover both, meaning 'language or dialect of a language'. The British linguist Trevor Hill used the term *tongue*; the American C.-J. Bailey talks of *lects*, and refers to multilingualism as *polylectalism*.

In principle, choice of language (tongue) and choice of register are independent of each other; they are determined by different sets of conditions. In practice, however, the two tend to be closely bound together. In most societies where more than one language or dialect is used, there is some kind of a 'division of labour' among them; certain kinds of activity, such as commerce or schooling, are carried out in one 'tongue', and others, such as informal conversation in the home or playground, in another, or in various others. In this way a particular register comes to imply a particular language or dialect; and this leads to the emergence of standard languages (which are really standard dialects) and national languages – varieties that are specially associated with those areas of activity that are supra-local in character. The influence of the register is so strong that even people from the same locality will often switch from the local to the standard variety when the register is one that by implication transcends local differences.

This interplay of language varieties, the tendency for a given register to determine a given dialect or language, reflects something that is a fundamental aspect of life in complex societies: namely the variable scope of social interactions. The exchange of meanings between two or more people at any one moment may involve the home, the neighbour-hood, the locality, the region, the nation or the world. All these represent, in an idealized sense, different speech communities, each with its own language or dialect; and since there are infinitely many homes in any one region or nation, most people are faced with the need to vary their dialect or language if they want to move very far along the scale. There are no doubt some who use the same dialect of the same language in all the social contexts in which they find themselves: the 'standard English' of an upper-middle-class speaker from London or Los Angeles may vary relatively little whether he is at home with his children or at an inter-national conference of heads of state. But such people are in a minority, and in most parts of the world, including all of Southeast Asia, there is considerable linguistic variation not only between different levels of social context but also within one level. In a typical multilingual society, the national language may differ from all the languages of home, neigh-bourhood or locality; and at any of these levels there may be more than one language in use, not only more than one home language but often more than one national language as well. At the upper end of the scale, in regional, national and international contexts, there is scope for language policy and planning; whereas at the lower end, whatever developments take place usually take place naturally.

In using these terms "local", "regional", "national", and so on, we are setting up a conceptual framework, one that will help in interpreting the variable scope of sociolinguistic interactions. Such a framework is of course an idealization; the actual situations of language use are by no means neatly separable into such clear-cut categories. It should be made

242

clear, moreover, that using language in a 'national' context does not necessarily mean communicating with people from outside one's locality or region; nor does an 'international' context necessarily imply a situation of talking to foreigners. These labels may simply indicate the subject matter of the discourse; as Blom and Gumperz discovered in Norway, even a group of villagers meeting in their own locality would tend to switch to the standard language when talking about national affairs. The labels are useful for indicating the extent of the communication network that is presupposed or implied by a particular instance of linguistic interaction. To say that a particular language is a "regional language" or a "national language" does not by itself tell us in what actual encounters any actual speaker will be using it. What it does tell us is the status that is accorded to that language in the community, the symbolic value that is placed on it by the members, and the meaning they attach to its use; and from this we can make intelligent guesses about the contexts in which it will typically be heard.

This scale of language status, from the home upwards, can also be interpreted as a developmental one, relating to how children learn language; it represents the widening linguistic horizons in the natural development of a child. A child begins by building up the linguistic patterns of the home, and he learns these almost entirely from his own family. Next come those of the neighbourhood, which are learnt mainly from his playfellows, the peer group. At this point society intervenes, and we put the child in school; he now starts to learn language patterns from his teachers. The school is a new environment for him, and may impose considerable discontinuity, both linguistic and cultural; for this reason it is all the more important to stress the essential continuity of the phases of language development through which he is passing as he grows up. Although a child coming into school may suddenly find himself coping with one or even more new languages, the linguistic experiences he is going through, and through which it is to be hoped the teacher is helping to guide him, are closely related to experiences he has been undergoing in one form or other since he was born; the more he is able to build on what he knows, the less formidable will be the task of assimilating what he does not know.

From an early age, a child is doing two things at once: he is learning language, and he is learning through language. At the same time as he is building up for himself the systems and structures of his mother tongue (or family tongues), he is also using these resources to build up something else, namely a potential for interpreting and interacting with his environment. It is often argued, in connection with second-language learning in school, that a language is most readily and naturally mastered through being used as a medium for learning something else. Those who make this point usually have in mind using the language as a medium for studying something else; studying geography in English, for example, as a way of mastering English. It could be pointed out in support of this view that this is in principle no different from what the child has been doing in his first language all along; he may not have been using it to study, but he has certainly been using it to learn. It is important to ask, then, what are the basic functions for which he has been learning his first language.

In the most general terms, there are two. First, the child has been learning to build up from experience a picture of the world around him, and of his own place in it. Second, he has been learning to interact with others; to act on them and, through them, on his surroundings. We shall call the first *experiential* and the second *interpersonal*.

In its experiential function, language enables a child to order his experience: to reflect on the processes that are taking place around him and inside him. Language provides him with names for things; with structures for representing events; and other resources for the narrative mode. With these resources he develops a range of semantic strategies which help him to learn. An example of one of these strategies is the strategy of partial analogy, or 'same but different'. Here is an extract from the speech of a little boy, Nigel, aged 1 year 11 months, showing this strategy at work. Nigel's parents were discussing plans for a visit to the aquarium, and Nigel was listening. He did not know what an aquarium was, but was trying to work it out from the conversation. This is what he said to himself: "We not going to see a rao [lion]. Vopa [fishes]. There will be some water." In other words: we're going somewhere that is like a zoo, but not with lions; with fishes instead – and water for them to live in. By relating the unknown word *aquarium* to something in his experience that was like it and yet different (a zoo) he was able to arrive at an understanding. It is very rewarding to listen to young children's speech, from this point of view, and to hear how they think things out for themselves.

In its interpersonal function, language enables a child to interact with, and to act on, the people in his environment: to take part in the goings-on, as distinct from merely talking about them. Language enables him to express himself, to influence others, and to engage in all kinds of conversational rhetoric – in this case, through the resources of the dialogue mode. Here the strategies the child develops are strategies not of learning but of 'doing'; they are ways of projecting himself onto other people. Since language by itself cannot change anything, then if language is to be a means of action, whereby the child exercises control over things, getting objects given to him and services performed, it has to be directed towards people so as to influence them to act for him. (This is why we use the term "interpersonal" to refer to language in its active function.)

These are the two basic functions of language. Language is at once a means of action and a means of reflection; and by the third year of life a child has learnt to do what adults do, namely to combine these two kinds of meaning in a single utterance. The utterance itself may be very simple, at least superficially; a 2-year-old may still talk mainly in one-word sentences. But in meaning these are already complex; even the simplest kind of message, say a demand such as *Drink!*, implies the experiential meaning '(I recognize) discomfort due to thirst, and (I know) what will relieve it' and the interpersonal meaning '(I want you to) pay attention to how I feel, and do something about it'. An adult form such as *Please will you get me a drink?* certainly contains more indications of good manners; but it conveys essentially the same twofold message. When the child starts to seek information by asking questions, which is a favourite pastime of children in all cultures, he is again using language in both its interpersonal (active) and its experiential (reflective) functions. So when Nigel at age 1 year and 9 months asked *Why broken that?* he was (i) expressing his own state of mind, together with a demand for appropriate action from the other person in the form of a response ('I want you to tell me – I don't know'), and (ii) exploring what was going on in the world around him. As soon as we use an adult-like language, one that has words and structures in it, these two modes of meaning, the active and the reflective, become inseparable.

This is perhaps the most significant aspect of the language that the child is building up for himself, and using as he builds it. The process of learning language is a continuous one; it starts, as we said, in the home, and continues in the neighbourhood and in the school. It is important to stress that language education does not begin in the classroom; as far as language learning is concerned, when a child goes into school the school is taking over responsibility for a process that has been happening for some years already, and that will continue to happen outside the school as well as inside it. What the school can do is extend the children's language experience along new paths and into new fields. Now, if the cultural context is a multilingual one, the principle of 'learn language, learn through language' applies with no less force. In the 'natural', pre-school and out-of-school environment, each language is a means of access to experience, a vehicle through which new knowledge can be gained. Teachers and educators who recommend teaching school subjects in a second language are applying the same principle; they want to use that language as a window on new realities. This is what lies behind the view that if we want primary school children to learn a new language, we should use that language for teaching a school subject. There are, of course, some circumstances under which all the teaching takes place in a language that the children do not know; this may be unavoidable. But where at least some of the instruction is in the mother tongue, or in a language that the children know well enough already not to have to be devoting their main energies to learning the language instead of using it to learn with, the learning of a second language in this kind of instrumental context, where they are learning it at the same time as, and as a by-product of, using it as a medium of instruction seems to make good sense to children, no doubt because that is the way they learnt their mother tongue in the first place.

Is learning through a second language a difficult task for a child? It is certainly not beyond children's normal learning powers. The nature and extent of the difficulty that is involved will be partly a matter of the gap between the languages concerned, the "language distance", as it has been called. Language distance is a complex notion, and a number of factors enter into it; but it includes one important component that we might call "socio-semantic" distance – that is, social and cultural differences in the meaning styles. Socio-semantic distance tends to be the product of two variables: (1) difference of status, along the dimension referred to earlier, of local–regional–national–international; and (2) difference of culture. The further apart two languages are along these two dimensions, the more difference there is likely to be between them in their characteristic modes of meaning and of expression.

The distance between two languages, in this sense, does not depend on whether the two languages are historically related. As Dr Nadkarni (1987) points out, although the Dravidian languages of South India are quite unrelated to Hindi, they have close cultural ties with it; so for children who speak a Dravidian language it is likely to be easier to switch to Hindi than to English. This kind of cultural affinity between unrelated languages is found in many parts of the world. Languages do not exist in isolation; they impinge on each other, mix, and grow alike. (I am not referring to their pronunciation, although it is also true that languages often grow to sound alike, as a kind of outward symbol of their semantic affinity.) In Singapore, for example, English and Chinese are growing more alike; they are gradually coming closer together in the kinds of meanings they express. But this process takes time. When languages start

246

to mix, as they tend to do in these multilingual contexts, the mixture both facilitates and symbolizes their concomitant development as alternative modes of expression for the same culture.

Other things being equal, it will usually be easier to learn another language from within one's own culture than one that is culturally remote, because there is the same reality laying behind it. Greater distance means more discrepant realities, and different realities create different semantic systems, between which translation may be extremely difficult. (Dr Sadtono's second-person pronominal studies are a case in point.) But we have to be careful here. As anyone knows who moves among different cultures, there is a relation between language and culture; but it is complex, indirect and difficult to define. It is a relationship that is to be sought in the whole system of meanings and meaning styles. We cannot, in general, relate isolated features of a particular language to isolated features of its culture. At the most we may be able to point to a certain number of lexical items, names of objects, institutions, social roles, and so on, which are found in this particular culture but not in others. But each language as a whole has its own characteristic patterns, and these have been shaped by, and also have helped to shape, the culture of which it is a part. This special flavour that each language has is what makes it difficult to translate it, to develop it in imitation of others and to teach it to foreign learners.

Teachers and language educators have been grappling with these fundamental problems with the aid of contrastive studies, in which two or more languages are systematically compared. The methods are promising, but the results so far have tended to be disappointing. This is partly, no doubt, because there has not yet been close enough collaboration between linguists and materials developers; but it is partly also because there is an inherent conflict here between two different kinds of assumption. The learner does some 'transferring' from his mother tongue, and it is important that he should do; there is so much that is in common among all languages, in their most fundamental patterns and functions, that a learner may take a great deal for granted (which he does quite unconsciously) and his assumptions will often turn out right. But when it comes to what is variable among different languages, the learner is being asked to create a new language for himself. Contrastive analysis will help us to predict the errors he is likely to make; and despite recent assertions to the contrary, errors of "transfer" or interference, although they are not the only kind of error a student makes, do account for a substantial proportion of them. But contrastive studies depend for their effectiveness on the careful and penetrating description and interpretation of each language in its own terms. It is the description that brings out the uniqueness of a language; a good description is one which enables the teacher to demonstrate that the language he is teaching, whatever language it is, is the very best language in the world, unique in its resources and its semantic power.

Good descriptions of languages are not a luxury sought after by idealistic linguists. They are a practical necessity, both for language educators and for language planners and developers. A language is much more than the sum of its dictionary words. For a language to function effectively as a vehicle of science, it needs not just scientific terms but scientific discourse; registers in which scientific concepts and arguments can be presented and discussed. In order to develop such registers it is necessary to understand how the language functions in its natural state; not only how it creates new terms (and every language has its own ways of doing this) but also how it is used in the casual encounters of daily life. The cornerstone of a language is spontaneous, informal, everyday conversation; if a language loses its base in the home and family, there is a danger of its becoming a fossil, a museum piece. There have of course been various instances where a language that was no longer anybody's mother tongue continued to be used for a long time for scholarly and administrative purposes, for example classical Chinese; but such languages had once been spoken, and had been in continuous use in the community from that time on. Nowadays, we no longer tolerate the scholarly and bureaucratic elites that these languages helped to maintain; we expect the language of learning to have its roots in the daily life of ordinary people. This is the problem with artificial languages, such as Esperanto: they have no children, no informal exchanges. A language that is used only for formal, official or learned purposes is rather like a computer language; one cannot express one's feelings in it – and it never changes. The leading edge of linguistic change is to be found in casual conversation among family members, friends or colleagues.

It follows from this that descriptive studies need to be made of all the languages of the community, whether international, national, regional or local; including the little languages, the vernaculars that may never find their way into a school or government office. These are the foundation of the national culture in family and neighbourhood, and need to be cared for and respected as long as there are speakers who live by them. It has sometimes been suggested that the serious cultivation of local vernaculars would pose a threat to the newly emerging national languages, still struggling for recognition and status. Many people felt that, when major efforts were needed to promote the recognition and development of languages such as Bahasa Indonesia, Bahasa Malaysia and Filipino, it would be a mistake to deflect any of the very limited resources that were available on to the local vernaculars, and to dedicate highly trained manpower to the tasks of describing them, developing writing systems for them and introducing them into the primary school. This is a very forceful argument; but nevertheless I think it must be rejected. There is good reason for thinking that, far from being in conflict with the national language, the local languages serve as one of its main supports. They are as it were at the base of the pyramid, solidly embedded in the daily lives of the people in the community. As Dr Sibayan implied, a language is both the symbol and the expression of cultural vitality; every language, however small, needs to be taken seriously and studied, not only by outsiders, but also by people from among those who speak it. Every language creates for its speakers a social and personal identity, a sense of the community they belong to; it is never easy for others to get the same 'feel' for a language as those who grew up with it have.

This process of creating a social and personal identity for ourselves is not something we set out to do deliberately, by conscious deployment of the functional resources of our language. Rather it is a natural result of our everyday use of language to reflect and to act. As children, we learn our language as a resource, a "meaning potential" for serving a range of different functions; and in so doing we use language to construct a picture of the world we live in. It is this world picture, our interpretation in words of the people and things around us, that defines our cultural identity.

I have recently been concerned, as linguistic adviser, with the making of a documentary film for use in teacher training. The film is a story of two adolescents who are applying for a job: we see them being interviewed for positions as sales staff in a department store; we see them starting work in the store, interacting with customers and with the other staff; we see them in school, at home and in the open, with their friends, their family and their teacher. The film is called *Demands on Language*. Its aim is to give an idea of the range of functions we expect our language to serve for us, the variety of purposes we expect to achieve by talking (and listening, and reading and writing) in the course of our daily lives. Despite the fact that the film is very short – less than half an hour – and is built up around a single theme, it gives a remarkably true picture of the way language works in different social-functional contexts.

This brings us back to the concept of "developing a language". Earlier in the chapter I referred to the question of register, the functional variation in a language that is associated with its different conditions of use. As I see it, the process of developing a language is essentially a functional one: that of step by step increasing its range of registers until it is used for all the functions for which the community uses any language at all. All languages have the potential for being developed in this way; equally, no language was born fully fashioned for life in the twentieth century. It is true that modern scientific research and international diplomacy cannot be carried out in a local vernacular; but neither could they have been carried out in Chaucer's English. The difference is that while English and French had three or four centuries in which to develop, today we expect the process to take place in three or four decades or even in three or four years. If we take a longer view, however, we can recognize that every language already is, in a deeper sense, a developed language – in the sense that at some time or other it has developed to meet the needs of the culture that produced it. There is no such thing as an "undeveloped" language. What language planners have to do is to ensure that the languages they are concerned with continue to develop, in whatever directions (including new directions) are needed, and at the speed that national development policy requires. It is not to be wondered at that a language that is subjected to pressures of rapid change tends to become mixed in the process. There is nothing new or surprising in this; no language could be more of a mixture than English, or Japanese, and these languages work quite efficiently in all their varied spheres of operation! It may turn out to be an advantage for a rapidly developing language to take in some of its innovative elements from outside.

For a linguist, questions of language development and language function are of interest not only for practical reasons but also because they help to shed new light on the nature of language itself. To put it in everyday terms, language is as it is because of what it does; or rather, since in itself language cannot 'do' anything, because of what people do with it. In other words, language has been shaped by the demands that are made on it by society. We see this most clearly when we start to look behind the vague conception of language as a means of communication, to establish what are the ways of meaning that all languages have in common – the basic semantic functions such as those of 'language as reflection' and 'language as action' that I was describing earlier; and then beyond these again to the words and structures through which the meanings are expressed. It then becomes clear that these semantic functions provide the principle on which the grammar of human languages has evolved. Grammatical systems are organized in such a way that in the production of an utterance, when a speaker settles on the meanings that he wants to express, he first selects the various semantic components – the different kinds of meaning – independently of each other, and then expresses all of them together in words and structures in a single combined operation.

The processes just referred to take place entirely unconsciously, at least in a language the speaker knows well. A theoretical interpretation of them, which forms the basis of a functional theory of language, might be considered to be of interest only to a professional linguist. But it has important implications when we come to describe a language for purposes relating to its use in the community, for example in the context of language education, or of national language development. To explain language in functional terms is to interpret language as a resource. From the community's point of view, that is what it is; but such an interpretation runs counter to what has recently been the prevailing mode of interpretation in linguistics, where language has been treated not as resource but as rule. This image of language as a set of rules, a system of formal operations for building structures, was inherited from traditional Western philosophical grammar and reinforced by the transformational syntax of the 1960s; it may have some interest for a theoretical linguist, or rather perhaps for a philosopher of language, but it is not very helpful to language educators and language planners, and has had a very negative impact on applied linguistic activities in general. For most applications of linguistics it is necessary to look beyond the forms of language at the meaning potential they express. For example, every language has certain resources for the expression of mathematical concepts, which can be taken up and used as the basis for teaching mathematics in that language (cf. UNESCO 1975). No grammar of sentence structures can adequately bring these out; they will appear only in a 'grammar' that describes semantic choices. If the descriptions of community languages are to be of real value to the community, the conception of language as a set of rules will need to give place to a conception of language as a treasury of resources.

Let me end by relating this point to three important aspects of language education in multilingual societies: language teaching and learning, materials production, and teacher training.

1 A language learner is learning to make choices: this word or that, this structure rather than that. In the process he makes mistakes, sometimes very subtle ones, like that of the Singapore student whose essay I was marking some years ago in which she had written the sentence *I like the taste of foreign furniture*. We know what she meant, and can guess what Chinese expression she had in mind when writing it; but it will not do in

English, because if you say in English that you like the taste of something it means you enjoy eating it. We can suggest various alterations to put it right: (i) choose the word *style* instead of the word *taste*; (ii) choose the expression *taste in* instead of *taste of*, which then must be personalized – it must be somebody's taste in furniture that I like; or (iii) choose the *please* type of clause instead of the *like* type, with *I* becoming modifier of *taste: foreign furniture pleases my taste*. All these can be seen as options to be explored, with different consequences following from each; they can be explained in the terms of a functional description of English.

2 The underlying aim of materials production for language teaching is in the fullest sense to bring out the meaning potential in language: the potential that inheres in the system of the given language, and the potential that inheres in its various contexts of use. For example, we may design materials through which the students can explore (i) the various possible ways of making a request in English, and (ii) the ways of making a request that will be most effective in a particular type of situation, such as in a shop, at a meeting, or in an enquiry office. The contexts may be those for which the language is actually being learnt, for example English for nurses, or English in banking; or they may be contexts that have been specially set up to facilitate the learning process. The principle is the same in either case: that of helping the learner to build up a resource for coping effectively with the demands that are made on language in real-life situations and tasks.

3 The training of teachers in language education is a specialized problem that needs separate discussion beyond the scope of this chapter. The only point I want to make here is again a linguistic one: it concerns the image of language that a language teacher has, and that he projects on to those he is teaching. In many instances this has been a rule-based image – often in fact a rule-bound image, in which a language is treated as if it was simply an inventory of rules of good behaviour. (This image has been reinforced by the tradition of "rules" in linguistics.) There has been a great deal of structure in the picture, but not nearly enough system. Taken by themselves, linguistic structures tend to appear at best arbitrary, and at worst downright perverse; in order to explain them, we have to look at the system that lies behind them. Of course, the structures do have to be mastered by anyone learning the language; but other things being equal it is easier to master something that makes sense than something that does not, or that has not been shown to make sense. Whatever else is achieved by it, the training that a teacher receives in language education should at least enable him to develop a feeling for the systems

252

of a language, so that he can make sense out of the medley of structural facts that language learners are typically presented with.

This will serve to make my final point. It is obvious that, in one sense, every language is arbitrary – there is no natural connection between the meanings and the sounds. A language may refer to H_2O as *water* or *acqua* or *shui* or *ayer* or *pani*; any one form is as good, and as neutral, as any other. This is the sense in which the term "arbitrary" is usually used in linguistics, although "conventional" is perhaps a better label for this concept in English. But in other respects languages are not really arbitrary. Grammatical structures reflect the meanings they express; differences between registers reflect the different functions for which language is being used. A functional linguistic theory is one that attempts to explain the forms of a language by relating them to the functions that language has evolved to serve. In a multilingual society those with responsibilities in the field of language education, whether in teaching, teacher training, curriculum planning, materials development or policymaking, are inevitably concerned with the community languages in their functional settings; descriptions of these languages in functional terms provide an important source of information for their work. It should not be forgotten that the converse is also true: the experiences and practices of language education in multilingual communities provide an important source of information about language for those who are trying to develop more useful kinds of linguistic descriptions.

Chapter Twelve

WHERE LANGUAGES MEET:
THE SIGNIFICANCE OF THE
HONG KONG EXPERIENCE
(1998)

We are constantly being reminded, nowadays, that we live in a global culture. Various nouns collocate with global: global economy, the global market, the global village, and so on; but one word that does not figure there is language. We have no "global language", only several "international languages" such as English. Yet if culture and language are interdependent, as we are often told they are, a global culture should imply a global language.

The problem lies with the word "culture", which is used in so many different senses – and likewise with its Chinese equivalent *wénhuà*. In one sense, the whole Eurasian continent, from China and Japan to Britain and Spain, is all one single culture, and has been for many generations: the culture of agricultural settlement, Iron Age technology, centralized political structures and the like. But there never was any common language; and while there were populations that did not share in this common culture, it was not language that kept them out.

There is a narrower sense of "culture", where we talk of Chinese culture, British culture, and so on, which does seem more closely tied to language: we are all familiar with the problem of trying to express Chinese concepts in English or English concepts in Chinese. This is because a language and a culture have typically evolved together: the culture is construed in the language. But the bond between language and culture is not a rigid one: it has often happened in history that a people have maintained their culture while taking over a different language; and on the other hand cultures are constantly changing, and the language does not hold them back. There is always a process of coadaptation taking place.

254

Very often when people refer to their own culture, they are looking towards the past: they mean the traditional culture they grew up with, and the reason they become aware of it is that it is already changing into something else. In that sense of culture, those of us taking part in this conference come from a number of different cultural backgrounds. But we are also, if we look around in the present, members of another culture that we share: the culture of education, with its classrooms and its conferences and committees and its books and teaching materials and all the rest. And this culture is, or is fast becoming, truly global; not everyone yet has access to it, but there is no section of the globe where some features of it are not in place.

Shared cultures defined in this way do tend to favour a common language, because they depend on verbal interaction: people need to write and talk to each other, so they can ongoingly exchange their experiences and their ideas. It is in this context that languages become internationalized, as has happened in the past (for example Arabic, in the Islamic world) and as has been happening with various languages today – principally English. No one planned this; no central authority decreed that it should happen, or which languages should be selected – if they had done, English might well have been rejected, because of its part in the older British and the newer American imperialisms. There is nothing special about English: it is no better, and no worse, than other languages in its potential for taking on this kind of role; it just happened to be around, in the right places at the right times. Of course, when I say "happened to be", there is always a particular historical reason: in Hong Kong, obviously, it was the language of the colonial power. Now, it is the language in which much of the world's computer software is written, consumer goods are advertised, and popular songs are sung; and for the time being, at least, it is the language of the world's only remaining superpower.

Why then do people not feel threatened by English, with its record of political and cultural domination? I think there are three main reasons. One is that people know they do not have to buy the culture along with the language: there are millions of people using English around the world who have no interest whatever in British or American culture. The second is related to this: they know they can co-opt English to their own uses, as it has been co-opted in many places as a medium for other literatures, other cultures, other forms of social organization. (To put this in technical linguistic terms, English gets *resemanticized* in African, Indian, Singaporean and other contexts.) And thirdly, people know that English is not the only language of world standing. Chinese and Spanish have similar numbers of speakers, and others such as German, Russian, French, Malay-Indonesian, Arabic, Hindi-Urdu and Japanese are all internationally current in one way or another. If English starts to lose the clear advantages it enjoys today, those operating in these global cultures will soon give it up in favour of something else.

It is in this sort of context, I think, that English will find its place, along with Chinese, in the Hong Kong of the immediate future. Hong Kong people are lucky, of course, in that both their languages have strong currency and high status. Their spoken form of Chinese, Cantonese, used not to have high status, at least within the Chinese-speaking community; but this has changed precisely because of the economic and cultural standing of Hong Kong itself. No one in Hong Kong thinks Cantonese will overtake Mandarin; but I should be surprised if it simply retreated to its previous position as a remote provincial dialect. Now the mother tongue, for children growing up in Hong Kong, is Chinese: the place of Chinese in their lives is entirely assured. The one that is problematic is English. If English is to have a place – not because Hong Kong was founded as a British colony, but because of its international role – this is going to require a steady input of energy, energy that is carefully fostered and also thoughtfully directed.

What has been learnt, in the last generation or so, that will enable Hong Kong people to direct that energy, to use their resources for language development in the most effective way? I have not been able to observe the Hong Kong scene for any continuing period at first hand; and I certainly would not presume to assess the successes or failures of your language teaching policy and practice. What I have are some impressions, from visiting, from talking to people, from reading your journals and attending your conferences and seminars; so what I am saying today should be heard as very tentative observations about present achievements and possible directions for the future.

It seems to me that there have been four great strengths in the Hong Kong experience of language education up to now: the universities, the government agencies, the professional supports and the teachers. The universities (and I include here all institutions of higher education, whatever their state of becoming) have given a lead in a number of important respects. This has been, first, in their own educational practice, in language centres, departments of education, and so on; second, in their research, in linguistics and related areas, including the application of linguistic theory in other fields (such as audiology) – where they have recognized that successful application must always be powered by effective theory; thirdly, in defining needs, goals and levels of attainment that are relevant in the Hong Kong context; and fourthly, in training teachers – without which no combination of the other three inputs, however powerful, could hope to succeed.

The Hong Kong government, faced with a massive demand for educating all its new citizens, recognized in good time what were the specifically linguistic elements in the task. They introduced the concept of 'language in education', and set up the special Institute for Language in Education, which inaugurated the highly successful series of international conferences beginning in the mid-1980s (notable for bringing together colleagues from China and from other Asian countries also). The Department of Education has carried out research projects, and supported research at other institutions, in the field of language education, and has set up educational goals and standards of attainment, curriculum models and guidelines and other instruments of educational policy.

Professional support has come, on the English teaching side, particularly from the British Council, who remain (despite constant tinkering from successive British governments) probably the most professional English language-teaching organization in the world. The Hong Kong Association for Applied Linguistics has maintained links with international professional bodies and institutions, and at least one internationally known publication (*Hong Kong Papers in Linguistics and Language Teaching*) has provided a forum for original researches by Hong Kong scholars. Again, increased professional contact with centres in China has been a very positive development in recent years.

It is obvious that the Hong Kong teachers themselves, faced with a rapidly growing school population, have had a strong commitment to their educational task. In this they were maintaining the traditionally positive Chinese attitude to education, but also recognized that if Hong Kong was to develop as a centre of industry and commerce its children had to be highly literate technologically. So the schools have been notably successful in nurturing a community of educated young people, as can be seen both in the quantity and in the quality of those going on to higher education, and in the standards that Hong Kong's tertiary institutions have attained.

We can say perhaps that these four agencies – the universities, the Hong Kong government, the professional bodies and the teachers – have collectively defined what I called "the Hong Kong experience" in the field of language education. If we first of all interpret "language education" more narrowly, as the teaching of languages, then they have had to do three things: to train all pupils in English; to train some pupils in other languages such as German, Japanese, French; and, more recently, to introduce Mandarin. People often compare Hong Kong with Singapore, usually to Hong Kong's detriment; and it is true that Singapore's language education has been notably successful. But Singapore is linguistically very diverse: there are substantial minorities of Malay and Tamil speakers, and the Chinese there speak many different dialects, so both Mandarin and English serve very obvious local needs: Mandarin as a unified language for the Chinese community, and English as a language for the nation – over and above the importance that each of the two has internationally. But Hong Kong has no local requirements of this kind. Hong Kong is very homogeneous language community: virtually everyone speaks Cantonese, and since Chinese is a language that has long been used as a medium of literature and technology there is no need to move into another language just in order to become an educated citizen.

I do not think it will be a problem for Hong Kong people to learn Mandarin once they come to interact regularly with people from other parts of China (although I will make a further comment on this in a moment). And since other languages are intended for limited numbers, the one remaining problem lies with English. Paradoxically, perhaps, as long as Hong Kong was a British colony most people didn't feel much need to learn spoken English: they took it for granted that some (those with tertiary education) could speak it fluently, and the country was on the international circuit anyway. In any case the status of English was rather ambivalent as between 'international language' and 'language of the colonial power'. But from now on the situation will be different. Under Article 9, English and Chinese are to be the official languages of the Hong Kong Special Administrative Region of the Chinese People's Republic; hence the status of English is much more clearly defined. This does not mean that we can predict exactly what the linguistic profile of Hong Kong will be in 2025; the language situation is continually evolving, and the world will be a somewhat different place. But it does mean that English will have a defined role in making the region "special"; and this in turn will make special demands on the new curriculum and on the resources that are made available to support it.

What have we learnt from the work of the recent past? It is easy to be sceptical, if we look back over the last 50 years, about the fads and fashions and fallacies that have come and gone in the theory and practice of language teaching – especially perhaps in teaching English as a foreign language. But some new things have been learnt, and some old knowledge has been reaffirmed and become more widely known. Here we need to adopt the wider interpretation of what "language education" means, because the context for evaluating these new or old ideas is the concept of language education itself. I see this as comprising two vectors. One is the vector of time: the development of the individual learner, from infancy through childhood and adolescence and into adult life. This is a continuous process, in which children's powers of language – their "meaning potential" as I call it – are all the time being developed and enlarged, first in home and neighbourhood and then also in primary and secondary school. The other vector is that of the domain of the learning: first language ("mother tongue"), second language(s), the subjects of the primary and secondary curriculum. All such educational learning is activated in, and mediated through, language: just as, when you learn your first language, you are also, at the same time, learning **through** that language, using it to build up your picture of the world, so also when you go to school and start learning about nature and about society, and then later on you move into the technical fields of physics, mathematics, history and so on, you are learning the **language** of these disciplines – "language across the curriculum", as it came to be called when this was first generally recognized. We could set this up as an informal matrix, as in Figure 12.1.

domain of learning \ age/stage of learner	infancy 0-1½	pre-school 1½-5	primary school lower 5-8	primary school upper 8-11	secondary school lower 11-14	secondary school upper 14-17	tertiary 17-
protolanguage	✓						
mother tongue (L₁)		✓	✓	✓	✓	✓	✓
second language(s) (L₂)		?	?	?	?	?	?
(initial) literacy (L₁ (?))			✓	✓	✓	✓	✓
primary subjects (numbers, nature, people)				✓			
secondary subjects (science and mathematics, humanities …)					✓	✓	✓

Figure 12.1 Matrix showing domain of learning with age/stage of learner

This shows that language is at the centre of all instructional learning (that is, where you learn by being taught), from initial reading and writing all the way through to the technical disciplines of natural science, social science and the arts.

We can take this together with certain things that we have known for a long time, but that are continually being exemplified and confirmed: that for people to become effectively multilingual, two conditions hold true. One is that they should start on a second language early in life, and certainly before the onset of puberty (and there is no doubt about this, even where for political or economic reasons it has been found expedient to deny it); the other is that they should encounter the second language in contexts of active participation and learning experience. If a second language is "picked up" in home or neighbourhood, this will automatically be the case; but where the second language is started and only kept up in school, then it needs to be used as the medium for studying something other than itself – or at least for some recognized sphere of activity in which the learners are required to participate. In other words it needs to be ongoingly "authenticated" in ways that make sense to a child.

The problem for educational authorities is this: that teaching a foreign language effectively to children is one of the hardest pedagogical tasks there is. You need a specialized professional training; and you need to know both languages well – both the language being taught (L_2) and the children's mother tongue (L_1). It is different if you are teaching adolescents or adults: in that case, if they are beginners, then the teacher needs to know their L_1 well (but need not have a vast knowledge of the L_2); while if they are advanced it is the other way round: the teacher needs to know the L_2 well (but need not have much knowledge of L_1, so heads of English departments who have on their staff native speakers of English who don't know much Cantonese exploit them for the advanced classes but keep them away from the beginners!) But when you are teaching children of primary-school age, you have to feel at ease in both languages; and this makes the task especially demanding.

Let me add one further comment on this. If you are teaching mathematics, then although the learners may ask you highly sophisticated questions, the problems they raise will always be instances of some well-defined mathematical system, one that rests on established general principles. But a language teacher may be confronted at any time with problems which – although there always are general principles behind them – are so complex and open-ended that every instance seems to bring up something new. However much you know about English tenses, for example, or the English definite article, or English phrasal verbs, you will always meet up with instances you cannot explain. So what non-native teachers need is constant access to data: some reliable source of information that can be easily consulted as and when it is needed. Such a linguistic database could go some way towards helping those many non-native-speaking foreign language teachers who continually feel exposed because of their imperfect knowledge of the language they are being expected to teach.

And this in turn raises another point: what is the future going to be of Hong Kong's English pronunciation? There will almost certainly be for a time what sociolinguists call a "lectal continuum", a spread in the way people pronounce the language ranging from 'most like English' at one end to 'most like Cantonese' at the other. (Similarly with Mandarin: there will be those who speak putonghua with a near-Beijing pronunciation, who can even distinguish *zhi chi shi ri* from *zi ci si*, and manage to get away from the strict syllable timing of southern speech; and others who will be barely intelligible in Mandarin except to another speaker of Cantonese.) I do not know how the goals for the pronunciation of English in Hong Kong have been, or are going to be, formulated; I do not imagine that Hong Kong people will try to sound like native Britons or North Americans – why should they? But there is still a significant distinction to be drawn. Educated Singaporeans who use English in regional or international contexts are readily understood when they speak it; whereas educated Japanese, who are typically highly competent at reading English, often fail to be understood in speech – because English has not been widely taught as a spoken language, and Japanese learners tend to pronounce it as they pronounce their English loanwords (as written in *katakana*). Now, if I may express a personal opinion, it seems to me that the biggest failure in language teaching in the last half century has been the failure to keep up the effective teaching of pronunciation. It is my impression that in China, where the standard of English among those (relatively few) who learnt it remained amazingly high right up to the 1980s, this has now been considerably undermined – I have heard Chinese professional tour guides whose English is largely unintelligible. But it is important to maintain standards of pronunciation, because (even in the age of e-mail) many Hong Kong people will need to interact with outsiders through spoken English – and also because the semantic foundations of any language lie in its spoken forms. In my view every teacher of a foreign language ought to be trained in phonetics, up to the level where they can **teach** their pupils what to do with their vocal organs in order to produce the appropriate sounds. I know this view is out of fashion today; it is regarded as unrealistic, or even undesirable. But I think this is a case where early investment in teacher training can both save the learners' time and significantly improve their performance.

Before I finish, let me mention two issues that often arise in discussions about language policy and planning. It is often said that people learn languages according to their perceived needs; what they don't perceive a need for, they won't learn. Like many such generalizations, this tends to be true by default – but it is not the end of the story. People tend to define their needs in a rather short-term perspective, and to be swayed by received attitudes rather than reflecting on their own experience. This means that it becomes the job of the authorities to foster and support a longer, more realistic view. And while adolescents and adults formulate their own perceptions, for children it is the grownups' perspective which counts – that of their teachers, and also that of their parents. Language attitudes begin and are reinforced in the family; if the family becomes the locus of rich language experience, the burden of the language educators is correspondingly lightened. That is something that takes time; but it would be wrong, in my view, to suggest that a community's perceptions of language needs cannot change. They can; and they not infrequently do.

The other issue that gets brought up a lot is that of what we might call coca-colonization. Many thinking people feel that if the community as a whole achieves a high level of competence in English they will be massively exposed to the English-based, media-dominated culture of modern commercialism: the high-powered consumerist advertising, the mindless sex-and-violence of television entertainment, the constant evangelizing of a particular political ideology and the like. These are real anxieties and need to be publicly addressed. I do not know the answer; but I am not sure there is clear evidence that people who know more English are necessarily more at risk. It might even be that they are better equipped to resist.

Not all multilingual societies are made up of multilingual individuals: there are some where each individual typically speaks only one of the community's languages. But the conception of a biliterate, trilingual Hong Kong does imply that each individual will be expected to be competent up to a certain level in Chinese and in English. This is not an easy goal to attain. But I believe it is immensely worthwhile. I well remember my own first experiences in learning to speak and read Chinese – and let me break off here to insert a personal note. It is almost exactly half a century since I first arrived in Hong Kong, on my way to

China to study Chinese at Peking University (where in 1995 I had the great honour to be made a guest professor); and it is nearly 20 years since I first met my co-presenter here, Professor Hu Wenzhong, one of the most distinguished scholars in the field of English language from China (who has himself been awarded an honorary doctorate by my own former University of Sydney). As I say, I remember my experiences in learning Chinese, which had a very practical purpose: for service in the British army in the Second World War, where Britain and China were allies. But beyond these very practical needs, where the languages were necessary for doing a particular job, I felt a greater sense of the richness of human experience, and of the versatility of the human brain. I don't want to romanticize about what is, in the last resort, a way of improving your chances – knowing languages is a means of getting as far as you can in a challenging and difficult world. The tasks of language education are hard work for all concerned. But this is, surely, a moment to celebrate: to celebrate what Hong Kong has achieved, linguistically, educationally and culturally, in the past; and to look forward to the unique status that Hong Kong will occupy in the next half century as a place where two major languages from the far ends of the Eurasian continent co-exist on truly equal terms.

PART FOUR

CONTEXTS OF LANGUAGE EDUCATION

EDITOR'S INTRODUCTION

"Language," writes Professor Halliday in 'The Notion of "Context" in Language Education' (1991), "is implicated in some way or other in all educational activity". Unless the resources for meaning have been put in place, one cannot truly be said to have 'learnt' something. Calling for theory-based research into the linguistic aspects of the learning process, he suggests approaching this "single, unitary process" from four perspectives, stated in terms of what the learner has to do: "(1) process and produce text; (2) relate it to, and construe from it, the context of situation; (3) build up the potential that lies behind this text and others like it; and (4) relate it to, and construe from it, the context of culture that lies behind that situation and others like it".

'Language Across the Culture'(1986) was first presented on the occasion of an RELC Seminar on *Language Across the Curriculum*. While at first glance, language across the curriculum would seem "a diversifying concept", in terms of both variation according to subject (e.g. scientific vs. literary language) and situation (e.g. group discussion, lecture notes), on the other hand, Professor Halliday sees it as "a unifying concept; not only because it embodies the unity of the curriculum itself, through the integrative notion of language as a means of learning, but also because it enables us to relate the registers of the classroom and the laboratory to their counterparts in the world outside – on the construction site, in the shopping centre, in the factory and on the farm." It is through its diversity, or "dynamic potential", that language is enabled to meet the diversity of demands put upon it, and maintain "the flow of meaning across the culture".

How can the language of a former colonial power become a positive force in a forward-looking post-colonial society? The answer lies in its potential for resemanticizing in response to new contexts and conditions. Out of this tension between two distinct semiotic systems emerges what Professor Halliday calls "a new meaning potential". Elaborating on this point in Chapter Fifteen, 'Contexts of English' (1994), Professor Halliday writes, "This appears clearly in the new literatures of the Commonwealth, which already feature many writers of international standing and acclaim. This kind of interpenetration is not new in the history of language; it has happened ever since human groups began splitting up and then recombining in new formations. What is new is the scale on which it is happening, the cultural distances that are traversed, and most of all perhaps the great diversity of semiotic contexts that are being created in this way (for example, the new literatures are widely read outside their place of origin, including by speakers of old varieties of English)."

Chapter Thirteen

The Notion of "Context" in Language Education (1991)

1 Language and language education

My concern here is with 'context' as a notion that is useful for thinking with when one is investigating language. But I want to consider it not in relation to linguistics as a whole but in relation to one particular domain of linguistic activity, namely language education. This does not mean that theoretical issues will be absent; but they will be approached from a specific angle.

Education, I take it, means enabling people to learn; not just to learn in the natural, commonsense ways in which we learn in our daily lives, but to learn in an organized, progressive, and systematic manner according to some generally accepted principles about what people ought to know. So when we qualify this as "*language* education", what have we added to the definition?

In one sense, nothing at all; all education takes place through the medium of language. I don't mean all **learning**: human beings learn a great deal without the medium of language. But all **educational** learning is mediated through language; so why "language education"? We have come to use this term, over the past 10–15 years, partly to make explicit that very point: to bring to the foreground a motif that emerged in the 1960s, of "language across the curriculum", when it was first widely recognized that there was an essential language component in learning science or learning history or learning anything else that had a place in school. But at the same time, in talking of language education we are asserting that there is a relationship between language as a **medium** of learning, in this sense of "language across the curriculum", and language as the **substance** of what is being learnt, in the teaching of foreign or

269

second languages, of the mother tongue, of reading and writing, of grammar, composition, and so on.

What is common to all these activities is expressed, in part at least, by the word "language". Language is implicated in some way or other in all educational activity; so we need to be aware of it, to recognize when learning problems are in some sense problems of language, and to conduct theory-based research into the linguistic aspects of educational processes. We know that this view is coming to be shared by the community when we see developments such as the Centre for Studies of Language in Education at the Northern Territory University in Australia, or the Institute of Language Education in Hong Kong. This tells us that there is a field of activity, or research and development, identified as the study of language in education, where we investigate how language functions in various educational contexts, and by doing so, seek to improve our educational practice.

I used the expression of language "functioning in educational contexts", and I think we have to bring this notion of language functioning in context explicitly into the discussion. What is distinctive about "educational linguistics", if I may be allowed to use that term as a shorthand for investigating language for educational purposes, is that we are concerned always with **language in context** (Martin 1993; Rothery in Hasan and Williams 1996). We are identifying certain kinds of activity in which language has a central place, and finding out just **how** language comes to play its part. What do people actually read, and listen to, and say, and write, when they are being 'educated'? What do they expect to achieve through using language; and how do we tell, and how do they tell, whether they have achieved it or not?

We generally take this notion of 'context' for granted. The context is some sort of environment; it's what's going on around, where language is somehow involved. And if we're talking English we then manipulate this in the typical English way, expanding the word by various derivations: we have the adjective *contextual*, as in *contextual features* or *parameters*; then the verb *contextualize*; and since language can be *contextualized*, it can also be *decontextualized*, and then of course *recontextualized* over again. And each of these, in turn, can become an abstract object, like *recontextualization*. So I think we should put this word "context" in inverted commas for a while and ask what it actually means: problematize it, if you like.

1.1 Context of situation

Originally, the context meant the accompanying text, the wording that came before and after whatever was under attention. In the nineteenth century it was extended to things other than language, both concrete and abstract: *the context of the building, the moral context of the day*; but if you were talking about language, then it still referred to the surrounding words, and it was only in modern linguistics that it came to refer to the non-verbal environment in which language was used. When that had happened, it was Catford, I think, who suggested that we now needed another term to refer explicitly to the verbal environment; and he proposed the term "co-text". But how did *context* come to be extended in this way?

Here is Malinowski writing in 1923, about what at that time was referred to as a "primitive" (that is, unwritten) language. He writes "In a primitive language the meaning of any single word is to a very high degree dependent on its context. . . . [An expression such as] *we paddle in place* demands the context of the whole utterance, . . . [and] this latter again, becomes only intelligible when it is placed within its *context of situation*, if I may be allowed to coin an expression which indicates on the one hand that the conception of context has to be broadened and on the other hand that the situation in which words are uttered can never be passed over as irrelevant to the linguistic expression" (Malinowski 1923: 306). (In passing, we might note that on the very next page he also wrote "The conception of meaning as *contained* in an utterance is false and futile".) Ten years or so later, Malinowski had changed his view that this was a special feature of "primitive" languages; writing in 1935 he said all languages were alike in that "the real understanding of words is always ultimately derived from active experience of those aspects of reality to which the words belong" (Malinowski 1935: 58; cf. Hasan 1985). By this time Malinowski is extending the notion of context still further: over and beyond the context of situation lies "what we might call [the] context of culture", so that "the definition of a word consists partly of placing it within its cultural context" (ibid.: 18). What this means is that language considered as a **system** – its lexical items and grammatical categories – is to be related to its context of **culture**; while **instances** of language in use – specific texts and their component parts – are to be related to their context of **situation**. Both these contexts are of course outside of language itself.

Although Malinowski was the first to use the expression **context of situation**, the concept of 'situation', in the sense of the events and actions that are going on around when people speak, had been invoked before in linguistics, in a very different domain of inquiry, namely dialectology. Linguistic field studies were not only of culturally exotic, unwritten languages such as those studied by anthropologists; they were also carried out with rural dialects, and the Swiss dialectologist Wegener had developed a "situation theory" to account for the "special" features of informal, spoken language – that is, features that **appeared** special at a time when the only form of text that was recognized in linguistics was a written text, preferably written in a language long since dead (i.e., no longer spoken at all) (Firth 1957b). What led linguists to take account of the situation was when they turned their attention to speech. Here, they had to recognize factors like reference to persons, objects and events within the speaker's attention (technically, *exophoric deixis*), as well as other, more oblique forms of dependence on and interaction with environment. What Malinowski was saying was that because of these things, in spoken language the "situation" functioned by analogy as a kind of context. The situation was like the text by which a piece of spoken discourse was surrounded.

Malinowski was an anthropologist, who became a linguist in the service of his ethnographic pursuits. His younger colleague J.R. Firth, who was a linguist, saw the possibility of integrating this notion, of the "situation" as a kind of context, into a general theory of language. Firth was also interested in spoken language; but not as something quaint or exotic like rural dialects and aboriginal languages. On the contrary, Firth was concerned with the **typical** – what he referred to as "typical texts in their contexts of situation" (Firth 1957a: 224), by which people enacted their day-to-day interpersonal relationships and constructed a social identity for themselves and the people around them. A text was an object of theoretical study in its own right; and what Firth did was to map the notion of "context of situation" into a general theory of levels of language. All linguistic analysis, Firth said, was a study of meaning, and meaning could be defined operationally as "function in context"; so to study meaning you took each of the traditional divisions of linguistic theory – phonetic, phonological, lexical, morphological, syntactic – and treated it as a kind of context. You could then include the *situation* as just another linguistic level. But the context of situation did have a special place in the overall framework, since it was here that the text as a **whole** could be "contextualized". (And if it was a written text it could be tracked through time, as it came to be "recontextualized" with changes in the contexts in which it was read and the cultural background and assumptions of those who read it.)

1.2 Context of culture

What about the "context of culture"? Firth made very little use of this idea. Although, to use Robins' words (Robins 1963:17), Firth considered that a language was "embedded in the life and culture of its speakers", he was actually very sceptical about general notions such as 'the language' and 'the culture', because he didn't see either a language or a culture as any kind of homogeneous and harmonious whole. The notion of culture as a context for a language – for language considered as a system – was more fully articulated in the work of their contemporaries Sapir and Whorf. Sapir did not use the **expression** *context of culture*; but he did interpret a language as expressing the mental life of its speakers, and from this starting point he and Whorf developed their powerful view of the interplay between language and culture, the so-called "Sapir–Whorf hypothesis". In this view, since language evolved as part – moreover the most unconscious part – of every human culture, it functioned as the primary means whereby the deepest perception of the members, their joint construction of shared experience into social reality, were constantly reaffirmed and transmitted. Thus in this sense the culture provided the context within which words and, more generally, grammatical systems were interpreted. (Many of Whorf's example involved what he called "cryptotypes": systems of meaning that were hidden rather deep beneath the surface construction of the grammar and could only be revealed by a penetrating and thorough grammatical analysis) (Whorf 1956).

These two founding traditions of the study of language in context, the British, with Malinowski and Firth, on the one hand, and the American, with Sapir and Whorf, on the other, are in an important way complementary to each other. The former stress the **situation** as the context for language as **text**; and they see language as a form of action, as the enactment of social relationships and social processes. The latter stress the **culture** as the context for language as **system**; and they see language as a form of reflection, as the construal of experience into a theory or model of reality. From these two sources, taken together, we have been able to derive the foundations of a functional semantics: a theory of meaning that is relevant to applied linguistic concerns.

2 Language and context, system and instance

So we come back to language education; but there is just one more general theoretical point to be made first. A functional semantics needs to be grounded in a functional grammar: a grammar that is likewise related to the contexts of language and language use. Here a major contribution came from a third source, this time on the European continent, namely the Prague school, whose founder Mathesius, another contemporary of Sapir and Malinowski, showed for the first time how the grammar of spoken language was organized so that it related systematically to the surrounding context, including both the context in its traditional sense – the "co-text", in Catford's term – and the context of situation. And now we can take the interpretation somewhat further and show that the entire construction of the grammar – the way all human languages are organized for creating meaning – is critically bound up with the situational and cultural contexts in which language has been evolving. As I wrote myself many years ago, language is as it is because of what it does: which means, because of what we do with it, in every aspect of our lives. So a theory of language in context is not just a theory about how people use language, important though that is. It is a theory about the **nature** and **evolution** of language, explaining why the system works the way it does; but with the explanation making reference to its use. (I should make it clear that this is not a teleological explanation; it says nothing about purpose or design. It is a functional explanation, based on a social-semiotic interpretation of the relations and processes of meaning.) And I think this last point is fundamental in relation to language education work.

In all language education, the learner has to build up a resource. It is a resource of a particular kind: a resource for creating meaning. I call it a "meaning potential". Whether someone is learning the mother tongue, learning to read and write, learning a second or foreign language, learning the language of science or mathematics, or learning the styles of written composition – all these are forms of meaning potential. What the learner has to do is to construe (that is, construct in the mind) a linguistic *system*. That is what is meant by "language as system": it is language as stored up energy. It is a language, or some specific aspect of a language, like the language of science, in the form of a *potential*, a resource that you draw on in reading and writing and speaking and listening – and a resource that you use for learning with. How do you construe this potential, and how do you use it when you've got it? You build it up, and you act it out, in the form of *text*. "Text" refers to all the *instances* of language that you listen to and read. And that you produce yourself in speaking and in writing.

I have suggested that the context for the meaning potential – for language as a system – is the context of culture. We will, of course, have

274

to problematize this term "culture" as well; I will come back to that later on. The context for the particular instances – for language as processes of text – is the context of situation. And just as a piece of text is an instance of language, so a situation is an instance of culture. So there is a proportion here. The context for an instance of language (text) is an instance of culture (situation). And the context for the system that lies behind each text (language) is the system which lies behind each situation – namely, the culture. (See Figure 13.1.)

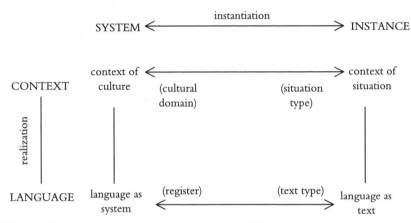

Figure 13.1 Language and context, system and instance

Note: Culture instantiated in situation, as system instantiated in text. Culture realized in/ construed by language; same relation as that holding between linguistic strata (semantics: lexicogrammar: phonology: phonetics).

Cultural domain and register are "sub-systems": likeness viewed from "system" end.

Situation type and text type are "instance types": likeness viewed from "instance" end.

2.1 The relation between system and instance: instantiation

However, there is a hidden trap to watch out for at this point. We have these pairs of terms, like culture and situation, or language as system and language as text; we need them in order to talk about what we do. But the implication is that these are two different things: that the "system" is one thing, and the "text" is something else, something different. Let me return to this concept of a "potential". The system is not some independent object; it is simply the potential that lies behind all the various instances. Although the actual texts that you process and produce will always be limited, the potential (for processing and producing texts) has to reach the stage where it is unlimited, so that you can take in new texts, that you haven't heard or read before, and also **interact** with them – interrogate them, so to speak, argue with them, and learn from them. (That, of course, is a high standard to attain.) And we can apply the same thinking to the situation and the culture. These also are not two different things; they are the same thing seen from different points of view. A situation, as we are envisaging it, is simply an instance of culture; or, to put it the other way round, a culture is the potential behind all the different types of situation that occur. We can perhaps use an analogy from the physical world; the difference between "culture" and "situation" is rather like that between the "climate" and the "weather". Climate and weather are not two different things; they are the same thing, which we call *weather* when we are looking at it close up, and *climate* when we are looking at it from a distance. The weather goes on around us all the time; it is the actual instances of temperature and precipitation and air movement that you can see and hear and feel. The climate is the **potential** that lies behind all these things; it is the weather seen from a distance, by an observer standing some way off in time. So, of course, there is a continuum from one to the other; there is no way of deciding when a "long-term weather pattern" becomes a "temporary condition of the climate", or when "climatic variation" becomes merely "changes in the weather". And likewise with "culture" and "situation": a school, for example, is clearly a cultural institution, a matrix of social practices governed by cultural norms and values. But we can also look at it as an assembly of situations: it consists of regular events called "lessons" in which people in certain role relationships (teachers and pupils) take part in certain forms of interaction in which certain kinds of meanings are exchanged. We can look at it as system (this is what we mean by education: the school considered systemically), or as text, repetitive instances of the processes of teaching and learning. We may choose to look at this phenomenon from either end; but it is still a single phenomenon, not two.

2.2 *The situational context in language education*

So much for the horizontal dimension. What about the vertical dimension: the relation between culture and language, and between situation and text? This is what we are calling the relationship of "context": culture and situation as the context, respectively, for language as system and for instances of language as text. But I have been talking for long enough in abstract terms; so let me now approach this question through some examples of language education practice. And since we are talking about language in context, let me start with one where we may feel that the language is somehow functioning out of context – a typical adult foreign-language class. (Many among us might feel that this is one of the most intractable problems on the language education scene!)

In traditional textbooks, single sentences and even single words were often presented in isolation: out of context, in the original sense of the term. Actually they had their own linguistic context: in a structure drill, for example, the context of a given sentence was the set of all the other sentences displaying a similar structure:

(1) Although they were poor, (yet) they were happy.
(2) Although the light was on, (yet) I fell asleep.
(3) Although she got the highest mark, (yet) she was not given a prize.

More recently, these tended to give way in favour of sentences having a similar function, as in the English lessons on Singapore Chinese radio:

(4) How long does it take to get to Silvertown?
(5) How long will it take me to get to Silvertown?
(6) How long does the journey to Silvertown take?

There is a co-text here; but since people don't go around talking in paradigms, the only context of situation is the one that is created by the language activity itself.

In the 1960s, when the theory of context became familiar in applied linguistics, teachers set out to improve learning materials by "contextualizing" them, and one early result of this was what came to be known as the "situational" approach. Instead of sentences related by grammatical structure this offered coherent passages having a recognizable situational setting, like "at the post office", "in a restaurant" or "in hospital". The parts of the text were now held together by the unities of the situation.

These materials were much criticized, on the grounds that the sentences were still readymade; people sensed that this conflicted with the basic notion of functioning in a context of situation. I don't myself share that objection; there are many situations in which the text is readymade, and I think readymade text has an important place in learning a foreign language. But there was a more serious objection to them, which was that the context of situation had been interpreted simply as a setting. But "context of situation" is not just equivalent to setting. The context of situation is a theoretical construct for explaining how a text relates to the social processes within which it is located. It has three significant components: the underlying social activity, the persons or "voices" involved in that activity, and the particular functions accorded to the text within it. In informal terms, the situation consists in what's going on, who is taking part, and where the language comes in. (These are referred to technically as the *field*, the **tenor** and the **mode**.) The setting, on the other hand, is the immediate material environment. This **may** be a direct manifestation of the context of situation, and so be integrated into it: if the situation is one of, say, medical care, involving a doctor and one or more patients, then the **setting** of hospital or clinic is a relevant part of the picture. But even there the setting does not **constitute** the context of situation; whereas the materials presented in the "situational" approach tended to relate exclusively to the setting and not to the cultur-ally defined social processes that lay behind it.

The point is, that the actual setting in which these texts had to func-tion was not, in fact, a post office or a hospital; it was a classroom, and this illustrates the contradiction that is inherent in 'teaching a language'. Consider an adult language class such as is typical of Australia and other countries where immigrants arrive knowing nothing of the majority language. What is the context of situation for the discourse of their language classes? The **immediate** situation is the activity of learning a foreign language, involving teacher, learner and fellow students, with the text functioning as instructional material (interspersed with other discourse, such as the teacher's classroom management); and in this con-text, the natural setting **is** a classroom. But beyond this immediate situation lies another layer of situation of which the learners are always aware, namely that of participating effectively in the life of their new community; and here the natural settings would be those of the workplace and the shopping centre.

2.3 The learning situation as context

So how have language educators tried to resolve this contextual contra-diction? One early approach was to engage with the setting of the classroom: to teach the students to survive in a world made of books and pens and blackboards. This obviously has its limitations! But note that it is possible to move on from there while still remaining within the **immediate** situation: that is, exploiting the language learning context, but going beyond the setting to the situation proper – using language that relates to learning language, to the roles of teacher and student, and even to the discourse itself. I have in mind the sort of work where students critique their own and each others' presentations, and reflect on and monitor their own learning experiences (cf. Jones et al. in Hasan and Martin 1989) Or – a third option – one may exploit the **outer** situation, that of participating in the community: following up the "situational approach" but again moving beyond the setting to engage with the social processes of which this situation is actually constituted. The value of "communicative" approaches is that they are based on a context of situation, not just on a setting; hence they do embody a real conception of text – language that is effective in relation to the social activity and the interpersonal relationships (cf. Breen and Candlin 1980). Applying this principle to the outer situation, one can simulate the workplace or shopping centre not just as physical surroundings but as the location where particular processes of production and exchange take place and particular kinds of interpersonal relationship are enacted.

To say "simulating" the workplace implies, of course, that the teaching is still actually taking place in a classroom. There is another way of dealing with the contextual contradiction, which is that the teachers move the operation out of the classroom altogether and teach the language in place, in the factory or the department store or the office. If this is done the activity becomes less like language teaching and more like language apprenticeship – though it is still a form of language **education**: it is guided and structured by a professional language educa-tor, so that the learner is not simply left to the casual goodwill of the workmates. You have to do without the facilities that the classroom offers (whether computer and tape recorder and reference books, or just the security of your own bit of personal space); but you avoid this huge disjunction between the immediate setting and what is perceived as the 'real' – that is, the outer – context of situation.

2.4 Exploring and creating the learning context

So is this kind of disjunction, this problem of language 'out of context', a feature of all the activities of language education? I don't think so. I think what I have just cited is an extreme case; most instances are much less contradictory, and in some there may be hardly any such conflict at all. Let me refer to some earlier experience of my own. In London in the 1960s I directed a curriculum development project, the Programme in Linguistics and English Teaching, in which we had primary, secondary and tertiary teachers all working together to apply some of the principles derived from linguistics to the teaching of English at various levels in school. This was English as a first language (there was a separate project for English as a Second Language), and we were aiming particularly at those sections of the population where the children were most likely to fail, which meant inner-city working-class and new-generation immigrants (Pearce et al. in Hasan and Martin 1989)

2.4.1 Programme in Linguistic and English Teaching: primary

The primary-school teachers, headed by David Mackay, were able to define their task more or less from the beginning: to develop a new programme for teaching initial literacy. They very quickly took up the relevant ideas, combined them with their own thinking and got down to work. For them, the context of situation was that of the school as an institution defined by the culture; there was no "outer" level of context conflicting with this one. (The "field" was the social practice of education: developing systematic knowledge in an institutional framework, as distinct from commonsense knowledge in home and family. The "tenor" was a teacher–pupil–peer group relationship, as distinct from one of child with parents, siblings and neighbours. The "mode" was that of explicit instruction, as distinct from learning through unstructured conversational interaction with other people.) The classroom setting, far from being in conflict, represents very precisely the situational and cultural context in which the activity of learning to read and write is situated, and also evaluated: namely, the children are learning to function in the world of educational knowledge.

In developing their materials, which were called *Breakthrough to Literacy* (Mackay et al. 1970), the primary teachers had to take various critical decisions; and they used their interpretation of the context in order to do so. Let me just refer to four of these. First, they recognized that the children were not just learning to read – they were learning to learn through reading; so they separated out the semantic aspects of reading and writing from the techniques, so that the children could get ahead with making sentences and constructing their own reading materials without having first to manipulate the written symbols and writing implements themselves. Second, they recognized that where the instruction is explicit the children need to be partners in the accompanying discourse; so they built into the programme a technical language so the children could always talk about what they were learning. (There had always been this strange discrepancy in infant schools: in arithmetic, everyone accepted that the children had to learn to talk about their number skills, like adding and taking away; but they were expected to master highly complex language skills without any systematic resources with which to talk about them.) Third, they recognized that, in order to relate their educational learning to their commonsense learning, the children had to be the authors of their own texts; so there were no primers – the first reading books were books the children made themselves. And fourth, they recognized that all language learning is highly interactive; so they designed the materials for the children to work with in groups, sharing their experiences instead of having to work through it all by themselves.

Initial literacy, then, is one kind of language education where the social process is defined by the notion of education; the cultural context **is** that of education, which is directly reflected, or "instantiated", in the situation of the classroom. Contrast this with the circumstances faced by the secondary teachers in the project. They were no less qualified and experienced; but when they came to their task, of producing materials for studying language in the upper secondary school, they took a very long time before they were able to get started. We can look at this also from the point of view of the context.

2.4.2 Programme in Linguistics and English Teaching: secondary

The problem faced by the secondary teachers was that, for them, there **was** no context. There was no culturally recognized activity of learning about language. "English", at that level in school, meant just the study of literature; and while they might have taken that as their context and developed materials on stylistics, that seemed both too specialized and too technical. This meant that, while creating their text, they had to be **creating the context** for it at the same time.

So how do you set about "creating" a context for language? You cannot do it by means of legislation, like decreeing that poems are to be written in praise of a national leader. The only way is for the text itself to create its own context of situation. Let me return for a moment to the earlier discussion.

I tried to suggest how this notion of context had evolved in modern linguistics. The "situation", and the "culture", were both taken as something "given" – as already in place, so to speak, to serve as the environment for language. Is this, in fact, a valid perspective? That depends on what you are trying to find out. If, like Malinowski, you are asking 'how do I explain the meaning of this text?' then you are bound to treat the situation in which the text was functioning as a "given" phenomenon: the reasoning is, 'now that we know what was going on, we can understand what was being said'. But in language education work we have to have a wider angle of vision. In any situation involving language and learning, you have to be able to move in both directions: to use the situation to construe the text, as Malinowski did, but also to use the text as a means to construe the situation. The situation, in other words, may not be something that is "given"; it may have to be constructed out of the text.

281

2.5 The relation between language and context: realization

Let us look again at this "vertical" dimension. The term that we usually use for this relationship, coming from European functional linguistics, is **realization**: the situation is "realized" in the text. Similarly the culture is "realized" in the linguistic system. This does not mean that the one somehow **causes** the other. The relationship is not one of cause. It is a semiotic relationship; one that arises between pairs of information systems, interlocking systems of meaning.

If the situation **caused** the text, the situation would have to exist first; and it would be impossible for the text to cause the situation – if *a* causes *x*, then *x* cannot also cause *a*. But text and situation come into being together; so whatever kind of order we set up between them, it must be such that we can start from either end. This is how Firth was able to integrate the situation into his model of linguistic levels, because the relationship between the levels **within** a language is already of this same kind. A language is articulated at the level of grammar, and also at the level of phonology; but neither of these two systems "causes" the other – the relation between them is this one of realization. We are able to project this relationship from language on to culture, and show that, in an analogous way, the text "realizes" the situation. And this is a relationship that can be traversed, or activated, in either direction.

If the culture, and the situation, are said to be "realized in" language, this means that they are also constructed by language – we could again use the term *construed* if we want to make it explicit that this is not a material process but a semiotic one. Thus the culture is construed by systems of language choice; the situation is construed by patterns of language use. I can give a simple illustration of this by just referring to the setting. If there was a storm starting up outside the window, I could say

(7) There was a flash of lightning.

That text makes sense in relation to a setting that is "given". But the day may be perfectly bright and clear; I can still say

(8) There was a flash of lightning –

and it still makes sense; I have started to tell you a story. I have **created** the setting by the device of using that text. We can say that the text has "construed" the setting; or, if you want to express this in terms of the mental processes of the interactants, you can say **you** have construed the setting out of the text. All fictional narrative depends on this construing power of language.

Coming back to our secondary teachers, then: they had no cultural context for teaching about language in the secondary school. Grammar had largely been disappeared from the curriculum, because the teachers in the schools found the traditional grammar boring and useless; but nothing had come in to take its place, and neither literature nor composition was taught with any real consideration of language or any proper value being accorded to it. We felt that students at this level, the upper secondary school, should learn about the nature and functions of language. But for this to happen, our teachers had not only to construct a new text; they had to make the text such that it would construct a new situation. In order to do this they produced a programme of materials entitled *Language in Use* (Doughty et al. 1971), through which teacher and pupils could explore language together (the teachers' book was called *Exploring Language*); and the concept around which they organized these materials was that of **variation** in language, especially functional variation of the kind we refer to as "register". They hoped in this way to be creating a new context within language education, in which the activity of investing language would become an integral part of developing educational knowledge.

Of course, no single project can transform the educational scene. But in the recent discussions of the national curriculum in Britain it was explicitly acknowledged that the work of these teachers back in the 1960s had been significant in reshaping the cultural context of language education. If they were able to play some part in this, it was because they understood that they had actively to construct the context for their work instead of merely taking it for granted. Language does not just passively reflect a pre-existing social reality. It is an active agent in constructing that reality; and in language education we often have to exploit that vast potential. (And of course that is what is being done whenever language education is used as an instrument of language policy and planning.)

3 The cultural context in language education

But you notice that I have now slipped from talking about the context of situation to talking about the context of culture. This is easy to do, given that, as I suggested earlier, "culture" and "situation" are not two different things, but rather the same thing seen from two different depths of observation. The culture is the paradigm of situation types – the total potential that lies behind each instance, and each class of instances. Thus just as the text realizes, and hence can construe, a context of situation, so the system, the potential that is inherent in that text – in this example, the potential built up by teachers and pupils as a discourse for exploring language – realizes, and hence can also construe, a context of culture.

But looking at **culture** in this way, as a context for our educational practices, we may come to view it rather differently from the way in which people usually understand it when they use expressions such as "teaching language, teaching culture". There it usually means the traditional lifestyles, beliefs and value systems of a language community. Many years ago, when I was still a language teacher, teaching Chinese at Cambridge University in England, I used to teach a class of scientific Chinese to a group of Cambridge scientists. They wanted to read scientific texts written by Chinese scholars: one was a plant geneticist, interested in Chinese work on hybridization, one was a mathematician, one was a psychologist, and so on. Now, they had no interest in Chinese culture in the traditional sense of the term; it wasn't necessary for me to teach them anything about Chinese history or family life, or about filial piety or other Confucian values. Did this mean, however, that there was no "context of culture" for my teaching? Of course not. There certainly was a context of culture; and you couldn't hope to learn scientific Chinese without knowing quite a lot about it. But "culture" here does not mean the traditional culture of China. It means the culture of modern science, whether practiced by Chinese or English or Australian or Vietnamese or any other nationality of scientists. When we talk of the cultural context for language education, we have to go beyond the popular notion of culture as something defined solely by one's ethnic origins. All of us participate in many simultaneous cultures; and language education is the principal means by which we learn to do so.

When people ask, as they often do, whether it is possible to learn a language without at the same time learning about the culture it belongs to, they usually mean the culture in the traditional sense, the ideas and the customs and the values inherited from the past. In that sense of culture, the answer is obviously: yes, it is perfectly possible. There are millions of people around the world learning English without learning anything about British or North American or Australian culture in the process. There is no need to involve the culture in that sense at all. In saying this, I'm not arguing **against** taking the cultural heritage into consideration in those cases where it's appropriate: there are situations in language education where traditional culture is very much part of the context, for example language maintenance in migrant communities, where the language is being taught precisely as an instrument for maintaining and transmitting the ethnic culture. (Even here, I think, such an activity is likely to be successful to the extent that it is forward-looking as well as backward-looking, having regard to the functional significance of the language in the new cultural context. This is in fact widely recognized, because in maintenance classes they usually teach the standard variety of the language, even though, as among Italians in Australia, and Chinese in many parts of the world, many parents feel that that is not the natural way to maintain the culture and it doesn't help the children to talk to their grannies.) But usually this sense of culture as tradition is not relevant as a cultural context for language education. When we talk of the "context of culture" for language activities we mean those features of culture that are relevant to the register in question. If we are looking at a secondary physics syllabus, then the cultural context is that of contemporary physics, combined with that of the institution of "education" in the particular community concerned (cf. Gunnarsson 1990).

3.1 Some examples of educational contexts

So I suggest that in our language education practice we interpret "culture" from a linguistic point of view: as a context for language, a system of meanings that is realized in language and hence can be construed in language. And just as in language education the term "language" does not usually encompass the whole of that unwieldy concept we call "English" or "Russian" or "Chinese" – it means the language in one particular variety or aspect, such as scientific Chinese, or Russian for interpreters, or initial literacy in English, and so on – so also the term "culture" will not designate some amorphous object such as 'Chinese culture' or 'Western culture'; it refers to something much more specific, that we can interpret in terms of some overall model such as the present one. I think one of the most penetrating studies in the field of language education is the work of Jay Lemke, Professor of Science Education at the City University of New York. In the early 1980s Lemke carried out some research into the teaching of science in American schools, on behalf of the National Science Foundation; his report *Classroom Communication of Science* (1983) was based on detailed observations of science classes in New York high schools, and he subsequently published a book, *Talking Science* (1990), which presents his ideas as they have developed since that investigation was carried out. As the title suggests, Lemke sees the activity of learning and teaching science as one of "talking": exchanging meanings through language. But this meaning-making activity is complex and has to be interpreted at different levels.

The text in Lemke's model is the discourse of the science class: he has recorded *instances* of teachers expounding scientific topics, with responses and interventions by the pupils. These belong in the southeast quadrant of our model. These texts are the *realization*, in language, of what Lemke calls "activity structures", the *situational contexts* in which the discourse sequences unfold. "An activity structure is defined as a socially recognizable sequence of actions" (198); or rather, he goes on, it is realized as sequences of actions, so that "the same activity structure can be realized in many ways" (ibid.). Among the activity structures that Lemke identifies in science classes are Triadic Dialogue, Teacher–Student Debate, Teacher Monologue, Groupwork. These are the modes of discourse of the specific situation types that make up the overall context of situation for talking science.

Moving now to the left-hand side of our diagram: the teacher is the one who knows the field – he has the *system* already in place. He has already constructed the meaning potential of the language of science; for him, the texts are instantiations of that system. For the pupils, however, the texts have to function so as to **construe** the meaning potential: they are learning the discourse of science. This system consists of what Lemke calls "thematic patterns", "shared patterns of semantic relationships" which can be "said" (instantiated) in various ways; but these, in turn, realize the underlying "thematic formations", the "webs of semantic relationships" that make up the context of culture for science education (87). "Thematic formations are what all the different texts that talk about the same topic in the same ways . . . have in common" (203); they are scientific constructs, typically realized in language but with other modes of expression also playing a part.

Thus the "context of culture" for any educational activity includes the structure of the relevant branch of educational knowledge, and Lemke explicitly interprets this in semiotic terms. "A scientific theory", he says, "is constituted of systems of related meanings"; it is "a way of talking about a subject using particular thematic patterns", that is "reconstructed again and again in nearly the same ways by the members of a community" (125: 99). So the wheel has now turned full-circle. If the culture is itself a construction of meanings, it has now become, not just context but "context", a con-text in the original sense of the term. The cultural context for the discourse of science, which these students are having to construe, is the world of scientific theory; but it is a world that is itself, as it were, made of meanings. And this is not a metaphorical way of talking about science just from the "applied" viewpoint of language education; it is a perspective that derives from the ideas of the scientists themselves.

The world of quantum physics, for example, in the widely accepted "Copenhagen interpretation", is a semiotic construction of reality. The universe is the way that we make it by turning it into meaning (Polkinghorne 1990).

My final example comes from Canada, from a language education project where the same general model can be found underpinning some activities of a very different kind. This is Bernard Mohan's "Vancouver project", in which primary-school children in a typically multilingual assortment, of the kind very familiar to us in Sydney and Melbourne, are learning how to learn: to construe educational knowledge and represent it in written English. While Lemke's project was one of research, Mohan's is curriculum development. His "texts" are information sources of every conceivable kind: writing, pictures, maps, diagrams, tables, news reports, any object or event that has a semiotic potential, that the children can use to construct their resource of knowledge. The context of situation is a classroom; but it is a classroom conceived of, and organized, as a repository of information (Mohan 1986).

The system that the children are construing from this text is one where language and subject matter are integrated; but it is not defined by subject matter – in terms of adult practices it is more like English for Academic Purposes than English for Specific Purposes. The meaning potential is that of language as the basis of learning: language construing and transmitting information – "content", in Mohan's terms – which may be about anything at all. So what is the context of culture for Mohan's work? As he sees it, the context of culture is a general theory of learning, and conception of educational knowledge, rather than the theories of particular disciplines. (Of course, both Mohan and Lemke include both a general theory of learning and particular, subject-based theories in their context of culture; the difference is one of orientation, between a secondary-level research project and a primary-level development project.) But this cultural context, as Mohan points out, often involves conflict with received ideas about education and about language that are dominant in the educational field. We should not forget that this general context of culture for language education – the dominant philosophy of education, if you like – is something that is already in place; and it is not something homogeneous and in perfect harmony, either with itself or with the transformed cultural context that our language education work is designed to bring about. In this connection Frances Christie finds it helpful to think of the school itself as a cultural context: instead of a system, or institution, of education in the abstract, with the school as simply the setting where this is instantiated, she prefers to see the school itself, in its guise as an institution, as the context of culture. This enables her to explain the emergence of special **language** systems as registers of education – what she refers to as "curriculum genres" (Christie in Hasan and Martin 1989).

3.2 Learning language, learning through language, learning about language

When I was working as a consultant to the Language Development Project in Australia, I used to sum up the scope of language education under the three headings of "Learning Language, Learning through Language, Learning about Language". "Learning language" means, of course, learning one's first language, plus any second or foreign languages that are part of the curriculum: including both spoken and written language – initial literacy, composition skills and so on. Here, language is itself the **substance** of what is being learnt. "Learning through language" means using language, again both spoken and written, as an **instrument**: as the primary resource for learning other things – language across the curriculum, in other words. "Learning about language" means studying language as an **object** in order to understand how it works: studying grammar, semantics, phonetics, and so on. Here language is a domain or branch of knowledge: typically in schools this is taken no further than a kind of linguistic nature study, with lists of parts of speech and rules of behaviour, but there is no reason why it should not become a properly constructed avenue of learning (Halliday 1981; Painter, Cloran, Rothery, Butt in Hasan and Martin 1989; Carter, van Leeuwen and Humphrey, Painter, Veel and Coffin, Macken-Horarik in Hasan and Williams 1996).

So language enters in as substance – we have to learn it to perform; as instrument – we have to learn with it, as a resource; and as object – we have to learn about it, as content. This is important because nothing else in our educational experience has all these three aspects to it. (Perhaps the nearest analogy would be a combination of mathematics and music – we can think of music as 'performing numbers'.) What is there that is common among these three, which enables us to model them in a coherent fashion? I think what is common is what is being expected of the learner. In all these activities, learners are having to transform text into system; that is, to construe the instances of language, what they hear and what they read, into a meaning potential. If we want to express the three aspects of that meaning potential as aspects of language, we can say that it is linguistic (that is, language skills), extralinguistic (knowledge of content), and metalinguistic (knowledge of language, as content).

288

For all this to be possible, we depend on the context of situation – hence the problem of "decontextualized" discourse, that I started with. Again, I don't just mean the setting. The setting, of course, is important: it is hard to learn science without laboratory equipment, and it is hard to learn anything, in the educational sense of learning, without writing materials and books. But I mean the context of situation as I have been talking of it; the coherent pattern of activities – activity structures, in Lemke's term – from which the discourse gains its relevance. These are so essential because the **system** that the learner has to construe for himself is also a system at that higher level – the context of culture, as I have been defining it. The advantage of interpreting this higher level as being itself a form of discourse, rather than in conceptual or cognitive terms, is that it enables us to model all the processes the learner has to go through using a unified theory of learning based on language. (It also helps us to diagnose the kind of partial learning that takes place when a student has construed the system at the linguistic level but not integrated this into a construction of the cultural context.)

In all educational learning, learners are being required to predict both ways: to predict the text from the context, and to predict the context from the text. This is something we do all the time in the casual, informal registers of speech; when small children are listening to stories, they are constructing the context in their imagination. But it can be very demanding, especially when too much of the total pattern is unfamiliar. The obvious example of this is if you are having to learn through text in a second language you haven't had much experience of; but it is not only a second-language problem – I have written elsewhere (Halliday and Martin 1993) about the problems that arise in learning science in the mother tongue when you have to construe, from technical and often highly metaphorical written texts, generalizations that you must recognize as relating to, but systematizing, your own previous everyday experience. Language educators have to be able to diagnose where specific effort may need to be expended in working on the language itself, instead of just taking it for granted that the learners are able to use the language for learning with. (For example, in learning how to construct technical taxonomies from the discourse of scientific textbooks; cf. Wignell et al. in Halliday and Martin 1993). If I have kept coming back to my little diagram, it has been partly in order to focus more closely on what we actually mean by "culture" in relation to language education; but mainly to suggest that, in educational learning, all four quadrants are involved. The learner has to (1) process and produce text; (2) relate it to, and construe from it, the context of situation; (3) build up the potential that lies behind this text and others like it; and (4) relate it to, and construe from it, the context of culture that lies behind that situation and others like it. These are not different components of the process, with separate activities attached to them; they are different perspectives on a single, unitary process. But to understand this process, and examine our own practices that are designed to bring it about, I think we need some in-depth, rich perception of language such as this. I think that, whenever we say that someone has "learnt" something, it means that all these resources for meaning are now in place.

Chapter Fourteen

LANGUAGE ACROSS THE CULTURE
(1986)

It is a pleasure, and a privilege, for me to be asked to be the first speaker on the occasion of this RELC Seminar on Language Across the Curriculum. I greatly value this opportunity to meet and exchange meanings with the many distinguished participants, not only because of the central importance of the topic we are discussing but also because we are discussing it at this particular juncture of place and time. The Southeast Asian Region, for which this Centre has such a fundamental task to perform, is a region of great diversity, with different social structures, different religions, different languages, and different language policies. At the same time there is a strong sense of a common purpose, perhaps reflecting at a very deep level a community of culture; and a sense of direction which seems to be lacking in many parts of the world, but which is manifested here, among many other ways, in the success of the language policies and planning in the Region. Of course, there have been problems, uncertainties, changes of direction; there always will be. But one cannot fail to be impressed by the achievements that have taken place, on the language and education fronts, in the years since RELC first came into being. National languages have emerged, their statuses have been strengthened and their functions extended and developed; and along with this process, educational policies have been adopted, and educational opportunities created, which are making it possible for the linguistic aspirations, the plans for language development which are often very far-reaching and require considerable use of resources, to become realized in the lives of today's citizens – and, even more, of their children, the citizens of tomorrow.

During the past two decades, an important concept has emerged which is playing a major part in these processes; that is the concept of "language education". You may in fact have come across two very similar expressions in English: "language education" and "language in education". The two are not really synonymous, and indeed they evolved by different routes; but they have now merged into a common frame and I shall just use the simpler one of the two, leaving the preposition out. "Language education" is a form of wording that can be interpreted in a very general sense: as education **in** language, or of course in languages; education **through** language – that is, the role of language in education; and even (if you stretch it a little) education **of** language – how a language itself changes as a result of its function in the educational process. We should not worry that the term is not more rigorously defined; a rigorous definition of a concept of this nature would be the first sign of its decay. What is significant is that language education is slowly coming to be recognized as a central concept in schooling, in teacher training and in applied language studies. There is a course given under this name in the English language programme at the National University of Singapore. A number of institutions in Britain, North America and Australia now have "language education" enshrined in their titles; and we are beginning to see journals of language education appearing on publishers' lists. The term is gradually becoming familiar.

It will be 40 years next month since I gave my first language lesson: it took the form of a dictation, in Chinese, to a class of British Air Force officers training for service in the East Asian theatre of war. This was not a very profound exercise in language education; but it was in an interesting context, since the language was being taught for a very specific purpose. Indeed that was one of the contexts in which LSP "Language for Specific Purposes" started – the course on which I was teaching was not one of those designed as LSP; but other courses that were being taught in London at that time **were** designed as LSP courses, the specific varieties being referred to as "restricted languages". It is 25 years since I started working as a linguist with teachers of language, both teachers of foreign languages (including EFL) and teachers of English as a mother tongue; their work would certainly qualify as "language education" today. At that time however no-one referred to anything of the sort. You could be 'learning a language', which meant any language other than your first one; or you could be 'learning to read and write' in your mother tongue – and later on, studying its grammar and its literature. But no one saw learning language as an educational process, and no one inquired into the role of language in enabling people to learn other things.

292

What has brought about the change, the emergence of new approaches and more positive attitudes? I think we can identify four strands in this event. First, the notion of children's language development: how children become articulate in their earliest language. Second, the notion of multilingual education: schooling in a linguistically complex environment. Third, the notion of language in the classroom: how teachers and pupils engage in verbal interaction. Fourth, the notion of language across the curriculum, the topic of the present seminar. I would like to say a little about each of the first three, before turning to the fourth topic as the one to be developed here.

First, then, language development. Children learn to talk; and they start doing so very early. They start listening as soon as they are born; and in fact even before they are born they can already hear the sounds and feel the rhythms of their mother's speech. As soon as they have got over the shock of being born they try communicating; not of course in language, to start with, but by the end of the first year of life they have started making up language for themselves and by the end of their second year they have learnt a considerable amount of the language that is going on around them. This process, the language development of each individual human being, begins in the home and continues in the neighbourhood and, nowadays, in the school. The neighbourhood may be a small country town, a kampong or village or a city highrise with a shopping centre attached; what matters is that it is a network of talk by which the child's linguistic experience is extended beyond his immediate household. Each of these environments, home, neighbourhood and school, adds to the demands made on the child's ability to communicate: his language is being stretched all the time to accommodate new functions and new meanings. In the past 20 years or so, not only have we found out a great deal about how children learn their first language or languages; equally importantly, we have come to see that the task of the school is essentially a task of continuing and carrying forward the same process. We go on developing our linguistic resources – our "meaning potential", as I like to express it – right through the years of our education; and if a child's language development fails to keep pace with the demands that are made on it by the school – by the teachers, the textbooks and the subject matter – then that child is going to remain "uneducated".

Now we come to the second component that has gone into the concept of language education: namely, multilingualism. Traditionally, educational institutions – not just the schools, but the supporting structures and materials – have been based on one language, even if the community at large spoke half a dozen, or spoke one that was very different from the official one. The community might be multilingual, but the educational system was monolingual; other languages appeared in the curriculum, but as subjects, not as media. And this is still often the case, where a modern standard or national language has taken the place that was once occupied by Sanskrit, or Arabic, or classical Chinese. But the world has changed, and there is more to learn now. We cannot devote three years of our lives to learning by heart sacred texts written in an unknown tongue. Educational languages have to be functional; they have to be tools for learning with, and learning with as quickly as possible. And where there is more than one language involved we have had to make the two complementary educational processes reinforce each other: to learn the subject through the language, and the language through the subject, both at the same time, perhaps with total immersion after the Canadian model. Sometimes two or three languages may function simultaneously as educational media, in a genuinely bi- or tri-lingual education system – languages chosen either because they are joint national languages, which everyone has to learn, or because we consider that the mother tongue can play a unique role in early learning experience, and we therefore want to give it a place in at least the earlier years of schooling. Either way the distinction between language as content and language as medium tends to be blurred, and we have come to think in terms of a more general, overarching concept – again, that of language education.

By paying attention to children's language development, on the one hand, and to multilingual experience on the other, we have gained a more broadly based conception of language development, in which the school is in partnership with the rest of society, and to which various languages may jointly contribute, even within the school programme; and at the same time, and partly as a result of this, we have become more aware of the role of language in the classroom. This – my third strand – can now be studied as it actually happens, in ways that were not possible until quite recently. With tape recorders first audio and now video as well, we can record what goes on between teacher and pupils, and check our hunches and our impressions against an exact account of what has taken place; and the development of "text linguistics", with grammars designed for analysing and interpreting language in real contexts of use, spoken as well as written, enables us to observe and understand how language is being used as a vehicle of systematic learning – what is being learnt; how well it is being learnt; and why it is often not being learnt as effectively as we should like. As Jay Lemke has said in his *Using Language in the Classroom* (Lemke, 1985),

> Classroom education, to a very large degree, is talk: it is the social use of language to enact regular activity structures and to share systems of meaning among teachers and students.

Lemke's own work, together with that of Sinclair and Coulthard and numerous others during the past ten years, has helped us to understand a great deal not only about classroom interaction but also about how language is used to learn, whether in or out of school. We have tended to forget in the past that learning is essentially an interactive process, and that language plays a far greater and a deeper role in this process than that of merely communicating a "content", the subject matter of some discipline that figures in the school timetable.

This leads me then to my fourth component of language education, which is the area that we shall be concentrating on this week: language across the curriculum. Let me first relate this to what has gone before. The notion of language across the curriculum is essentially that of language as a medium – language functioning as a medium of instruction. But while when we talk about "English-medium" or "Malay-medium" education we are simply referring to **which** of a number of possible languages is used as the means of instruction, when we refer to "language across the curriculum" we are concerned with **how** the language is used: what kind of English, for example, or what kind of Thai is involved in learning science, or in learning history or mathematics.

This question is equally valid and relevant no matter what language is being used, and no matter whether the language in question is one among many or is the only language having a place in the educational system. Wherever there is teaching, language is being used to teach with; from the teacher's talk in the classroom, through the students' reports and essays, the textbooks, up to the syllabus outlines and curriculum documents – these are all made of language. (So, of course, are the minister's policy statements and the references to educational aims set out in the national constitution.) Language is truly present all across the board.

What "language across the curriculum" specifically refers to, of course, is the fact that not only is language at the centre of all transmission of educational knowledge, whether arts, social science, natural science or technology, but that as one moves across from one subject area to another language is likely to be functioning in rather different ways. Consider for example the varied range of writing that a pupil is expected to produce. A narrative of personal experience is very different from a history essay, which is different again from a scientific report. So my fourth component of the "language education" concept embodies the notion of "functional variation" in language. Language varies; and it varies, not randomly, but systematically according to **what we are doing** – what we are using language to achieve.

This, you may say, is an interesting observation; but is it any more than that? Why do we need to take account of it? Will it affect our practice in any way? The reason we need to take account of it is the usual reason for which we take account of anything: because we hit a snag, a problem; something goes wrong, and we are stuck. Students are finding difficulties in learning, let us say in learning science – physics, or chemistry; and some of them are failing to learn altogether. Maybe they don't know enough English, we say, if English is not their first language. And yet in other respects they seem to know a lot of English – and anyway, many native speakers of English, for whom it **is** the first language, also have these problems, or very similar ones. So the science teacher blames the English teacher: "You haven't taught them how to write English," he says; and the English teacher replies "It's not my job to teach them the kind of English **you** want – that's your job." But the science teacher has not been trained in linguistics, and all he can think of is a list of technical terms – and this turns out not to be the real problem: learners have little difficulty with technical vocabulary. So he may try out some pet theory of his own, like a former professor of chemistry at Sydney who was convinced that all would be well if only his students understood about prepositions; so he coached them in the use of prepositions – prepositions across the curriculum, as it were. I do not know whether the experience did anything to improve their chemistry.

Clearly, if the notion of 'language across the curriculum' is to be of any use, we need to be able to derive some form of activity from it – there has to be what I have seen referred to recently as an "operationalization" of the concept. (It has to be operationalizationalized?) So we need to understand the nature of this functional variation in language, both in principle and as it is realized in specific instances. What insights have we got, at the present stage?

I have found it useful to refer to functional variation in language as register variation, using the term "register" in a way that is parallel to "dialect", the two being different ways in which a language can vary. Just as dialect variation can be defined along various different lines, and to varying different degrees of discrimination, or "delicacy", so also there are various different factors that determine variation in register; and we can classify registers as finely, or as grossly, as we need. Then we can bring

both dialect **and** register under the same general theory when we need to (this arises particularly in relation to standard forms of languages: in Singapore, for example, all the more highly valued registers of Chinese are associated with Mandarin). A register is a variety of a language that is oriented to a particular context: to a certain type of activity, involving certain groups of people, with a certain rhetorical force.

One feature that we can often specify, for a given register, is the kind of text structure that is appropriate to it. Sometimes this is obvious, and may indeed be specified by the teacher: your science report must begin by stating the purpose of the experiment, followed by the materials used, the method adopted, the observed result and finally the principle you were able to derive from it. But often the text structure is left implicit, even though it may be just as determinate as that of the science report: for example, my colleagues Martin and Rothery found (*Writing Project Report* 1980, Sydney) that primary school teachers had very definite expectations regarding the structure of the stories they were expecting children to write, even though they never told the children what it was they expected from them – because the teachers were unaware of it themselves. In other words they knew, unconsciously, what kind of text structure a narrative of personal experience had to have; but they had not brought this knowledge to consciousness, just as we do not ordinarily bring to consciousness our command of the grammar or the sound system of our language. Even the very informal registers of casual conversation tend to have some kind of structure associated with them; while most of the registers that pupils have to use in school are structured rather tightly, and it may be helpful to them if these are presented and explained.

When it comes to the more strictly linguistic features of a particular register – the meanings that are expressed in it, and the grammar and vocabulary used to express them – we are in greater difficulty. We can of course list the technical terms; but, as pointed out by Dr Nadkarni in his paper to the 1977 seminar here at RELC, that is not really the issue. The more important question is what are the semantic styles, the ways of meaning that are characteristic of this or that kind of discourse; and these we know much less about. It is not the case, however, that we know **nothing** about them; and I shall return to this point in a moment. Before that however I want to refer to the way in which register theory has already been taken into account in the teaching of English to speakers of other languages.

I mentioned earlier that special-purpose language teaching goes back at least to the time of the Second World War; but it was not until the mid–1960s that it came to be recognized as a particular type of language programme. This happened first and foremost in TEFL, where it came to be known as ESP, or English for Special (later changed to Specific) Purposes. Specific purpose language learning is not, of course, tied to English; so I shall go on referring to it as LSP, "Language for Specific Purposes", instead. But so far as I know it has been mainly in English teaching that this principle has been implemented in practice.

Now, I think it is important to point out that, while the LSP concept, and the practices that derived from it, have proved extremely fruitful in language teaching, there is a sense in which these did not fully exploit the notion of register. Let me first give a different example, where another related concept derived from linguistics was taken over into English teaching but without being fully thought through; that was situation theory. The so-called "situational" method, although it was labelled, along with some of the materials, by the use of this term, did not in fact exploit the very rich linguistic notion of 'language in the context of situation'; this concept is much more accurately represented in the more recent practice of communicative language teaching. The communicative approach embodies the 'situation' in its true linguistic sense, as distinct from its rather partial and superficial interpretation as something equivalent to 'setting'.

A similar thing happened with the notion of register as incorporated in ESP. Register has tended to be interpreted in the rather narrow sense of 'subject matter'. Now the subject matter is, certainly, one aspect of the 'field' of the discourse – it is one component in the nature of the social activity that is taking place. But it is only one aspect even of the field; and the field, in turn, is only one alongside two or three other factors that together form the background to the discourse. One also has to take account of the tenor, the social relationships among the participants; and the mode, the specific role that is being allocated to the text. A good example of the difference that this makes is the design of language materials and programmes for those entering tertiary studies in an English-speaking country. If register is defined simply as subject matter, then we should expect to provide subject-oriented courses: English for students of economics, English for students of law, English for students of physics, and so on. But if register is understood in its richer sense, as a combination of meanings of different kinds, representing not only what is being achieved, such as learning economics, but also who are the people involved and in what way are they using language to achieve it, then we should predict that there will be a good deal in common to the language requirements of all forms of tertiary study: the student has to interact with lecturers and tutors, use English in certain ways – to take notes, write essays, and so on; and we should think in terms of courses such as English for university studies, English for technical courses and the like. I am not saying, of course, that this particular theory of register is necessarily the best one; I am saying that if it is understood in the sense in which it was intended, it is likely to lead to certain practices (course design, materials, and so on) being adopted rather than others.

To return for a moment to the question of the ways of meaning that are characteristic of particular registers. Teachers are familiar with the important distinction between different levels of formality: you do not talk to your teacher as you would to your younger brother or sister, and you do not write an essay as you would a letter to a personal friend. They are familiar with certain special linguistic features that have become stereotypic: science English is supposed to be written impersonally with lots of passives, for example. But the distinctive character of a register is very hard to pin down, and this for two reasons: first, what distinguishes one register from another is a matter of probabilities rather than certainties – certain patterns occur more frequently than elsewhere, others less often; and second, many of these features have to do with grammar rather than vocabulary, and grammar is much less obvious to the language user. We notice words; they spring to our attention very easily. It is much harder to notice grammatical patterns.

Let me give an example to show what I mean by this. Here are four different English wordings relating to a particular state of affairs; all of them are quite typical forms of expression:

1. People in southern Sudan have still not got enough to eat.
2. Food is still very scarce in southern Sudan.
3. There is still a shortage of food in southern Sudan.
4. The famine in southern Sudan is still continuing.

If I ask teachers or students of English to compare these wordings, even though I have made the grammatical distinctions among them very obvious, they always react first to the vocabulary: they mention the difference between *eat* and *food*, between *not enough* and *shortage* and *scarce*, and between the different combinations of these, such as *shortage of food*, on the one hand, and the single word *famine* on the other. But what really makes these clauses into different messages is the grammar. They are all fairly informal, even the last; but the information they convey is strikingly different, and different in a number of respects. Let me mention briefly three respects that I would consider most important. (1) The **thing** that is presented as the main entity is different in every case:

people in the first, *food* in the second, *shortage* in the third and *famine* in the fourth. These are the words that function as Head in the nominal group. (2) The **theme** is different in every case: *people in southern Sudan* in the first, *food* in the second, *there* (the existential pronoun, meaning 'something exists') in the third and *the famine in southern Sudan* in the fourth. The theme is the point of departure: what the message is being said to be about. (3) The informational prominence, or the **news value**, of the main event, the famine, is different in every case. In the first, it is fore-grounded, given maximum prominence as an item of news. In the second and third it gets progressively less prominent, until in the fourth example it is fully backgrounded, presented as something that is to be taken for granted. Taken by themselves, of course, these clauses do not constitute different registers; only a piece of discourse can be identified as a particular register, not a single sentence. But the grammatical, or rather lexicogrammatical, variation that I have illustrated is typical of what is likely to be associated with a shift between one register and another. And every one of these patterns might occur as we move with our language across the school curriculum.

I have deliberately chosen an example where the difference is **not** in the subject matter, because I think it is important to get away from the image of language across the curriculum as simply a shift from one content area to another. The variation illustrated in these examples is a variation in the mode of discourse rather than the field; and it leads me to the other factor I want to bring into the discussion of register here: the difference between speech and writing. In any culture that is literate, there will always be a difference between the spoken and the written language. Not usually a clear-cut distinction into two different languages, though this can happen and used to be common enough; nowadays the two are generally closer together, and we have mixed forms, with very colloquial styles of writing and rather bookish kinds of speech – nevertheless the fact that we recognize some speech as bookish, and some writing as colloquial, means that there must be patterns that are typical of speech and others that are typical of writing; otherwise we could not characterize the one as being like what we expect of the other. Now the four examples just given were not sharply distinct in this respect; but they were different enough for us to be able to say that the first was more 'spoken', and the last more 'written', with the other two somewhere in between. If they occurred in school, the first would be likely to be an answer to a teacher's question in class, while the last would have occurred somewhere in a pupil's essay. This is because the background-ing effect that is bought about by nominalizing *the famine in southern*

Sudan is typical of written language, which packages its information very differently from spoken language. There is a significant difference here between speech and writing. The detailed picture of this is fairly complex; but the principle is not difficult to state. Spoken language treats everything as happenings, and trots out each happening as a piece of news in its own right; whereas written language regards the world as a construction of objects, and presents a large part of it in tableau form, as background to what it has to say. Written language thus involves a great deal of grammatical metaphor, whereby one kind of phenomenon is dressed up to look like another – typically, happenings are represented as if they were things. In this particular example, each variant was slightly more metaphorical (in this special sense of grammatical metaphor) than the last. *People have not got enough to eat* is a straightforward account of people and their condition of life. In the second version, *food was scarce*, the 'thing' referred to is food, and the 'state of affairs' that is presented is the quantity of it available. The third refers to a *shortage of food*: in other words, the main protagonist is now a quite fictitious object called a shortage; while in the final version the whole complex phenomenon has become a *famine*, a purely abstract entity, that is then pushed into the background by the definite article *the*, meaning 'you know all about this anyway'.

It is this last form of expression that is characteristic of written language. Taken to great lengths, as it often is, it can be very difficult to follow, and can also lead to ambiguity if you don't know the subject matter. On the other hand, you have more time to work at a written text and to think about it than you have with spoken language; and this is an important factor if you are learning through a language that is not your childhood tongue.

It is useful to be reminded that for most of the history of the human race people managed very well without writing; and although all cultures may eventually choose the path of literacy, there is much insight to be gained from seeing how oral cultures, those communities whose languages never have been written down, interact with their natural environment. When a culture becomes literate, writing tends to take over; it is then the written language that carries authority. So while people in all cultures use language to **teach** their children, those in literate cultures use it to **educate** them – and educational knowledge is knowledge expressed in writing. Hence when we come to school, we are taught to read and write; and from then on, that is how we are expected to learn – through books and magazines, and through the written variety of the language. And teachers sometimes seem to think that before their pupils come to school, before they become literate, in effect they have no knowledge at all. But of course a 5-year-old knows a great deal; he has been learning hard, for five years; and much of what he knows he has learnt through language – which means, for him, through spoken language. He has learnt by listening and by talking.

There has been a considerable amount of research into the role and functions of spoken language in non-literate cultures. But because of the great prestige of writing, there has been very little notice taken of the role of speech in literate cultures. And yet we do not stop talking, when we are able to read and write; and – what is important here – we do not stop learning through talk. Language across the curriculum includes language that is spoken as well as language that is written. Of course, the amount and the kind of talk that goes on in classrooms is very variable; in some parts of the world teachers expect their pupils to listen in silence, and allow them to talk only so they can perform – recite, read aloud, and so on. But they talk about their work among themselves, or with their families at home; there is a spoken language of schoolwork as well as a written one. On the train on which I travel to the university each day there are always a lot of schoolchildren; and they are often talking about their school homework. I have listened regularly to one group of high-school students, about 16 years old, arguing about mathematics. It is, of course, typical informal teenage discourse; but it is strongly task-directed, and highly effective. A great deal of learning can take place in this way.

An effective policy of "language across the curriculum" depends on a linguistic theory of learning, and of the role of language in the learning process. We have to take seriously the contention that people learn **by using language**. And since speech and writing present complementary pictures of the world, each has its place as a vehicle of understanding and of knowledge. No doubt much of what we know could have been learnt equally well either way, either through reading and writing or through talking and listening. But while the written language is good for organizing dense and complex structures, which we can work on in our own time and with fully conscious minds, spoken language is good for following intricate chains of argument that move along at a rapid pace and may even remain slightly below the level of our conscious attention. And, to move to another part of the curriculum, the study of literature, while most kinds of prose may be essentially written discourse, meant for reading, surely most poetry is made to be listened to and spoken aloud.

The distinction between speech and writing is of course just one of the respects in which language varies according to its use. I have chosen it here as my main illustration in order to suggest that, when we talk about language across the curriculum, we are not simply referring to variation in subject matter but to a wider spread of functional variation in language. We still do not know a very great deal about this, and a lot of research is needed into how such variation works. Here are some examples, just a few of the kinds of question that need to be investigated in our research into language across the curriculum:

- What are the text structures required by the different kinds of writing task that are assigned to students? How are these structures made explicit?
- What kinds or logical-semantic connections are typically found in particular kinds of discourse (e.g. biology textbooks, literary critical essays, engineering reports)? Are they usually made explicit, and if so how?
- What is common to different kinds of spoken and written discourse associated with the same subject area (e.g. lecture, seminar, informal discussion, textbook, learned article, popular article)?
- What differences are found among different registers of the curriculum in the way information is organized and presented (balance between old and new information, foregrounding and backgrounding, etc.)?
- How much use is made of grammatical metaphor, and what kinds of grammatical metaphor are most in evidence?
- Is the usual assumption of a common core lexicogrammar justified, and if so how is it defined? Is it essentially a statistical concept?
- What are the characteristic patterns of cohesion? Can we also define the broader concept of coherence in a systematic way, in any of the registers in question; and if so, how?

I have expressed these questions in terms that relate them to English, because it is in English that most of the research up to now has been done. But this raises the even more fundamental question: how far are such features universal? To what extent will the characteristics that we find in English across the curriculum – the English of a physics or chemistry textbook, or the English in which the teacher discusses a poem or short story, or the English of a student's history essay – also turn up in similar contexts in Thai, or in Malay and Indonesian, or in Filipino? Will it always happen, to take one of the fundamental issues, that the language of science, and of scientific cultures (the language of development, we might say, since it is all organized and institutionalized knowledge that is in question, not just science) must be based on nouns rather than verbs? Are all languages following the same path as English, putting nearly all content into nominal constructions? And if they are, is this because people began by translating the textbooks from English (or French, or Russian, all of which have followed the same road)? Or is it because this is an essential step that every language has to take in order that its speakers can apprehend the world in a certain way? Or is it (and this is a third possibility) not an essential step, but one that is desirable in order to maintain the unity of knowledge in the world – it helps if scientific Malay is like scientific English, because then it is easier to move from one to the other. And if we do all submit to the tyranny of the noun, is this then going to hold us back at the next stage of human development when perhaps we shall want to interpret our experience once more in terms of processes rather than of products – as a world that consists of being, becoming, moving, changing rather than just of things? This last part is all speculation; but the serious issue, one that is of immediate relevance to everyone, is what are the consequences of having to function across the curriculum for each language that is now being used, or being developed, as a medium of formal education. Every language is changing, all the time; but what directions do these present changes take?

In linguistically diverse communities, there is always a danger of isolating the language of education, the language in which science and technology, law and government are carried on, from the languages of daily life; the one based on writing, the other on speech – as if these were somehow two different communication systems each with its own domain but with little interaction between them. If you isolate intellectual language, you will isolate intellectual life, and that means you isolate the intellectual from the rest of the community. This is the problem with diglossic situations, where the language that goes across the curriculum may never move outside the curriculum, across the culture as a whole.

But the curriculum is a microcosm of the culture – condensed, distilled, a little rarefied perhaps; but not a different order of reality. The school is part of the community, and the language of education is part of the community's linguistic resources. The continuity between the curriculum and the rest of the culture is thus again a linguistic continuity: it is expressed through language – through the use of the language, in parent-teacher discussions, in public debates, in letters to the press, and so on; but also through the forms of the language – including the way that the registers of education infiltrate into ordinary discourse, which takes over many of the wordings and modes of expression from science and technology (as well as from other highly valued domains). This again is an important process; if it did not happen, then in an age like ours when technology and science are racing ahead year by year the continuity could easily be lost. Our technical educational knowledge is now so far removed from everyday, commonsense knowledge that only common language can keep them in touch. A significant role is played here by such things as popular computing magazines, which combine sophisticated technical language with ordinary everyday discourse, often in a highly entertaining, if linguistically unorthodox manner.

So while language across the curriculum is in one sense – one very important sense – a diversifying concept, in that it embraces the differences, the variation that there must be, between, say, scientific language and literary language, or between teacher language and text-book language, or among essays, group discussion, class notes, formulae and the like – in another sense it is a unifying concept; not only because it embodies the unity of the curriculum itself, through the integrative notion of language as a means of learning, but also because it enables us to relate the registers of the classroom and the laboratory to their counterparts in the world outside – on the construction site, in the shopping centre, in the factory and on the farm. Our teachers need this vision of language for very practical purposes: so that they can evaluate the achievements of their pupils and understand (and help them to understand) why they have succeeded – or why they have not succeeded – in relation to particular goals. This is the diversity of language, matching the diversity of the demands that are made upon it. But in gaining access to this diversity we are also made aware of the unifying effect that derives from it. It is this dynamic potential that language has, which we recognize in the way that it is deployed across the curriculum, that enables our languages to function as they do in maintaining the flow of meaning across the culture.

Chapter Fifteen

CONTEXTS OF ENGLISH
(1994)

Language has always been at the centre of human evolution. This was true of our evolution as a **species**: an essential component of this process was the evolution of a new kind of semiotic, a way of meaning that was qualitatively different from what our predecessors had had. We can still see the traces of that earlier semiotic in the "protolanguage" of very small children, which they develop during the first year of life, before embarking on the mother tongue.[1] It has also been true of every stage of our **cultural** evolution, as each major social and technological trans- formation – we refer to these as "ages": the age of settlement, the iron age, the scientific age, and now the age of information – each of these trans- formations in the human condition has been acted out in language, with important consequences for the system of language itself. Whenever a certain section of the human race changes its basic design for living, language is at one and the same time both a **part** of that change and also a **means** by which the change is brought about. This is the ultimate context for human language.

Consider the "age of science", known to Westerners as the "Renais- sance" and often characterized by the term "modern" (now sometimes opposed to "postmodern"). The old land-based power structures that had dominated agrarian life in most of our Eurasian culture band (the so-called "feudal system") were destroyed, in Western Europe, and replaced by new political formations. These had to be strong enough, and centralized enough, to permit a free and reliable exchange of the products of human labour; so in place of the shifting and unwieldy "empires" of the previous age there emerged relatively stable "nation- states". Like every other political institution, a nation-state is a semiotic entity, a construction of discourse; and this means not only the *texts* through which it is enacted, each with its own particular context of *situation*, but also the *system* that lies behind those texts, the total meaning potential (which we call "language") whose context is the overall context of *culture*. Of course the earlier political formations had been likewise constructed and maintained through language; but what changed was the **role** of language, the demands made by individuals, and by society as a whole, on the semiotic resources available. They now expected to achieve a great deal more by their use of language. The contexts for language were different from what had gone before.

It is probably true to say that with every major change in the human condition the total semiotic resources tend to expand, although one has to be cautious in interpreting what this means. One aspect of this is the technological change that takes place; with the nation-state, this was the introduction of printing. This might seem not to impinge on the system of language; but it does, because it changes the relationship between writer and reader. Writing now takes place in a new context, in which the text is addressed to a readership not only unseen but also unknown, who may have shared little common experience with the writer. But at the same time the potential of language rapidly expands; each language comes to accommodate greater variation than before, and the nature and significance of this variation changes.

At first sight this seems to conflict with what we know – that each language (English, French, German, Italian, Spanish) has previously been a patchwork of different dialects, whereas now there emerged a single variety as the "standard language" of the state. The "dialects" became confined to the fields and to the kitchen, where even if they survived in recognizably distinct form their status was drastically reduced. But while this was happening, the dialect, or dialect mixture, that had gained status as the standard language was itself beginning to grow, to accrue to itself a whole range of new varieties. These new varieties, however, are not of the old dialectal kind, different forms of expression distinguishing one county's speech from that of its neighbours. They are *diatypic* varieties, or "registers", marked out not by region but by **function** – by the contexts they are called on to construe. Since in the new political structures many people, including all those in positions of power, participate in a variety of different contexts in the course of their lives (indeed typically in the course of a single day), such people are polyglot; they control a range of different registers, and shift among them. (Of course this sort of thing had happened before; but on a much more limited scale.) Thus a standard language does not just take over in contexts that existed before.

Rather, it creates new contexts for meaning; and its meaning potential inevitably tends to grow.

What do we mean when we say that a language grows? Most people think that language is made of words; so when a language grows, this means that its vocabulary increases. Like most folk views on language, this contains a part of the truth: new contexts often do engender new words. Linguists do not usually try to count the words in a language, and there are good reasons for this. In the first place, it is hard to know what to count. Words are often not very clearly defined, either syntagmatically or paradigmatically; we cannot tell where they begin and end, nor do we know what are two words and what are two variants of the same word – if the same lexical item is both noun and verb, without change, as typically in Chinese, is it two words or one? are the past and present tense forms of a verb, in English, say, or in Japanese, the same word or not? or the various cases of a noun, as in Russian? Of course it is always possible to devise some answer to these questions; but it is extraordinarily difficult to provide an answer which will be valid for all languages, or even for the same language at different stages in its history.

But there is another, more important reason for not trying to count words, and that is that words are part of grammar ("lexicogrammar" is a more accurate term). What one language may achieve by lexical means another language may accomplish in the grammar; furthermore since words are grammatical constructs, new ones can always be created. This can of course be achieved by "borrowing", the kind of mixing of languages that goes on all the time: either borrowing at the phonological level ("loanwords"), as is commonly done in English and in Japanese, or borrowing at the lexicogrammatical level ("calques"), as is the norm in Chinese. But every language has resources for making new words out of its own stock, like the derivational and compounding principles that are being used all the time in English. The COBUILD corpus project at the University of Birmingham in England has an ongoing programme for monitoring the new words that appear each week in the various written sources that it surveys. So there is no very meaningful way of counting the total number of words in a language. At the same time it is clear that there are more words in use now in English than there were, say, a thousand years ago; and – the significant point – that the difference is an outcome of the range of functional variety in which the language is now involved. By and large, when a language does more work, its meaning potential expands; and words are one source of this semantic power.

308

In a language such as modern English, which does a great deal of work of a very varied kind, a best guess of the number of words currently disposable, if we include all the technical vocabularies, might be somewhere in the seven-figure range: more than a million, and less than ten million. But of course no individual speaker uses them all. Any one person, using English regularly in a typical adult register range, might call actively on, say, between one per cent and five per cent of the total; they would no doubt understand many more, especially in a living context, or at least have some sense of what they were about. But that still leaves a vast number that would mean nothing to them at all. I myself, for example, would have no access to the vast inventory of medical, chemical and pharmaceutical terms that are recognized as part of modern English. None of us can participate in more than a fraction of the semiotic contexts that make up today's English-speaking culture.

So if we say a language grows, this is a functional-semantic concept; it means that it expands its meaning potential, extending the scope and depth of its existing contexts and also moving into new ones. And it is important to make a distinction at this point. Every language – and that means every language that is somebody's mother tongue – is capable of expanding its meaning potential indefinitely in the way that languages such as English and Chinese and Russian have done. But only a very small proportion of human languages have in fact expanded in this way. It requires particular historical conditions; and it requires a considerable amount of time. What we call a "standard" language is one that has set out along the road of functional expansion, becoming a resource for at least some of the complex semiotic contexts of a modern nation-state.

There has always been some functional variation in language, alongside variation of a dialectal kind. Speakers of unwritten languages typically make distinctions between religious and secular speech, poetry and prose, narrative and dialogue, forms of political rhetoric, and so on; and are often aware of differences between some functionally marked variety and the language of daily life, just as we who live in written cultures are ourselves. These may also include some esoteric words – Malinowski used to refer to the "coefficient of weirdness" of magical in contrast with pragmatic speech. But words are only a part of the resources available, and not even a necessary part; we often find texts that are clearly in some fairly specialized register but which use hardly any terms from outside the daily language. (One way of putting this is to say that not every special register of a language is *technicalized*.) What is it, then, that people are responding to when they identify the particular context of a given piece of discourse in their language?

Here is a passage of English, which one can easily assign to a source:

> Rain showers will be scattered across the central lake region today. Elsewhere variable cloudiness is expected. Skies will become clear tonight. Tomorrow will be mostly sunny. High temperatures will be in the middle 70s, lows will be near 60 degrees.

It is a weather forecast from the *New York Times*. It has some special words in it, such as *cloudiness*. But the main lexical effect is the **collocation** of words from one semantic domain (*rain, shower, skies, sunny, temperatures*); and the co-occurrence of these with words from another set, that of time, and specifically time relative to the present day (*today, tonight, tomorrow*). Each word by itself is very ordinary; what we respond to is the way they go together.

But the way the words go together is not simply a matter of co-occurrence. They are not presented to us in a list; they are a part of the total **wording**, the lexicogrammatical construction of the discourse, which includes also the grammatical features of all kinds: the structure of the clauses, phrases and groups, and the particular options selected within each. For example, unlike typical conversation, where people like to join as much as they can together grammatically, this passage is rather fragmented, with each clause standing more or less on its own. Along with this we notice the higher lexical density, which is characteristic of writing rather than speech. Most of all perhaps we are aware of one or two specific grammatical features. One of these is the pattern of tense choices: out of six finite clauses, five are in the future tense. Another is the structure found with *cloudiness is expected*, instead of, say, *it is expected to be cloudy* (compare, in another example, *gradual clearing will follow* instead of *it will gradually become clear*), where a noun *cloudiness* is used in place of the more usual adjective *cloudy*.

Now neither of these patterns, the future tense or the nominalized verb or adjective, is in any way remarkable in itself. We derive nouns from verbs and adjectives all the time; and the future tense is part of the core grammar of English. But locutions such as *cloudiness is expected*, *clearing will follow*, are more likely to occur in more technical contexts; while in almost all forms of discourse the future is notably less frequent than the past or the present – whereas here it leaps out in front as the most highly favoured choice of tense. And this provides a clue to the nature of register variation.[2]

Register variation is variation in the **setting of linguistic probabilities**. Most of the time, when speakers of a language develop that language in new functional contexts, they do not invent new grammatical

310

forms. They exploit and extend those that are already there. In so doing, they realign the probabilities of the system. The future tense is a case in point: in weather forecasts, the probability of future shifts from being way below that of past or present to being significantly above the sum of those two together. There is no surprise in this; a weather forecast is, obviously, a text that is concerned with the future. But the fact that this semantic feature is explicitly realized in the grammar, by the perturbation of the frequency pattern of the tense system (perhaps with other realizations also, for example special lexical selections such as *expect*, *predict*, *forecast*), enables the reader to locate the text in its semiotic environment. In other words, the text **construes** its own context of situation by its overall quantitative profile.

"Setting the probabilities" means, in fact, resetting them in contradistinction to other register varieties – that is, by reference to the general probabilities inherent in the linguistic system. It is important to understand, therefore, the probabilistic nature of grammar itself. The grammar of a natural language is a system of probabilities. If we say, for example, that the finite verb in English has three primary tenses, past, present and future, what does this statement mean? First of all, it means that these three stand in a paradigmatic relationship each to the others: that there is a specific environment, in the grammar of English, where the speaker must choose one, but only one, out of these three options. In other words, in the terminology of system-structure grammar, they form a **system**. But that is not the whole story. In order to characterize that system adequately, we need to add **with certain probabilities attached to each of the terms**. Similarly when we say that a clause is positive or negative, a nominal group is singular or plural, a clause is declarative, interrogative or imperative, a verbal group is either active or passive, and many other such key grammatical systems: what we have to explain is not merely that these are alternatives that arise at a defined location in the grammar, but that they are alternatives that carry with them a particular weighting. And the weighting, in relative probability, of each one of its terms is an essential part of the meaning that the system brings into the text.[3]

Until very recently, if grammarians wanted to include quantitative information of this kind, they had to guess at it by extrapolating from very small samples. But now the situation is changing. With very large modern corpuses, such as the COBUILD English Language Corpus at the University of Birmingham in England, under the direction of Professor John Sinclair, it is possible to gain access to very large bodies of discourse.[4] The Birmingham project now has a corpus of 200 million words on line; and it is classified according to the register, so that in principle it is possible to establish both the overall, global probability pattern of a grammatical system, and its local probabilities as "reset" for any particular register. We can thus follow up the important work begun by Svartvik in the 1960s when he used the original data of Professor Quirk's Survey of English Usage in London to examine the relative frequency of active and passive in text samples of about 12 different varieties of written English.[5]

I said that "in principle" it is possible to establish the patterns of probabilities; but this needs to be stringently qualified! Since we need to take into account not just thousands but millions of instances, we cannot access them manually; the program must identify them for us. But no parser is yet accurate enough – and, more to the point, no parser is yet **fast** enough – to be able to undertake the task. Therefore, we have to be able to devise pattern-matching procedures that will work directly on the corpus as it is stored and indexed, and identify the instances of the categories we are interested in within an acceptable margin of error. This is really the major challenge that is posed by this kind of work; and in tackling problems of this kind we learn a great deal about the grammatical profile of the language.

If grammatical probabilities vary systematically from one register to another, this suggests that at some level of consciousness speakers of the language are aware of them – that is, they are a part of what it means to "know" a language. It was shown some time ago that speakers are aware of the relative frequencies of words: a speaker of English knows, and can bring the knowledge to conscious attention, that for example *go* is more frequent than *grow* and *grow* is more frequent than *glow* – or, to use words related in meaning rather than in sound, that *go* is more frequent than *walk* and *walk* is more frequent than *stroll*. By contrast with lexis, grammar is buried more deeply below the level of our conscious attention, so people cannot usually answer questions about grammatical frequencies; but this is partly because it is difficult to do so without using abstract labels for the grammatical categories, which they are not familiar with. But they are rather sensitive to **fluctuations** in grammatical frequencies, and very likely could bring at least some of these patterns to consciousness if some means could be found of probing them. If I may be allowed to refer for a moment to my own personal history, the context in which I myself originally began raising questions about grammatical frequencies was as a language learner, and subsequently as a language teacher. When learning a foreign language I had wanted to know which options in the various grammatical systems were more likely to be selected than others; it seemed to me to be an essential element in the meaning of the system, as well as important knowledge for a learner to have access to (as a child has, when learning the mother tongue), and when I taught a foreign language I wanted to be able to pass such information on to my students. (At that time, of course, I was not aware of its importance in distinguishing one register from another.)

The reason that there can be systematic variation of this kind is of course that it is not arbitrary; it is semantically motivated. That is to say, there is variation in the kinds of meaning that are being construed – and therefore in the words and structures that construe them (that "realize" them, to use the technical form of wording). We sometimes tend to forget this, because it is precisely when such variation ceases to be semantically functional, and becomes **ritualized**, that we become most keenly aware of it. Thus, for example, using the **passive**, in scientific English, became at a certain time round about a hundred years ago a kind of ritualistic claim for objectivity, for the authority attached to impersonal observations; writers of scientific reports and papers were enjoined to use the passive, to say *it was observed that* rather than *I observed that*. (Eventually, of course, this led to a reaction **against** the passive and people started to be told **not** to use it, which is equally silly.) But it did not start this way. The reason the passive was used in early scientific writing was no different from the reason for which it is used in ordinary English conversation, where it is also a normal feature: namely, to distribute the information contained in the wording of the clause. For example, here is a little snippet out of the middle of a piece of conversation:

She said she wished that everybody would take the thing seriously when they were told

– where it would be rather unnatural to use anything but the passive in the final clause: the word *they* is the natural Theme, since it is already given, so it comes first, whereas the New information, that which the listener is needing to attend to, is contained in the verb (which needs no active participant, since it doesn't matter who told them, and can therefore come in the position of prominence, at the end). Now considerations of this kind, relating to the flow of information, are very important in scientific prose discourse; and when Isaac Newton and his contemporaries began developing a register of experimental science they followed normal speech patterns and used the passive where it gave the appropriate balance. Here are two examples from Newton's *Opticks*, one with an Agent and one without:

313

This is the reason of the decay of sight in old Men, and shews why their sight is mended by Spectacles.

For if the Rays, which at their entering into the Body are put into Fits of easy Transmission, arrive at the farthest Surface of the Body before they be out of those Fits, they must be transmitted.

Note that these passives have nothing to do with being objective or impersonal; indeed Newton showed no coyness about saying "I" did this and that – the previous sentence in the last example starts *In this Proposition I suppose the transparent Bodies to be thick*. Another example of something in the grammar which people became aware of because it got ritualized in this way is that of turning verbs and adjectives into nouns, which I exemplified earlier with the word *cloudiness* in the weather forecast. I have written about this elsewhere;[6] again, it was originally motivated, when it first emerged as a prominent feature in the same period of scientific writing, very clearly by the requirements of the discourse; the need to build up a logical argument in which material previously introduced as new information could then be "packaged", so to speak, in a nominalized form so as to serve as the point of departure for the next step in the argument. Here again is a brief example from Isaac Newton, taken from the same passage concerned with the decay of sight:

If the Humours of the Eye by old Age decay, . . . the Light will not be refracted enough, and for want a sufficient Refraction will not converge to the bottom.

Notice how the clausal expression *will not be refracted enough* has been turned into a nominal one, *want of a sufficient Refraction*, so as to function as the Theme of the following clause. This was the typical discursive context for such nominalizations.

But in the centuries that followed this pattern steadily became ritualized, first as a key signature of the language of physical science, because of its high prestige, and then as a feature of the elaborated discourses of bureaucracy and power, where it typically has no local semantic motivation at all.[7]

But establishing large-scale probability profiles of very general grammatical systems, such as active and passive, or past and future, important though it is to our understanding of the system of the language and its potential for functional variation, is only one aspect of the power of today's computerized corpuses. The modern corpus is an extremely powerful theoretical instrument for linguistic research, and among other things it enables us to make the entire concept of functional variation explicit in lexicogrammatical terms. Thus the concept of the resetting of probabilities applies to lexis as well as to grammar. But in lexis it has different implications. On the one hand, there are often lexical items which occur **only** in a particular register – this is the commonsense understanding of a "technical term"; and on the other hand, where the variation lies in the different **distribution** of the lexical items within one register and another, the notion of probability has to be differently defined. Lexical items do not function in paradigmatically closed systems; so there is nothing in lexis analogous to shifting the probabilities between active and passive in the grammar. But they do occur in two kinds of syntagmatic environment, one lexical the other grammatical. Lexically, they occur in *collocational* patterns, better–than–random associations of one word with another; grammatically they occur with specific functions in clauses, phrases and groups. As far as the vocabulary in concerned, therefore, the major distinction between different registers is likely to be found in the way the words are deployed in their lexical and grammatical environments. The COBUILD team in Birmingham is undertaking systematic research in both these areas, leading to significant new conceptions both of the dictionary and of the grammar.

To return for a moment to the conception of a language growing, or becoming bigger: it could be argued that, if the probabilities are just being "reset" in this way, so that one pattern of collocation is replaced by another, or there is a shift in the relative frequency of the terms in a grammatical system, the language has not grown any bigger; only by accumulating **new** words, or **new** grammatical structures, can it increase in size. There is of course no virtue in simply growing bigger; indeed we might argue that in language, as in other domains of our experience, "small is beautiful"! But there is an issue of some relevance here. If you switch around the probabilities of a system, you may increase its overall meaning potential. I say "you may" because this will in fact depend. If one profile is merely replaced by another, such that the first one disappears as a functioning system, then of course there is no gain. But if the first continues in use, such that the two patterns now co-exist, then the overall meaning potential has increased. When the probabilities of the tense system come to be reset, as in the language of English weather fore-casting, it has become in a significant sense a different system. A new dimension of meaning potential has been added to tense in the verb: it can now construe a form of reality, a "universe of discourse", in which the norm, the unmarked temporal state, is that of the future. We now have two different temporal perspectives: and if we also take into our consideration a third perspective, already construed in the register of narrative fiction, in which the unmarked temporal reality is that of the past, we can see how the existence of these two registers, that of forecasting the future and that of fictionalizing the past, adds a new dimension to our semantic space if we compare it with a universe of discourse in which only the present appears as the temporal norm. (We do not yet know, incidentally, whether there is a systematic distinction between fictional narrative and other registers in this respect; the quantitative analysis still remains to be done.) What is significant, here, is that the variation we are observing is *semantic*; it is variation in the grammar's construction of meaning (just as, if we find collocational differences among different registers this is variation in the lexical construction of meaning). Thus any language in which weather forecasts are a recognized context for meaning construes a future-based model of reality, whether or not its verbs have a future tense. Grammars have many different ways of construing the meanings that go to make up human experience.

Of course some registers die out. I do not know whether we still have a register of falconry in English or not, but I have certainly never come across it. But in the modern period, at least, wherever a standard language has evolved it has consistently enlarged its register range. We do not know whether there is any limit to this process: whether a language can get overloaded, so that it fragments into smaller pieces (like the fragmentation of dialects into different languages in the past). But provided that does not happen – provided, that is, the language continues to develop new contexts for meaning without these becoming in some sense different languages – then in the course of growing it is also bound to change. Each new expansion of the meaning potential, whether it is powered by new forms of wording or by shifts in the alignment of existing forms, inevitably affects the overall character of the language. There is no insulation between the various registers; the meanings leach into one another in the course of time, even the most highly technical and specialized registers ultimately impinging, however indirectly, on the most everyday, functionally non-specialized form of discourse, casual conversation among family or close friends. The semantic styles of today's casual conversation in English are vastly different from those of a hundred years ago. This is not something immediately visible in the outward appearance of the language: I am not talking of those changes that take place at the formal level, in phonology and grammatical structure, without affecting the meaning potential – the sort of changes that have taken place in languages everywhere throughout their history.

316

On the contrary; standard languages, since they are written down and institutionalized, tend to change less in this respect than those that are non-standard, or non-standardized. But in their meaning potential they change more, because they are constantly moving into new contexts and new functional domains.

Needless to say there can be a great deal of variation in the conditions under which standard languages emerge, and in the relationship between the standard language and the vernaculars in everyday use as "mother tongues". In the course of its evolution as the standard language of the nation-state in England, standard English took over in political and administrative contexts from French and in scientific and ecclesiastical contexts from Latin; while in commercial and industrial contexts English functioned from the start. In communities characterized by what is known by Charles Ferguson's term "diglossia", there is an ongoing disjunction between the everyday spoken languages and the standard language of education and political and cultural life. Ferguson's own researches were focused on the Arab world of today, where the situation is largely of this kind: there is a considerable gap between standard ("classical") Arabic and the colloquial varieties spoken in the Arabian peninsula, Iraq, Jordan, Palestine, Egypt and the other countries of northern Africa. Even here, however, there is continued exchange of meaning between the "high" and the "low" varieties; the "high" form, even if it is nobody's mother tongue today, had been at some time in the past, and is clearly recognized by its users as a variety of their own language – albeit a special one, appropriate for the more elaborated functions. (It is thus quite distinct from an artificial language such as Esperanto, which has never functioned as a mother tongue to anyone.) The meanings construed in the extensive register range of today's classical Arabic can readily be adapted into the various forms of colloquial Arabic; and on the other hand, the classical language itself is constantly being modulated by the semantic styles and motifs of everyday discourse. One may compare it in this respect with Latin in medieval Europe, which was very different from the spoken Latin of the classical period, having adapted to the semantics of the European vernaculars; or with classical Chinese, which although retaining much of the formal characteristic of the pre-Han language, had by Sung times a very different semantic foundation, and was different again by the time it was overtaken by the modern standard language in the present century. Even in such situations there is no total disjunction between the elaborated semiotic of knowledge and power and the ordinary everyday language in which people live their daily lives.

317

Indeed there cannot be. There is bound to be a regular two-way traffic between the discourse of commonsense and the discourses of educational knowledge and social power. This follows inevitably from the functions that language plays in human existence, the essential continuity between the contexts of these two semiotic modes. At the most fundamental level, all language serves a twofold function: on the one hand, we use language to construe our experience, to make operational sense out of what goes on around us and inside our bodies; and on the other hand, we use language to enact our interpersonal relationships, to take part in social processes and to identify our selves at the intersection of those processes. (We refer to these in systemic theory as "metafunctions": the experiential metafunction, and the interpersonal metafunction.) This is how we learn our mother tongues, as the semiotic resource that enables us to do these things. But the new forms of understanding, and new patterns of behaviour, which are construed and enacted in the elaborated registers of the standard language, are simply extensions of these original metafunctional resources. The interplay of knowledge and power which is enshrined in a standard language is built up on the interplay between the experiential and the interpersonal components in the grammar of the mother tongue.

Of these two aspects of the meaning potential, knowledge and power, it is that of knowledge which primarily concerns us here. The point is, then, that educational and scientific-technical knowledge is built upon commonsense knowledge; hence the *grammar* in which educational knowledge is construed is a direct extension of the grammar that we learnt at our mother's knee. Each one of us, in our first encounters with our mother tongue, built up a formidable potential for meaning, a semiotic powerhouse that enabled us to make sense out of our environment and to act successfully on it. How did we do this? We did it by constructing for ourselves *contexts* of language use, situations in which a resonance was set up between the grammar and some other part of our experience. (Lemke explains this resonance by his theory of "meta-redundancy" in semiotic systems.[8]) Or rather, one should say: in which a resonance **could be** set up, because small children are constantly **challenging** their grammar, setting it tasks which stretch its potential up to and beyond its current limits. They are doing this in order to construct a theory of experience – because that is what a grammar is (I mean the grammar of a natural language), or at least it is one of the things that a grammar is. But by the same token, this ensures that the same grammar will continue to serve as the foundation for all future extensions of that theory, including its extension into the realm of educational and technical knowledge. A scientific theory is itself a semiotic system, a kind of grammar; and even the most abstruse discourses of scientific theory-making depend for their effectiveness on the grammar of daily life. They depend on it both as a **means** and as a **model**. It is the means because scientific theories are construed in natural language grammar; aided of course by mathematics, but never entirely replaced by it (and mathematics itself has its ultimate foundations in natural language). It is the model because it itself evolved as a theory for construing human experience, and its role in building a scientific theory is thus an extension of one of the primary contexts by which its own structure was originally shaped.

The problem facing students of a foreign language (or one of the problems – there are many!) can be formulated in these terms. They want to move into it at the adult level, typically in order to grapple with some of the elaborated registers of educational knowledge, or at the very least to engage in meaningful encounters with adult writing and speech. And this is a reasonable expectation; after all they have mastered one mother tongue, maybe more than one, so they know what a language can do and they have used it to construe their own primary experience. They certainly have to build on that semiotic foundation; but it is not sufficient to guarantee success, because there are many possible ways of construing human experience, and not all languages do it in exactly the same way. Many years ago I used to teach Chinese to a group of scholars, university teachers and graduate students in science and other fields, who wanted to read Chinese academic writings in their own particular disciplines. They were well acquainted with the intellectual contexts in question; and they did not need to know anything of the background of traditional Chinese **culture** – their interest was in Chinese contributions to twentieth-century scientific research. But I found that I needed to teach them how meaning is constructed in the ordinary everyday Chinese **language**: for example, which meanings are grammaticalized in Chinese but not in English (e.g. aspect and phase) and vice versa (e.g. tense and number); the principle whereby systems in Chinese typically have an unmarked term (contrast English past, present or future, where it must be one or the other, with Chinese perfective or imperfective, where it can also be neither); the way that information is organized (here Chinese is remarkably similar to English, although there are differences, including subtle patterns of rhythm which play a part in written discourse), and so on. These are all features of everyday spoken Chinese; but their resonance is felt even in the most elaborated forms of the written mode. The Chinese physicist and linguist Y. R. Chao pointed out many years ago how it is that many people find it difficult to learn a language only in its written form (I discovered early on in adult life that I myself could never do this, so I understood very well what he meant!). Language learners, as we know, fall into different types according to where they find themselves to be located along certain basic learning dimensions, and many can in fact learn purely written languages without much trouble; but Chao's point is a valid one – there is a sense in which the experience of a language in its spoken mode gives access to meanings that are assumed in the written language but not easily accessed solely through written discourse.

What one tries to do, as a teacher, for the adult learning a foreign language is what one tries to do in any teaching situation: if the learners lack certain important dimensions of prior experience we try to identify other aspects of their experience which will be relevant to the learning task. If you are studying scientific and technical Chinese, it helps greatly if you already speak everyday conversational Chinese. But if you don't, you can at least build some expectations on the knowledge you have of scientific and technical varieties of your own mother tongue – English, in the example I was discussing. That is to say, if you can't move vertically, to the same language in a new context, at least you can try to move sideways, carrying over the same context to a new language. (The biggest problem arises when a learner has to move both upwards and sideways in a single diagonal leap.)

In other words, we can try to exploit, in the learning task, the kinds of context which are shared between one human culture and another. There are some quite significant differences between scientific English and scientific Chinese; but there is also a great deal in common, and the learner already familiar with the discourse of a scientific discipline in his own language can make use of this experience in trying to master that in another. No doubt the same general pattern of relationship (though different in its specifics, of course) would hold among scientific varieties whatever the language. Since the disciplines of science and technology are a part of our world culture, there is much in common to these contexts, and to the discourse that is associated with them, in whatever language it is couched. At the same time we should note, perhaps, that even in the most internationalized of disciplines, like physics, chemistry and mathematics, there may be considerable differences in the way that discourse is organized at the level of rhetorical structure. Clyne has pointed out that even between English and German, which are closely related both in language and in their contexts of culture, there are noticeably different traditions of scholarly writing.[9] And it seems that the further you move away from the physical sciences, the greater such differences are likely to become. Again perhaps we can explain this in linguistic terms.

As I expressed it earlier, human language evolved in two primary functional contexts: construing personal *experience*, and enacting *interpersonal* relations. Every human language instantiates these two metafunctions, its lexicogrammar constructing a meaning potential in which they become integrated in unitary acts of meaning (and the grammar has evolved a third component, the *textual*, whereby such acts of meaning become discourse, a kind of virtual reality in semiotic form). Since all of us live on the same planet, and we all have the same brains, there are limits – even though they are quite generous limits – to the possible, or at least plausible, semiotic constructions of experience. Hence those aspects of scholarship which depend more on the experiential component in the semantics of everyday discourse, like the physical sciences (primarily experiential) and mathematics (depending on a fourth and final component, the *logical* element in natural language), will tend to be more readily translatable between one language and another. But there is much less constraint on the variation among human cultures; so in those sciences which deal with human society and its relationships, with systems which embody a concept of *value*, we derive relatively more of our understanding from the interpersonal component in the everyday language. In sociology, therefore, and in psychology, there is much greater scope for each language to import its own cultural preconceptions into the field, whether in the interpretation of its own culture or of that of other human groups. (The most problematic field of all, of course, is linguistics; but that is another story.)[10]

In the very long term, no doubt, there is a tendency for the contexts of any one language to become the same as those of every other language: the move towards a unified and homogeneous world culture that we sometimes hear people talk about. But I cannot see this on the agenda yet, nor even until some way into the future. I tend to look at the question first and foremost as a linguist, which is only one of the possible angles of vision – but a relevant one, since culture is largely constructed out of language. Here the most striking thing that is happening is that many languages are disappearing; this has been identified by UNESCO as an ecological disaster and an international committee has been set up, under the chairmanship of Professor Stephen Wurm, to seek out possible remedies. At the same time, and as a related phenomenon (though not identical with it), many human cultures are drastically changing, as people are forced to abandon their traditional ways of living. Those whose cultures are most at risk are those whose lifestyles are most sharply at variance with, indeed in conflict with, our so-called "modern" methods of exploiting the resources of the planet – the "hunting-and-gathering" communities who do not form permanent settlements. We do not usually find communities speaking large-scale languages such as English or German undergoing such catastrophic cultural transformations; indeed they don't. But this does not mean that there can be no significant discontinuities in the cultural contexts of these languages. I recently gave an overseas audience an example of the dialect spoken by some of my older relatives at the time when I was still a child – not my own dialect, because I grew up in a big city, but the "original" dialect of the country region roundabout, which I had learnt to understand. Needless to say, the audience found it unintelligible (as would most native speakers of English!). I have not been back to that part of the north of England for many years; but I imagine that nobody speaks that dialect any more, except perhaps as a museum piece – that is, it is no longer learnt as a mother tongue, which means that, effectively, it has died. And the patterns of culture that went with the dialect, whereby some folk perhaps never went out beyond their own valley throughout the whole of their lives, have also disappeared – that is to say, the local culture has been transformed into something quite different from what it was. The contexts of English have changed, and continue to change all the time.

This does not mean, of course, that English no longer functions as a language of family and neighbourhood, of the home and the street (something that learners of English as a foreign language often tend to forget!). Whatever its contexts on the global scale, it is still the mother tongue for hundreds of millions of people; that is what keeps it alive. But its local contexts have evolved into new situations and settings. The centre of gravity of the home has shifted; the neighbourhood has become the shopping centre; and the meanings that are construed by the grammar and vocabulary of the language are now urban rather than rural, commercial rather than communal, leisure-oriented rather than work-oriented.

And here there are conflicting tendencies in play, just as there were in seventeenth-century England when the new discourses of physical science first impinged on the language of daily life. On the one hand the changes in semiotic style have made the everyday language much more permeable to the elaborated languages of technology and science; meanings move across much more easily than they could do into the traditional semantics of the countryside. But at the same time – and by the same token, in fact – these discourses of the modern world may come to seem alien and remote, and the English in which they are constructed may seem to many to be setting up an increasingly esoteric and hostile reality (which is then mediated through another semiotic, the modern fairy tale – space fantasies, horror movies and the like). Linguistically speaking, it is primarily the nominalizing structures in the grammar, together with the complex of related features that I have referred to collectively as "grammatical metaphor", which have the effect of construing a world that is distant and disjoined from experience, a world made of abstract and technical things; so that, while building directly on the resources that evolved in the mother-tongue grammar, the resulting discourse seems to invoke contexts that are incompatible with the forms of experience which the mother tongue first construed. This is perhaps the major problem for language education in contemporary Western societies.

But while this is happening with the older varieties of English, at the same time the language is extending into new contexts of a very different kind. These are the context of the "new varieties of English" (called "NVEs", as I first learnt in Singapore), where English functions in India, Africa, South-East Asia and elsewhere as a living semiotic resource for the cultures of the region. Here the language of the former colonial power has come to take on the positive values of a forward-looking post-colonial society. What makes this possible is that the language takes on board the meanings that have evolved within these cultures; in other words it becomes ***resemanticized*** in response to its new contexts and conditions. But the result is a new meaning potential, which is different both from the "old" varieties of English and from the local languages. It is still English, and so brings with it the semantic patterns with which English itself evolved; but these now come face to face with the meaning potential of other, non-European cultures. The result is a tension between two distinct semiotic systems, out of which emerges something that is not the same as either of the components which made it up. This appears clearly in the new literatures of the Commonwealth, which already feature many writers of international standing and acclaim. This kind of interpenetration is not new in the history of language; it has happened ever since human groups began splitting up and then recombining in new formations. What is new is the scale on which it is happening, the cultural distances that are traversed, and most of all perhaps the great diversity of semiotic contexts that are being created in this way (for example, the new literatures are widely read outside their place of origin, including by speakers of old varieties of English).

What is the outcome of this multiplicity of different contexts? Kachru prefers to talk about "Englishes" rather than just "English"; his work has done more than anyone's to describe and interpret what is happening.[11] The late Professor Peter Strevens, a thoughtful observer of the global linguistic scene, was one of the first to argue for recognizing these local varieties of English as legitimate norms and standards: "Indian English", "West African English", "Singapore English", and so forth. This does not mean that English is breaking up into "daughter" languages, like the language families of the past; what is happening is more complex than that. On the one hand, what evolve in such situations are "creole continua", scales of dialectal varieties that evolve wherever a standard language is imported from outside – as for example with Mandarin Chinese in Singapore. At the "acrolectal", upper end of the scale, the language has international currency; at the "basilectal", lower end it has only local compass. This is dialect-like variation, mainly in the lexico-grammar and phonology. On the other hand, semantically the new varieties of English add further dimensions to the overall semantic space that goes by the name of English. (Here perhaps the problem with Kachru's term "Englishes" is that it is too discrete. All these varieties shade into one another. A mass noun such as "Englishness" might be more appropriate!)

This multidimensional semantic space is the meaning potential defined by all the contexts of English taken together. Of course no speaker of the language controls it all. But it is a relevant concept to work with. Probably no other language has ever covered quite such a disparate range of human experience and human relationships. To avoid any misunderstanding, let me say clearly that this has nothing to do with its inherent qualities as a language; it is the product of its unique history. Any other language that happened to have been in those places at those times under those sociopolitical conditions could have developed in comparable ways; they would not have been identical, of course, because each language has its own special characterology; but they would have been no less complex and diversified. As I said, no one can control it all. But speakers of English can move about within this semantic space exploring where they want. You can use it to listen to Billy Joel or Michael Jackson, to sell computers to people, or to immerse yourself in the living cultures not only of the Anglo-Saxon world but of many regions of Asia, Africa, the Caribbean and the Pacific. In hardly any of these contexts would I hear the English that I grew up with, with its particular vowels and consonants, its rhythms, and its characteristic forms of expression. But that happens to anyone, whatever their mother tongue, when they move among changing contexts in a changing world.

Notes

1. For the "protolanguage" see my (1975) *Learning How to Mean: Explorations in the Development of Language*, Edward Arnold, London; Elsevier, New York, 1977. See also Clare Painter (1984), *Into the Mother Tongue: A Case Study in Early Language Development*, Pinter Publishers, London and New York.
2. For a detailed theoretical treatment of register and context, see Christian Matthiessen (1993) "Register in the round: diversity in a unified theory of register analysis", in Mohsen Ghadessy, ed., *Register Analysis: Theory into Practice*, Pinter Publishers, London and New York.
3. See my "Corpus Studies and Probabilistic Grammar", in Karin Aijmer and Bengt Altenberg, eds (1991), *English Corpus Linguistics: Studies in Honour of Jan Svartvik*, Longman, London and New York.
4. For an account of the COBUILD corpus project and the programme of research based on the corpus, see John M. Sinclair, ed. (1992), *Looking Up: An Account of the Cobuild Project in Lexical Computing*, Collins ELT, London and Glasgow.
5. Jan Svartvik (1996), *On Voice in the English Verb*, Mouton, The Hague.
6. A brief historical account appears in my "On the language of physical science", in Mohsen Ghadessy, ed. (1988), *Registers of Written English: Situational Factors and Linguistic Features*, Pinter Publishers, London and New York. See also M.A.K. Halliday and J.R. Martin (1993), *Writing Science: Literacy and Discursive Power*, Falmer Press, London and Washington DC.
7. For discussion and illustration of this point see J.L. Lemke (1990), "Technical discourse and technocratic ideology", in M.A.K. Halliday, John Gibbons and Howard Nicholas, eds, *Learning, Keeping and Using Language: Selected Papers from the Eighth World Congress of Applied Linguistics, Sydney 16–21 August 1987*, Vol 2., Benjamins, Amsterdam and Philadelphia.
8. The concept of "metaredundancy" is introduced and explained by J.L. Lemke in Chapter 3 of his (1984) *Semiotics and Education*, Victoria University, Toronto Semiotic Circle Monographs, Working Papers and Prepublications, No. 2, Toronto.
9. See the article "Directionality, rhythm and cultural values" by Michael Clyne (1991) in Frances Christie, ed., *Literacy in Social Processes: Papers from the Inaugural Australian Systemic Networks Conference, Deakin University, 18–21 January 1990*, Northern Territory University, Centre for Studies of Language in Education, Darwin, NT.
10. The metafunctional foundations of lexicogrammar, and their significance in the construction of higher level semiotic systems, have been discussed

in many places within systemic linguistics. See, among others, articles by J.R. Martin and Paul Thibault (1991) in Eija Ventola, ed., *Functional and Systemic Linguistics: Approaches and Uses*, Mouton de Gruyter, Berlin and New York, and articles by Kristin Davidse, M.A.K. Halliday and Christian Matthiessen (1992) in Martin Davies and Louise Ravelli, eds, *Advances in Systemic Linguistics: Recent Theory and Practice*, Pinter Publishers, London and New York.

11. See Braj B. Kachru (1985), *The Alchemy of English: The Spread, Functions and Models of Non-native Englishes*, Pergamon Press, Oxford; (1990) University of Illinois Press, Urbana, IL.

PART FIVE

EDUCATIONAL LINGUISTICS

EDITOR'S INTRODUCTION

In the summer of 1981, *The English Magazine* ran an article in which three linguists, M.A.K. Halliday, Noam Chomsky and Dell Hymes, replied to a series of six questions. The replies of M.A.K. Halliday to these questions have been extracted from that article, and now appear in Chapter Sixteen, 'A Response to Some Questions on the Language Issue' (1981). Responding to the first question on whether analytic methods of linguistics have done justice to the richness and inventiveness of language use, Professor Halliday shares how linguistic analysis has added to his appreciation of the richness of language: "One of the things that has always struck me since I started working on texts, back in the early 1950s, is how much a linguistic analysis (actually I would prefer to say a linguistic interpretation) adds to my enjoyment of the text. The process of discovering why it means what it does reveals so much of the covert patterning in the text that by the end one's appreciation of it is immensely heightened." The majority of questions, however, dealt with the contribution of linguistics to educational practice in particular, and society in general. While, on the one hand, forewarning against expectations of immediate payback, Professor Halliday still maintains that linguistics has a role to play "in the cause of education for a just society". It can do so "by trying to raise the general level of community discussion of language, and the general efficacy of language education in school".

The next two chapters, 'Some Basic Concepts of Educational Linguistics' (1988), and 'On the Concept of "Educational Linguistics"' (1990) outline Professor Halliday's approach to 'educational linguistics', which he sees as the intersection of what he describes as "the theme of 'how people mean'" and "the theme of 'how people learn'". The goal of educational linguistics is not to work towards a theory of language, but rather a language-based theory of teaching/learning. Professor Halliday identifies the following five important aspects of language in education: first language development, the expansion and elaboration of the semantic potential, language as reality construction, language contact and mixing, and functional variation in language, including spoken and written varieties.

If our goal is to understand how children learn, and how teachers can more effectively contribute to this process, then as Professor Halliday explains in the final chapter, 'A Language Development Approach to Education' (1994), we need to explore a language development approach to education, understanding better the metafunctional foundation on which the child construes knowledge.

Chapter Sixteen

A Response to Some Questions on the Language Issue (1981)

[Editor's note: The following was extracted from an article, "Mark these linguists", appearing in *The English Magazine* (Summer 1981) in which three linguists (Noam Chomsky, Dell Hymes and M.A.K. Halliday) replied to the following six questions. M.A.K. Halliday's response to these questions is presented below.]

1. How far do you think the analytic methods of linguistics have really done justice to the richness and inventiveness of language use? What kinds of work are still to be done?
2. Many people would say that linguistics ought to be interesting and yet it appears to be boring and arid. Have these people got it wrong?
3. Linguistics on the whole has paid relatively little attention to texts. How much would you say linguists have contributed to our understanding of the production and reception of written texts?
4. Educationalists have attempted to draw from the work of linguists implications for educational practice. What is your experience of this process, particularly with reference to your own work?
5. Teachers have turned to linguists for help in understanding why working-class children and ethnic minorities have failed in school. It has become something of a growth industry. How would you assess their contribution? Can linguists contribute to a more just society?
6. The study of language has recently become an explicit part of the curriculum in some schools. What aspects of language do you feel it is particularly important for people to understand?

Isn't the first question slightly off the mark? It seems to me rather like asking whether the analytic methods of acoustics have done justice to the richness and inventiveness of musical composition – or even whether mathematical astronomy does justice to the beauty of the heavens. I'm trying to make clear to myself what "have really done justice to" means, and to imagine what kind of analytic methods would lead someone to answer 'yes' to this question; but I find it difficult.

Precisely for that reason, perhaps, it's a good question to ask. It shows up, I think, a mismatch (not really anything to do with linguistics) between the notion of 'analytic methods' and the evaluative concepts of 'richness and inventiveness' – between the process of understanding a thing, and the value that thing has in someone's mind, or in the value system of the culture.

Let me relate this to the study of discourse, or "text" as linguists call it. Suppose we analyse a text in linguistic terms, which means in such a way as to relate it to the system of the language. What are we trying to do? We are trying to explain why it means what it does. (This is not the same thing as saying what it means; that, in general, is not a technical linguistic exercise, although the linguist's search for explanation often does, in fact, suggest new meanings which had not been obvious before.) How the text comes to mean what it does – that is the primary goal. There is a further goal, more difficult to achieve, which relates to the question being asked here; namely, why is the text valued as it is in the culture? This is obviously important in stylistics (the linguistic study of literature): we would like to be able to explain why one work is more highly valued than another. Now, if the question means, can we, by the analytic methods of linguistics, explain not only why a text means what it does but also why it is valued as it is, then I think it is very clear question, and I would answer it by saying: no, not yet; that is a very high goal to aim at; but we are trying hard, and we think we have some ideas and some partial results.

However, linguistics is much more than a body of analytic method. Linguistics is often defined as the systematic study of language; that is all right, provided we point out that a discipline is defined not by its terrain but by its quest – by what it is trying to find out, rather than by what phenomena it is looking at; so whereas lots of people other than linguists – nearly everybody, these days – are engaged in studying language, for them language is an instrument, which they use for asking questions about something else, such as culture, or the brain, or why children fail in school. For linguists, on the other hand, language is an object. To say you are doing linguistics means that language is your object of study; the questions you are asking are questions about language itself. In order to answer those questions, of course, you have to investigate a lot of other things over and beyond language; so here the boot is on the other foot – what is 'object' for an anthropologist, say non-linguistic semiotic systems in a culture, for us become 'instrument', additional evidence that we can use to shed light on the nature and functions of language.

The critical step

Naturally (glancing for a moment at question 2), linguistics isn't everyone's cup of tea; what I find interesting is not what someone else may find interesting. There have always been people fascinated by the study of language – linguistics is one of the oldest sciences; you find it in ancient China, India, Greece and Babylon – and others who find it arid. Personally, I have always found it very exciting; whereas when I tried to take up psychology many years ago, I found it boring and arid, and had to give it up. But I take that to be a fact about me, not about psychology; and of interest to no one but myself. The reason for taking up this point, however, is that I think there are special problems that some people have with the study of language; connected, I think, with the fact of its unconscious nature, stressed by the great American linguists Boas and Sapir. Some people find it threatening to have to bring language to the level of consciousness; and many others, though they may not feel threatened by it, find it extraordinarily difficult. And I think until you have taken that critical step the study of language may tend to seem rather arid. Once you have taken it (and you'll know you have when you begin to be able to listen to grammar, and words, and sounds, as well as to meanings), you are likely to find it fascinating.

One of the things that has always struck me since I started working on texts, back in the early 1950s, is how much a linguistic analysis (actually I would prefer to say a linguistic interpretation) adds to my enjoyment of the text. The process of discovering why it means what it does reveals so much of the covert patterning in the text (presumably this is the "richness" referred to in question 1) that by the end one's appreciation of it is immensely heightened. So although the analytic methods of linguistics have not yet done full justice to the richness of language use, they certainly help us to appreciate it. And I hope it is clear that I am not just talking about the study of literature. It tends to be in the most unconscious uses of language – ordinary everyday spontaneous dialogue – that the richness of language is most fully developed and displayed.

But the methods of linguistics are not designed only to explain texts. They are aimed at establishing the system that lies behind the text. In my view one of the great weaknesses of twentieth-century linguistics has been its sharp separation of system and process. Saussure made the distinction very clear, back in the 1900s: the **process** that we observe, as speech or writing, is the outward manifestation of a **system** (what I have called a "meaning potential"); and we use our observations of the process, or rather of the product, in the form of text, as evidence for construing the system. But, as Hjelmslev (who I would say is the greatest theoretical linguist of this century) always insisted, system and process have to be interpreted as one; whereas linguists have tended to study the system in isolation from the process, describing it in ways such that it is hard to see how it ever could engender real text. (Likewise many people who study the product – text – do so in ways that make it impossible to conceive that it could ever have been engendered by any system.) But text is only understood by being referred to the system that generated it. (This is why it is very hard to learn a foreign language by the old "literature" method, which is based on the assumption that a learner can construe the system from a very few instances of highly valued text, mapped on to the general conception of a linguistic system that he brings from his own mother tongue. It is an interesting notion, and it does seem to work with a few people, but I think they are rather exceptional.) You appreciate poetry in a language because you have been talking and listening in that language for a long time; you can relate it to the whole of the rest of your experience – not piecemeal, but as that experience has been incorporated and "coded" into the system of the language as you control it.

If I may be allowed to invert Chomsky's dictum, I would say that language is an infinite system that generates a finite body of text. This means that we can never do full justice to the system. But we can do justice to its nature as a system, as a resource for living and meaning. (That last sounds like a slogan, but it is intended to be taken seriously. Language is a resource for meaning, and meaning is, for human beings, an essential component of living.) Linguistic theories have mostly been theories of linguistic structure: inventories of sentence formulae, with devices for relating one sentence to another. There, 'a sentence' is one thing, and its 'relatedness' to other sentences is another thing, distinct from the sentence itself. In a theory of the system there are not two phenomena here but one; a sentence, or any other linguistic entity, is simply a set of relationships, a complex process of choice, or of choosing let us say, within an intricate web of meaning potential. This is what I understand by the richness of language; and the inventiveness of language use I take to refer to the way in which speakers and writers explore, exploit and expand that potential in the process of creating text.

Can linguists help?

Can linguists contribute to a more just society? Linguists are a cross-section of the human race, and obviously differ in the weight they would give to this question, and in their understanding of what it means. Personally I set store by the social accountability of theories in general; at the same time I don't always expect an immediate payoff. (This is the great problem for teachers, which I'll come to in a moment.) I do feel committed to the usefulness of linguistics, and have tried to organize work in the subject, where this has been my responsibility, in such a way that those who are researching, teaching and studying it maintain strong links with the community and an interest in community problems. For me this has meant that a lot of my work has had an educational focus; and I have tried to work with teachers on problems of literacy and language development, language in the classroom, mother tongue and foreign language teaching and so on. In London in the 1960s I was able to bring together the Nuffield/Schools Council team of primary, secondary and tertiary language educators who produced *Breakthrough to Literacy* and *Language in Use*, and subsequently *Language and Communication*. In Sydney we have built up a Department of Linguistics all of whose members are involved in community language problems and language education: language problems of multicultural education, and the 'language profile' of the community; the language of school texts, and their difficulties for the migrant learner; the development of children's writing, in different registers; and the place of linguistics in teacher education. We recently held a week-long "Working Conference on Language in Education", with nine simultaneous workshops examining different aspects of language education in the Australian context. And I myself have been active from the start in the "Language Development Project" of the Curriculum Development Centre in Canberra, which focuses particularly on language development in the middle school years.

Now, in one sense none of this has to do with educational failure. That is to say, we're not producing remedial language materials for the disadvantaged or devising tests for predicting children's performance in school. In common with most linguists, I think, we would hold the view that the underlying causes of educational failure are social, not linguistic; but there are obvious linguistic links in the causal chain, and it is reasonable – indeed necessary, if only to help get the picture straight – to look to linguistics as a contributory source of ideas and practice. The point I would make is that, given the nature of the problem (and of language), the contribution of linguistics will be indirect and global rather than direct and local. In other words, it is by trying to raise the general level of community discussion of language, and the general efficacy of language education in school, more than by special language-stimulating projects aimed at particular groups, that linguistics can be of most help in the cause of education for a just society.

This is not to belittle the importance of special programmes designed to help those who are at risk. It is simply that here the guiding considerations are pedagogical rather than linguistic. Linguistics comes in, once again, as background knowledge and ideology: providing descriptions of languages, and of varieties – dialects and registers – within languages; and, in the process, helping to raise the status of those languages and varieties that are part of the symbol-package by which a particular group is marked off, and marked out, for discrimination and abuse.

Implications for practice

With any academic discipline (turning to question 4), there is always a problem of "implications for educational practice": what do you teach, out of the huge accumulation of knowledge, and how does your teaching relate to the theorizing of the practitioners in the field? Experience in science education and maths education shows how big a problem this is even in these subjects.

The relationship is even more complex in the human sciences, and especially in the sciences of human behaviour. What implications does one draw from sociology, psychology and linguistics? Whatever else, you don't draw your content from them. Traditionally (that is, for the past hundred years or so), the answer has been: from psychology you get the basic theory and practice of education, and from sociology and linguistics you get nothing. This dominance of psychology over sociology in the theory of education reflects Western obsession with the individual, and the conviction that learning is an individual rather than a social process. It would help if we had a more balanced contribution from these two disciplines – especially in countries where different cultures mix (which means all English-speaking countries, now).

From linguistics, of course, it is not true that nothing has been drawn; there is a long tradition of taking content from linguistics, in the form of 'school grammar', the version of classical and medieval linguistic scholarship that went into the making of humanist descriptive grammars. It is not a bad grammar; but it is not very useful in school. It is formal; rigid; based on the notion of rule; syntactic in focus; and oriented towards the sentence. A more useful grammar would be one which is functional; flexible; based on the notion of resource; semantic in focus; and oriented towards the text. Hence the recurrent cycle of love and hate for it: 'we thought it would help children to write; it doesn't, so we abandon it; they still can't write, so we take it up again', and so on.

When I say that no implications have been drawn from linguistics, I'm not intending to denigrate classroom grammar, where linguistics has supplied the content of the teaching. But by "educational implications" I understand not the content but the theory and practice of the educational process. I think linguistics is of central importance here, and yet this aspect of its value is still very largely ignored.

In working with our Language Development Project I have suggested that language development is three things: learning language, learning through language, and learning about language. Again, perhaps, by making it sound like a slogan I may stop people from listening to what it means; but, again, I mean it to be taken seriously. Let me take up the last part first.

Learning about language is, of course, linguistics; this refers to the importance of the study of language (as an 'object') in school. This does not have to be grammar; when *Language in Use* was written, at a time when grammar was 'out', the authors found no difficulty in devising 110 units for work on language in secondary school without any reference to grammar at all. Now, I think, we are reopening the question of 'a grammar for schools'. I think it will be possible to develop a school grammar that is interesting and useful; I have some idea of what it might be like, but I don't think we have one yet. But even given an ideal grammar, it would be only one part of the "learning about language" that needs to go on in school.

Learning through language refers to the fact that almost all educational learning (as well as much learning outside school) takes place through language, written and spoken. This notion came into educational parlance as "Language Across the Curriculum". A child doesn't need to know any linguistics in order to use language to learn; but a teacher needs to know some linguistics if he wants to understand how the process takes place – or what is going wrong when it doesn't. Here therefore linguistics has the role of a background discipline, such as psychology and sociology. I think it is probably as important as they are, and needing about the same emphasis in teacher education. Of course,

337

not all branches of linguistics are equally important (that is true of any background subject); but it is not too difficult to identify those that matter.

Learning language means construing the mother tongue – and before that the 'child tongue', the protolanguage with which an infant first exchanges meanings with those around him. There is a special branch of linguistics – child language studies, or "developmental linguistics" – that is concerned with how children learn their mother tongue; it has made enormous strides in the past 20 years, probably more than any other branch of the subject; and its findings are of tremendous importance for education. For one thing it has shown that children take certain steps in their semantic development – that is, control certain meanings and meaning relationships – well before they have been thought to do in cognitive-psychological representations of the learning process. Since, presumably, a child's semantic system does not run ahead of his cognitive system (I don't even know what that would mean, I suspect that these are merely two different ways of looking at the same thing), we may have to revise some of the prevalent notions about cognitive development. More important: by supplementing the cognitive model with a semantic one (which relates meaning to its 'output' in words and structures, sounds, and writing) we get a much more rounded picture of the nature of learning, and the relation of learning to environment.

I have always been an 'applied linguist': my interest in linguistics is in what you can do with it. But there must be something to apply. Applied linguistics is not a separate domain; it is the principles and practice that come from an understanding of language. Adopting these principles and practices provides, in turn, a way in to understanding language. In this perspective, you look for models of language that neutralize the difference between theory and application; in the light of which, research and development in language education become one process rather than two. But this means selecting, refining, adapting; and being prepared to hasten slowly. The one difficulty I have always had in working with teachers is that they so often expect immediate results; the latest findings translated there and then into effective, not to say magical, curriculum design, or classroom processes. Now, I think we can often make intellectual, research applications of our latest findings right there, on the spot (partly because no one will get hurt if they turn out not to work). But for shaping what we do, with children, or adult learners, I think we have to depend more on the indirect, oblique and thoughtful application of the accumulated wisdom of the past. I get worried by the fashions in language teaching, which are sometimes only a half-baked application of ideas about language which themselves were only half-baked in the first place.

Knowledge about language

There are lots of other 'customers' for linguistics. But the questions are about "aspects of linguistics and education"; and educational applications are perhaps predominant, certainly in terms of the number of people affected. What aspects of language are most important for people to understand (your question 6)? I think we have to balance two things: (i) those aspects of language that people are already interested in, and (ii) those aspects of language that you have to understand in order to understand the rest. (Linguists tend to ignore the first and everyone else tends to ignore the second.) Senior students are likely to be interested already in such questions as; translation and its problems; language policy and planning; dialect and accent; language and the power structure; language and the media; ambiguity and failures of communication; language and literature; rhetoric and the writing process. All of these are valuable topics to explore. (I am not suggesting one should explore all of them in one course!) But I do think that, in order to understand any of these properly, and to derive benefit from exploring them, you need to have some fundamental grasp of the nature, functions and ontogenesis of language. This means knowing something about speech sounds and sound systems, including the rhythm and melody of language; about grammar and vocabulary; about meaning; about language variation; about writing systems; about language development of children; about language and social context; and about language universals and variables – what all languages have in common, and what may vary from one language to another. If you don't know something of the topics listed under these second headings, your appreciation of those listed under the first headings may be superficial, or even distorted. But again, it is often not so much the content of what is studied as the level of understanding brought to it by the teacher that determines the value of the work.

People know quite a lot about language simply by virtue of the fact that they listen and talk – that they have been listening and talking, in real situations with real purposes to be achieved, since the very first year of life. This is gut knowledge, not head knowledge; it is very difficult to bring it to the level of consciousness. I have found it quite useful sometimes to begin with a kind of folk linguistics, discussing the concepts which are the very earliest of the linguistic concepts mastered by a child; things such as 'say' and 'mean' and 'call', 'make up' and 'tell' and 'rhyme' (usually expressed by verbs rather than nouns). You can build up a very perceptive account of language without any formidable technical apparatus. This may be the best way for those whose feelings about linguistics lie behind the two questions posed at the beginning of the list!

Chapter Seventeen

SOME BASIC CONCEPTS OF EDUCATIONAL LINGUISTICS (1988)

It is a pleasure and a privilege to me to be asked to address the opening plenary session of this international seminar on "Languages in Education in a Bilingual or Multilingual Setting", organized by the Institute of Language in Education of the Department of Education in Hong Kong. In accepting this commission I could not help being struck by the many signs of the times that are evident in the organization of this particular event:

- first, it is noteworthy that there **is** such a thing as an Institute of Language in Education;
- second, it is noteworthy that it is established within a government Department of Education;
- third, it is noteworthy that it is holding an international seminar on this scale and of this quality;
- fourth, it is noteworthy that it is taking a multilingual setting as the norm, as its point of departure for the discussions;
- fifth, it is noteworthy that it takes for granted the relevance of a number of different settings as contexts of experience:
    obviously, Hong Kong itself;
    also, that of the original language-exporting countries, Britain, the USA, Canada and Australia;
    but also, that of other countries of Asia and the Pacific: India, Sri Lanka, Thailand, Malaysia, Singapore, the Philippines, Japan, Brunei, Indonesia and Papua New Guinea;
    and, of course, China.

(All these countries are represented in the programme.)

341

These 'signs of the times', as I called them just now, embody – and also symbolize – two rather new developments that have taken place over the last decade or so. One of these is new forms of **participation** in the processes of language education. Until rather recently, those who worked in this field were ready to recognize their own responsibilities (e.g. "I teach college level English in Hong Kong"), and might look for help in carrying them out – typically, ideas and resources from Britain and North America; but they would not normally think of themselves as participating in a wider endeavour (and so would not have said, e.g., "let me exchange ideas with those who are teaching in Indonesia or in Thailand"). Now, on the other hand, it seems entirely natural to interact in this way; and most people recognize that, while no two language situations, or language learning situations, are ever identical, there is much to be learnt from the experiences of those who are working in different educational contexts. Agencies such as the Regional Language Centre (RELC) in Singapore, and the Central Institute of English and Foreign Languages in Hyderabad, India, have played an important part in bringing about this changed perception.

The other new development I have in mind is that of the concept of language education itself (or "language in education": both formulations are used). This concept is far from being universally accepted; and even by those who do accept it, it is not always understood in the same way. But it has evolved, especially over the last ten years, out of – I was going to say a synthesis; but it is not a synthesis. It has evolved, rather, out of the interaction among practitioners in various domains of educational practice: teaching second languages, especially English as a second language; teaching first languages, or the mother tongue; language across the curriculum – the language of science, of history and so on; and bi-/multi-lingual education in plural, linguistically complex societies. We now have a concept of 'language across the multilingual curriculum' which includes something from all these different components.

There seems to be no doubt that these two developments (the sharing of experience, on the one hand, and the language education concept on the other) are related to one another. Both involve extending the horizons – the horizons of linguistic practice; one interpersonally, extending the communication network of those that are taken as one's colleagues – as sharing in a common endeavour; the other ideationally, extending the field of action, the range of activities that go to make up this common endeavour and give it substance. The broader your concept of what you yourself are engaged in, the greater the number of others you will see as being engaged in the same process. And vice versa, of course: each of these two perspectives implies the other.

But how far does this broader conception correspond to any reality? In what sense do all these often very diverse domains of practice constitute a unified field that we can call "language (in) education"? There is an obvious and immediate demonstration of this unity in what is going on around us in practically every Hong Kong household: children are growing up being educated in (a variety of) the mother tongue, learning a second language, maybe also a third one, and learning 'across the curriculum' in one or the other or both. Now what strikes us here is this: a child who is studying science in his second or third language does not feel as if he is engaged in two quite distinct operations (in the way that, say, learning to play football would be a distinct operation). The reason is, I think, that both learning a second language and learning science are essentially linguistic activities. So is learning the mother tongue, of course – with the difference that, in that instance, the learning experience is outside, and prior to, the school.

So the unity of language education is displayed in front of our eyes, case by case, in the form of the individual learners that all of us know – that we meet, in their homes and in the classroom. But while in the informal, commonsense learning environment of the home, the neighbourhood, the housing block and the street, the children's learning experience is unstructured, without any clear boundaries (there is certainly no boundary, for a small child, between **learning** his first language and **using** that language as a means of learning about other things), when children enter the formal, educational learning environment of the school we do, in fact, create boundaries for them, by separating these activities off from one another: there is the Chinese class (first language), the English class (second language), and the science class (language across the curriculum). Each is seen as having its own sphere, its own content: "science" (physics, chemistry, etc.) in the one case, "English" (that is, a **language** as 'content') in the second, and "Chinese" (another language) in the third – assuming, that is, the case of a Chinese child growing up in Hong Kong, speaking Chinese at home, and learning English in school. Of these three areas of content, it is the mother tongue as content that has traditionally been the most problematic; a typical formula for resolving the problem has been some mixture of literature, composition and a few marginal exercises in grammar. But the three are seen in school as different learning activities, and they occupy distinct 'subject' slots in the curriculum. So if we are constructing a concept of 'language in education', it is not enough to point

343

out that these activities all form part of the experience of the one individual. There must presumably be a more substantive, and also more theoretical, basis for claiming that language in education is a meaningful construct.

Let me then consider the important factors that seem to me to constitute this complex notion of language in education. I shall treat these under five headings:

1. early childhood and pre-school language development;
2. language as a process of meaning, and the nature of discourse;
3. language as reality construction: how language construes all our experience, including what we learn in the course of education;
4. language in contact: how one language impinges on another; and
5. functional or "register" variation in language, including spoken and written varieties.

I would like to say a few words about each of these in turn.

1 The very first language a child construes is not, in fact, that child's mother tongue; or anybody else's mother's tongue. It is something that precedes the mother tongue, which I called the "protolanguage" – we could call it "child tongue" if you prefer. Typically, children build a protolanguage in the period from around 9 months to 16 months of age, the period known to some psychologists as that of "secondary intersubjectivity"; and the protolanguage appears to be unaffected by what language is being spoken in the environment. That is to say, while there is obviously some variation among individual children at this age in the meanings they express, and the sounds or gestures they use to express them, both meaning and expression are constructed by the child himself – they are not imitations of adult language. Thus Qiu Shijin's study of children growing up in Shanghai, whose parents speak the Wu dialect of Chinese, shows that at the protolanguage stage it is impossible to tell these children apart from children who are growing up in an English-speaking environment such as Nigel, Hal and Alison (see Qiu 1984; Halliday 1975; Painter 1984; Oldenburg 1986). So it appears that for a critical period in children's early lives their language activity, while it may be affected by other variables of a sociocultural kind, is not apparently affected by which particular language is spoken in their environment – or presumably by whether what is being spoken in their environment is one language or two or more.

When the child moves out of the protolanguage into the mother tongue, in a transition taking place typically in the middle to latter half of

344

the second year of life, then of course the language becomes differentiated: he now starts learning Chinese, or English, or whatever language is around. But whatever language it is there are certain very important invariants: universals, if you like, although they are not the universals of formal grammar, they are functional-semantic universals. All children learn the fundamental principle that language has two distinct functions: reflection and action. Every language is both a means of understanding one's environment (building up a picture of reality that makes sense of your experience), and a means of controlling, or at least interacting with, other people; and each of these "metafunctions" (as they are called in systemic theory) has its own semantics, or meaning potential, and its own grammar, or wording potential. Furthermore the meaning potential of all languages has a great deal in common. The details vary – Chinese, for example, construes time differently from the way English does; but the overall semantic space is essentially the same.

When children learn their mother tongue what they are doing is elaborating that semantic space; and this will lead us into the next heading. Before leaving this one, however, let me just add one point. While the Chomskyan myth of the 'deficient input' is still around (for example in a recent paper by Lydia White, 1985), in fact the linguistic environment of most children (as distinct from, say, those who are born deaf) is amazingly rich in all the features which they need in order to construe these complex resources of meaning and of wording. By the age of 5 the average child has heard from a quarter of a million to half a million clauses, practically every one of them communicatively successful and relevant to its context. This is more than enough to allow him to construct a linguistic system, or even two or three different ones simultaneously (apparently up to six or seven, if the opportunity arises!). **2** So to my second heading, which was language as meaning and as discourse. Learning language is learning how to mean, and that implies two things: that the driving force is functional and semantic, rather than formal and syntactic, and that the operational unit is discursive rather than sentential. The **wording** – that part of the system we call lexicogrammar, or just the grammar for short – is of course syntactic and sentential: there has to **be** a grammar, a structured form of output/input, with its own underlying system of ordered relations; and as that system comes into being it then enters into a dialectic relation with the semantics and so becomes a powerful source of meaning in its own right. In other words, the grammar becomes a partner in the meaning-generating process. But the crucial element in building up a language is the semantic one; and this involves both extension and elaboration of the semantic space. That is to say, the learner **both** extends the frontiers of the system **and** elaborates progressively within it, adding finer and finer 'shades of meaning', or semantic differentiation.

Researchers in second-language development are now coming to interpret this also as a process of semantic elaboration (for example Ellis 1985; Brindley 1986). In this view the learner language progresses by enlarging and filling in the meaning potential, the accessible semantic space. This is usually expressed in terms of the development of grammatical functions (e.g. Wagner-Gough 1978); but as Gibbons and Markwick Smith (1992) have pointed out it is more powerfully and more explanatorily modelled in terms of the development of grammatical systems, as these are understood and formalized in systemic theory. Relative to the learner's mother tongue, of course, the process of second language development will typically appear as semantic simplification, as the learner reverts to becoming a linguistic child (or perhaps we should rather say becomes an aphasic); but in its own terms the second-language meaning potential is being elaborated just as the first one was – not of course along the same route as the first language (because the point of departure is quite different – and anyway it is impossible to do anything for the first time twice), but by a process that is by now well-tried and familiar.

3 And this leads in turn to my third heading: how language construes our experience – or rather, how we construe experience by means of language; and here I take up another thread from my first heading. Much has been written on the analogies between first and second language learning; so let us not lose sight of what it is that is unique about learning the first one. We often draw the distinction between learning language, on the one hand, and on the other hand learning **through** language – that is, using language as a means of learning something else. As children learn their first language they simultaneously use that language to construe their experience and make sense of the world that is around them and inside them. Now for analytical purposes, when we want to study and understand these things, it is useful for us to distinguish between these two aspects of learning: between learning language, and using language to learn. But in doing so we also create a pseudo-problem, of how the two relate one to the other; and it may be more helpful to think of a single, multi-level construction process, in which the language – that is, the semantic system – **is** the representation of experience in the form of knowledge. In this perspective, language is not the means of knowing; it is the form taken by knowledge itself. Language is not **how we know** something else, it is **what we know**;

knowledge is not something that is encoded in language – knowledge is made of language.

This view is as valid for educational knowledge as it is for the commonsense knowledge that precedes it. My colleagues Martin, Wignell and Eggins have been studying the construction of school subjects in the first years of secondary school; and they have given detailed accounts of learning geography and learning history that are expressed in linguistic terms, showing how learning a discipline is learning the discourse of that discipline.[1] These are, of course, technical disciplines, and the knowledge involved is educational knowledge, designed in the form of what Lemke (1985) interprets as "activity systems" and "thematic structures". But these design features are also present in the language – it is the language that embodies the design; and thus the part played by language in constructing this more specialized bit of reality is not essentially different from what it is in daily life. There is a continuity from the commonsense knowledge of the home and neighbourhood to the educational knowledge of the school – provided, that is, that the learners have access to the language in which the educational knowledge is enshrined.

In this regard, the second-language learner is playing a very different game. He is not engaged in this multi-level construction process – because the upper levels are already installed. In artificial intelligence terms, he already has a knowledge base, and his task is to slot in a new input/output system (the lexicogrammar) underneath. This, at least, is the view that was implicit in traditional methods of second-language teaching, which rest on the assumption that the learner can cross over from first to second language while remaining at the lower levels (finding word equivalents, grammatical category equivalents; using translation, and so on). But as we now know there are problems with this view. One is that different languages embody different realities; only very slightly different, it is true, by comparison with how much they share – but nevertheless problematic, the more so because the differences are subtle and cryptotypic: they lurk hidden in the least accessible strata of the informal, subconscious, everyday, spontaneous spoken language. The other problem – a more serious one, I think – is that there is an internal contradiction in learning a language in this way, when it has no job to do. It is as if, subconsciously, the learner is saying to himself: "I need language in order to construct reality. But I already have a reality, thanks to my first language; so why do I need to learn a second one?" The way we now try to get round this problem, in communicative language teaching, is to foreground the **other** primary function of a language: the metafunction of action, instead of reflection. We set tasks for the learner to perform.

At first these were largely transactional, like buying a ticket; latterly they have been more interpersonal ones, like apologizing or offering condolences on bereavement. These can be more readily motivated, since they involve doing rather than knowing; furthermore they foreground the interpersonal areas of the grammar, which are more closely culture-bound and therefore more obviously variable from one language to another (so the learner readily accepts that this is something he has to learn).

The significance of this for language in education is, I think, the following. The notion of language as reality construction is a powerful one, linking especially first-language learning in the home with language in school. It also bears forcefully on second-language learning – with the reminder that 'reality' is interpersonal as well as ideational: that what language constructs for us, or what we construe in language, is not just a way of thinking, a reflective representation of experience, but also, and simultaneously, a way of doing – a model of, and hence a resource for, social action.

4 Up to now, I have taken for granted the two categories of 'mother tongue' and 'second language', treating them as clearcut and discrete. Again this is a traditional point of departure; but one that is often rather remote from the realities of educational practice. In Sydney, at least, where something like one-quarter of the population are first or second generation non-English-speaking immigrants, there is a continuum of 'Englishness': at one end there are those for whom English is clearly the sole mother tongue, and at the other end those for whom it is clearly a second language; but there are also people at all possible stages in between. In such a situation instead of the ESL specialist – or rather in addition – one has to think of providing every teacher with some basic ESL awareness and training.

It is from sociolinguistics and creolization studies that we have gained insights into the complex phenomena of language contact and language mix, and also some measure of understanding of both societal and individual bi- and multi-lingualism. John Gibbons in his study of code mixing and code choice in Hong Kong (1987) finds it useful to identify four "codes" as the significant varieties along the Cantonese–English continuum: Cantonese only, and English only, as two extremes, and then two mixed varieties in between, the one predominantly English, the other predominantly Cantonese. The last of the four, that which is predominantly Cantonese but with some English incorporated into it, is the one that interests him in particular; he gives a characterization of this variety in lexicogrammatical terms, and then relates it to certain environments (who the interactants are and what they are doing; certain values of the field, tenor and mode variables, in systemic terms). A typical scenario in which this mixed variety is used would be, as one would expect, informal casual conversation of tertiary-level students on matters of educational concern.

This kind of mixed code is, as Gibbons rightly contends, a valid and effective communication system in its own right. As a matter of fact, some languages that have attained a high degree of respectability in the modern world have had just such creolizing phases in their own previous history: Japanese, for example, and English. When such a process becomes stabilized, as part of the history of a language, we call it large-scale borrowing; there is no clear definition of "large-scale", but one noticeable effect is that the intrusive forms may break the bonds of the host language's phonological system (cf. Gibbons' examples of ri˳sœf 'reserve' and stɛtɪ 'steady (boy/girlfriend)' in Cantonese mix) and may eventually set up a phonological sub-system of their own, as happened with Chinese elements in Japanese, Graeco-Romance elements in English and Sanskrit elements in Thai. I doubt whether this will happen in Cantonese. But the extensive use of this form of mix is a very relevant feature of the language education scene in present-day Hong Kong.

5 So to my fifth heading, which is that of functional variation in language, with some specific attention to the difference between spoken and written. Wilga Rivers' book (1987) on interactive language teaching contains some interesting contributions on the place of poetry and drama in language learning; Brumfit and Carter have devoted a book to the role of literature (1986); and the experience of teaching 'language for specific purposes' over a number of years has helped to enrich our conception of language for general purposes by reminding us that a language is simply the sum of all its varieties, and that to experience a language in the round learners need to be given access to a fair range of its registers, or functional varieties – not automatically restricted to just those they are likely to use, although not so remote as to have no possible context for them (as often happened with traditional literature-based language teaching).

I referred earlier to the work of Martin and his colleagues, published under the rubric of the Writing Project Report; let me return briefly to another aspect of the work of this project as described in various publications by Martin and Rothery (1980–86; cf. Martin 1984b; Hammond 1987). They are concerned with the development of writing skills – composition and written language – by children in primary school; and they point out that this essential component in the children's educational success is often denied to them, simply through the impoverished view of language that prevails in education, where all writing activities are reduced to 'telling a story' and even then the learners are given no guidance on what constitutes effective story writing. Martin and Rothery have developed a "genre-based approach" to writing development in which they introduce other registers that are more relevant to the educational needs of the children; for example, expository writing and reports. Furthermore they assign to each of these registers an explicit generic structure that enables the teachers to give explanations of what goes wrong and guidance on how to put it right. (There is no suggestion that these structures have to be taught to the children, although in fact they master them and use them with obvious relish when they are taught.) The typical Sydney primary classroom is rich in multilingual variety, with children at all points along the Englishness continuum; and it is not improbable that one of the effects of genre-based writing will be to reduce the gap, so that the ESL children are less at a disadvantage in comparison to their native-speaking peers.

Under this heading I would also like to refer to the work of Frances Christie, reported last year at the RELC International Seminar, on what she calls "curriculum genres" (1987): those varieties of a language that evolve as special registers in the context of the school classroom. It is the processes of education itself that engender these special varieties, patterns of language that are specific to learning in school – including not only 'teacher talk' but also the language of textbooks and other learning materials. In terms of Hasan's distinction (1981) between institutionalized and individuated contexts, the school is, obviously, strongly institutionalized; it is to be expected that the discourse of the classroom will be in many respects highly predictable, and it is in fact important that it should be, if it is to provide an environment in which learning can take place. The notion of curriculum genres proves to be a valuable working concept which relates to all three of my initial contexts for language in education: mother tongue, second language and language across the curriculum.

We should remind ourselves here that language in education includes spoken language as well as written. However central the place that is given to reading and writing, it remains true that much of what children learn they learn through talk, including of course talking among themselves. This is one of the factors that enables them to maintain the continuity between home and school, and between commonsense knowledge and educational knowledge, that is necessary to educational success. More importantly, it ensures that what they learn in the various technical disciplines in the highly metaphorical wording of the written language maintains contact with reality as already represented in the spontaneous spoken language they use outside. And this becomes even more important if the two are very far apart – if children are being educated in a language that is quite different from the one they grew up with in the home.

I think it will have appeared, in this very brief survey of some of the salient aspects of language in educational contexts, how features which at first sight seem to be specific to one context or another turn out to be relevant to two or even all three of those I began with. In other words, it is not just that one and the same individual engages in first language, second language and across-the-curriculum learning; there is also a deep sense in which all these three learning contexts can be interpreted as **working on language**. Whether or not the contexts themselves overlap (a clear instance where they do all overlap would be a Hong Kong classroom with students learning science, talking in Cantonese and reading in English), the **activities** all embody at least three and often all five aspects of language in education that I identified: first language development, the expansion and elaboration of the semantic potential, language as reality construction, language contact and mixing, and functional variation in language. And I suggest it is because these pervade almost all of people's learning activities that we find it possible – and also necessary – to operate with this overall organizing concept of 'language in education'.

But – and this is an issue that must be faced – it demands a very high level of linguistic awareness if one is to be sensitive to all that is going on. Without this awareness, no teacher can be expected to diagnose all the problems that a learner may be having. Yet it is quite unrealistic to expect that in the course of a few half-day or weekend workshops and some guided reading such awareness can somehow be achieved. The demands a teacher makes on the learner's language sometimes seem minor ones by comparison with the demands a learner makes on the teacher's language awareness (and see Thornton 1986 on linguistic "flat-earthers").

I can perhaps, in the short time remaining, make just a few remarks on the kind of image of language that we will somehow have to project as the image of language in education. It has to be one – and this is almost the most difficult part – in which language is seen to be at once both system and text. That is to say, 'language' is, at the same time, both a **potential** – a resource for meaning – and the **use** of this potential in the form of discourse. This seems very obvious and simple; yet it is a balance that almost everyone, linguists included, fails to maintain (for most people it is one **or** the other, and for some it never manages to be either). It would take another paper to elaborate on this point; but I hope that what I have said so far is sufficient to make clear what I have in mind.

The system of a language, then, has to be modelled as a resource, a potential for making meaning. I was struck by a formulation used by a contributor to the first number of *Language Learning and Communication*, Ai Zuxing 艾祖星: writing about the communicative goals of language teaching, he said (1982: 51): 學習英語和學習其它語言一樣：目的是為了社會交際；因此教學的最終目的應是交際能力的培養，即語言的能力的運用。

'Learning English is like learning any other language: the purpose is for social communication; and therefore the ultimate purpose of language teaching must be to develop communicative power – that is, the use of the power of language.' The use of the power of language (or linguistic potential) is a very good definition of communicative power; and the "power of language" corresponds well with this conception of the system. It follows that we must be able to represent the system as variable in extent and in elaboration, in order to show how its power increases as the learner makes progress. We have been able to do this with the language development of small children as they learn their mother tongue. We still need to find out how to do it with learners of a second language. The systemic concept of 'delicacy', the progressive differentiation within a semantic space, is highly relevant here.

Our conception of grammar, as the resource wherewith the semantic power of language is activated, has I think to be a functional one. This is partly because a functional theory of grammar is oriented towards the semantics, explaining the **general properties of grammar** by reference to general semantic categories; and partly because it is oriented towards the text, explaining **specific grammatical structures** as organic configurations of functional roles – (the "cases" of case grammar are a special instance, but there are many other types of grammatical function besides these). So the grammar shows what **function** each **part** is playing by reference to the whole, and what **kind of meaning** is created by the **whole** of which it is a part.

The conception of language itself needs to be problematized: not so as to deconstruct it out of existence, as some people try to do, which is a self-defeating piece of reductionism, but so as to reconstruct it dynamically – that is, as something that evolves in constant interaction with its environment. In order to function as it does, a language must be continually changing; it must vary in a way that is sensitive to its environment; and it must maintain contact with others of its kind – other languages. Particularly in a language education perspective, we need to take a dynamic view of language in all three dimensions of its variation: dialectal (regional/social), diatypic (functional) and diachronic (historical). To put this in less technical terms: for any theory of language in education, it should be seen as the norm, rather than the exception, that the community of learners use a variety of codes (languages and/or dialects), that they use a variety of registers, and that none of these ever stands still.

With this step we approach the point where we can venture to talk about an 'educational linguistics'. But there will still be one element missing, the fourth corner of the dynamic perspective just referred to: namely the developmental one. In other words, while language has these dynamic properties, as an evolving, metastable system, it also has one more: it can be learnt. It is in fact caught on the wing by every human infant. That this is possible is because the input that the child hears is so highly structured, especially in quantitative terms, that he can model it ongoingly according to his own maturational level and needs. But it also follows from what I was saying earlier that learning language is not, simply, learning language. Learning language equals learning, since learning anything at all means turning it into language. Thus in fact educational linguistics, while in some respects it is much less than a theory of language (since it can ignore many features of language as irrelevant to its concerns), in another respect it is more than a theory of language: it is a theory of learning. It has sometimes been objected that specialists in language education ignore the need to subscribe to some recognized learning theory. A valid objection, perhaps; but there is a reason for it. They cannot subscribe to learning theories in which language has little or no place; and that leaves very few contenders. Instead, they seek to provide a learning theory of their own, one that not merely accommodates language in some cosy corner but one that is actually **based on** language – because language defines both the process of learning and that which is being learnt.

I do not think that any of us has such a theory yet. But I believe that conferences such as this one – and institutes such as the one that is organizing it – provide the necessary context; the only possible environment, in fact, where we can hope to develop the discourse out of which such a theory may emerge.

Note

1   See Wignell, Martin and Eggins 1987; Eggins, Wignell and Martin, 1987.

Chapter Eighteen

ON THE CONCEPT OF "EDUCATIONAL LINGUISTICS" (1990)

What is meant by "educational linguistics"? As I understand it, this term refers to something that people do. If we take part in certain activities, guided by certain principles, we are doing educational linguistics.

Who are the "we", in this context? Typically a learner, or several learners, and a teacher. And because in some educational discussions the part of the teacher has come to be treated as secondary, as a kind of optional extra, I should like to emphasize rather that in my opinion learning and teaching cannot be separated from one another. They are two aspects of a single process. I shall return to this point later, right at the end.

What are the "doings"? At the most general level, of course, they are teaching and learning through language. But this is too general to be of much use, so let me suggest a more detailed account. Below is a tentative and schematic listing of the activities that might be thought of as falling within educational linguistics.

I Teacher/researcher:

studying school textbook language
   [how learners engage;
    how writers write]

describing textbook registers
   [the languages of 'subjects']

studying classroom discourse
   [how learners engage;
    how teachers teach]

describing curriculum genres
   [the languages of learning]

studying intermodal learning processes
   [discourses of classroom; textbooks; teachers' notes; learners'
   notes, essays, discussions, homework/etc.]

developing general theory of learning through language
["language across the curriculum" → "role of language in
learning" → "language-based learning theory"]

investigating 'institutional' variables, esp. learners' language background
[when language of education is learners' 1st/2nd/foreign language]
and different institutional models
[remedial; withdrawal; bilingual education]

Such 'activities' range along reflection ←→ action scale: research into these
issues, and intervention in relevant contexts:

curriculum development   teacher education
          organization of bilingual programme
textbook writing   classroom praxis

Overarching theory is likely to include:

                              general model of ontogenesis of
                                knowledge:

general model of literacy;   pre-educational ("commonsense")
  theory of literate cultures   spoken; events define things
                                    non-technical, non-
                                    compartmentalized

  general model of meaning systems
    (semiotic theory)   primary-educational (transitional)
                                    spoken→ written; domains
                                    emerging

    general model of language   secondary-educational
                                    ("organized")
                                    written; things define events
      (i) as system   technical,
      (ii) as institution   compartmentalized

        general model of bilingualism   general model of
          (individual and societal)   language development in
                                          sense of 'learning how
                                          to mean'

II Learner:

school grammar ('formal' grammar)
  [parsing; parts of speech, etc.]   language usage
                                       [literary and non-literary language;
language as institution   register variation]
  [microlinguistic profile of
  home and neighbourhood]

                                   foreign languages in school

functional grammar and discourse
[stylistics; media studies;
language of science, politics, etc.]

Again, such "activities" range along reflection ←——→ action scale,

e.g. (1) functional grammar ("grammatics") as way of:

understanding the language of poetry (and therefore poetry)
revealing ideology of journalistic, technocratic etc. forms of discourse
understanding how science, history etc. are constructed as text
mastering written language
mastering highly valued writing styles (essays, reports etc.)
mastering foreign languages; translating, interpreting

e.g. (2) microlinguistic profile as way of reflecting on dialect/register variation; also of controlling such variation, mastering standard language etc.

Overarching theory is general theory of place of study of language, as system and as institution, in educational experience.

I have assumed that the term "educational" here means that we are talking about school: that is, the teaching/learning is going on in some institution that has been created for this purpose. Hence my headings do not include children learning at home, from their parents, elder siblings and others. Obviously, children have learnt a great deal through language before they ever go to school. We would not usually say they have been taught. They have learnt by participating, in processes where they are simultaneously both learning language and learning through language. The others around them have displayed the meaning potential of language by using it as part of their lives; and this has enabled the children to master it through their own contextualized practice.[1]

It could be maintained that, in the course of this experience, the others have in fact been **teaching** the children a great deal. Hasan and Cloran bring this out very clearly, showing the essential continuity of home learning and school learning: see for example their account of Kristy learning to join up the dots to make an outline, where her mother is actively teaching her how and why.[2] The way mother and daughter are talking to each other in this context illustrates very effectively how language is used in this shared activity of teaching /learning.

Yet we are presumably not going to suggest that the mother is doing something called "domiciliary linguistics". There is a significant difference between home and school, in how language is used to enable children to learn. In school language becomes a thing in itself; it is something that has to be worked on, first of all in learning to read and

356

write, and then increasingly as a "subject" with spelling, grammar, composition, foreign languages, and so on. In the course of all this, language becomes as David Butt puts it "detached from culture".[3] Instead of relating to things that are already happening around it, school language has to create its own new world of experience; and while this does also happen in the home, when children listen to stories, the world that the stories create, while it may be different and richly imaginative, is still at the same level of abstraction as daily life. It is made up of persons and things who act and interact in a theatre of space and time. Language in school, on the other hand, has to create different kinds of knowledge, based on generalizations and abstractions that are removed from daily life and relate only very indirectly to the learners' own personal experience. These generalizations and abstractions, in turn, draw on different linguistic resources; the languages of education have their own meaning styles and their own grammar to go with them, seen not only in the disciplinary discourses of the secondary school but also already in the "curriculum genres" of the primary.[4]

As a consequence, the activity of 'teaching' gets transformed. Parents are often teaching very actively; but they do not typically reflect on the fact, or on the activity itself. Teachers in school know that they are teaching, and inevitably therefore they are also engaged in research: they are finding out about the learning that their activities are bringing about. Exactly how these activities are bringing about learning is complex and far from clear – I once tried to explore this issue through an analysis of the sentence

The teacher taught the student English

which can be interpreted grammatically in a number of different ways, corresponding (it seemed to me) to different facets of the teaching process.[5] But however it may be happening, "education" is something that both parties are aware is taking place; and the teacher is observing, monitoring, evaluating, checking whether the learner is learning or not. These too are linguistic processes. Thus it is a feature of educational linguistics that one cannot separate the personae of teacher and researcher. What distinguishes teachers from parents is not that teachers are teaching and parents are not, but that teachers are reflecting on the process and ongoingly monitoring its outcome. Furthermore, in order to understand and promote the learning that takes place in school, the teacher/researcher has to understand the learning in home and neighbourhood that preceded it – and which of course is going on all the time. In other words, although the **practices** of educational linguistics are institutionally located, these practices are based on principle and the principles derive from considering the whole of the learning experience, not just that of the institution itself. Educational linguistics involves more than the linguistic practices of education.

What could we say about its relationship to linguistics? The term "educational linguistics" might suggest a subdivision or branch of the subject, like comparative linguistics or the various other branches that arose during the evolution of linguistics as an academic discipline. But it is obviously not a branch of linguistics in the usual sense. Alternatively it might be understood as an intersection of two disciplines, along the lines of those which have emerged since the 1950s with names like socio-logical linguistics, or sociolinguistics. This suggests an interdisciplinary perspective; but it is still not the right one, since (as Kress has remarked about "sociolinguistics") it would imply that there are two things, educa-tion and linguistics, which are then put together and in the process lead to some new domain of practice and research – whereas here there are not two things, but only one. The nearest parallel, perhaps, would be clinical linguistics, meaning the theory, and practices based on that theory, that have to do with language in clinical contexts. Like clinical linguistics, educational linguistics is not a part of linguistics, nor is it a kind of linguistics; in fact it is not a disciplinary concept at all. The perspective is thematic rather than disciplinary.

A discipline (or "subject", in school parlance) is typically defined by its content: by what it is that is under study. The structure of educational knowledge in the twentieth century has been strongly disciplinary in this sense, with the social, or human, sciences – sociology, psychology, linguistics – being modelled on the earlier, natural sciences with their divisions into physics, chemistry, zoology, botany, geology. It was assumed that the methodology of a discipline was essentially determined by its content: in other words, that the question of how something was to be studied was determined by the inherent nature and properties of that something, its status as a phenomenon.

The disciplines have been remarkably successful as a model of know-ledge. But the problem is that, when we do need to transcend them in order to go further, their methodologies turn out to be so different that no dialogue can take place between them. It is true that effective dialogue depends on difference;[6] but there must be a dimension of shared meanings for dialogue to take place at all. These dimensions of shared meanings are often referred to as "themes". The structure of knowledge in the twenty-first century is likely, I think, to be thematic rather than disciplinary. A theme, in this sense, is not an object under study; it is not a content but an angle, a way of looking at things and asking questions about them, where the same question may be raised with respect to a wide variety of different phenomena.

The earliest theme in Western thinking was mathematics: this was a way of understanding things by measuring them. If you measured anything, you were doing mathematics. And mathematics has always been the odd one out in the school curriculum, because it is not a subject like the others; it has no content. In the modern world, as constructed by experimental science, there have been two broad types of thematic approach: one which emphasizes how things are organized, and another that emphasizes how things change – respectively, the "synoptic" and the "dynamic" perspectives; with a periodic swing of the pendulum between them. The major theme of eighteenth century thought was that of natural law, which embedded the dynamic perspective within the synoptic: laws were structural principles determining how things behave. In the nineteenth century the bias shifted in favour of the dynamic, the dominant theme being that of evolution. With the twentieth-century theme of structuralism, the pendulum swung to the opposite extreme. In recent decades, these two themes have re-emerged but have been elevated on to a more abstract plane: evolution has itself evolved into the study of how things change, sometimes called "cladistics", which recognizes three fundamental kinds or contexts of change; while structuralism has been reinterpreted as semiotics, the study of how things mean. It seems likely that the end of the millennium will be celebrated by a resynthesis of the synoptic and the dynamic in the form of a theme having to do with all phenomena seen as system-and-process – perhaps construed by a re-synthesis of spoken and written language. This might provide a way of transiting into another, no longer Western-dominated, intellectual era. Let me summarize this movement as follows, and then go on to relate it to our present topic (see Figure 18.1).

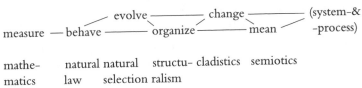

Figure 18.1 Some themes in Western intellectual history

In order to engage effectively with language in educational contexts, we have to adopt a perspective that is at least as much thematic as disciplinary. It is not language as phenomenon that we are concerned

359

with; we are concerned with how people learn by making and exchanging meanings. They do this, of course, by means of language; but they do it in other ways as well, and even in order to understand how people make meaning in language it helps to put language into a thematic context of systems-and-processes of meaning. This theme of "how people mean" then intersects with the theme of "how people learn" to provide the perspective of an educational linguistics.

We can I think trace the progression towards a thematic perspective of this kind if we look back over educational thinking about language during the past 50 years. Up until about the 1950s, language was thought of in fragmented "subject" terms. Literacy ("reading and writing") was a skill, or set of skills, to be acquired first; then language figured as content under the subsequent rubrics of spelling, grammar and composition. But the **word** *language* was very rarely used in curriculum or policy statements (except in the expression *modern languages*), and there was little overall awareness either of language as system and text or of children's language development. Grammar was largely concerned with the marginalia of linguistic good manners, and the only texts considered as worth studying were the highly valued texts of mainstream literature (poetry, the novel, drama).

Educators in the 1950s began to take account of other, non-literary registers; to recognize the concept of "usage" as well as "correctness"; and to allow a place to spoken language as a vehicle of learning. Then in the 1960s we had "language across the curriculum", whereby it was acknowledged that there was a language of science, a language of history and so on, and that anyone learning these subjects had to master their special registers – in English language teaching this took the form of "language(s) for specific purposes". Next we came to hear of "the role of language in learning", suggesting that learning in school involved not just the language of the disciplines as found in textbooks but a great deal else besides: the language of lessons ("classroom discourse"), of class handouts, of displays and other materials, of teachers' notes, of students' notes, of students' essays, library sources, peer group discussion, and homework. The ELT analogue of this was "English for academic purposes". At the same time teachers were moving towards an integrated conception of language development, with the understanding that children started learning language at birth and that there was continuity between home, neighbourhood and school as environments for learning, as well as continuity in the children's own experience. These two strands, the institutional and the developmental, then came together in a more "constructivist" view of language education. "Reality", the human experience of what is out there – and also of what is "in here", the reality inside the head – is not something readymade and waiting to be acquired. It has to be construed; and language is the primary means we use for construing it.

This is consistent with the standpoint of systemic linguistics; not a coincidence, since systemic linguistics evolved in action, and especially perhaps in the context of language education practice (for example the work on *Breakthrough to Literacy* and *Language in Use* at University College London in the 1960s). Looking at the notion of reality construction linguistically, however, we might want to break it down into two or three distinct but interpenetrating components. (1) There is the component of construing experience: using language to know about the world. (2) There is the component of enacting interpersonal relationships: using language to act on the world. Both of these are ways of constructing reality, but they are complementary: in (1) the reality is construed in reflection, with language in its "third person" function; in (2) it is constructed in action, with language in its "first/second, person" function. Reflection and action each embodies the other as a submotif: we act on the reality that we have construed in reflection (like a baby dropping things from the side of its chair, or a structural engineer), and reflect on that which we have constructed in action (like a baby musing on itself and its mother, or a theoretical sociologist).

There is then also (3) a third component, that of constructing the discourse as itself another kind or aspect of reality: language is used to construct reality, but it is itself also part of reality, and has to be constructed in its own right.[7] These three components are present in the grammar of every language; we refer to them as ideational, interpersonal and textual. In fact this tripartite structure is the basic principle around which language is organized, as a potential or resource for meaning – something that a deep analysis of the plane of content will reveal.

Following up the work of the 1960s I tried to suggest the direction of movement towards a more thematically conceived body of educational linguistic theory and practice by using the expression "social semiotic" borrowed form Greimas.[8] With the more explicit notions of "social meaning-making practices" and the development of the linguistic theory in the direction of discourse, genre and ideology, we have been learning to critique – and hence to intervene in – the registers of educational discourse, and to bring into range the other processes that go with them, both the semiotic processes other than language and the non-semiotic, material processes.[9] In the series of workshops of which this is the latest one we have been building up a store of experience and understanding on the basis of which it is possible to examine, criticize and, we hope, improve our own practices as teachers and as co-workers with teachers. By the same token we are also learning – often painfully, but we hope significantly for the future – what are all the things that now need to be done: to be problematized so that we are forced to enrich the theory. Let me round off this talk by mentioning some of the fields of current enquiry that might form part of an educational linguistics which we could usefully pursue in approaching the twenty-first century. In no sense, of course, is this a comprehensive or definitive list; rather, it is a sample of the work that needs to be done so as to ensure that it will continue to be fruitful for educators to engage with language. I will give them headings:

1. Exploring synoptic and dynamic perspectives
2. Deepening and extending the "grammatics"
3. Investigating semantic variation
4. Continuing to explore the "higher" strata
5. Working towards a language-based theory of teaching/learning

1 Exploring the synoptic and dynamic perspectives. We have been making a lot of use of these terms since the distinction was first introduced into our discourse (in conversation among Jay Lemke, Jim Martin and myself some ten years ago): but it is important to recognize that they are not different classes of phenomena. They are not two things, but two ways of looking at things – as entities, and as happening. They are complementary, in the sense that while they contradict each other (no phenomenon can "be" both object and event) both are valid and indeed necessary modes of interpretation: each sheds light on different aspects of a phenomenon, as in the prototypical example of wave and particle as complementary models of light. All dualities tend to get co-opted into the roles of "good" vs "bad", and we are now living in a phase in which the dynamic is cast as the good; but there is of course no difference of value between them. There is a difference, however, in how accessible they are: it is much harder to apprehend and construe things in dynamic terms.

In the experimental paradigm, phenomena are held still, synoptically, while we study them. But in order to view them dynamically, we may have to account for three different histories, which might involve all three types of change recognized in cladistics: evolution, growth and individuation.[10] The system of language, and of a particular variety of a language (a register or dialect), evolves; so for example we can talk of the evolution of scientific English. The way language is developed by a child, however, is a process of growing; while the unfolding of a particular instance of language – a text – is a process of individuation. When we try to apprehend a linguistic phenomenon, such as grammatical metaphor, dynamically we may need to construe it in terms of all these histories: its evolution in the system, its growth in the learner, and its individuation in the text.

2 Deepening and extending the "grammatics". Perhaps the most significant domain for the operation of the dynamic/synoptic complementarity is in the grammar itself. As we use language to construe the domains of our experience, the features that are more accessible, more specific, and more volatile are construed in words (as vocabulary), and the more hidden, more general and more lasting features are construed as grammar. This means that the grammar of a natural language is a general theory of experience. For example, the grammatical system of transitivity (types of process, their participants and circumstantial relations) constitutes a theory about events in the real world – including of course the world inside our heads, and the world of language. So when we construct a theory about grammar, in order to understand how the grammar constructs a theory about experience (or rather, how speakers do this, using grammar as their strategic resource), our theory is already a theory of a second order – a theory about a theory. I have called this higher order theory of grammar "grammatics".

Now, grammars (the grammars of natural language) embody many of their own complementarities: that is, different and in principle contradictory ways of interpreting some field of experience. An example would be tense and aspect as complementary theories of time. One of these complementarities in the grammar is precisely that of interpreting what goes on either as a construction of objects or as a flow of events: the contrast between *his fear of possible retaliation* and *he was afraid they might strike back*. In other words, the grammar can take either a synoptic or a dynamic view of the world it evolved to construct.

But if we are to understand how the grammar embodies such complementarities, our grammatics has to probe beyond the grammar's more accessible reaches into the realm of what Whorf called "cryptotypes". These are the patterns, largely hidden from view, that carry the ideologically pervasive message of our species and its diverse cultures. Since these patterns depend for their potency on large-scale quantitative effects, then as the corpus-based study of grammar comes to be feasible such a "cryptogrammatics" can reasonably appear on the agenda.[11]

3 Investigating semantic variation. A fundamental issue for educational

linguistics is that different human groups tend to mean in different ways. This variation arises not only between different cultures but also between different populations within one culture, as Bernstein showed with his 1960s studies of "sociolinguistic coding orientation".[12]

Ruqaiya Hasan has been finding out how the linguistic interaction between mothers and children shapes the way the children learn: their forms of reasoning and of knowing, the ways in which they construe experience, and the dimensions of the semiotic space within which their consciousness develops. Her primary database contains over 20,000 "messages" of spontaneous conversation in the home, and she has constructed a semantic system network to represent the total paradigm of significant options. She has then used cluster analysis to study systematic patterns of variation in semantic choice – for example in the way mothers answer their children's questions; the programme "clusters" those sets of features that contribute most to this semantic variation, and one can then note what variables in the population are being constructed by it. Hasan's findings show that on linguistic grounds the population is structured very clearly along two dimensions; and these turn out to be those of class and sex – the sex of the child, and the social class status of the family.[13]

The immediate educational significance of this particular work is very obvious, and is specifically brought out in a number of further studies being undertaken by Hasan and her colleagues David Butt, Carmel Cloran and Rhondda Fahey. But the results also show that the concept of systematic semantic variation, as embodied in terms such as "meaning style" or "fashions of speaking", can be made explicit provided it is backed up by large-scale quantitative studies of naturally occurring discourse and by a paradigmatic interpretation of the meaning potential such as is represented in a system network.

4 Continuing to explore the "higher" strata. Hasan's work just referred to is clearly about the construction of ideologies – higher-level meaning systems that constitute what we think of as "a culture"; and in the ten years since the appearance of Kress and Hodge's *Language as Ideology* there has been a substantial forward movement on these frontiers by educationally involved linguists working from a systemic point of view. Martin's genre theory has been critical in two respects: in providing a way in for teachers wanting to use linguistic insights in their teaching (as Joan Rothery saw at the start, the grammar is not the best point of entry, but the route must **lead on to grammar**, which the register studies in *Language in Use* had not been able to do); and in provoking the most thoroughgoing debate about the place of **linguistics** (i.e. explicit

attention to language) in classroom activities. But genre is also, for Martin, the way of modelling a higher level of organization whereby language construes the culture, and hence is central to all educational issues. Education involves the entire set of social meaning-making practices of the cultures, as well as the linguistic construction of specific hierarchies such as race and sex, and of higher-order systems of all kinds, such as for example the semiotics of verbal art.[14] These higher-level patterns are critical for educational linguistics in at least two respects. First, they pervade the **discourses** of education, as we see from studies of the teacher's talk in the classroom, of textbooks in the various disciplines, and so on; and second, through Lemke's "thematic systems" as an intermediate construct, they determine the underlying directions of educational praxis and educational change.[15]

5 Working towards a language-based theory of teaching/learning. This is one of the urgent tasks: to use the "grammatics" to work towards a greater understanding of the processes of learning and teaching. I have suggested elsewhere what seem to me to be essential features that need to be integrated into any learning theory that takes language as its point of departure.[16]

These derive in the first place from our understanding of children's language development; but they also include other problem areas where a consideration of language suggests general insights into how people learn – for example, the dialectic of system and process, whereby each instance is both an addition to the repertory of "text" and a trigger for the construction of "system".

Lemke has shown that predisposition to learn is always matched by predisposition to teach – no matter whether we are talking of physical, biological, social or semiotic systems.[17] At the same time, all these systems have their own special properties. Since most human learning (and all educational learning, in the sense in which I defined this at the beginning) involves a semiotic component – typically language – it is important to ask specifically how **semiotic** systems come to grow. How are the internal processes of growth engendered by exchanges with the external environment? The environment, of course, is the teacher – with *the teacher* here first to be read as Value (it is the environment that functions as teacher) and then re-read as Token (it is the teacher that functions as environment – in other words, that **constructs** the context in ways such that the learner will learn).[18]

These are some of the areas which have proved critical for educational linguistics in the past decade – and which for that very reason now need to gain much greater theoretical force. The headings are selective (reflecting what I happen to have been thinking about lately!), and are not being put forward as exhaustive or even as of highest priority. Their relationship to educational practice is two way: as input, to inform and to challenge current praxis from the most abstract statement of goals to the most down-to-earth classroom activities; and also as output, areas where our theoretical understanding of language and of the semiotic construction of reality has derived significantly from the educational contexts in which systemic linguists have always worked.

Notes

1. For an account of these processes see Hasan and Martin (eds) 1989, especially papers by David Butt, Carmel Cloran, and Clare Painter.
2. See Hasan 1988; Hasan and Cloran 1990.
3. See Butt 1989.
4. For the disciplinary discourses as constructed by textbooks used in Years 7 and 8 see Wignell, Martin and Eggins 1987, and Eggins, Wignell and Martin 1987. For the "curriculum genres" of the primary of school see Christie 1988.
5. In Halliday 1976.
6. As implied by the title of the present conference.
7. The interpretation of the textual metafuction as the construction of semiotic reality is put forward by Christian Matthiessen 1992.
8. The term was used by Greimas in his paper in International Days of Sociolinguistics, the conference held in Rome in 1971.
9. For the concept of "social meaning-making practices" see Thibault 1991a, Lemke 1989, 1990. For genre theory see Martin 1984a, 1984b, 1992. For language and ideology see the papers collected in Threadgold et al. (eds) 1986; also Threadgold 1988. For the relation of genre and ideology see Kress and Threadgold 1988, Threadgold 1988, 1991, and Martin 1991. For reports of earlier workshops in the series see e.g. Hasan (ed.) 1985 and Painter and Martin (eds) 1986.
10. From J.L. Lemke, paper given to the Newtown Semiotics Circle, November 1989.
11. As example of this kind of grammatics see Martin (1988), and Matthiessen (1991).
12. For Basil Bernstein's fundamental contribution, based on research carried on throughout the 1960s, see his *Class, Codes and Control*, Vols 1 and 2 (1971, 1973), and the series of books deriving from this project (of which these titles formed a part) brought together as *Primary Socialization, Language and Education* and published at various times during the 1970s. For Bernstein's more recent work see *Class, Codes and Control*, Vol. 4 (1990).

13. See Hasan and Cloran 1990. A number of other papers reporting on this project are in the course of publication, or have already appeared. (See the forthcoming Vol. 2 of Ruqaiya Hasan's Collected Works, London: Equinox, in press.)

14. Cf. publications referred to in note 9 above; also McGregor 1990; Poynton 1985. For the semiotics of verbal art see Hasan 1985, O'Toole 1989, Butt 1987 and the authors represented in Birch and O'Toole 1985.

15. See J.L. Lemke 1988, *Using Language in the Classroom*, Oxford: Oxford University Press, 1988; and his book *Talking Science* referred to in note 9 above.

16. These were set out in a paper entitled 'Towards a linguistic theory of learning', presented at the Conference on Language and Learning, Kuala Lumpur, July 1989 (see Halliday 1993*b*).

17. See J.L. Lemke 1984, *Semiotics and Education*, Toronto: Victoria University (Toronto Semiotic Circle, Monographs, Working Papers and Prepublications), 1984.

18. For Token and Value see Halliday (1967/68, 2005; and 1985, especially Chapter 5); also Toolan 1990 for insightful discussion of these conceptions.

Chapter Nineteen

A LANGUAGE DEVELOPMENT
APPROACH TO EDUCATION
(1994)

It is a great pleasure for me to be here in Hong Kong on this occasion, and to be taking part in the International Language in Education Conference "ILEC 93". The theme for this year's conference is "Language and Learning", and I have tried to locate my own contribution squarely within that topic. For me the conference comes towards the end of a few weeks' stay in Hong Kong, during which I have been working with colleagues in the language education area; and one of the issues that we have been exploring is that of the relation between commonsense learning and educational learning – between the kind of learning that children are involved in, more or less from birth, in the family and among their own peer group, and the kind of learning they engage in when they come to school, where learning is institutionalized (that is, after all, what a school is: an institution designed for learning in). These two aspects of children's learning experience, commonsense learning and educational learning, are not of course insulated one from the other: there is continuity between the two; but there is not perhaps as much continuity as there could be, and some people might feel that the two are kept rather too far apart. In Hong Kong this is probably thought of as a consequence of the language situation, given the distance that typically separates the language of home from the language of school. This obviously plays some part. But lack of continuity between commonsense and educational learning is not just a feature of societies that are linguistically complex. Even where home and school share essentially the same language of interaction, there is typically a considerable discontinuity in children's experience of learning, as they move between these two learning environments.

Now this is not the principal focus of my talk today; but I need to look a little further into the phenomenon of learning discontinuity, in order then to look behind it and beyond it. What is the nature of this discontinuity between home and school, and how does it arise? One factor is presumably the linguistic medium: commonsense learning, in the preschool years at least, is thoroughly grounded in the spoken language; whereas after children become literate, at the very beginning of their stay in school, it is typically assumed that what they learn in class will be learnt essentially through reading and writing. But this is clearly not the whole of the picture. After all, even in school the teacher talks to them, and they discuss what they are learning both with the teacher and with each other; and on the other hand, before children ever go into school their parents are often reading to them out of books, and some children learn to read quite a lot all by themselves. So there is no exact equation such that commonsense learning equals learning through speech and educational learning equals learning through writing. Nevertheless the difference between speech and writing is a significant factor – although we should concentrate, rather, not on the medium itself but on the difference between spoken language and written language. It is not the difference between media that are relevant so much as the different kinds of meaning that are typically associated with them.

What we are observing, in this context, is a discontinuity between educational and commonsense forms of knowledge: between two different ways of construing human experience. It is obviously impossible to characterize this difference adequately in a few short sentences; it is something complex and many-sided. But I can try and capture one or two salient points. (1) Commonsense knowledge is fluid and indeterminate, without clear boundaries or precise definitions: it does not matter too much exactly where a particular process begins and ends, or what is one phenomenon and what is another. Educational knowledge is determinate and systematic: the categories of experience are organized into conceptual structures with defined properties and explicit interrelations. (2) Commonsense learning foregrounds processes – actions and events, including mental and verbal events; of course it is also concerned with things, but their main significance is in the way they enter in to all the various processes. Educational knowledge foregrounds the things: persons and concrete objects, then later on increasingly abstract and virtual objects that are needed to explain how the things behave. (3) Commonsense knowledge is typically construed as dialogue, and built up interactively, or "intersubjectively", by the human group. Educational knowledge is typically construed monologically, and built up by each individual – the "others", in our present educational system at least, tend to be competitors rather than collaborators. (4) And commonsense knowledge is typically unconscious: we do not know what we know; whereas educational knowledge is conscious knowledge – and so it can be rehearsed, and therefore monitored and assessed. There are no examinations for knowledge of the commonsense kind.

James Britton, in his influential book *Language and Learning*, written about a generation ago, distinguished in students' writing between the private, "expressive" kind and the more public kinds demanded by the school, "transactional" on the one hand and "poetic" on the other. Britton saw the expressive as the learner's point of departure, the natural mode of meaning that children brought with them from the experience of their early years. The priority that Britton gave to the expressive category derived from his own rather individualistic ideology of education; but his work had considerable influence on educational practice in England and elsewhere – for example, in the way primary school writing came to be dominated by stories, on the assumption that the bridge from commonsense to educational learning was to be built out of personal narrative. (See Britton 1970.) Narrative is, in turn, the term that Jerome Bruner uses to name one of his two modes of "cognitive functioning", the narrative and the paradigmatic. The paradigmatic mode "attempts to fulfil the ideal of a formal, mathematical system of description and explanation. It employs categorization or conceptualization and the operations by which categories are established, instantiated, idealized, and related one to the other to form a system." By contrast, "the imaginative application of the narrative mode leads instead to good stories, gripping drama, believable (though not necessarily 'true') historical accounts. It deals in human or human–like intention and action and the vicissitudes and consequences that mark their course." These two modes of cognitive functioning each provide, according to Bruner, "distinctive ways of ordering experience, of constructing reality". (See Bruner 1990: 11–13.)

We see this dichotomy transformed and built in to educational knowledge if we compare the language of natural science and the language of the humanities, as Martin and his colleagues have done in their detailed studies of these discourses in the secondary school (see Halliday and Martin 1993: esp. Chapter 11). The grammar of science constructs elaborate technical taxonomies, using nominalizing metaphors and complex nominal group structures to create virtual objects and build them into sequences of logical argument. The grammar of the humanities, on the other hand, constructs schemata made up of individual semi-technical abstractions, simpler in structure (often single nouns) because not taxonomized, but each one charged with value and coming together as a whole to make up an ideological stance. Compare the following two passages, the first taken from a geography textbook and the second from a textbook of history:

> *As air is moved upward* away from the land-water surface or downward towards it, very important *changes occur in the air temperature. Air moving upward* away from the surface comes under lower pressures because there is less weight of atmosphere upon it, so *it stretches or expands.* Air moving downward towards the surface from higher elevations encounters higher pressures and *shrinks in volume.* Even when *there is no addition or withdrawal of heat* from surrounding sources, the temperature of *the upward or downward-moving air* changes because of *its expansion or contraction. This type of temperature change* which results from *internal processes* alone is called *adiabatic change.* (G.T. Trewartha, *An Introduction to Climate*, 1968: 1361)

I have used italics to mark examples of how the grammar constructs technical entities and organizes them into logical sequences; e.g. *[air] stretches or expands . . . because of its expansion or contraction; changes occur in the air temperature . . . this type of temperature change . . . is called adiabatic change.*

> Wars are costly *exercises.* They cause *death* and *destruction* and *put resources to non-productive uses* but they also *promote industrial and technological change.* This *benefit* does not mean that war is a good thing, but that sometimes it *brings useful developments.*
>
> The Second World War further *encouraged the restructuring of the Australian economy* towards *a manufacturing basis.* Between 1937 and 1945 the value of *industrial production* almost doubled. *This increase* was faster than otherwise *would have occurred. The momentum was maintained* in the post-war years and by 1954–5 *the value of manufacturing output was three times* that of 1944–5. *The enlargement* of Australia's *steel-making capacity,* and of chemicals, rubber, metal goods and motor vehicles all *owed* something to the *demands* of war. The war had acted as a hot-house for *technological progress* and *economic change.* (H. Simmelhaig and G.F.R. Spencely, *For Australia's Sake*, 1984: 121)

Here the italics show instances of abstract expressions of a semi-technical kind (e.g. *exercises, put . . . to non-productive uses, brings . . . useful developments*) and terms with a clear evaluative loading (e.g. *destruction, non-*

productive, promote, benefit, useful, increase, momentum). The ideological motif of 'growth is good' is foregrounded throughout (cf. Halliday 1993a: 25 ff.).

I will refer again to these examples later on. Here the point I am drawing attention to is this: the kind of variation that we find here at secondary level, between the discourses of science and the humanities, is an elaboration of the same dichotomy; this dual motif runs throughout the educational process, and there seems no reason to assign priority to one variant or the other. Yet in much of contemporary learning theory and educational practice in the West it is assumed that the narrative mode (in Bruner's sense) is somehow cognitively prior, and that commonsense learning is overwhelmingly in terms of "good stories". Bruner himself acknowledges (p. 127) that his own early model of the child was "very much in the tradition of the solo child mastering the world by representing it to himself in his own terms"; and this model readily lends itself to (and in practice typically co-occurs with) a "story-telling" interpretation of childhood. I think that we, as educators, should challenge and be prepared to reject this kind of "childist" model. If we accept any such dichotomy as that proposed by Bruner (and it may be helpful as a tool for thinking with, although we might adapt it to become less dichotomized and more explicitly grounded in language), we probably need to recognize that both these modes of meaning, the paradigmatic as well as the narrative, contribute equally to children's commonsense ordering of experience.

If we are seeking a model from educational theory that we can relate to the distinction between commonsense and educational knowledge as this is manifested in children's early language development – where the commonsense reality is construed in language before the educational one – we might do well to re-examine Bernstein's theory of code, deriving from a sociological rather than a psychological perspective on learning. Commonsense and educational learning construe reality in terms of different codes. While these do not correspond exactly to Bernstein's "restricted" and "elaborated" varieties (there can be various features of elaborated code in the linguistic construction of commonsense knowledge), they are related at a general level; and more specifically, in that educational knowledge as at present constituted cannot be construed without the semantic resources that Bernstein identified as "elaborated". This applies equally both to the discourse of science and to that of the humanities.

What we have been lacking, however, it seems to me, is a perspective on learning that starts from language itself, instead of first being formulated from outside language and then mapped on to observations of language as an afterthought. Of course we have moved some way from the views of Piaget, who saw language as essentially a means for the expression of thought processes. Both Bernstein and Bruner, arguing for a constructivist view (and citing Vygotsky as a pivotal figure), foreground language as a central factor in the process by which reality is constructed. But if reality is constructed in language – or, as I would prefer to put it, if human experience is construed in the form of language – then the way in which language itself comes into being must give us an insight into the fundamental nature of learning. After all, children are at the same time both learning language and using language to learn with (as Gordon Wells has documented very richly in the course of his work). It is we who distinguish these two processes, as we have to do for purposes of analysis; as far as the children themselves are concerned, learning language and learning through language are just one integrated process – namely, learning. Might we not take more account of what has been found out about children's language development, when we try to increase our understanding of the nature of learning in general?

It seems to me that there are certain aspects of what we know about language development in children, if we start from the earliest phase before they move into the mother tongue, that are relevant and suggestive in such a context. I am not going to try to enumerate them all – I have written about this elsewhere (Halliday 1993b); but I should like to discuss one or two of theses features of children's learning that I think are particularly relevant to the present situation here in Hong Kong. Let me refer first of all to the very general principle of linguistic function, and ask: what are the functional contexts in which language first appears?

1 Very early in life, children find that they can use language – not yet the mother tongue, but a "child tongue", a little protolanguage they construct for themselves in interacting with parents and others – in a number of different ways: to get things done for them, or given to them; to get others to join in some activity, or else just to attend to them and "be together"; and to express their own feelings and curiosity about the outside world. When they start to learn the mother tongue, however, and thus get ready to construe their experience in the distinctively human mode, children typically adopt a simple but very powerful strategy: they re-construe these functions by setting up a very general opposition – that between language to act with and language to think with. In this period, round about the second half of the second year of life, it has often been observed that children's utterances are of one or other of these two kinds: either pragmatic – they want something done for them; or what I called

373

"mathetic", meaning by this the learning function – they are learning to name things and to describe what is going on around them. This strategy then turns out to be a transitional one leading to something much more pervasive and lasting: before very long each utterance comes to include a combination of both functions, having both an active and a reflective dimension of meaning. Now, from the language point of view, what we are seeing here is the birth of grammar, as (i) the opposition between pragmatic and mathetic evolves into the mood system (indicative/ imperative, and so on), while (ii) the experiential content (of both types) evolves into the system of transitivity: transitivity and mood are the two fundamental components of the meaning-making resources of every natural language. But we also see here something that is significant from the point of view of learning in general: namely, that construing experience is inherently an interactive process – there can be no content without also a speech function. The mood system is the resource for constructing dialogue; and it is only when the experiential content is mapped into a dialogic form that the child's world begins to take semiotic shape. Commonsense knowledge is not a purely experiential construction; on the contrary, it is built out of the impact between the experiential and the interpersonal modes of meaning. Learning involves both thinking and doing.

2 In the course of this impact, something else takes place. At the beginning of the transition from protolanguage to mother tongue, the child's mathetic utterances are as it were annotations, or footnotes to experience – a commentary on what is going on at the time, or an account of happenings from that past. They are not yet statements: that is, the child does not address these utterances to anyone who is not, or was not, a party to the happenings in question. Children may simply say these things to themselves. But if they are directed to another person, that person must be someone who is sharing or has shared the experience with them. Adults are frequently surprised to discover this; mother says, after an outing with her little boy, "Tell Granny what we saw" – but the child cannot do so. He may turn back to mummy, and tell her the whole story; but if he turns to look at granny, he is tongue-tied: – how can I tell Granny? She wasn't there. At this stage, language is a construction of shared experience – it is not a surrogate for it; and it is only when the two dimensions of meaning come together, when transitivity and mood combine to form a clause, that children can construe experience as news, using language not just to say but to tell. And once they can tell, of course, they can also ask. Again, when we trace the origin of telling and asking, we are looking at the child's development from a language point

of view. What is the relevance to a general learning theory? It is that "information", something that we usually take for granted (it is after all built in to the concept of teaching), is not an inborn capability. Telling is a capability that has to be constructed – constructed in the course of learning language. It is only when you have learnt to tell that you can share experiences symbolically, as information, with those who have not been present with you to share in the events themselves.

The last two paragraphs have concerned developments that take place long before children go to school; they lie at the foundations of our unconscious, commonsense knowledge. There are other aspects of language learning that stretch out over much more extended periods of time. Let me turn next to two examples of these. The first I shall call the "interpersonal gateway".

3 I have suggested that language, in its distinctively human, adult sense, is an interplay of action and reflection: of the interpersonal and the experiential "metafunctions", in the terms of systemic functional theory. In every human language, whenever we speak (or write) we are typically at once both construing some aspect of experience and enacting some interpersonal force – the second of these includes both expressing our own angle on the matter and engaging in some relationship with another person, or other people. Both these components of meaning are present in all discourse. They are installed there by the grammar; hence, the grammar also makes it possible to foreground one or other of the two. It seems to be the case that when children are taking a major step forward in language learning they typically do so in contexts that are strongly loaded interpersonally. One example could be drawn from my last heading, learning to tell: this step is likely to be taken under pressure from the expressive domain, when a child needs to convey that something unpleasant has happened – he has hurt himself, perhaps, and is needing sympathy. Another example, from a little later on, is that of learning to construe conditions: logical-semantic relations such as those expressed in English by *if, unless, although*. These are learnt in the first place, as Clare Painter (1989) and Joy Phillips (1986) have observed, in the context of threats and warnings: the adult says things like "if you touch the iron you'll hurt yourself", or "unless you stop banging that pan I shall take it away from you" – and the children then address such remarks to themselves, or to a younger brother or sister if one is available. In these and numerous other such examples, the meanings they are learning to make are primarily experiential in nature, semantic configurations that are going to play a central part in constructing knowledge, both commonsense and educational knowledge (like conditions); but the child's

way in to these meanings is through the interpersonal gateway. And this again has implications for a general model of learning: the greater the conceptual distance that has to be traversed, in some particular learning task, the more critical it may be to set the task in an interpersonal environment – some context with which the learner is likely to be positively and interactively engaged.

4 The next feature is one that extends throughout the entire process of language development: the movement towards abstraction – children's progress through the semantic territory of the general, the abstract and the metaphorical. This too is a development in the potential of the lexicogrammar, and we can observe it as we track how children construct their grammatical resources. When they first move into the mother tongue, children learn to generalize: that is, they make the leap from "proper" to "common" terms – from naming individuals to naming classes, classes of things (persons and objects), of processes (actions and events) and of properties. These phenomena are construed in the open-ended word classes of every language, prototypically the nouns and the verbs. Children have no problem in construing as general terms the concrete domains of their "outer" experience: they readily master cups and dogs and buses, big and red, falling and hitting and breaking; and soon afterwards they also learn to construe their own "inner" experience of hurting and liking and remembering and seeing, and so on. What they cannot yet cope with at this stage are words with purely abstract referents: words such as *real* and *habit* and *choice* and *manage* and *delay*. Since one needs abstract meanings when learning to read and write (the teacher will often refer to *words* and *sentences* and *complete sense* and *information* and the like), it is at the age when children typically come to master this kind of language – round about 5 – that we put them into school. But it is not the actual skills of reading and writing so much as the entry into educational forms of knowledge that will make this demand on their language abilities. The primary phase of education depends on the learner being able to understand the meaning of abstract discourse.

But there is still another semiotic hurdle remaining to be crossed: the move from the abstract to the metaphorical. And this typically requires another four or five years of development. It is usually not until the age of 8 or 9 that children begin to accommodate metaphor in their grammar; and it takes them two or three years to sort it out and domesticate it. Now, while the educational knowledge of the primary school depends on abstractness, the discipline-based knowledge of the secondary school depends on metaphor: the sort of discourse that I illustrated earlier in the extracts from geography and history. Both the humanities and the sciences rely extensively on metaphor in the grammar, though in rather different ways. The history text talks about *war* and *peace* and *benefits* and *influences* and *supporting* and *promoting* and *progress towards a manufacturing basis*: these are metaphoric manipulations of abstract or institutionalized entities, which the learner has to relate to each other and assign appropriate connotations of value. The geography text talks about *withdrawal of heat, expansion, contraction, condensation, humidity, drainage, frontal uplift* and the like: these are processes and properties (get cooler, expand, shrink, condense, humid, drain, push up from the front) but they have been nominalized – that is, transformed metaphorically into virtual objects, the component parts of a systematic technical taxonomy. It is only by the time of adolescence that children are fully at home with this metaphorical mode of construing experience: when they move over from the primary stage of education into the secondary.

Thus it is the development of grammar that reveals most clearly the maturational principles that lie behind the structure of education – not only of educational knowledge but of the institution of education itself, the division of schooling into primary and secondary, with (in some systems) a middle or junior high school dedicated to helping children make the transition. Of course, the linguistic factors that I have picked out here as being critical in this developmental process are not suddenly appearing in isolation from everything else; they are part of the grammar's overall construction of experiential meaning. The grammar opens up a multidimensional semantic space through clusters, or syndromes, of related systemic features. To give just one example, at the same time as children are mastering these metaphorical nominalizations they are also, in English, developing the use of non-finite clauses, which are another element within the same area of semantic potential. But we can often identify certain specific components within the grammar which turn out to be critical for a particular "moment" in children's construction of knowledge.

I would like now to refer to three further linguistic features that illustrate my general thesis; but I will deal with them very much more briefly. They are, as those already discussed, aspects of children's language development which seem to me to offer pointers to the nature of learning in general. The three headings – somewhat opaque in themselves, but to be clarified, I hope, in what follows – are: the movement between system and instance; semiotic regression and reconstruction; and the synoptic/dynamic complementarity.

5 In learning language, children are all the time moving between the system and the instance. That is to say, they are construing the

system – the potential of language, its semantic, lexicogrammatical and phonological resources – out of instances that they listen to and read; and, on the other hand, they are using these resources in speaking and in writing: from the system they are producing instances of their own. It is the dialectic between these two that constitutes learning. We can often observe this movement when a child says something new, describing an event, perhaps, with a grammatical pattern that is extending the frontiers of his system; the child may then repeat the same account, many times, over the next few weeks and months, using precisely the same sounds and the same wording – by which time the system has moved ahead, and the instance now sounds like a fossilized relic of an earlier stage (which is exactly what it is).

6 In this particular case, there is no actual regression: the child's progress only appears to be stilted because we are hearing, at one and the same time, instances that were first worded at rather different times. But in one type of context there is a pattern of regression and reconstruction; this happens in the transition from commonsense to educational learn-ing – it is an aspect of the discontinuity that I referred to right at the beginning. When children move into school, they face a considerable task of semiotic reconstruction: they have to reorganize their ways of meaning along new and unfamiliar lines. They have to re-form their language into a new medium, that of writing; and at the same time, or shortly afterwards, they have to restructure the discourse semantics so as to construe their knowledge systematically in a conscious form. In this process they often regress to earlier modes of meaning, on the one hand in their writing, so that a 6-year-old, fluent and sophisticated in speech, will often write using the language of a child of 2 or 3; and on the other hand in their understanding, so that they are learning over again things they already know perfectly well, but learning them now within an organized structure of knowledge. Children sometimes do not realize that something that is being presented to them in the written mode, and with all the majestic authority of the textbook, is actually something that has been part of their unconscious knowledge for some considerable time. I often cite the example from an upper primary science textbook, *some animals protect themselves with bites and stings*: in Australia, at least, children have known this since the age of 2 – it is important for their survival! They would not, of course, construe it in this way grammatically; they would say *they bite and they sting*, using verbs to express the actions, whereas the textbook is intro-ducing them to scientific discourse and transforms these processes metaphorically into nouns: *bites and stings*. The experience is being

reconstrued for them, by the grammar, as part of a different universe of knowledge.

7 And this leads me to the final heading, which I expressed technically (using grammatical metaphor) as "synoptic/dynamic complementarity". Here in fact this very fundamental notion of grammatical metaphor becomes central to the interpretation of learning. When children first construct the grammar of their mother tongue, they are able to do so very quickly because it provides them with a theory for explaining their own experience. So the structure of a clause, in English, or in Chinese, is a theory about actions and events; it provides (i) a class of words for the process that is taking place, the doing or happening – this we call a "verb"; and (ii) another, distinct class for the participants in the process, the persons and concrete objects that do things, or have things done to them – these are the "nouns". So the child construes a model of experience in which the basic unit is an action or event, comprising a process and one or two participants, with the process represented as a verb and the participants as nouns. Thus the prototypical meaning associated with a noun is that of a person, animal or concrete object; that associated with a verb is doing or happening. Other aspects of the total phenomenon also have their typical forms of wording: adjectives construe properties, conjunctions construe logical-semantic relations, and so on. Since the grammatical mode is clausal, which foregrounds doing and happening, the resulting picture of reality is a fairly dynamic one.

But later on, as we have seen, the grammar undergoes a change; it is reconstructed in different forms, with nouns, or rather nominal groups, taking over from clauses as the basis for organizing experience. Now if children's grammar had started out in this way there would be nothing metaphorical about it; the noun would have been the everyday, typical resource for talking about phenomena of every kind. But it did not. In their commonsense learning, nouns were names of things. The grammar is not now neutral any more; it is already semantically charged, and the nouns carry this semantic prosody with them wherever they go. So when experience is reconstrued, with educational discourse, into a nominalized form, this sets up a semantic tension, a complementarity of perspective. If students read about *evaporation*, and *seepage*, and *rainfall runoff*, in their hydrology text, these have the semantic features both of happenings, processes (water evaporates and seeps through, rain falls and then runs off) and of things, this being the prototypical meaning of a noun. We might want to say that no phenomenon can be both process and thing at the same time: the two are mutually contradictory. But that is precisely what *evaporation* and *seepage* and *rainfall runoff* are. Just one or two random instances by themselves would have no noticeable effect; but when the entire edifice of knowledge takes on this bivalent form it makes a profound difference to the learner's picture of the world.

The two conflicting forces, however, do not meet on entirely equal terms. Commonsense knowledge is deeply installed in our brains and in our bodies; but it is unrecognized – whereas the more lately developed perspective carries not only the full authority of educational discourse ("what the textbook says") but also the immense power of a knowledge that is organized and systematic: either in systems of values, typical of the humanities, or as in the sciences, where the grammatically constructed logical argument is further reinforced by the taxonomic resources of the lexicon. (Such taxonomies depend entirely on construing every phenomenon as a "thing".) The effect of this is to provide a less dynamic, more synoptic vision of the world, in which reality is as it were held still, rendered fixed, bounded and determinate, so that it can be observed, measured and, if possible, explained.

This suggests that we, as educators, need to be aware of the technical language of the scientific disciplines and to see it not as a "jargon", a set of unnecessary and often complex and cumbersome terms, but as a powerful grammatical resource with which experimental science reinterprets human experience. We might note here that technical taxonomies are rather less forbidding in Chinese than in English – whereas in its technical grammar, on the other hand, Chinese is the more problematic of the two (see Halliday and Martin, 1993: Chapter 7). But the implications for learning theory go rather further than this. It is not simply that we should be aware of how reality is construed in language, first in the language of the home and then later reconstrued in the languages of education. More especially, to a significant extent the process of learning consists in adopting complementary perspectives on experience: on seeing reality in ways which are at one level mutually exclusive, and even contradictory, and yet which taken together provide a deeper insight than either perspective adopted by itself. In one sense, the entire division into commonsense knowledge and educational knowledge, of which we tend to emphasize only the negative effects (and these there certainly are), may also have its positive function, if it is from the clash between these two very different modes of meaning that wisdom is ultimately attained.

I have made use of seven headings, as follows:

1. the functional multiplicity of grammar: "action and reflection"
   – enacting interpersonal relationships ["interpersonal"] and construing human experience ["experiential"]
2. "information" as dialogic exchange: "telling and asking"
   – combining mood (interpersonal) and transitivity (experiential) as the foundation of commonsense knowledge
3. the interpersonal "gateway" to learning
   – engaging with what is being learnt, through involvement of the "self" in interaction with others
4. the move towards the abstract
   – from generalization to abstractness to metaphor: creating new dimensions of semantic space
5. the dialectic of system and instance
   – construing grammar out of discourse, and construing discourse out of grammar
6. semiotic regression and reconstruction
   – accommodating the written medium, and reorganizing knowledge in systematic and conscious form
7. complementary perspectives on experience: "dynamic and synoptic"
   – maintaining the tension between reality as process (clausal) and reality as thing (nominal)

What these seem to suggest, if we put them together, is that learning, when seen from the vantage point of language, is a highly complex endeavour – but one that is achieved through the interplay of a number of different meaning-making processes each of which by itself is rather simple. It is perhaps better to try and summarize them in a different order. (4) Children are progressively reconstruing experience, away from the immediate and concrete, using likeness (or analogy) to construe general categories, then abstract categories, then metaphorical categories. Adopting a topological framework we can say that each step creates, or rather allows the learner to create, new **dimensions** of semantic space. (7) The metaphoric categories require the learner to adopt simultaneously two complementary **perspectives** on experience. Three further factors also play a part in enabling children to learn: (2) knowledge first becomes dialogic, such that it is expanded by telling and by asking – the learner is **exchanging** meaning; (6) the learner often regresses and reconstructs, returning to the same experience at a "higher" semiotic level – the familiar phenomenon of **spiralling**; (3) major steps involve renewing connection with the self, and the axis of "you and me"

381

– let us say that the learner is **engaging** with what is being learnt. (5) Throughout these processes the learner is always involved in the dialectic between the **system** and the **instance**; in language, this means building a grammar out of the discourse and building a discourse out of the grammar. (1) Finally, the concept of "language development" suggests that children are recapitulating, or re-enacting, the history of human knowledge – I do not mean modelling it in detail, but developing a semiotic, namely language, which is at one and the same time a mode of reflection and a mode of action. In other words, the learner is developing the **metafunctional** foundation on the basis of which knowledge itself is construed.

You may feel that considerations such as these are merely the abstract musings of a grammarian who (like the grammarian of folklore) is a dealer in symbols, far removed from the daily activities of the classroom. Some might think that nothing in the theory of grammar would be relevant to educational practice. But we are now educating the citizens of the twenty-first century; and the demands that are going to be made on their intellectual resources – their understanding of the world, and of their own situation within it – are truly formidable. The points I have raised here are my own perception of how aspects of the learning of language may relate to learning, and to teaching, in general. They may not be the main issues; they may ever be wide of the mark. But if we want to understand how children learn, and how we, as teachers, can effectively contribute to this process, I think it can be helpful to explore a language development approach to education.

BIBLIOGRAPHY

Abdulaziz, M.H. (1971) 'Tanzania's national language policy and the rise of Swahili political culture', in Whiteley (ed.).

Abercrombie, David (1965) *Studies in Phonetics and Linguistics*, London: Oxford University Press.

Ai, Zuxing (Ai Tsu-hsing) (1982) 'Some personal experience in teaching Chinese students basic English', *Language Learning and Communication* 1.1 (in Chinese: 艾祖星 '談談我對教好中國學生基礎英語的一點探索' 中英語文教學 第一卷 第一期).

Albrow, K.H. (1972) *The English Writing System: Notes Towards a Description*, London: Longman (Schools Council Programme in Linguistics and English Teaching, Papers Series II, Vol. 2; reissued London: Schools Council, 1981).

Anderson, J. (1985) *C.O.M.P.U.T.E.R.S in the Language Classroom*, Perth: Australian Reading Association.

Bailey, Charles-James N. (1976) 'The state of non-state linguistics', *Annual Review of Anthropology*, 5.

Bernstein, Basil (1971*a*) *Class, Codes and Control, Vol. 1: Theoretical Studies Towards a Sociology of Language*, London: Routledge & Kegan Paul (Primary Socialization, Language and Education).

Bernstein, Basil (1971*b*) 'Social class, language and socialization', in Bernstein (1971*a*).

Bernstein, Basil (ed.) (1973) *Class, Codes and Control, Vol. 2: Applied Studies Towards a Sociology of Language*, London: Routledge & Kegan Paul (Primary Socialization, Language and Education).

Bernstein, Basil (1975*a*) *Class, Codes and Control, Vol. 3: Towards a Theory of Educational Transmissions* London: Routledge & Kegan Paul (Primary Socialization, Language and Education).

Bernstein, Basil (1975*b*) 'The classification and framing of educational knowledge', in Bernstein (1975*a*).

Bernstein, Basil (1990) *The Structuring of Pedagogic Discourse (Class, Codes and Control, Vol. 4)*, London and New York: Routledge.

Bernstein, Basil and Henderson, Dorothy (1973), 'Social class differences in the relevance of language and socialization', in Bernstein (ed.)

Birch, David and O'Toole, Michael (eds) (1985), *Functions of Style*, London: Frances Pinter.

Blom, Jan Petter and Gumperz, John J. (1972) 'Social meaning in linguistic structure: code-switching in Norway', in John J. Gumperz and Dell H. Hymes (eds), *Directions in Sociolinguistics*, New York: Holt, Rinehart and Winston.

Bloom, Lois (1973) *One Word at a Time: The Use of Single-word Utterances before Syntax*, The Hague: Mouton.

Bohm, D. (1980) *Wholeness and the Implicate Order*, London: Routledge & Kegan Paul.

Breen, M.P. and Candlin, C.N. (1980), 'The essentials of a communicative curriculum in language teaching', *Applied Linguistics* 1.2.

Brindley, Geoff (1986) 'Semantic approaches to learner language', *Australian Review of Applied Linguistics*, Series S no. 3.

Britton, James (1970) *Language and Learning*, London: Allen Lane, Penguin Press.

Brown, Roger (1973) *A First Language: The Early Stages*, Cambridge, MA: Harvard University Press.

Brumfit, Christopher J. (1997) 'Theoretical practice: applied linguistics as pure and practical science', in Mauranen and Sajavaara (eds).

Brumfit, Christopher J. and Carter, Ronald A. (eds) (1986), *Literature and Language Teaching*, Oxford: Oxford University Press.

Bruner, Jerome (1990) *Acts of Meaning*, Cambridge, MA: Harvard University Press.

Butler, C.S. and Hartmann, R.R.K (eds) (1976) *A Reader on Language Variety*, Exeter: University of Exeter (Exeter Linguistic Series 1).

Butt, David (1988*a*) 'Randomness, order and the latent patterning of text', in Birch and O'Toole (eds).

Butt, David (1988*b*) 'Ideational meaning and the "existential fabric" of a poem', in Robin P. Fawcett and David J. Young (eds), *New Developments in Systemic Linguistics, Vol 2: Theory and Application*, London and New York: Frances Pinter.

Butt, David (1989) 'The object of language', in Hasan and Martin (eds).

Candlin, Christopher N. (1990) 'What happens when applied linguistics goes critical?', in Halliday, Gibbons and Nicholas (eds), Vol. 2.

Carroll, John B. (1962) 'The prediction of success in intensive foreign language training', in Robert Glaser (ed.), *Training Research and Education*, Pittsburgh: University Press.

Chafe, Wallace L. (1982) 'Integration and involvement in speaking, writing and oral literature', in Deborah Tannen (ed.), *Spoken and Written Language: Exploring Orality and Literacy*, Norwood, NJ: Ablex (Advances in Discourse Processes IX).

Chesterfield, Ray and Kathleen (1985) 'Natural order in children's use of second language learning strategies', *Applied Linguistics* 6.1.

Christie, Frances (1987) 'Young children's writing: from spoken to written genre', *Language and Education: An International Journal* 1.1.

Christie, Frances (1988) 'Curriculum genres', *Linguistics and Education* 1.1.

Christie, Frances and Martin, James R. (eds) (1997) *Genre and Institutions: Social Processes in the Workplace and School*, London: Cassell.

Clark, I.F. and Cook B.J. (eds) (1986) *Geological Science: Perspectives of the Earth*, Canberra: Australian Academy of Science.

Clyne, Michael (1991) 'Directionality, rhythm and cultural values', in Frances Christie (ed.), *Literacy in Social Processes: Papers from the Inaugural Australian Systemic Networks Conference, Deakin University, 18–21 January 1990*, Darwin, NT: Northern Territory University, Centre for Studies of Language in Education.

Corder, S.P. (1967) 'The significance of learners' errors', *International Review of Applied Linguistics* 5.

Corder, S.P. (1975) 'Error analysis, interlanguage and second language acquisition', *Language Teaching & Linguistics Abstracts* 8.14.

Davidse, Kristin (1991) *Categories of Experiential Grammar*, Nottingham: University of Nottingham English Department (Monographs in Systemic Linguistics).

Davidse, Kristin, Halliday, M.A.K. and Matthiessen, Christian (1992) in Martin Davies and Louise Ravelli (eds), *Advances in Systemic Linguistics: Recent Theory and Practice*, London and New York: Pinter.

Davies, Martin and Ravelli, Louise (eds) (1992) *New Directions in Systemic Linguistics*, London: Frances Pinter.

Day, Ruth S. (1975) 'Language and cognitive configuration', in Robin P. Fawcett et al. (eds), *Semiotics of Culture and Language*, London: Frances Pinter.

Delbridge, Arthur and Bernard J.R.L. (1966) *Patterns in Language (English Language for Senior Students Vol. 1)* Sydney: Angus & Robertson.

Dore, John (1976a) 'Children's illocutionary acts', in R.O. Freedle (ed.), *Discourse Relations: Comprehension and Production*, New York: Erlbaum.

Dore, John (1976b) 'Conditions on the acquisition of speech acts', in I. Markova (ed.), *The Social Context of Language*, New York: Wiley.

Doughty, Peter, Pearce, John and Thornton, Geoffrey (1971) *Language in Use*, London: Edward Arnold (Schools Council Programme in Linguistics and English Teaching).

Doughty, Peter, Pearce, John and Thornton, Geoffrey (1972) *Exploring Language*, London: Edward Arnold (Schools Council Programme in Linguistics and English Teaching).

Douglas, Mary (1966) *Purity and Danger: An Analysis of Concepts of Pollution and Taboo*, Harmondsworth: Penguin Books.

Douglas, Mary (1971) 'Do dogs laugh? A cross-cultural approach to body symbolism', *Journal of Psychosomatic Research* 15.

Durrell, Gerald (1956) *My Family and Other Animals*, London: Hart Davis.

Eggins, Suzanne and Slade, Diana (1997) *Analysing Casual Conversation*, London: Cassell.

Eggins, Suzanne; Wignell, Peter and Martin, J.R. (1987) 'The discourse of history: distancing the recoverable past', *Writing Project Report 1987* (Linguistics Department, University of Sydney, Working Papers in Linguistics 5), 66–116.

Elliott, Blanche B. (1962) *A History of English Advertising*, London: Business Publications and Batsford.

Ellis, Jeffrey and Ure, Jean N. (1982) 'The contrastive analysis of language registers', in W. Nemser (ed.), *Trends in Contrastive Linguistics*, The Hague: Mouton.

Ellis, Rod (1985) *Understanding Second Language Acquisition*, Oxford: Oxford University Press.

Eltis, K.J. and Cooney, G.H. (1983) *Project Languages: Languages Other than English in the Senior Secondary Curriculum*, Sydney: Macquarie University.

Ervin-Tripp, Susan M. (1973) 'Structure and process in language acquisition', in *Language Acquisition and Communicative Choice: Essays by Susan M. Ervin-Tripp Selected and Introduced by Anwar S. Dil*, Stanford, CA: Stanford University Press.

Ervin(-Tripp), Susan M. (with Charles E. Osgood) (1954) 'Second language learning and bilingualism', in Charles E. Osgood and Thomas A. Sebeok (eds), *Psycholinguistics: A Survey of Theory and Research Problems (Journal of Abnormal and Social Psychology 20)*. Reprinted in Susan M. Ervin-Tripp (1973).

Fawcett, Robin (2002) *The Functional Syntax Handbook: Analyzing English at the Level of Form*, London and New York: Continuum.

Fawcett, Robin (2003) *The Functional Semantics Handbook: Analyzing English at the Level of Meaning*, London and New York: Continuum.

Firth, J.R. (1957*a*) *Papers in Linguistics 1934–1951*, London: Oxford University Press.

Firth, J.R. (1957*b*) 'Ethnographic analysis and language, with reference to Malinowski's views', in Raymond Firth (ed.), *Man and Culture: An Evaluation of the Work of Bronislaw Malinowski*, London: Routledge and Kegan Paul.

Forsyth, Ian J. and Wood, Kathleen (1977) *Language and Communication*, London: Longman.

Gerot, Linda; Oldenburg, Jane and van Leeuwen, Theo (eds) (1988) *Language and Socialization: Home and School: Papers from the Working Conference on Language in Education, Macquarie University 17–21 November 1986.* Sydney: Macquarie University School of English and Linguistics.

Gibbons, John (1987) *Code-mixing and Code Choice: A Hong Kong Case Study,* Clevedon and Philadelphia: Multilingual Matters (Multilingual Matters 27).

Gibbons, John and Markwick-Smith, Mary (1992) 'Exploring the use of a systemic semantic description', *International Journal of Applied Linguistics* 2.1.

Gomes de Matos, Francisco (1984) '20 years of applied linguistics: AILA Congresses 1964–1984', in Jos Nivette, Didier Goyvaerts and Pete van de Craen (eds), *AILA Brussels 84: Proceedings,* Vol. 5.

Goodman, Kenneth D. (1971) 'Psycholinguistic universals in the reading process', in Pimsleur and Quinn.

Gorman, T.P. (1971) 'Sociolinguistic implications of a choice of media of instruction', in Whiteley (ed.).

Gouin, François (1880) *L'Art d'enseigner et d'étudier les langues,* Paris: Fischbacher. English translation by H. Swan and V. Betis (1924) *The Art of Teaching and Studying Languages,* London: Longman (first published in 1893).

Graff, Harvey J. (1987) *The Labyrinths of Literacy: Reflections on Literacy Past and Present,* London: Falmer Press.

Greenfield, Patricia Marks and Smith, Joshua H. (1975) *Communication and the Beginnings of Language: the Development of Semantic Structure in One-word Speech and Beyond,* New York: Academic Press.

Gunn, J.S. and Eagleson, R.D. (1966) *Survey of Language (English Language for Senior Students, Vol. 2),* Sydney: Angus & Robertson.

Gunnarsson, Britt-Louise (1990) 'The LSP text and its social context: a model for text analysis', in M.A.K. Halliday, John Gibbons and Howard Nicholas (eds), *Learning, Keeping and Using Language,* Vol. 2, Amsterdam: John Benjamins.

Hagège, Claude (2000) *Halte à la mort des langues,* Paris: Odile Jacob.

Halliday, M.A.K. (1967/68) 'Notes on transitivity and theme in English', *Journal of Linguistics* 3.1, 3.2, 4.2, in *Collected Works,* Vol. 7.

Halliday, M.A.K. (1971) 'Language Acquisition and Initial Literacy', paper presented to the Thirty-eighth Annual Claremont Reading Conference, Claremont Colleges, California, February 1971.

Halliday, M.A.K. (1974) *Language and Social Man,* London: Longman (Schools Council Programme in Linguistics and English Teaching. Papers Series II, Vol. 3).

Halliday, M.A.K. (1975) *Learning How to Mean: Explorations in the Development of Language,* London: Edward Arnold, in *Collected Works,* Vol. 4.

Halliday, M.A.K. (1976) ' "The teacher taught the student English": an essay in applied linguistics', in Peter A. Reich (ed.), *The Second LACUS Forum,* Columbia, SC: Hornbeam Press.

Halliday, M.A.K. (1978) *Language as Social Semiotic: The Social Interpretation of Language and Meaning*, London: Edward Arnold.

Halliday, M.A.K. (1981) 'Three aspects of children's language development: learning language, learning through language, learning about language', in Yetta L. Goodman et al. (eds), *Oral and Written Language Development: Impact on Schools*. International Reading Association and National Council of Teachers of English, in *Collected Works*, Vol. 4.

Halliday, M.A.K. (1985*a*) *An Introduction to Functional Grammar*, London: Edward Arnold. Second (revised) edition, 1994.

Halliday, M.A.K. (1985*b*) *Spoken and Written Language*, Geelong, Vic.: Deakin University Press. Reissued Oxford: Oxford University Press, 1989.

Halliday, M.A.K. (1988) 'On the language of physical science', in Mohsen Ghadessy (ed.), *Registers of Written English*, London: Pinter, in *Collected Works*, Vol. 5.

Halliday, M.A.K. (1989) 'Some grammatical problems in scientific English', *Australian Review of Applied Linguistics* Series S, no. 6 (reprinted in Halliday and Martin 1993), in *Collected Works*, Vol. 5.

Halliday, M.A.K. (1991) 'Corpus Studies and Probabilistic Grammar', in Karin Aijmer and Bengt Altenberg (eds), *English Corpus Linguistics: Studies in Honour of Jan Svartvik*, London and New York: Longman.

Halliday, M.A.K. (1993*a*) *Language in a Changing World*, Canberra: Applied Linguistics Association of Australia (Occasional Paper 13).

Halliday, M.A.K. (1993*b*) 'Towards a language-based theory of learning', *Linguistics and Education* 5:93–116, in *Collected Works*, Vol. 4.

Halliday, M.A.K. and Martin, J.R. (1993) *Writing Science: Literacy and Discursive Power*, London and Washington: Falmer.

Halliday, M.A.K., Gibbons, John and Nicholas, Howard (eds) (1990) *Learning, Keeping and Using Language: Selected Papers from the Eighth World Congress of Applied Linguistics, Sydney, August 1987*, Amsterdam: John Benjamins.

Hammond, Jennifer (1987) 'An overview of the genre-based approach to the teaching of writing in Australia', *Australian Review of Applied Linguistics*, 10.1–2.

Hammond, Jennifer (1990) 'Oral and written language in the educational context', in Halliday, Gibbons and Nicholas (eds).

Hasan, Ruqaiya (1973) 'Code, register and social dialect', in Bernstein (ed.).

Hasan, Ruqaiya (1981) 'What's going on: a dynamic view of context in language', in James E. Copeland and Philip W. Davies (eds), *The Seventh LACUS Forum 1980*, Columbia, SC: Hornbeam Press.

Hasan, Ruqaiya (1984) 'Ways of saying: ways of meaning', in Robin P. Fawcett et al. (eds.), *The Semiotics of Culture and Language, Vol. 1: Language as Social Semiotic*, London: Frances Pinter (Open Linguistics Series).

388

Hasan, Ruqaiya (1985*a*) *Linguistics, Language and Verbal Art*, Geelong, Vic.: Deakin University Press (reissued Oxford: Oxford University Press, 1989).

Hasan, Ruqaiya (1985*b*) 'Meaning, context and text: fifty years after Malinowski', in James D. Benson and William S. Greaves (eds), *Systemic Perspectives on Discourse*, Vol. 1, Norwood, NJ: Ablex.

Hasan, Ruqaiya (ed.) (1985) *Discourse on Discourse*, Canberra: Applied Linguistics Association of Australia (Occasional Paper 7).

Hasan, Ruqaiya (1986) 'The ontogenesis of ideology: an interpretation of mother–child talk', in Threadgold et al. (eds).

Hasan, Ruqaiya (1988) 'Language in the processes of socialization: home and school' in Gerot et al. (eds).

Hasan, Ruqaiya (1995) 'The conception of context in text', in Peter H. Fries and Michael Gregory (eds), *Discourse and Meaning in Society: Functional Perspectives – Meaning and Choice in Language*, Vol. 2, Norwood, NJ: Ablex.

Hasan, Ruqaiya (1996) 'Literacy, everyday talk and society', in Ruqaiya Hasan and Geoff Williams (eds), *Literacy in Society*, New York: Longman.

Hasan, Ruqaiya (in press) *The Collected Works of Ruqaiya Hasan Vol. 2, Semantic Variation: Meaning in Society*, London: Equinox.

Hasan, Ruqaiya and Cloran, Carmel (1990) 'Semantic variation: a socio-linguistic interpretation of everyday talk between mothers and children' in Halliday et al. (eds).

Hasan, Ruqaiya and Martin, J.R. (eds) (1989) *Language Development: Learning Language, Learning Culture: Meaning and Choice in Language*, Vol. 1, Norwood, NJ: Ablex.

Hasan, Ruqaiya and Williams, Geoff (eds) (1996) *Literacy in Society*, London and New York: Longman.

Henderson, Dorothy (1973) 'Contextual specificity, discretion and cognitive socialization: with special reference to language', in Bernstein (ed.).

Hill, Trevor (1958) 'Institutional Linguistics', *Orbis* 7.

Hu, Zhuanglin (ed.) (1990) *Language System and Function: Proceedings of the 1989 Beijing Systemic-Functional Workshop*. (語言系統與功能) Beijing: Peking University Press (in Chinese).

Hu, Zhuanglin (1995) *Contemporary Linguistic Theories and Applications*. (當代語言理論與應用) Beijing: Peking University Press (in Chinese).

Huddleston, Rodney D.; Hudson, Richard; Winter, Eugene and Henrici, Alick (1968) *Sentence and Clause in Scientific English: Final Report of the O.S.T.I. Programme in the Linguistic Properties of Scientific English*, London: University College London, Communication Research Centre.

Jespersen, Otto (1904) *How to Teach a Foreign Language*, London: Allen and Unwin.

Kachru, Braj B. (1985) *The Alchemy of English: The Spread, Functions and Models of Non-native Englishes*, Oxford: Pergamon Press.

Kachru, Braj B. (1990) 'World Englishes and applied linguistics', *World Englishes* 9.1.

Kress, Gunther and Threadgold, Terry (1988) 'Towards a social theory of genre', *Southern Review* 21.

Lance, Donald (1969) *A Brief Study of Spanish–English Bilingualism* (Final Report, Research Project Orr-Liberal Arts 15504), College Station, Texas: Texas A. and M. University.

Lemke, Jay L. (1983) *Classroom Communication of Science: Final Report to National Science Foundation*, ERIC Document Service no. ED 222 346.

Lemke, Jay L. (1984) *Semiotics and Education*, Toronto: Victoria University (Toronto Semiotic Circle Monographs, Working Papers and Prepublications 1984.2).

Lemke, Jay L. (1985) *Using Language in the Classroom*, Geelong, Vic.: Deakin University Press.

Lemke, Jay L. (1989) 'Semantics and social values', *Word* 40.1–2.

Lemke, Jay L. (1990) 'Technical discourse and technocratic ideology', in M.A.K. Halliday, John Gibbons and Howard Nicholas (eds), *Learning, Keeping and Using Language: Selected Papers from the Eighth World Congress of Applied Linguistics, Sydney 16–21 August 1987*, Vol 2, Amsterdam and Phila-delphia: Benjamins.

Lemke, Jay L. (1990*a*) *Talking Science: Language, Learning and Values*, Norwood, NJ: Ablex.

Lemke, Jay L. (1990*b*) 'Technocratic discourse and ideology', in Halliday, Gibbons and Nicholas (eds).

Lewis, M.M. (1953) *The Importance of Illiteracy*, London: Harrap.

Lightbown, Patsy M. (1985) 'Great expectations: second-language acquisition research and classroom teaching', *Applied Linguistics* 6.2.

Luke, Carmen; de Castell, Suzanne and Luke, Allan (1989) 'Beyond criticism: the authority of the school textbook', in Suzanne de Castell, Allan Luke and Carmen Luke (eds), *Language, Authority and Criticism: Readings on the School Textbook*, London: Falmer Press.

Mackay, David; Thompson, Brian and Schaub, Pamela (1970*a*) *Breakthrough to Literacy*. [For the pupil: (i) *My Sentence Maker*, with insert word cards and stand; (ii) *My Word Maker*, with insert letter cards; (iii) *Breakthrough Books* (24); (iv) *Big Breakthrough Books* (2); (v) *Sally go round the sun* (LP record). For the teacher: (i) *Teacher's Sentence Maker*, with insert word cards and stand; (ii) Magnet board, magnets and figurines; (iii) *Teacher's Manual*], London: Longman.

Mackay, David; Thompson, Brian and Schaub, Pamela (1970*b*) *Breakthrough to Literacy, Teacher's Manual: the theory and practice of teaching initial reading and* *writing*, London: Longman (Schools Council Programme in Linguistics and English Teaching), revised (illustrated) edition, 1978.

Mackey, William F. (1967) *Bilingualism: A World Problem*, Montreal: Harvest House.

Malinowski, Bronislaw (1923) 'The problem of meaning in primitive languages', Supplement I to C.K. Ogden and I.A. Richards, *The Meaning of Meaning*, London: Kegan Paul.

Malinowski, Bronislaw (1935) *Coral Gardens and their Magic, Volume 2*, London: Allen and Unwin.

Mann, W.C. and Thompson, S.A. (eds) (1992) *Discourse Description: Diverse Linguistic Analyses of a Fund-raising Text*, Amsterdam: John Benjamins.

Martin, J.R. (1984*a*) 'Language, register and genre', in *Children Writing: Reader*, Geelong, Vic.: Deakin University Press (ECT 418).

Martin, J.R. (1984*b*) 'Types of writing in infants and primary school' in L. Unsworth (ed.), *Reading, Writing and Spelling*, Milperra, New South Wales: Macarthur Institute of Higher Education.

Martin, J.R. (1985) *Factual Writing: Exploring and Challenging Social Reality*, Geelong, Vic.: Deakin University Press (reissued Oxford: Oxford University Press, 1989).

Martin, J.R. (1986) 'Grammaticalizing ecology: the politics of baby seals and kangaroos', in Threadgold et al. (eds).

Martin, J.R. (1988) 'Grammatical conspiracies in Tagalog: family, face and fate', in James D. Benson, Michael J. Cummings and William S. Greaves (eds), *Linguistics in a Systemic Perspective*, Amsterdam: John Benjamins.

Martin, J.R. (1990) 'Literacy in science: learning to handle text as technology', in Frances Christie (ed.), *Literacy in a Changing World*, Melbourne: Australian Council for Educational Research (reprinted in Halliday and Martin 1993).

Martin J.R. (1991a) 'Intrinsic functionality: implications for contextual theory', *Social Semiotics*, Vol. 1, no. 1, pp. 99–162.

Martin, J.R. (1991b) 'Nominalization in science and humanities: distilling knowledge and scaffolding text', in Eija Ventola (ed.), *Functional and Systemic Linguistics: Approaches and Uses*, Berlin and New York: Mouton de Gruyter.

Martin, J.R. (1992) *English Text: System and Structure*, Amsterdam: Benjamins.

Martin, J.R. (1993*a*) 'Technology, bureaucracy and schooling: discursive resources and control', *Cultural Dynamics* 6.1–2.

Martin, J.R. (1993*b*) 'Genre and literacy – modelling context in educational linguistics', *Australian Review of Applied Linguistics* 13.

Martin, J.R. and Rothery, J. (1986) 'What a functional approach to the writing task can show teachers about "good writing"', in Barbara Couture (ed.), *Functional Approaches to Writing Research*, London: Frances Pinter (Open Linguistics).

Martin, J.R. and Rothery, J. (1980, 1981, 1986) *Writing Project Report 1980/1981/1986* (Working Papers in Linguistics 1/2/4) Sydney: University of Sydney Linguistics Department.

Martin, J.R., Christie, F. and Rothery, J. (1985) 'Social processes in education – a reply to Sawyer and Watson (and others)', *Working Papers in Linguistics* 5, Sydney: University of Sydney Linguistics Department.

Martin, J.R. and Thibault, Paul (1991) in Eija Ventola (ed.), *Functional and Systemic Linguistics: Approaches and Uses*, Berlin and New York: Mouton de Gruyter.

Martin, Nancy; D'Arcy, Pat; Newton, Bryan and Parker, Robert (1976) *Writing and Learning Across the Curriculum*, London: Ward Lock Educational (Schools Council Publications).

Mathesius, Vilēm (1964) 'On the potentiality of the phenomena of language', in Josef Vachek (trans. and ed.), *A Prague School Reader in Linguistics*, Bloomington: Indiana University Press (Czech original, 1911).

Matthiessen, Christian M.I.M. (1991) 'Language on language: the grammar of semiosis', *Social Semiotics* 1.2.

Matthiessen, Christian M.I.M. (1992) 'Interpreting the textual metafunction', in Davies and Ravelli (eds).

Matthiessen, Christian M.I.M. (1993) 'Register in the round: diversity in a unified theory of register analysis', in Mohsen Ghadessy (ed.), *Register Analysis: Theory into Practice*, London and New York: Pinter.

Matthiessen, Christian M.I.M. and Bateman, John M. (1991) *Systemic Linguistics and Text Generation: Experiences from Japanese and English*, London: Frances Pinter.

Mauranen, Anna and Sajavaara, Kari (eds) (1997) *Applied Linguistics Across Disciplines [AILA Review No. 12, 1995/6]*.

Maw, Joan (1971) 'Sociolinguistic problems and potentialities of education through a foreign language', in Wilfred H. Whiteley (ed.), *Language Use and Social Change: Problems of Multilingualism with Special Reference to Eastern Africa*, London: Oxford University Press.

McGregor, William P. (1990) 'The linguistic construction of the racial other', in Halliday et al. (eds).

McKellar, G. Bruce (1987) 'The place of sociosemiotics in contemporary thought', in Ross Steele and Terry Threadgold (eds), *Language Topics, Vol. 2*, Amsterdam: John Benjamins.

McNeill, David (1965) *Some Thoughts on First and Second Language Acquisition*, Cambridge, MA: Harvard University Centre for Cognitive Studies.

Meadows, J. (1989) *Info-technology: Changing the Way We Communicate*, London: Cassell.

Mear, Annie (1971) 'Experimental investigation of receptive language', in Pimsleur and Quinn.

392

Mohan, Bernard A. (1986) *Language and Content*, Reading, MA: Addison-Wesley.

Moore, Helen (1990) 'Process vs product, or down with the opposition', in Halliday, Gibbons and Nicholas (eds).

Mountford, John (1990) 'Language and writing systems', in N.E. Collinge (ed.), *An Encyclopedia of Language*, London and New York: Routledge.

Nadkarni, M.V. (1987) 'Cultural pluralism as a national resource: strategies for language education', in Arthur Yap (ed.), *Language Education in Multilingual Societies, RELC Anthology 4*, Singapore: Regional Language Centre.

Nelson, Katherine (1973) *Structure and Strategy in Learning to Talk*, Chicago: Society for Research in Child Development (Monographs, 38.1–2).

Nelson, Katherine (1977) *Individual differences in language development: implications for development and language*, New York: City University Graduate Centre.

Nickel, Gerhard (ed.) (1974) *Applied Contrastive Linguistics*, Heidelberg: Julius Groos (Third AILA Congress, Copenhagen 1972; Proceedings, Vol. 1).

O'Halloran, Kay and Judd, Kevin (2002) *Systemics 1.0: Software for Research and Teaching Systemic Functional Linguistics (SFL)*, Singapore: Singapore University Press.

Oldenburg, Jane (1986) 'The transitional stage of a second child – 18 months to 2 years', *Australian Review of Applied Linguistics* 9.1.

Oller, John W., Jr. (1971) 'Language communication and second language learning', in Pimsleur and Quinn.

Olson, D.R. (1989) 'On the language and authority of textbooks', in Suzanne de Castell, Allan Luke and Carmen Luke (eds), *Language, Authority and Criticism: Readings on the School Textbook*, London: Falmer Press.

O'Toole, Michael (1989) 'Semiotic systems in painting and poetry', in M. Falchikov et al. (eds), *A Festschrift for Dennis Ward*, Nottingham: Astra.

O'Toole, L.M. (1990) 'A systemic-functional semiotics of art', *Semiotica* 82, (3/4).

O'Toole, L.M. (1994) *The Language of Displayed Art*, London: Leicester University Press.

Painter, Clare (1984), *Into the Mother Tongue: A Case Study in Early Language Development*, London and New York: Pinter.

Pakir, Anne (2002) 'The making of Englishes', *World Englishes Today Symposium*, University of Illinois at Urbana-Champaign.

Painter, Clare (1984) *Into the Mother Tongue: A Case Study in Early Language Development*, London: Frances Pinter (Open Linguistics series).

Painter, Clare (1986) 'The role of interaction in learning to speak and learning to write', in Painter and Martin (eds).

Painter, Clare (1989) 'Learning language: a functional view of language development', in Hasan and Martin (eds).

Painter, Clare and Martin, J.R. (eds) (1986) *Writing to Mean: Teaching Genres across the Curriculum*, Applied Linguistics Association of Australia, Occasional Paper No. 9.

Palmer, Harold E. (1922) *The Principles of Language-Study*, London: Harrap (reissued London: Oxford University Press, 1964).

P'Bitek, Okot (1971) *Song of Lawino*, Nairobi: East African Publishing House.

Pearce, John, Thornton, Geoffrey and Mackay, David (1989) 'The Programme in Linguistics and English Teaching, University College London, 1964–1971', in Hasan and Martin (eds).

Perren, G.E. (ed.) (1969) *Languages for Special Purposes*, CILT Reports & Papers 1, London: Centre for Information on Language Teaching.

Phillips, Joy (1986) 'The Development of Modality and Hypothetical Meaning: Nigel 1.7–2.7', *Working Papers in Linguistics* 3, Sydney: University of Sydney Linguistics Department.

Pimsleur, Paul and Quinn, Terence (eds) (1971) *The Psychology of Second Language Learning. Papers from the Second International Congress of Applied Linguistics, Cambridge, 8–12 September, 1969*, Cambridge: Cambridge University Press.

Polkinghorne, J.C. (1990) *The Quantum World*, Harmondsworth: Penguin Books.

Pottier, Bernard and Bourquin, Guy (1966) 'Preface' to *Actes du premier Colloque international de Linguistique appliquée*, Nancy: Faculté des Lettres et des Sciences humaines de l'Université de Nancy (Annales de l'Est, Mémoire 31).

Poynton, Cate (1985) *Language and Gender: Making the Difference*, Geelong, Vic.: Deakin University Press (reissued Oxford: Oxford University Press, 1989).

Qiu, Shijin (1984) 'Early Language Development in Chinese Children', University of Sydney MA (Honours) Thesis.

Ravem, Roar (1969) 'Language acquisition in a second language environment', *International Review of Applied Linguistics* 6.

Reibel, David (1971) 'Language learning strategies for the adult', in Pimsleur and Quinn.

Reid, I. (ed.) (1987) *The Place of Genre in Learning: Current Debates*, Geelong, Vic.: Deakin University Press.

Rivers, Wilga M. (ed.) (1987) *Interactive Language Teaching*, Cambridge: Cambridge University Press.

Robins, R.H. (1963) 'General linguistics in Great Britain 1930–1960', in Christine Mohrmann et al. (eds), *Trends in Modern Linguistics*, Utrecht: Spectrum.

Rodgon, Maris Monitz (1976) *Single-word Usage, Cognitive Development and the Beginnings of Combinatorial Speech: A Study of Ten English-speaking Children*, Cambridge: Cambridge University Press.

Rothery, Joan (1984) 'The development of genres – primary to junior secondary school', in *Children Writing: Study Guide*, Geelong, Vic.: Deakin University Press.

Sawyer, W. and Watson, K. (1987) 'Questions of genre', *The Teaching of English* 52.

Selinker, Larry (1971) 'The psychologically relevant data of second language learning', in Pimsleur and Quinn.

Senate Standing Committee on Education and the Arts (1984) *Report on a National Language Policy*, Canberra: Australian Government Publishing Service.

Simon, W. and Lu, C.H. (1942) *Chinese Sentence Series* Vols. I–III, London: Arthur Probsthain.

Sinclair de Zwart, Hermine (1969) 'Developmental psycholinguistics', in David Elkind and John H. Flavell (eds), *Studies in Cognitive Development: Essays in Honour of Jean Piaget*, New York: Oxford University Press.

Sinclair, John M. (ed.) (1992) *Looking Up: An Account of the Cobuild Project in Lexical Computing*, London and Glasgow: Collins ELT.

Skinner, B.F. (1957) *Verbal Behaviour*, New York: Appleton-Century-Crofts.

Sorensen, A.P., Jr. (1967) 'Multilingualism in the Northwest Amazon', *American Anthropologist* 69. Revised version in J.B. Pride and Janet Holmes (eds) *Sociolinguistics: Selected Readings*, Harmondsworth: Penguin Books (1972).

Steiner, Erich and Yallop, Colin (eds) (2001) *Exploring Translation and Multilingual Text Production: Beyond Content*, Berlin: Mouton de Gruyter.

Strevens, Peter (1985) 'Language learning and language teaching: towards an integrated model', Forum Lecture to the LSA/TESOL Institute, Georgetown University, Washington, DC.

Svartvik, Jan (1996) *On Voice in the English Verb*, The Hague: Mouton.

Sweet, Henry (1899) *The Practical Study of Languages: A Guide for Teachers and Learners*, London: Dent.

Taylor, Charles (1979) *The English of High School Textbooks*, Canberra: Australian Government Publishing Service (Education Research and Development Committee, Report No. 18).

Teich, Elke (1999) *Systemic Functional Grammar and Natural Language Generation: linguistic description and computational representation*, London and New York: Continuum.

Thibault, Paul J. (1987) *Text, Discourse and Context: A Social-Semiotic Perspective*, Toronto: Victoria University (Toronto Semiotic Circle Monographs, Working Papers & Prepublications 1987.3).

Thibault, Paul J. (1991a) *Social Semiotics as Praxis: Text, Social Meaning Making and Nabokov's 'Ada'*, Minneapolis: University of Minnesota Press.

Thibault, Paul J. (1991b) 'Grammar, technocracy, and the noun: technocratic values and cognitive linguistics', in Eija Ventola (ed.), *Recent Systemic and other Functional Views on Language*, Berlin: Mouton de Gruyter.

Thornton, Geoffrey (1986) *Language, Ignorance and Education*, London: Edward Arnold (Explorations in Language Study).

Threadgold, Terry (1986) 'Semiotics–ideology–language', Introduction to Threadgold et al. (eds).

Threadgold, Terry (1988*a*) 'The genre debate', *Southern Review* 21(3).

Threadgold, Terry (1988*b*) 'Stories of race and gender: an unbounded discourse' in Birch and O'Toole (eds).

Threadgold, Terry (1989) 'Talking about genre: ideologies and incompatible discourses', *Cultural Studies* 3(1).

Threadgold, Terry (1991) 'Postmodernism, systemic-functional linguistics as metalanguage and the practice of cultural critique', in Frances Christie and Elwyn Jenkins (eds), *Social Processes in Education: Proceedings of the First Australian Systemic Network Conference, Deakin University, January 1990*.

Threadgold, Terry; Grosz, Elisabeth; Kress, G.R. and Halliday, M.A.K. (eds) (1986), *Semiotics, Ideology, Language*, Sydney: Sydney Association for Studies in Society and Culture (*Sydney Studies in Society & Culture* 3).

Thumboo, Edwin (2002) 'Breaking the ramparts: liberating the study of E(nglish-) literatures', *World Englishes Today Symposium*, University of Illinois at Urbana-Champaign.

Toolan, Michael (1992) 'Token and Value: a discussion' in Davies and Ravelli (eds).

Tucker, Gordon H. (1998) *The Lexicogrammar of Adjectives: A Systemic Functional Approach to Lexis*, London and New York: Continuum.

Turner, Geoffrey J. (1973) 'Social class and children's language of control at age five and age seven', in Bernstein (ed.).

UNESCO (1975) *Interactions between Linguistics and Mathematical Education: Report of a Symposium Sponsored by UNESCO-CEDO-ICMI, Nairobi, September 1974*, Paris: UNESCO (ED-74/CONF 808).

Unsworth, Len (ed.) (2000) *Researching Language in Schools and Communities: Functional Linguistic Perspectives*, London and Washington: Cassell.

Ure, Jean N. and Ellis, Jeffrey (1972) 'Register in descriptive linguistics and linguistic sociology', in Oscar Uribe Villegas (ed.), *La Sociolinguistica actual*, The Hague: Mouton.

Van Leeuwen, Theo and Humphrey, Sally (1996) 'On learning to look through a geographer's eyes', in Ruqaiya Hasan and Geoff Williams (eds), *Literacy in Society*, New York: Longman.

Wagenaar, Willem A. (2002) 'False confessions after repeated interrogation: the Putten murder case', *European Review* 10.4.

Wagner-Gough, J. (1978) 'Comparative studies in second language learning', in

396

Evelyn Hatch (ed.), *Second Language Acquisition: A Book of Readings*, Rowley, MA: Newbury House.

Watson, K.L. and Eagleson, R.D. (eds) (1977) *English in Secondary Schools: Today and Tomorrow*, Ashfield, NSW: English Teachers' Association of NSW.

Wells, Gordon (1986) *The Meaning Makers: Children Learning Language and Using Language to Learn*, Portsmouth, NH: Heinemann.

White, Lydia (1985) 'The acquisition of parameterized grammars: subjacency in second language acquisition', *Second Language Research* 1.1.

Whiteley, Wilfred H. (1969) *Swahili: The Rise of a National Language*, London: Methuen (Studies in African History 3).

Whiteley, Wilfred H. (ed.) (1971) *Language Use and Social Change: Problems of Multilingualism with Special Reference to Eastern Africa*, London: Oxford University Press.

Whorf, Benjamin Lee (1956) *Language, Thought and Reality: Selected Essays, edited by John B. Carroll*, Cambridge, MA and New York: MIT Press and Wiley.

Wignell, Peter; Martin, J.R. and Eggins, Suzanne (1987) 'The discourse of geography: ordering and explaining the experiential world', *Writing Project Report 1987* (Working Papers in Linguistics 5), Sydney: University of Sydney Linguistics Department.

Williams, Geoff (1994) *Using Systemic Grammar in Teaching Young Learners: An Introduction*, South Melbourne: Macmillan Education.

Winitz, Harris and Reeds, James A. (1973) 'Rapid acquisition of a foreign language (German) by the avoidance of speaking', *International Review of Applied Linguistics* 11.

Zhu, Yongsheng (2005) *A Dynamic Study on Context*. (語境動態研究). Beijing: Peking University Press (in Chinese).

INDEX

398